Feminist Theory across Disciplines

Defying traditional definitions of public and private as gendered terms, and broadening discussion of women's writing in relation to feminist work done in other fields, this study addresses American women's poetry from the seventeenth to late-twentieth century. Engaging the fields of literary criticism, anthropology, psychology, history, political theory, religious culture, cultural studies, and poetics, this study provides entry into some of the founding feminist discussions across disciplines, moving beyond current scholarship to pursue an interpretation of feminism's defining interests and assumptions in the context of women's writing. The author emphasizes and explores how women's writing expresses their active participation in community and civic life, emerging from and shaping a woman's selfhood as constituted through relationships, not only on the personal level, but as forming community commitments. This distinctive formation of the self finds expression in women's voices and other poetic forms of expression, with the aesthetic power of poetry itself bringing different arenas of human experience to bear on each other in mutual interrogation and reflection. Women poets have addressed the public world, directly or through a variety of poetic structures and figures, and in doing so they have defined and expressed specific forms of selfhood engaged in and committed to communal life.

Shira Wolosky is Professor of English and American Studies at the Hebrew University of Jerusalem, Israel.

Routledge Interdisciplinary Perspectives on Literature

1 **Environmental Criticism for the Twenty-First Century**
Edited by Stephanie LeMenager, Teresa Shewry, and Ken Hiltner

2 **Theoretical Perspectives on Human Rights and Literature**
Elizabeth Swanson Goldberg and Alexandra Schultheis Moore

3 **Resistance to Science in Contemporary American Poetry**
Bryan Walpert

4 **Magic, Science, and Empire in Postcolonial Literature**
The Alchemical Literary Imagination
Kathleen J. Renk

5 **The Black Female Body in American Literature and Art**
Performing Identity
Caroline A. Brown

6 **Narratives of Migration and Displacement in Dominican Literature**
Danny Méndez

7 **The Cinema and the Origins of Literary Modernism**
Andrew Shail

8 **The Gothic in Contemporary Literature and Popular Culture**
Pop Goth
Edited by Justin D. Edwards and Agnieszka Soltysik Monnet

9 **Wallace Stevens and Pre-Socratic Philosophy**
Metaphysics and the Play of Violence
Daniel Tompsett

10 **Modern Orthodoxies**
Judaic Imaginative Journeys of the Twentieth Century
Lisa Mulman

11 **Eugenics, Literature, and Culture in Post-war Britain**
Clare Hanson

12 **Postcolonial Readings of Music in World Literature**
Turning Empire on Its Ear
Cameron Fae Bushnell

13 **Stanley Cavell, Literature, and Film**
The Idea of America
Edited by Andrew Taylor and Áine Kelly

14 **William Blake and the Digital Humanities**
Collaboration, Participation, and Social Media
Jason Whittaker and Roger Whitson

15 **American Studies, Ecocriticism, and Citizenship**
Thinking and Acting in the Local and Global Commons
Edited by Joni Adamson and Kimberly N. Ruffin

16 **International Perspectives on Feminist Ecocriticism**
Edited by Greta Gaard, Simon C. Estok, and Serpil Oppermann

17 **Feminist Theory across Disciplines**
Feminist Community and American Women's Poetry
Shira Wolosky

Feminist Theory across Disciplines
Feminist Community and American Women's Poetry

Shira Wolosky

NEW YORK LONDON

First published 2013
by Routledge
711 Third Avenue, New York, NY 10017

Simultaneously published in the UK
by Routledge
2 Park Square, Milton Park, Abingdon, Oxon OX14 4RN

*Routledge is an imprint of the Taylor & Francis Group,
an informa business*

© 2013 Taylor & Francis

The right of Shira Wolosky to be identified as author of this work has been asserted by her in accordance with sections 77 and 78 of the Copyright, Designs and Patents Act 1988.

All rights reserved. No part of this book may be reprinted or reproduced or utilised in any form or by any electronic, mechanical, or other means, now known or hereafter invented, including photocopying and recording, or in any information storage or retrieval system, without permission in writing from the publishers.

Trademark Notice: Product or corporate names may be trademarks or registered trademarks, and are used only for identification and explanation without intent to infringe.

Library of Congress Cataloging-in-Publication Data

Weiss, Shira Wolosky, 1954–
  Feminist theory across disciplines : feminist community and American women's poetry / by Shira Wolosky.
    pages cm. — (Routledge Interdisciplinary Perspectives on Literature ; 16)
  Includes bibliographical references and index.
  1. American poetry—Women authors—History and
criticism. 2. Feminism in literature. 3. Feminist theory—United
States. 4. Women and literature—United States—History. I. Title.
  PS152.W45 2013
  811.009'9287—dc23
                                                         2012051063

ISBN13: 978-0-415-81794-3 (hbk)
ISBN13: 978-0-203-58268-8 (ebk)

Typeset in Sabon
by IBT Global.

 Printed and bound in the United States of America
by IBT Global.

Contents

Acknowledgments		ix
Preface: Public and Private in Feminist Theory and Poetics		xi
1	Modest Muses: Feminist Literary Criticism	1
2	Muted Groups, Veiled Discourses: Feminist Anthropology	23
3	Recovering Women's Voices: Feminist Psychology	47
4	Separate Spheres: Feminist History	69
5	Public Women, Private Men: Feminist Political Theory	93
6	Civic Feminism and Religious Association	116
7	The Subject of the Body: Foucault and Culture Studies	139
8	Feminist Poetics and Aesthetic Theory	162
	Notes	183
	References	211
	Index	233

Acknowledgments

This has been a project of many years. I would like to thank the Institute for Advanced Study at Princeton for Fellowship support toward researching this project, and I would like especially to thank Caroline Bynum. I would also like to thank Beverly Haviland, Cristanne Miller, Tova Hartman, and Shuli Barzilai for their support and interest in this feminist project. I want to thank Harold Bloom and Sacvan Bercovitch for their continuing support and friendship. I dedicate the work here to my daughters Tali, Tamar, and Nomi; to my son Elazar; to my sisters Rickey and Leslie; and to my husband Ariel.

This book contains material published in the following articles:

"Public Women, Private Men: American Women Poets and the Common Good," *Signs*, Vol. 28, No. 2, Winter 2003, 665–694.
"The Ethics of Foucauldian Poetics: Women's Selves," *New Literary History*, Vol. 35, No. 3, Summer 2004, 491–506.
"Medical-Industrial Discourses in Muriel Rukeyser's 'Book of the Dead,'" *Literature and Medicine*, Vol. 25, No. 1, Spring 2006, 156–171.
"Relational Aesthetics and Feminist Poetics," *New Literary History*, Vol. 41, No. 3, 2011, 571–592.

Permission to quote poetry has been granted by:

The Poems of Emily Dickinson: Variorum Edition, Ralph W. Franklin, ed. Cambridge, Mass.: The Belknap Press of Harvard University Press, Copyright © 1988 by the President and Fellows of Harvard College, Copyright © 1951, © 1955, © 1979, © 1983 by the President and Fellows of Harvard College.

I'm Wife	J 199 / F 225
A solemn thing	J 271 / F 307
I took my power	J 540 / F 660
Fitter to see him	J 968 / F 834

x *Acknowledgments*

Poems by Gwendolyn Brooks: Reprinted by Consent of Brooks Permissions

Marianne Moore, "To a Snail," "Blessed Is the Man," Faber and Faber Ltd., "To a Snail". Reprinted with the permission of Scribner, a Division of Simon & Schuster, Inc. from *The Collected Poems of Marianne Moore* by Marianne Moore, Copyright © 1935 by Marianne Moore, renewed 1963 by Marianne Moore and T.S. Eliot. All rights reserved.

Sylvia Plath, "Face Lift" from *Crossing the Water* Copyright © 1971 by Ted Hughes. Reprinted by permission of HarperCollins Publishers.

Adrienne Rich, 6 lines from "Novella," *Adrienne Rich: Poems Selected and New, 1950–1984*, 1984. Reprinted with the permission of W.W. Norton and Company. This selection may not be reproduced, stored in a retrieval system, or transmitted in any form without prior permission of the publisher.

Muriel Rukeyser, *The Collected Poems*, New York: McGraw-Hill, 1978, by Muriel Rukeyser. Used by permission. All rights reserved.

Preface
Public and Private in Feminist Theory and Poetics

This book began with curiosity about feminism in different fields: how are the varieties of feminist study connected to each other? Most discussions of feminist theory are organized along ideological lines. I instead was interested in the work being done in specific disciplines of study and understanding how these might bear on each other and enrich each other. Therefore, I do not organize my discussions through ideological categories—liberal and radical, cultural and difference feminism, Marxist and Socialist, or, following a different set of criteria, first, second, and third Wave, or Anglo-American historicist against French psychoanalytic theory.[1] Instead, this book is organized according to disciplines: the fields in which most feminist work is actively pursued. Nor do I attempt to be comprehensive as to the feminist writing that is available—something that has grown to a massive body of material. I do not offer surveys. Instead, I focus in each chapter on work that has been foundational in each field considered and out of which much other work has been generated, then investigating each through poems by American women.

This book thus can serve as an entry into some of the founding feminist discussions across a range of fields. Feminist study has almost by definition pursued a strong interdisciplinary commitment. In terms of women's writing, how the writer is located, her access to education, social roles, and the status of literature cannot be ignored when the writer is female—or, as gender studies exposes, when the writer is male as well.[2] There is an inextricable intercrossing of historical, social, cultural roles and their ideological contexts in any study of gender. Yet the conduct of feminist inquiry remains, understandably, largely disciplinary—notice the many collections of essays devoted within each field. Here I attempt to bring some of the various strands of feminist study into fuller relationship with each other; with literature, for reasons I investigate, a site in which their intercrossing becomes both accessible and dramatic.

As I worked through different feminist disciplines, I further became aware of a thread running through them. The Second Wave of feminism in which I grew up emphasized personal liberation, self-realization, and self-determination. But as I immersed myself in feminism through a range of approaches, I realized that this was only one mode of feminist imagining. Both historically and theoretically, women's lives and their accounts of it have been defined not mainly through categories of self-determination and self-assertion, but as part of the social and community life to which they foundationally contributed. This contribution has been undervalued, indeed unacknowledged and often invisible. What emerged as I worked was a recognition of what I am calling 'civic feminism' (in relation to and distinction from 'civic humanism' and 'civic republicanism'): the active contribution of women to common and community life as a long-standing and authentic trend in the history, activities, and writings of women. Civic feminism contests the description and ascription of women to domestic privacy, recognizing instead their contribution to social life in both the family and the community. It also challenges definitions of the self as autonomously defined, self-enclosed units who exist prior to or outside of the relationships that constitute human being while also affirming individual responsibility and creativity.

Civic feminism affirms a strand of feminism and of women's experience that Second Wave feminism, again understandably, challenged. The achievements of Second Wave liberal feminism are great, and all women, including myself, have benefitted immensely from the opportunities it created. But the Second Wave tended to push out of view other women's commitments, which have been and remain a fundamental basis for community and our shared lives as human beings. This in turn has created tensions within the feminist movement, causing many women to draw back from it (even as they continue to benefit from the options it has opened for them).[3] To acknowledge this community commitment is to bring to visibility the public contributions women have made and to represent these as an authentic feminism that in fact speaks to and for many women. This is to challenge not only problematic accounts of women in history, society, and culture, but also to affirm the values of community responsibility that women have and continue to uphold. But women's commitment to community—which includes, as I shall argue, family not as a private but a primary social unit—should be seen as a framework and not only as an obstacle to the possibilities of individual achievement. How to combine both commitment to the self and commitment to others has been a major concern of women and of feminist writers, and it remains a primary challenge today. Current feminist theory has interestingly returned to some of the terms and concerns of earlier nineteenth-century feminism in which women's social commitments were the defining framework—not as isolated 'domesticity' but as direct public activism.

This question of community proved to be inevitably also a question of selfhood, as each defines the other. What is a self? How is it historically, culturally, and politically situated and defined? How is selfhood expressed by women? One persistent trend in many different areas of feminist theory and poetics pointed toward a sense of the self as deeply embedded in community, defined in responsibility to it. This is not the autonomous, self-determined self of the Lockean tradition, but a self whose structures, purposes, and values emerge from and are directed toward the social world. Cultural anthropologists underscore how any person is thickly embedded in culture, emerging from and through it.[4] This is true of the liberal individual as well. Liberal individualism is also a cultural construction, one that, however, obscures its own cultural and social basis in its ideology of independence. Women, however, are not only inscribed in culture: they are, and have traditionally been, invested in it. What distinguishes women's traditions is the way they have acknowledged and embraced their embeddedness and seen it as a positive value.

If this recognition of women's investment in community is in some ways obvious and traditional, in other ways it presents a marked reversal in the traditional ways that women have been viewed. As I discuss throughout this book, women have been assigned from the outset of Western discourses to a private domain.[5] The approach to women's selfhood as inscribed within community in fact runs counter to the long tendency to relegate women to the private domain and men to the public one: an assignment that is continuous through philosophy and political theory, history and economics, anthropology and classical psychology, theology and religious history, and also literary study. Women's lives have been relentlessly defined as private and domestic through a multitude of political discourses and historical paradigms, psychological norms, cultural ideologies, and religious assignments. Men's lives, conversely, are defined as public. The meanings of these terms have shifted from period to period and in interrelationship with each other. Nonetheless, they have consistently privileged men's positions as 'public' and demoted women's positions as 'private.' Hegel sums this up, locating women in the family where they "are not made for activities which demand a universal faculty, they cannot attain to the ideal."

> If women were to control the government, the state would be in danger, for they do not act according to the dictates of universality, but are influenced by accidental inclinations and opinions. [For women]the particular is to be the prime factor in determining conduct. Thus the ethical seems to be discarded and superseded.

Hegel's civil society is one in which "each member is his own end, everything else is nothing to him," an autonomous individuality that nevertheless requires a centralized state to give it real universal meaning.[6] But women are barred from this universalization.

Carole Pateman observed in 1983 that "the dichotomy between the public and the private . . . is ultimately what the feminist movement is about."[7] These terms, enduring from Greek philosophy onward, prove themselves to be deeply gendered. Rather than merely describing either geography or activities pursued and performed, they reflect hierarchies of values, proscriptive norms, and power distributions. The terms 'public' and 'private' presuppose fundamental models of selfhood as these define what make up a self, a self's relationship to itself and its surrounding culture, and also judgments of the self's measure: what attributes give value to a self. What emerges in the contexts of women's cultures is an essential instability in the terms 'public' and 'private,' which, far from describing gender in neutral terms, find their origin deeply embedded within gender ideology. Public and private, that is, are highly circular, gendered terms from the outset. They ground gendered assignments rather than describe them. Through various evolutions, they are ideological and unstable. Through all its various usages, however, the term 'private' as assigned to women denies their involvements and contributions to the social world, making their presence invisible and devaluing their fundamental and necessary work. It has been an important task of feminist theory across disciplines to investigate these definitions of 'public' and 'private' and the models of selfhood and the hierarchy of values they have consistently enforced.

Feminism here is meant as the critical study of gender as one—although not the only—foundation of social experience and cultural expression.[8] Gender is conceived as a historical, social, and cultural category—a matrix marking how women and men have been traditionally situated in their roles, definitions, undertakings, self-reflections, and the discourses in which these take place. It is as historical and social manifestation that womanhood has been enacted in history; and therefore it is only as historical and social that womanhood can be addressed and analyzed, regardless of any other biological or psychic phenomena—phenomena that in any case would be mediated through social and cultural categories. This is a position shared by most feminisms.[9] Joan Kelly-Gadol called it the notion "basic to feminist consciousness, that the relation between the sexes is a social and not a natural one," and "that women's situation is a social matter." Changes in history itself involve "changes in the relation of the sexes."[10]

To argue, however, that gender is historical and socially constructed is not to claim that the self is fully determined and disciplined by social institutions in ways that eliminate or obstructively and negatively compel choice, as is implied, I will argue, in Foucauldian discussions, where social institutions are seen fundamentally in coercive terms. Nor is gender entirely performative, in the sense of free play open to any alteration, as Judith Butler argues in *Gender Trouble*. Butler's claim that even sex in biological senses is always culturally interpreted is a persuasive and powerful hermeneutic of gender. But social construction by definition situates within society and thus is never entirely free from it in play or performance. Social construction anchors identity even as it releases identity from essential, fixed categories and characteristics. As Seyla Ben-Habib observes, to be situated is not the same as to be fictive.[11] Individuals are placed within social situations and gain definition in terms of them while nevertheless attaining freedom for self-definitions through the variety of contexts in which they participate, the interactions between them, personal and cultural histories, and other factors and strategies. The self is a site of transformation as well as commitment through multiple and changing factors, which renders each self unique and studded with options: a selfhood rooted deeply in social forms that is also subject to activism and change.

POETIC ENGAGEMENT

Literary criticism is offered here as one of the fields of feminist study—one in which interdisciplinary work has taken strong root, especially in reference to history and Culture Studies. I pursue and expand these cross-disciplinary interests with an eye to how the study of gender does not merely extend a field of study to include a new set of considerations or parameters, but transforms the discipline, bringing into it new methods, new orientations, and new definitions. In this book, literature provides a site of intersection among such diverse disciplines. A range of different fields are brought to bear on literature while literature in turn is brought to bear on other fields of study. The goal is to have the texts illuminate the fields and the fields illuminate the texts. Textual engagement, on the one hand, provides concrete material for investigating and applying theories and methods proposed within specific disciplinary domains. But the poetry is not reduced to mere illustration. Instead, each chapter's methodological approach opens avenues into the literary text in ways that enlarge our sense of literary power and possibility. On the other hand, the texts enact, actualize, and extend issues examined within different disciplinary approaches.

Throughout this study, American women's poetry provides a body of material for investigating and analyzing women's self-representation and its cultural inscriptions. Indeed, one goal is to include poetry in the cultural conversation of feminism, as broadly engaged in its issues and as a major source and scene of their enactment. Most discussions of American women poets focus either on specific periods, or topics, or individual authors. I have set out to bring into one continuing discussion the work of a wide range of American women poets from Anne Bradstreet to twentieth-century writers. This situates my discussion of feminist topics within a delimited and specified historical framework and set of conditions, through a defined body of material in which trends can be followed. Reciprocal interdisciplinarity also opens questions of feminist poetics itself: what is a feminist poetics? How does it alter traditional notions of textuality and aesthetics? Poetry has, I argue, special powers and claims to just such reflection in terms of cross-disciplinary trends. Literature, and not least poetry, has an extraordinary power to act in and address many fields, bringing them into encounter with each other. Poetry becomes a site of interaction among different realms of experience. A poem can be a historical document, a psychological introspection, a philosophical meditation, an ethnographic artifact, a xvi *Preface*

religious devotion, and a political declaration in ways none of these can be each other. Indeed, poetry can be several of these different modes at once, bringing them into mutual interrogation. As against the usual assumptions of poetics and aesthetics, I argue that it is the cultural place and aesthetic power of the poem not to enclose language in a separate, self-referring realm, but rather to bring a variety of experiences into mutual recognition, reflection, address, critique, and encounter. Poetry in particular has tended in the twentieth century to be bracketed out of cultural discourses as a self-enclosed, formal language as if it is only, or mainly, about 'itself.' But poetic texts engage and register, mark and are marked by the discourses surrounding them—indeed, poetry offers an extreme self-consciousness to cultural practices exactly as discourses, that is, in their linguistic conduct and its effects.

W. H. Auden once said that poetry makes nothing happen. Here, on the contrary, I pursue poetry as an event, making things happen between and among the diverse areas of human experience. As I discuss in a final chapter on poetics, engagement with and between various domains of experience is what constitutes literature's aesthetic power. This is especially the case for a feminist poetics. By including questions of gender, a feminist poetics transforms the notions of poetic text and aesthetics from a space of detachment and self-reflection to one of intersection, transformation, and event. As gendered, the approach to poetry must be cross-disciplinary. This does not mean reducing the poetic text to historical, political, or cultural terms, making the text a mere demonstration or instance of them. Rather, I set out to explore how poetry reassembles in new ways and in terms of each other historical, political, religious, psychological, and other trends.

In this book, I pursue a civic construction of the self in its various aspects from chapter to chapter, as this emerges and links the different forms of feminist theory in their analysis and deployment of models of selfhood. The disciplines I consider include literature, anthropology, psychology, history, political theory, Culture Studies, religion, and finally aesthetics. I necessarily omit large areas. I do not, perhaps most notably, give a separate chapter to psychoanalysis and related questions of sexual constitution. This is partly because these have been so often treated, partly because they involve their own specialized vocabularies, and partly because my emphasis falls more on questions of community: how selves, and particularly the selves of women, define themselves in communal, and hence historical, political, and ultimately civic frameworks.[12] Such interests are not specifically opposed to psychoanalytic subjectivities, but the emphasis differs. Since, however, psychoanalytic discourses enter into most feminist discussions, they also are considered at various points in the course of the study.

Literature remains the anchor of the book, as the continuing engagement through the variety of its discourses. The first chapter thus begins with feminist literary criticism. This has been, I show, focally concerned with questions of literary tradition: women's exclusion or inclusion from tradition, how women have been represented within it, the problems of women's authorship, and the recovery of women's writings. Literary history of women writers governs here. Yet there are also core theoretical questions within literary history, notably concerning questions of authorship distinctive from those in the male-authored traditions. Women's authorial selfhood has been described as lacking authority in the mode of self-constituted originality. But women's poetic self-representation takes on, I argue, a different form of authority, one that derives less in personal genius than as constructed through a sense of commitment to issues and to others with whom authors feel strongly connected and responsible. In this, women's senses of literary roles intercross with their cultural and community embeddedness. Theirs tend to be voices of attachment rather than self-assertion, of address rather than personal emphasis.

The second chapter turns to feminist work in anthropology that has focused on language in ways powerfully suggestive for the reading of literature. There, theories of 'dominant' versus 'muted' discourses have developed (as they have also in Marxist theory) to account for the inaccessibility of women to anthropological investigation. The notion of a dominant discourse and the way words mean in it, proves to be rich in implication for analyzing poetic presentation when contrasted against subgroup discourses which may use the dominant words but as they mean within the subgroup culture. Women constitute such a subgroup. How words mean when they appear in women's writings, drawn from but with different intention and function than their uses in general circulation, opens windows into women's viewpoints on dominant meaning systems that are critical, exposing, and revisionary.

Similar questions of the muting of women's voices emerge in the third chapter, as uncovered in feminist psychology and its critique of standard models of development. Traditional models are exposed as assuming autonomous individuation to be the mark of the highest levels of maturity and moral judgment. While such individuation remains an important part of psychological and moral development, the work of Carol Gilligan and other feminist psychologists and moral philosophers has come to propose a coordinate model in which responsibility and commitment rather than or alongside of independence and autonomy are core values in both psychological health and moral development. The traditional privileging of assertive, autonomous selfhood has resulted in an undervaluation of women's historical forms of selfhood, and hence a loss of voice and authority for women, whose senses of self are, by social but also by moral commitment, enmeshed with others as part of their self-definition.

The next chapters address the construct of separate spheres in historical context and how these have been treated in feminist political philosophy, focusing on the private/public distinction—a distinction that has pervasively governed both women's lives and the interpretation of them, which is a major concern of feminist discussion across fields. Here I argue that these categories distort the understanding of women's experiences and writing. The public/private distinction in fact each projects distinctive forms of selfhood whose divergence from each other remains unexamined and unacknowledged. These differences are concealed under the ideology of individualism, which actually encompasses different kinds of selves that persons can have, selves which in some ways converge but also conflict. The kind of self that claims and is modeled on autonomy constitutes an economic individualism, committed largely to self-interest. But civic feminism, as an expression of civic selfhood, affirms the self as it participates in communal and civic interests. It is this form of selfhood that often finds expression in women's writing—not as private, as is traditionally claimed, but as oriented in public and indeed republican directions. In the course of American history, such civic selfhood, however, has been increasingly obscured and dominated by economic individualism, which has pushed other forms of selfhood to the side, overriding and demoting them in ways that also override and demote women in their communal commitments.

The chapters on history and politics are followed by a chapter addressing women and religion. Religion can and has been a conservative force working against the emancipation of women. But in American contexts, religious association has also been a central forum for women's participation and activism in social life. The civic self historically derived, in part, in a religious selfhood deeply committed to community. American women, including poets, have often drawn on, and expressed, religious vision and religiously grounded authority as a context and basis for their activities and their writings. Their writings become a scene that both appeals to and yet also resists religious norms, which have continued to frame women's undertakings and writings even in the twentieth century.

The seventh chapter of this book turns to the challenges that Culture Studies poses to notions of selfhood, specifically with reference to the work of Michel Foucault. Foucault's critique of the self as caught within disciplinary systems has provided a powerful tool for feminist analysis. But Foucauldian anti-institutionalism can also conceal and preclude the ways in which selfhood takes shape and draws strength from commitments to surrounding selves in community, out of which selves emerge but which they also shape and define. This positive sense of community can be seen in such radical women poets as Muriel Rukeyser and Gwendolyn Brooks.

A final chapter reflects back on the methods and discussions throughout this study to consider the aesthetic implications of literature as a feminist and cross-disciplinary site. I argue here that literature, in its aesthetic power, is an arena in which the different domains of life encounter, interrogate, confirm, and contest each other. Far from being, as traditionally defined, a detached realm, literature emerges exactly out of relationship among diverse domains of understanding and experience. It is just this status as arena for intersecting realms that defines it *as* literature. Poetry can provide an especially intensive space for such encounter. Within recent historicizing trends in literary study, women's fiction has generally attracted more interdisciplinary and specifically historical analysis than poetry has. Fiction's apparently direct representation of its surrounding world has seemed more hospitable or plausible to relationships beyond its own aesthetic boundaries. Poetry, in contrast, has traditionally tended to be seen as removed from history, a lyric space outside of time. But the enclosure of poetry into an aesthetic object is a historical phenomenon whose sources can be traced to early twentieth-century literary movements and aesthetics.[13] Nineteenth-century poetry, in contrast, openly addressed, and defined itself as engaging, issues of public concern, offering especially to women an avenue for participation in social and political debate. Twentieth-century aesthetics regards poetry as a separate, pristine, and more or less self-enclosed art object, a remote island in a glass aesthetic sea. Women's writing underscores how the poetic text, against this view, invokes and interprets other discourses and the domains of experience they shape, reflect, and represent.

In each chapter, a different selection of poets is discussed, as their work on one side exemplifies that chapter's particular disciplinary concerns, and on the other explores how different disciplinary approaches can open new understandings of poetry. The order of poets in this study is not chronological, although in its course most major American women poets are explored. Some poets are discussed recurrently throughout since their work is outstandingly multi-dimensional and multi-domainal, illuminating different fields and approaches as a great range of concerns and experiences come in their poetry to especially intense mutual interrogation.

CIVIC FEMINISM

Current discussions of feminist theory are deeply divided over how to define the feminist venture. Heightened recognitions of differences among women have rendered the term 'woman' problematic as a category, undercutting what served as the organizing focus of feminism. The result has been "ever proliferating positions as to the objects, goals, and definitions of feminism," a "splintering" of the feminist project.[14] Various kinds of 'postfeminism' mark the critique or abandonment of earlier feminist positions. 'Third Wave' and poststructural feminists focus on the multiplicity of subjectivities, warning against treating 'women' as a fixed and unitary category.[15] Feminist interchanges can become caught in a stalemate of categorization: sameness against difference, equality against separation, justice against care, and rights against responsibility, with postmodern theory radically questioning subjectivity and selfhood as such.

Here I do not attempt to address 'women' in general but the specific body of women poets writing within American cultural and historical contexts, mediated through modes of poetry, and focusing on questions of women's involvements in community in what I call 'civic feminism.' Within this category and context, distinctive constructions of the self and distinctive feminist goals emerge. As to goals, feminism's project has been repeatedly and consistently claimed as liberatory. This has been the case through socialist, radical, Marxist, and liberal feminisms, from Alison Jaggar's early call to "all those who seek, no matter on what grounds, to end women's subordination to help us to achieve the fullest possible liberation" onward.[16] But pure emancipatory desire omits the ties, connections, and relationalities that are central to much women's writing as well as their lives, as has been especially explored in feminist ethics. Emancipation assumes a pre-established autonomous or authentic subject before or beyond social life to be freed from its distortions—the kind of essentialist categories much feminist work has contested. In historical terms, the liberatory model projects, as Sabah Mahmood has explored, one specific social form as a 'universal norm,' restricting "the notion of agency to the space of emancipatory politics." But Mahmood, citing the example of Muslim women, argues that the "desire for freedom and/or subversion of norms is not an innate desire that motivates all beings at all times" and who may have other goals and ties.[17]

To the extent that liberation calls for revolt against institutions as such, it invests in a kind of romantic fantasy that imagines a pure selfhood formed outside of human relationships. Yet as Mary Douglas writes, "external form is a condition of existence . . . as a social animal man is a ritual animal. Social rituals create a reality which would be nothing with them. It is impossible to have social relations without symbolic acts."[18] A revisionary goal would then be not to abolish all institutions but rather to establish good ones. A good deal of feminist work points to definitions and affirmations of the self as inscribed in community, responsible to and for it—a selfhood that strongly emerges in much American women's poetry, whose speakers and topics often critique pure autonomy and speak as selves committed to projects through an engaged selfhood larger than an individualism in which the self is foremostly self-interested. Rather than *emancipatory*, the model for such civic selfhood is *participatory*. Selfhood would both emerge from and be brought to participatory experience, in ongoing processes that remain anchored in the relationships, histories, and purposes that link selves together. These would be contributory but not merely self-sacrificing. They would claim recognition for the work that women have done in building and maintaining human community and society. Civic feminism embraces responsibility rather than seeking freedom from it, a manner of extending the self beyond its private self, in the tradition of republican commitment to public affairs and a common good. To be a participant is to constitute selfhood as part of larger projects. But these are never unitary. The multiplicity of participations and purposes provide critical stances from which to judge and alter each other in given situations. Activism would include but not be reducible to resistance only, which emerges in much feminist discourse as the core mode of emancipation.[19] But besides emancipation, there is transformation, in which not only resistance plays a part, but also alliances and allegiances, identifications and reformations, drawing on institutions and social forms even while adjusting and redirecting them. Women through such alliances have been a vital part of the public sphere in America. Theirs has been a civic involvement and participation that is deeply embedded in the senses of selfhood that women have historically embraced, attested to by their poetic expression, which gather together into mutual encounter the many spheres of their endeavors.

1 Modest Muses
Feminist Literary Criticism

Literature has been among the earliest and most important entries for women into the public world, and literary criticism has been a foundational area of feminist study. Its first, central task has been to redefine its very field, which has meant reviewing and rewriting literary history. Feminist criticism has typically set out to ask: what place have women had in what has been a resolutely male tradition of literature? How have women been represented, and how does this affect their own self-representation? What have been the (male) models of authorship, and how do these serve—or not—as models for the authorship of women? Are there gendered aspects of literary genres, of imagery, of language itself? What do we even mean by a 'women's' literature? What would distinguish it from 'men's' literature, other than the fact that women have written it?

Feminist literary criticism thus has largely taken as its core concern literary tradition: investigating and recovering women's writing; asking questions of the place in and displacement of women's writings in literary canons; and formulating what a women's tradition might look like, with consequent interrogation of the very principles of tradition and canon, the criteria for inclusion and exclusion, and the aesthetic assumptions that have governed such choices as being exclusionary and demanding revision. It has tried to conceptualize what happens when women are introduced into a literary tradition from which they have been kept outside in so many senses and when gender becomes part of literary analysis. The absence of available female literary models, the exclusion or subordination of women in traditional genres, and the problems of female poetic voice have stood at the center. Such critical questions have extended into theoretical ones concerning the very category of 'women' as a literary measure, in terms of writer, reader, style, and textual construction itself.[1]

What identifies gender in literary texts? It is possible to assemble and specify a number of gender markers in compositional terms. These include: female speakers; female experiences, such as pregnancy and childbirth; female roles, such as wives, daughters, and sisters; traditionally female activities, such as child care and sick care; cooking, sewing, and cloth-making; and traditionally female spaces, such as domestic settings and enclosed spaces. In addition, topics, images, basic stances, viewpoints, formal choices, and core assumptions concerning the poet's roles and self-conception may be gendered. Certain genres may be considered feminine historically or may be transformed in women's hands. There may be feminized uses of male images and feminized readings and transformations of the male literary past, which regender male forms into female ones.[2] Such gendered revision was a self-conscious project of many women poets. Already in nineteenth-century America, many poems took up female figures from the classics or, especially, the Bible, to reread the experiences of women characters, giving them voice.[3] These strategies have continued well into the twentieth century in such poets as H. D., Adrienne Rich, Muriel Rukeyser, and others.[4]

Running through this feminization of literary elements—of speakers and images, genres and settings—there is a prior concern regarding the poet's right to be a writer altogether. This has given rise to certain literary conventions or *topoi* that are especially characteristic of women's writing. Among these issues are naming and having a name, speaking and being silent, public appearance and the lack of access to it, and, crucially, authorship itself. Issues of poetic identity, poetic authority, and poetic self- representation become central. What it is to be an author and poet proves not to be simply gender-neutral. How a man conceives of himself as a poet may differ from the way a woman conceives of herself. The senses of authority, of creative claims and confidences as well as stances and approaches, tend to produce different kinds of self-representation and distinctive conceptions of the female poet's roles in relation to her social ones.

Questions of voice and silencing emerge with immediate historical force in the core project of feminist criticism to recover women's texts that have disappeared from literary history. Since the time of the Renaissance, and even after women began to write and publish in significant numbers in the late eighteenth and nineteenth centuries, their works have tended not to be republished, anthologized, or included in literary curricula or canons. Women's has been a discontinuous tradition.[5] Even nineteenth-century American women's poetry, despite wide popularity in a variety of publishing venues during their lifetimes, was immediately buried with their authors on their deaths. In the past decades, an immense and continuing effort has gone toward recovering these lost texts, restoring them to the light of literary day. But this recovery underscores the prior lack of access to a women's tradition. Until quite recently, each woman writer has had to begin, as it were, over again, with little sense of what other women before her might have written. Each has confronted anew questions about what it might mean for a woman to write; how gender shapes authorship; what subjects, interests, viewpoints, idioms, settings, or genres gender may affect; without the benefit of referring to past efforts by past women in similar or dissimilar circumstances. She would not have a tradition of women writers available to her.

The task of recovery is one example of how literature and history are bound to each other, closely tied to other questions of women's social histories. That women wrote texts which have failed to remain in circulation reflects the lack of access to literary distribution, as well as to the material resources Virginia Woolf dramatized in *A Room of One's Own*. To write at all, women have needed access to literacy. To be literary requires being literate: to be able to read and write, as well as have exposure to literary culture through an education that introduces the individual to her textual heritage. Until quite recently, these conditions have rarely been met. Gerda Lerner estimated that no more than 300 women left written records before the seventeenth century. This number has been revised as further texts have been discovered and the genres of women have been recognized. Still, the relative quantities of women's writing remain small.[6] Literacy, and even more higher education, was until recent modernity almost exclusively available to men, if mainly to members of the nobility or the church. The church, it is interesting to note, was the framework for much of the early women's writings that havebeen preserved, although some of these were dictated to male confessors, advisors, or directors rather than being written directly by the women themselves.[7]

The American context is distinctive. Its combination of Protestant emphasis on reading the Bible the better to obey it, extended to girls. Later Revolutionary principles in which education was recognized as essential for self-government to some extent included women, leading to the establishment of seminaries and then colleges for women. New literary markets created by higher literacy, and new technologies in production and distribution, made writing by women possible in new ways and on a new scale. It became a financial resource to which genteel women, barred from most other professions or incomes, could turn, as well as an avenue allowing for the direct address to public issues otherwise difficult to access.

These questions of literacy and access to publication underscore the direct linkage of literature to historical and social forms. Women's social positions framed, and often posed obstacles to, literary production. These positions involved social roles within ideologies defining who women were and what was proper to them, which did not include public exposure. What remains challenging is balancing the limitations that social contexts imposed on women while also recognizing and exploring the terms through which women positively negotiated their own authority, self-definitions, and voices.

WRITING ANXIETY

Many discussions of women's place in literary tradition and the sources of creativity available (or not) to them were first framed in response to Harold Bloom's transformative theories of literary influence and the questions of authority, originality, and anxiety that he defines as fundamental to authorship. Bloomian theory centrally draws on Freudian (among other) structures to unveil creativity itself as a scene of both inheritance and rivalry, identification and displacement.[8] Before Bloom, literary influence was seen mainly as a matter of homage and allusion, of prior creations generating subsequent works through imitation and reverence. Bloom instead sees literary creativity as a highly charged drama of admiration, competition, appropriation, and repression, accompanied by anxiety. Influence is as overwrought as it is inevitable. Literary creation inevitably emerges from prior literary creation. Texts are written out of other texts. But this is an agonistic struggle, not a decorous bequeathing. Influence is expressed not only through citation and imitation, but also via gaps and omissions, swerves and counter-thrusts and negations. The poet's relationship to his poetic precursors in the tradition is thus like repression and displacement in general, with an analogy to the Oedipal struggle of son against father. While the poet-son imitates and admires the precursor-father, he also fears and seeks to displace him, to assert his own prowess by overcoming the father in competitive striving. To attain his own imaginative assertion and autonomy, he must wrest from his precursor-fathers—the great writers of the past—their authority and power.

What the poets and precursors compete over is the Muse. The Muse is Bloom's figure for poetic inspiration and authorization. In his creative drama, the male poet's effort to wrest authority from tradition takes shape as a sexual competition over the female Muse who, imaged as a desired lady, inspires and rewards poetic creativity. Since the dawn of literature, erotic energy has been invested as poetic desire. In Bloom's Freudian terms, eros is directed toward the Muse as a figure for the mother and her female substitutes, over whom the poet-son, in Oedipal contest, struggles with past poets, who act as precursor-fathers. Through this competition and desire, the Muse serves to inspire poetic venture. The Muse figure, thus, represents the inspiration that incites creativity in the poetic contest that is writing itself. Creativity, as in Freud, is deeply eroticized, and its characteristic poetic form becomes erotic pursuit, courtship, seduction, or quest. Bloom underscores how the Quest-Romance serves as an overarching pattern for poetic creativity itself, especially in Romantic writing.[9] Romance provides a figure for poetry as a quest for the Muse. But such poetic creation is highly conflictual. It involves both adoration and rivalry, service and assault on the father as an image and owner of tradition. Likewise, the female Muse of desire inspires, but attaining her may, as the end of quest, also signal the poet's own demise, the end of his creativity, figured in death.

This Bloomian vision of poetic tradition as erotic rivalry extends across the centuries, with the Muse as a presiding figure in Greek lyric, in Troubador and then in Renaissance poetry as the idealized and frustrating Lady. In this guise, the Muse is basic to the sonnet form and other lyric modes, underwriting the persistent lyric subgenre of seduction. She then emerges as a central impulse in Romantic quest lyric. Sexuality is no accidental or decorative feature of poetic form. It is deeply implanted in the sources, impulses, and forms of poetry. Bloom's terms underscore this erotic element but also the ambivalence and indeed violence that it imports into poetic creativity. Poetry is born out of tradition, but as Bloom insists, it is a difficult birth. Far from being a harmonious accumulation or transmission, poetic production is instead a fraught, anxious, and ambivalent effort. The poet would claim the tradition while denying all debt, would repress sources while wresting them from his precursors, to claim as his own. In offering an erotics of poetry, where the tradition stands as father and the Muse as mother/lady, Bloom collects and focuses age-old images but gives them a sharp and explosive clarity that has powerfully altered our notions of literary history altogether. From an orderly inheritance, literary history becomes instead a siege and campaign, claiming and counter-claiming possession in a highly sexualized contest and with an undercurrent of ferocity.

However, what happens to this model when the poet is not a man, but a woman? A generation of Bloom students and readers that coincided with Second Wave feminism noted that Bloom's Oedipal model, like Freud's own, is highly gendered. It assumes from the outset a male protagonist. The poet is Oedipal son to the authority and power of tradition as precursor-father, in competitive conquest of the female mother/lady/Muse. The structure is intrinsically gendered. Would the same model, with the same distribution of roles and processes, arise if the poet were a woman? How does a woman poet stand in relation to tradition as (male) precursors? Who is her Muse, and what is her relation to her or him? What might the sexual identities of both precursor-tradition and inspiring Muse look like, and how would these position the poet if the genders were switched? What would be the erotic shape of the poem, the shape of its creator's desires?

These questions were taken up in a series of works on women writers and poets: first by Sandra Gilbert and Susan Gubar in *The Madwoman in the Attic*, which in many ways inaugurated American feminist literary criticism along Bloomian lines.[10] The shift in gender from male to female writer proved to have large implications for the Bloomian model of tradition and creativity. First, the relation of poet to precursors changes from son/father to daughter/father. Since literary tradition is made up overwhelmingly of male writers, the precursor/tradition/father remains largely male, with an authority that the female poet, like the male one, has to confront. But the poet-daughter's relation to the father is not the same as the poet-son's. The core relationship between poet-son and precursor-father is, in the Oedipal model, one of competition and aggression, but also of strong and enabling identification. The son could compete with the father because he was like him, could vie to take his (male) place. But the relation of poet-daughter to precursor-father (with few precursor-mothers at first available) would be more like daughter to father. Would this relationship still be structured through competitive identification? Would the daughter-poet have the strength and self-confidence for the agonistic struggle? Would some other relationship to past poets instead emerge, one with less rivalry if also less identification? Would it be more collaborative and less competitive? In Freudian terms, daughter/father relations have their own problematic issues as a model for creativity. The daughter's stance toward her father is in Freud one of envy and despair at not possessing the male organ. Instead of contending and identifying with the father and his male substitutes, the daughter submits herself to him and them. Such a role, both as interior drama and expressive structure, would from the outset dam the female poet's creative energies.

Other problems arise along social-historical rather than psychological lines. The role of poet generally contradicts, or at least tensely confronts, the traditional roles of womanhood. If the poet is daring, venturesome, and forward, with confidence in himself to take up his pen against the challenge of the fathers who wrote before him, then the woman is severely schooled against any such ventures or stances. The woman has traditionally been submissive not assertive, passive not active, circumscribed not daring, as in fairy tales where women wait for knightly rescue and without the self-confidence and authority that forms the basis and provides the strength for authorship. What then are her creative resources? What in her experience is worth telling about, and who would listen? How can the female poet dare to assert herself against the precursor-father tradition, to embark on a quest to claim and wrest the domain of the father as her own?

The relation of female poet to father-precursor is thus a deeply perturbed one. Her relation to the Muse is no less so. Indeed, for women writers, the whole figure of poetic creativity as erotic quest and courtship runs counter to her given social role. A woman does not set out on quests to court erotic objects, no more than she traditionally stands in rivalry against fathers. In the assigned positions of heterosexual romance, the woman is not courtier but courted, to be at last attained and possessed. This is embodied in the feminized position of the Muse, which has a certain sway to bestow or withhold inspiration, to elude or invite. Yet the Muse's dominance only persists as long as the quest remains incomplete. Once the courtship ends and her favors are obtained, she loses her power to both evade and allure. And even while courted, her power is a positional rather than an active one. The Lady-Muse remains passive. It is hers to wait, attract, and promise, not to pursue or initiate. Once she is attained, she loses even this passive authority, reverting to the subordinate position of a woman claimed and conquered, with no further commanding role. Hers becomes the settled female position: subordinate to the authority of the male who possesses her.

How then is the female poet to proceed? To take the active role of courtier or quester is to go against traditionally authorized modes of female behavior in literature and society. It is to claim a mobility that women have almost never had, an avenue of venture largely denied them, with its active and competitive pursuit of desire. The woman's anomalous position as poetic seeker is compounded, with regard to the Muse, by the problem of sexuality. Who exactly is the woman poet courting? One possibility is to continue to imagine the Muse as female. But this would shift the poetic structure from heterosexual to homoerotic or autoerotic, perhaps transforming entirely the model of courtship and erotic relationship. Or, feminist critics have speculated, if the model for creativity were based in intra-female relationships, it might be reshaped in terms of sisterhood: a non-Oedipal structure replacing rivalry, dispossession and conquest with collaborative, mutual inspiration.[11]

Or the Muse can instead be imagined as male, in reverse symmetry with the male Quest-Romance and in continued accordance with heterosexual norms. But such a male Muse would seriously constrain the woman poet's position. It is socially and normatively odd for her to actively pursue a male, in ways both dictated to and internalized by her. Beyond this strain in traditional roles, attaining a male Muse might bring defeat to the woman poet rather than achievement. For if the female poet's courtship were successful, there is the danger that her relation to her male Muse would not be one of expression but rather of subordination, the ordinary power relation between the sexes. The male Muse would possess and command the female poet, not she him. Her relation to the sources of inspiration would be not empowering, but instead overpowering and engulfing. Courting the male Muse would not involve seeking him as an act of creative power, but rather being dominated by him, under his authority and command as women normatively are to men.

With regard to poetic authority in Bloomian theory, then, the female poet's position requires a counter-normative role. She cannot identify with tradition as a male poet can, nor is she authorized to do so. Yet to be cut off from tradition is to threaten to cut her off from poetic resource, while to claim or court male poetic power is to be threatened with subordination to it. The object of desire may overpower and silence rather than confirm and reward her approach, and its pursuit goes against her social identity. The normative male authorization of literary history escapes her.

MODEST RESOURCES

The approach to women's poetry through the psycho-erotics of literary tradition ultimately focuses attention on the figure of the poet herself and questions of female authorization and self-representation in poetry. As Gilbert and Gubar formulate it, Bloom's "anxiety of influence" becomes in women writers an "anxiety of authorship." In the face of their lack of models, as well as their social roles and literary representations as submissive and colorless "angels in the house," or alternatively as dark-lady sexual fiends, women find it hard to find their literary voices. What is lacking, Gilbert and Gubar argue, is the autonomy and authority that make authorship possible. To become writers, women must resist what Gilbert and Gubar describe as "the feelings of self-doubt, inadequacy, and inferiority that their education in "femininity" almost seems to have been designed to induce."[12] Women, to be writers and poets, have to overcome obstacles both internal and external to them, obstacles deeply inscribed into literary conventions and its representations of women as against men.

This emphasis on obstacles and constraints to autonomy, however, can overlook the resources women have from within their own cultural position and to adopt dominant and largely male models as the measure of authorship. Are there models that draw on women's own senses of identity? These have been seen mainly (and with justification) negatively, as bounded by injunctions to be "chaste, silent and obedient," which keep women from the autonomy and authority enjoyed by men writers.[13] The result is a struggle internal as well as external to women, who must, in Gilbert and Gubar's account, pursue the "difficult task of achieving true female literary autonomy by simultaneously conforming to and subverting patriarchal literary standards."[14] But this focus on autonomy in a sense adopts standards of men's culture for women. It means embracing what have been male models of authorship, so that the problem of women becomes their exclusion from the autonomy and self-assertion that male writers have. This is the view in a good deal of feminist literary history. In *The Madwoman in the Attic*, Gilbert and Gubar write, "For all literary artists, of course, self-definition necessarily precedes self-assertion: the creative 'I AM' cannot be uttered if the 'I' knows not what it is."[15] Similarly, in *Women Writers and Poetic Identity* Margaret Homans, another student of Bloom, sees the problem of the woman writer to be her lack of identity: "Without subjectivity, women are incapable of self-representation, the fundamental of masculine creativity." But women have "difficulty in creating a central sense of self in poetry."[16]

However, women poets' modes of expression also affirm a female sense of values and commitments, as these historically differed from men's. Women poets rarely claim to be speaking out of their own sublime genius, their own commanding visions. They tend not to see their poems as focused on themselves and their creative force. Instead, they are apt to speak for or to some purpose beyond themselves, certainly up until the twentieth century and even surprisingly into it.

Women in this sense can be seen to draw poetic authority from resources within women's culture and their own senses of who they are speaking for and to. These alternative resources derive from within the historical and social, religious and legal positioning of women, not only as scenes of restriction, although they certainly were also that, but as the contexts for women's own self-definition and self-representation in poetic venture. These contexts can be summed up under the heading of modesty. Modesty is in a sense the master virtue underlying or connecting other key feminine attributes such as the "piety, purity, submissiveness and domesticity" listed by Barbara Welter as making up the "Cult of True Womanhood" in the nineteenth century.[17] Norms of modesty of course antedate the nineteenth century's specific confirmations of it. Modesty runs backward through women's history as a regulative requirement across centuries, cultures, and geographies. In the United States, it took its own particular turns, under the religious, economic, geographical, cultural, legal, and ideological circumstances peculiar to American experience. Its persistence in women's culture places it at the center of many questions of women's literary history: the possibilities and images of authorship, the access to publication or circulation, the modes of self-representation, and the boundaries of women's experiences.

Within the parameters of women's literary history, modesty has been mentioned in literary analysis almost entirely as a repressive force denying to women freedom and self-determination. It is fundamental to women's assignment to the private sphere, limiting the reach and stature of their work and silencing their voices regarding public concerns and public presentation. As such modesty has been roundly condemned. Mary Kelley, for example, describes it, in its role of shielding "the female's person . . . from public scrutiny," as making publication itself into a transgressive act.[18] Gilbert and Gubar group together "submissiveness, modesty and self-lessness" as invidious constituents of the "angel" image that men have imposed and women have absorbed to the detriment of their "literary autonomy."[19] Mary Poovey contrasts the proper lady against the woman writer, where the act of publication "jeopardizes modesty, that critical keystone of feminine propriety; for it not only hazard[s] . . . disgrace, but cultivates and calls attention to the woman as subject, as initiator of indirect action, as a person deserving of notice for her own sake."[20] As Elaine Hobby puts it, "the primary 'necessity' for women was that they be 'modest,'" where modesty entails chastity and privacy.[21]

These claims are largely fair. Modesty without doubt has been and remains a means for circumscribing women, a barrier confining them to male-defined roles, spaces, possibilities, and, not least, dress and bodily comportment. Yet modesty is a complex structure that is not reducible only to suppression. This is specifically the case for women writers. As basic to their inscription in social systems, modesty has been a pivotal aspect of women's identity. As such it has also been part of the way women represent themselves. Indeed, for women writers, modesty is a central mode *of* self-representation, a way they have put themselves forward as a voice, author, and speaker, shaping how they present themselves, even as it also constrains their self-presentation. Modesty as a mode of presentation can be and has been, despite restrictions, in effect a counter-force against silencing. Even more, modesty may positively register a structure of values that women have articulated and embraced, not only as a limitation inflicted on them (although it has also been that) but also as an ethos to which they are committed: one that counters certain forms of aggressive, self-aggrandizing behaviors.

Modesty in its more complex senses has been acknowledged by critics, but then almost entirely as a "strategy," a disguise donned to evade social strictures while seeming to accede to them. Modesty is then said to be deployed out of the need to "find a repertoire of devices to make their writing a modest act" in order to conform to, and hence evade social strictures.[22] Certainly modesty also has strategic functions. It offers a concession to social expectations as a way of disarming them, acknowledging the limits on women in order to circumvent those limits, thus gaining for women some hearing at all. As tactic and strategy, it thus concedes limitation and bows to social prejudice, but it also opens a territory in which women are able to speak and be heard.

But modesty is rarely only strategic for women writers. Complex and ambivalent, modesty at once accepts restraint but also may define the self in terms other than self-assertion.[23] Even as a tactic, modesty may serve to express genuine senses that women have of themselves as historical and social beings. It is no mere external gesture to trick an audience. For many women writers, modest self-representation is a sincere image of who they considered themselves to be. And while modesty involves internalization of strictures imposed on women, raising problems of complicity in their own confinement, modesty also contains an aspect of women's identity in a positive sense, within a framework of cultural values women have represented and embraced. In this sense, it opens a window into women's culture, into the lives they have lived and the values they have been pledged to. These are values of obligation and community, of duty and a sense of self as embedded in and serving ends larger than the self. It involves a sense of limitation on the self as part of the self's engagement with others and creation of a joint social world. In these senses, the antonym to modesty is not simply freedom but the relentless pursuit of self-interest. Against this opposite extreme, modesty stands as a positive virtue, and indeed ethic, as a limitation of selves who would otherwise consume the world for themselves. This complex modesty can be seen in much of women's poetry. There modesty emerges as a characteristic topos, not only as abasement but as critical of the self-assertion and self-advancement that became increasingly dominant and obsessive goals in the development of American culture.

Modesty even as restraint is not exclusively a feminine virtue. Humility is a generally Christian ideal. But in social contexts, modesty has defined and restrained women more than it has men. Yet at the same time, from the viewpoint of women's culture, modesty can also be thought of as a positive value leaving room for others, as against self-promotion. Modesty would then not be mere self-erasure, but a structure of the self that confirms selfhood, as in one sense limited in relation to other selves and in another sense enlarged to engage and address others. As Marianne Moore puts the distinction in the poem "Silence," "The deepest feeling always shows itself in silence; not in silence, but restraint" (*CP* 91). Restraint is not simply silence, but rather a relationship between self and other, as well as a defining value of selfhood (in order to restrain a self you must first have one), leaving room for selves to act and speak in respect and also connection with each other.

That modesty as a social practice has been assigned to women rather than to men reflects gendered roles, but also divergent values characteristic in women's and men's cultures. Margaret Ezell has cautioned that current views of modesty are tied to a twentieth-century ideology, which sees "traditional configurations of the feminine as repressive and distorting," which she claims does not apply to women in the coterie culture of manuscript circulation in seventeenth-century England.[24] Recent discussions of early modernity have begun to explore a complicated hybrid of feminist positions whose political affiliations and cultural values were royalist as well as sectarian, Tory as well as Whig or radical.[25] America offers its own distinctive configurations of hybrid modesties, containing both conservative and progressive elements.

Law in general followed a different course in America, under different conditions and customs in economic and social terms than those obtained in England. Above all, as America moved into the Revolutionary period, women's relationships to public life began to alter, with republican claims to citizenship inaugurating in America new notions of women in the public sphere.[26] In this new context, modesty takes on new senses and implications. It emerges not only as a religious structure and social norm, but as a value with public implications, changing with the changing roles women in America began to assume. As will be argued throughout this book, women in America began to acquire a special sense of civic virtue, of the self as committed to others in community life and toward common goods. Modesty acquires new dimensions in this context, as the acknowledgment and embrace of self-limitation as self-enlargement, the sense that the self is part of a larger world.

This redefined sense of modesty in political senses emerges in the writings of Mary Wollstonecraft. Wollstonecraft is best known for focusing on questions of individual rights as these pertain to women. Yet in the *Vindication of the Rights of Woman*, she includes a chapter on "Modesty Comprehensively Considered and Not as a Sexual Virtue." Modesty represents there "the reserve of reason," a stance "equally distant from vanity and presumption, though by no means incompatible with a lofty consciousness of our own dignity." As such reserve, modesty takes its place within a network of women's social norms, norms women in America have upheld and enacted against drives of self-interest that occlude and indeed can abuse the good of others and the common interest.

Such complex modesty is especially pronounced for women writers, who by definition have pledged themselves to forms of self-expression. For American women poets, modesty in fact emerges as a major construction of identity and a foundational topos of feminine writing.[27] In this it acts as an avenue of self-representation and not only a mode of its prevention and suppression: a door out into public space rather than one only closed against it. Tropes of modesty include the problematics of naming and of silencing, central concerns of much of women's poetry; the placement of women in various spheres of society; modes of address; and the evocation and structure of the poet's role, of her poetic authority, of the right or possibility of her writing. Modesty is thus deeply embedded in women's self-representation in poetry, in their poetic conduct, and in a characteristic vision of the world. It provides a mode of self-presentation connecting the writer to her woman's culture while negotiating the masculine culture around her, even launching a critique of it in terms of her own values and sense of self. At issue here is not only complaint or compliance at exclusion from male modes of opportunity, but also questions about the costs and values of male cultural norms in the name of commitments that women historically have upheld and the structure of selfhood these imply. It involves the recognition of limitation of the self, and of obligation to society, as a positive, civic, and critical virtue. In this sense of self-limitation as against pure self-interest, modesty is value as well as constraint, functioning as an expression of women's selves and especially of ethics to which they have been committed. This complex stance is one of critical modesty or ethical restraint.

As a woman's topos, modesty is thus many-sided, highly complex, and multi-functional. On one level it is strategic, where conceding female limitations then allows the woman poet to exceed them, proceeding to her own expression and claiming some domain as properly her own. Modesty then serves as a mask, a way of disguising and circumventing restrictions it negotiates by acknowledging them. Yet it is more than a calculated gesture adopted for strategic ends. It also serves historically as a genuine expression of aspects of women's identity, at times as an internalized insecurity, but also as a positive expression of values that women hold and uphold. While expressing uncertainty as to both the ability and right to poetic venture, the modesty topos also provides the woman writer with an avenue of self-representation and emergence. It forms a familiar part of feminine discourse, and also of her commitment to certain values associated with and upheld by women. It becomes, Muse-like, a mode of authorization, at least for women poets willing to redefine it from subordinative to positive senses. Approached this way, modesty represents not only a barrier but also an avenue to women's writing, as a mode not of silence but of voice.

FEMALE MODELS OF POETIC SELFHOOD

Modest expression is a typical mode for women's poetic voices. In modesty, women poets partly accede to restrictions, partly circumvent them, but also partly articulate a different set of values, critical of the values of self-promotion and self-advancement as these became increasingly obsessive in American society. For the female artist, the problem is not simply the lack of an assertive selfhood denied to her and whose denial she must subvert and resist. Women poets, especially in the nineteenth century, offer models of selfhood based on different values with its own literary expression. These women's values, and the identities embedded in them, are not merely failed male identities based on the exclusion from yet hope of attaining some absolute autonomy and virile self-assertion. Instead, women's writing makes visible how such assertive individual identities can be problematic. Thus, women's poetic construction and self-representation are not only or primarily frustrated but are also critical and creative, projecting other voices, other modes of selfhood and authority distinct from those traditional to male poets.

Harold Bloom's recasting of poetic creativity as Quest-Romance in terms of poet, precursor-tradition, and Muse-inspiration offers a model that helps chart and distinguish women poets' senses of inspiration and authorial role. The image of writing as an Oedipal activity of the male poet in quest of his Muse, in order to wrest her from tradition in assertion of his own creative power, illuminates complexities for the woman poet in encountering these roles. In social terms, the woman is not normally the one who pursues and then claims and commands the object of desire. Rather than proclaiming their own originality and unique power, women poets tend to seek other positions from which to speak and address. This can include the critique of the male roles and norms, or of the place of women within them.

Emily Dickinson (1830–1886) is such a critical writer. Her speakers struggle with the paradox of the woman author for whom modesty makes it awkward to launch the activity and authority of creative writing, yet is a value that she embraces in complex ways. In that the poetic tradition is itself essentially male, Dickinson has difficulty in claiming it as her inheritance and taking her place in it, in terms of both models for speaking voices and its audiences and regarding the materials she treats and addresses. As to the experiences of inspiration, in both tradition and desire, this comes to her gendered male. Male ambition and desire are traditionally directed at the Muse as woman, a figure the male poet normatively courts and commands. Female poetic desire as directed toward a male object, however, threatens to command the woman writer, not she him. Rather than being inspired, the woman poet is at risk of being overpowered, something vividly shown in Dicksinson's abject letters addressed to a "Master." This is one level of the ambivalence that pervasively defines Dickinson's positions. In Bloomian terms, as Joanne Feit Diehl particularly shows, Dickinson courts but also flees from the male Muse whom she seeks but also wards off, both inviting and evading him.[28] As Diehl notes, in Dickinson there is a persistent retreat alongside invitation: "We shun it ere it comes. . . . And lest it fly / Beguile it more and more." (J 1580/F 1595).

But the modesty of the female position—as passively pursued rather than pursuing, as desired goal rather than desiring—does not simply compromise the conduct and possibilities of Dickinson as a woman poet. Dickinson also makes modesty into a strong poetic voice, fashioning it as a force of critical power. In her, the complexity and ambivalence of modest inscription becomes a cultivated art. Dickinson in her life of reclusion at once obeyed, exposed, and transmuted the modest norms that constituted her woman's culture. In her work, she makes modesty and its interlocking attitudes of concealment and disclosure, disclaimer and claim, a core poetic technique as well as a topic.[29]

Poems such as "I Meant to Have but Modest Needs" and "The World Stands Solemner to Me" name modesty directly as a scene of contention. The poem "Fitter to See Him" (*J* 968/*Fr* 834) examines more obliquely the archetypal position of the sequestered female, waiting for a man to come and recognize and rescue her, with its structural implications for poetic venture. But in Dickinson, the authorities of each position are powerfully redistributed. The poem renders in exemplary manner the modest assignment of women to passive confirmation and also its unmasking. It opens with the speaker in a state of waiting, suggesting the castle incarcerations of fairy tales, the fantasies of gendered romance, and also a religious anxiety that Dickinson shows to correlate with these: "Fitter to see Him, I may be / For the long Hindrance—Grace—to me— . . . To make me Fairest of the Earth / The Waiting—then—will seem so worth." In this poem, it is almost as if Dickinson has asked herself: what is the lady doing and thinking during all that time she is imprisoned in the castle while her rescuer is out and about? The poet imagines the lady to be in a state of intense anxiety about the self the hero will find, but she is also in profound critique of the whole arrangement and the criteria he will apply to her. "Fairest of the Earth" suggests romance and fairy tale while "Grace" suggests religion as deploying a similar structure, where the awaited male is God. But in either case, the speaker is disturbed. She is worried about being unworthy, but she is also angered at the position in which she has been placed. "I shall impute with half a pain / The blame that I was chosen—then—." Being at last "chosen" might make the "Waiting" indeed "worth," but it will erase only "half" the "pain" and "blame" that the lady feels.

As so often in Dickinson, opening positions are steadfastly complicated as the text proceeds, often to the undoing of what the poem seemed at first to say. At the start, patient waiting is apparently embraced as a proper romantic and religious attitude before a male authority, who alone can initiate, decide, and bestow ultimate judgment. But both the patience and the ordeal become exposed as unjust and tormenting. Seemingly acquiescent language turns into critical attack. As the poem proceeds, "Time to anticipate his Gaze" promises to justify the lady's immobilized and anxious attendance as readying her for her lover/redeemer's advent. But the initial "Delight" becomes "Surprise," not as pleasure but rather as alarm. What the lady finally faces is an inspection by the "Gaze" of the arrived quester, "turning o'er and o'er my face," seeking "Evidence it be the Grace." But what if this "Grace" is denied? Then the "Delay" to test the woman's "worth" may herald not bliss but harsh judgment using questionable criteria. Dickinson's waiting woman, unlike those in fairy tales, is not protected from the ravages of time and change. She may have aged so that the male inspector may seek an "Excellenter Youth." Even worse, what may disturb the hero is not the lady's loss of youth and beauty, but even her gains: "I only must not grow so new," "I only must not change so fair." What he may dislike is exactly her having grown and changed into a self that fails to conform to his image and desire of her.

The poem brilliantly balances an ecstatic language of redemption, both sexual-social and religious, against suspicion of it. The lady's fantasy of final rescue, to "Elsewhere go no more" whether as marriage or heaven (with a suggestion of entrapment?), is at the cost of a selfhood that may differ from the one the hero—or God—judges by. The poem's end offers a highly equivocal entanglement of these counter-crossing discourses. What looks like exuberant justification—"I shall not lack in Vain"—becomes a paradoxical claim to "gain—thro loss" and "obtain" through "Grief" only partly convincing. Nor is it clear just what the lady in the end does "obtain." She is finally reduced to mere "Beauty" as "reward" for the male courtier. As to herself, the best outcome seems to be not gain but relief: "The Beauty of Demand—at Rest." At least her anxious waiting comes to an end, with all the demands and expectations that are as much a prison as her confined quarters.

In this text, the traditional position of woman as the object of male quest and male poem is adopted but radically transformed. Dickinson here is less lady-in-waiting than lady-in-ambush. Yet neither does she simply reverse roles. She waits, but in doing so she exercises her own judgment and offers her own version, her own sense of what is or is not "fair."

Emily Dickinson's verse provides an intense scene of conflict between gendered positioning and strenuous authorship, with the relations among poet, precursor-tradition, Muse-inspiration, and the roles of each placed under severe pressure. Modesty, however, is a scene of contention long before Dickinson. In America, it begins with the first published poet, Anne Bradstreet (1612–1672). Bradstreet's work almost uncannily introduces features and elements that remain enduring throughout the whole subsequent course of American women's poetry. Modesty almost defines her self-representation as a woman poet. In her, however, while modesty is an obstacle and a form of self-demotion, it is also a critical claim and a source of authority. Bradstreet contests as well as claims precursors, and also contemporary men, often in the name of women's culture and values, which in their own way emerge as her Muses.

Modesty fundamentally defines Bradstreet's poetic voice, tying it to women's social as well as religious roles, as a constraint but also as representing values for which Bradstreet speaks. Her sense of self works among three distinct identities. She is at once Puritan, woman, and poet. Given how tense the relationship among these different selves can be, Bradstreet is remarkably balanced in her life and work. Educated in the private library of the Earl of Lincoln whom her father served as steward (her brother attended Cambridge), she was both daughter and wife to governors of the Massachusetts Bay Colony, associating her more with Massachusetts' civic than religious elite, if at one remove. As a magistrate, her father presided at the trial of Anne Hutchinson in the antinomian controversy, in which Bradstreet's own sister was also implicated. Yet Hutchinson's female rebellion, claiming inner voice against the authorities of the established (male) ministry, seems not to have deeply marked Bradstreet. Her own memoir, left for her children's edification, mentions early trials of faith, safely passed, but she was no outright rebel.[30]

Bradstreet's poetic self-representations are firmly anchored in her womanly roles: as daughter, as wife, as mother. This is the case even in her main body of work, which was devoted to public rather than private affairs. These public poems founded her reputation in her own day, although it is her more personal poems that are now read and admired. Her writings generally lean toward mundane rather than theological concerns, although always within the framework of Puritan religious attitudes. Bradstreet appears to be comfortable in her religious community and its roles. Among these, modesty is formative. The story of how she came to be published illustrates. Bradstreet insisted that not she, but her brother-in-law, had her work published without her consent or knowledge. Anonymity or adopting male names to protect the female author's modesty, as well as excuses or justifications for publishing, are standard practices well into the nineteenth century, during which many women also excused publishing as a necessity due to their family's financial need or in the context of religious or civic calling. In Bradstreet's case, apologia structures her now famous "Prologue" (*Works* 15) to her collection of public poems, where she concedes that it is not for her

> To sing of wars, of captains, and of kings,
> Of cities founded, commonwealths begun,

No such epic topics are suitable to her, since hers is a "mean pen" for such "superior things." Her "obscure lines" should not "dim the worth" of real "poets and historians." But as it turns out, her "main defect" is gender itself, what she later calls having "a weak or wounded brain." Hers is a "foolish, broken, blemished Muse," faults that "no art" can "mend, . . . 'Cause nature made it so irreparable."

What is striking in this and other self-deprecating Bradstreet texts, however, is the rhetorical mastery with which she elaborates her tropes of incompetence. Modest female inadequacy is gainsaid by the firm accomplishment of her performance, so that failings are attested with complex wit, and claimed dullness is brilliantly conducted. "From schoolboy's tongue no rhet'ric we expect," she writes, but then she goes on to cite the "sweet consort" of Pythagorean cosmic music, Demosthenes as "sweet tongued Greek," the "nine" Muses and "Calliope" as "poesy's" mother. As a claim to ignorance and inability, the poem quite fails.

It then turns to counter-attack, in what emerges as a trove of feminized tropes:

> I am obnoxious to each carping tongue,
> Who says my hand a needle better fits,
> A poet's pen all scorn I should thus wrong,
> For such despite they cast on female wits;
> If what I do prove well, it won't advance,
> They'll say it's stol'n, or else it was by chance.

Bradstreet's images of writing as mending and of the needle for writing recur as women's topoi. Her use of commonplace phrases such as women's "obnoxious . . . carping tongue," as a way to contest their accepted social meanings, is a practice of invoking and questioning dominant phrases and words that many women writers pursue. This verse in fact unmasks the prevailing "despite on female wits" as circular and self-confirming, since even when what women do "prove well" it is then denied as "stolen" (as occurred in the case of Phyllis Wheatley) or "by chance." Finally, Bradstreet's modesty works as a disarming concession that opens ways for her to be heard:

> Preeminence in all and each is yours;
> Yet grant some small acknowledgement of ours.
>
> And oh ye hi-gh flown quills that soar the skies,
> And ever with your prey still catch your praise,
> If e'er you deign these lowly lines your eyes,
> Give thyme or parsley wreath, I ask no bays;
> This mean and unrefined ore of mine
> Will make your glist'ring gold but more to shine.

Men, she grants, have "preeminence," while all she seeks is "small acknowledgement." Yet this is still a claim to be acknowledged. In the last verse, "Preeminence" emerges as a suspect value, with modesty in contrast actually the superior virtue. Male verse, with its "high flown quills that soar the skies," is exposed as birds of "prey" hunting "praise." If they "deign" to look in disdain at hers as "lowly lines," this is not here a sign of her failure but a critique of those (male) writers who seek praise ravenously. Her "mean and unrefined ore" then shines as genuine, against false values that are likened to "glist'ring gold." Bradstreet's lowly modesty thus emerges as having a superior claim, something valuable to offer as against male poetic ambition. In her conclusion, Bradstreet's own language displaces those that would silence her. In a gesture at once modest and affirming, she denies any claim to bay wreath crowns and instead is content with "thyme or parsley leaf." The bay wreath originates in the rape of Daphne, who to escape Apollo was turned into a tree. It marks competitive poetic glory. In its stead, Bradstreet says she seeks a crown of kitchen herbs drawn from her ordinary and domestic domain, which she thus renders poetic.

Modesty thus stakes out a feminized territory for the poet, in many ways limited but also claiming value for itself against ambitions that prove predatory and aggressive. The complexity of this modesty topos is even more pronounced in a poem that Bradstreet prepared for a second printing of her book, which she did not live to see. Found among her papers, "The Author to Her Book" (*Works* 221) offers an extended and elaborate conceit comparing authorship to motherhood, through an intensified modesty topos that invokes but also challenges its own abject forms:

> Thou ill-formed offspring of my feeble brain,
> Who after birth didst by my side remain,
> Till snatched from thence by friends, less wise than true,
> Who thee abroad, exposed to public view,
> Made thee in rags, halting to th' press to trudge,
> Where errors were not lessened (all my judge).
> At thy return my blushing was not small,
> My rambling brat (in print) should mother call,
> I cast thee by as one unfit for light,
> Thy visage was so irksome in my sight;
> Yet being mine own, at length affection would
> Thy blemishes amend, if so I could:
> I washed thy face, but more defects I saw,
> And rubbing off a spot still made a flaw.
> I stretched thy joints to make thee even feet,
> Yet still thou run'st more hobbling than is meet;
> In better dress to trim thee was my mind,
> But nought save homespun cloth " th' house I find.
> In this array 'mongst vulgars may'st thou roam.
> In critic's hands beware thou dost not come,
> And take thy way where yet thou art not known;
> If for thy father asked, say thou hadst none;
> And for thy mother, she alas is poor,
> Which caused her thus to send thee out of door.

In the intricate extended simile this poem elaborates, author is to mother as book is to child. Retelling the story of the book's unintended publication, each step of authorship correlates with a stage of mothering in subtle and masterful puns. Kidnapped from her nursing "side," the book/child is "exposed to public view" through printing, dressed in "rags"/paper, whose "halting" trudge of faulty metric makes it a "rambling" brat in both linguistic and ambulatory senses. "Blemishes" of skin and type-setting are attended by "Rubbing off a spot" as both face-washing and paper-erasing. "Even feet" correct both walking and prosody.

More complex still is the mother/author's attitude to her offspring. To be "ill-formed" is to be monstrous, and the poet seems to speak mainly of shame and dissatisfaction with what she has produced. Yet what also comes through is care and attention, and ultimately an embrace of what she has created: "Yet being mine own, at last affection would / thy blemishes amend." Even negative terms prove double-edged. The author/mother's "brain" may be "feeble," but its book/child springs from it as Athena did from Zeus's head. To be dressed in "homespun" is to be dressed plainly, but also to wear only what she herself has made. If the book/child has no "father," it is illegitimate but also created by herself alone. And the mother/author is committed to protecting her creation against presumably male "critics." Above all, the extreme accomplishment of this poem utterly belies its self-deprecation. Bradstreet's concluding claim to be "poor" serves to protect herself as well as her writing from attack, and also to expose negative expectations as unfounded prejudice. One might say that the figure for the Muse here is not seductive female but mother. Rather than quest, there is birth. In an act of self-naming deeply characteristic of women's poetry, Bradstreet bids the child should her "mother call (in print)." And for all the poem's hedging, it ends with acknowledging it as her own and sending it "out of door" into the public arena. Disclaimer thus turns into claim, or rather, counter-claim. Its main argument of defective writing is masterfully belied and overturned by the masterful poetic conduct in which it is put forward. And although it concedes, it ultimately also affirms and defends what she called in the "Prologue" "lowly lines" which, in her poetic doing, gives validation to women's experience as a topic for writing.

MODESTY AND MODERNITY

Anne Bradstreet's feminized tropes, in which she draws on women's experiences and domains as the source of her imagery; her strategies of self-representation in which she claims the role of poet but through concession and disclaimer; and not least her critique of male values in the name of alternative standards and commitments, continue to shape the poetry that comes after her, in the nineteenth and twentieth centuries. Marianne Moore, in many ways a bridging figure from nineteenth- to twentieth-century poetics, combines the radical experimentation of the latter with the senses of restraint of the former, now clearly claimed as critical and positive. Often her modesty has been seen as merely restrictive, often associated with the private sphere. Randall Jarrell describes Marianne Moore's (1887–1972) poems as having "the manners or manner of ladies who learned a little before birth not to mention money, who neither point nor touch, and who scrupulously abstain from the mixed, live vulgarity of life."[31] Adrienne Rich similarly describes Moore as "maidenly, elegant, intellectual, discreet." To Cheryl Walker, Moore is among the poets who have led "quiet lives, applauded gentility, preferred intellectual reflection over gestures of social outrage, and amused themselves with playful experiments."[32] Betsy Erkkila sees in Moore "traditional notions of feminine virtue and reticence" whose "fundamental Protestant faith set her apart, aesthetically and morally, from the sordities of the times."[33] This maidenly, mannerly, and modest impression is confirmed by Elizabeth Bishop, although she also associates herself with such muted compliments. Bishop bids Moore, in "Invitation to Miss Marianne Moore," to "please come flying," "Bearing a musical inaudible abacus, / a slight censorious frown," to a Manhattan "awash with morals this fine morning."[34] But "Efforts of Affection," Bishop's memoir of Moore, concludes with a meditation on the letter M that exactly proposes Moore's manner as a mode of ethics: "Marianne's monogram; mother; manners; morals; and I catch myself murmuring, "Manners and morals; manners *as* morals? Or is it morals *as* manners?"[35] Conversely, Moore wrote of Bishop, in a review essay called "The Modest Expert," "Why has no one ever thought of this, one asks oneself, why not be accurate and modest."[36] Here Moore both invokes and undermines rigid gender terms in which modesty is self-effacement, associating it instead with a fidelity that does not focus on the self as its center.[37]

Moore repeatedly makes modesty a trope, variously figured, for her own poetic voice, and indeed for poetics itself, closely tied to her ethical commitments. In "To a Snail" (CP 85), the snail, a popular image of womanly domesticity and modesty in literary history, here becomes an image for poetics itself.[38]

> If "compression is the first grace of style,"
> you have it. Contractility is a virtue
> as modesty is a virtue.
> It is not the acquisition of any one thing
> that is able to adorn,
> or the incidental quality that occurs
> as a concomitant of something well said,
> that we value in style,
> but the principle that is hid: . . .
> in the absence of feet, "a method of conclusions"
> "a knowledge of principles,"
> In the curious phenomenon of your occipital horn.

Poetry's hidden meanings—"the principle that is hid," are intensely compressed in its language and never fully exhausted or unveiled, is compared with the "virtue" of "modesty." Here "style" is a "grace," first in its "contractility" of the self as against either confessional or other poetries in which the poet's vision or person stands out, insisting on itself as the poetic center. Modesty further stands against the economic appetite of "acquisition," the vanity and reduction of what merely "is able to adorn," the self-admiration of "something well said." If modesty is a womanly quality, it is also here poetic and moral, in the name of what "we value" and against its betrayal into more aggressive assertions.

Moore's poetic forms in many ways practice the modesty she preaches. Hers is very much "the principle that is hid," including her reticent rhyme patterns (as in repetitions of virtue, virtue; style, style; the off-rhyme of said/hid; and then the surprising full rhyme of adorn/horn); subtle puns ("in the absence of feet," which applies to both the snail and the poem); visual play (this is almost a shape poem); respectful attention to marginal creatures, who, as here, are often protected and concealed; and incorporation and conscientious quotation of words taken from others. Yet with "a knowledge of principles," patterns become apparent, in prosody, rhyme, and image.

Modesty has emerged in recent discussions of ethics and virtue largely as a matter of self-regard, involving questions of attributing or claiming credit, accurate appraisal of levels of accomplishment, and issues of personal temperament.[39] But in Moore, modesty is less focused on the attitudes of the self to itself than a stance toward others. As a "contractility" that contracts, it does not erase the self, but allows place to others. It claims a constraint against imposing self on others, showing regard for them, as a strength, and indeed a claim to style and virtue.

Modesty as moral stance surfaces in another twentieth-century poet, far removed from Moore's proprieties. Gwendolyn Brooks' (1917–2000) writing uncannily recalls Bradstreet's. Brooks's 1950s sonnet sequence "The Womanhood" is one of several spoken in the voice of a mother, whose self-representation concerns her powerlessness in facing the social-historical obstacles she and her children face. As one poem asks, "What shall I give my children? Who are poor" (*B* 116).

> What shall I give my children? who are poor,
> Who are adjudged the leastwise of the land,
> Who are my sweetest lepers, who demand
> No velvet and no velvety velour;

The children are those to whom the poet is most deeply attached and obligated, but her personal and social means to meet their needs are severely constrained. In a world where her children, as African-Americans, are "adjudged" my authorities remote from them; are "leastwise of the land," excluded as "lepers" (although to her "sweet"), Brooks concedes at once the limitations to her powers and yet their urgent necessity. This in turn becomes an elaborate figure for poetic creativity itself. These poem/children

> have begged me for a brisk contour,
> Crying that they are quasi, contraband
> Because unfinished, graven by a hand
> Less than angelic, admirable or sure.
> My hand is stuffed with mode, design, device.
> But I lack access to my proper stone.
> And plenitude of plan shall not suffice
> Nor grief nor love shall be enough alone
> To ratify my little halves who bear
> Across an autumn freezing everywhere.

Her children, like her art, have "begged me for a brisk contour." But her ability, as mother/poet, is restricted. Far from claiming potent genius, she portrays herself as struggling with both an external world that denies her means—"I lack access to my proper stone"—but also with her own imperfection, leaving her child/art "unfinished, graven by a hand / Less than angelic, admirable or sure."

As a sonnet, "What Shall I Give My Children" raises aesthetic questions about constraints and creativity. Sonnet structure, with its rigors of limitation, becomes a form of inventive power, in ways not unlike Marianne Moore's careful craft. Limit and creativity are inextricably intertwined. As in Bradstreet's poem "The Author to Her Book," this sonnet is spoken by a mother who is also a poet, each presented as a figure for the other, while the children in turn represent creative art. The mother becomes a Muse figure, a source of inspiration, drawing not on traditional authority but a woman's culture that emphasizes devotion. Birth and care are the tropes for creativity. But these are not merely private concerns. They are placed in wider frameworks, with both mother/poet and the children/poetry she cares for located in a "freezing" world that leaves little room for them. Brooks is in fact bounded by both gender and race, economic and social situations that construct her. She resides in a world that she does not control. Yet the poet/mother's hand still reaches to engrave. It is "stuffed with mode, design, device." Although her skill and devotion are "not enough alone to ratify" (in legal language) her creative efforts, she continues them. The world, and her work in it, remains one that she both embraces and protests. Modesty registers this ambivalence and also dedication. Her work remains "graven by a hand / Less than angelic, admirable or sure." But this sense of incompletion deepens her commitment to a future and a world outside, and in many ways beyond herself. However modest and limited her power to reshape her reality, in this sonnet, the artist, like the mother, devotes herself to the creation of other possible worlds.

2 Muted Groups, Veiled Discourses
Feminist Anthropology

Some of the most original and compelling feminist work was originally launched in the field of anthropology. Anthropologists were among the first to pose underlying and overarching questions defining the categories for feminist discussion. What makes an experience or a structure gendered? What continuities are evident across societies regarding the place(s) of women? How are differences and similarities from society to society to be systematically coordinated and assessed? Do the marked differences in different societies make generalizations about gender and women's experiences impossible? Sherry Ortner describes the creative tension in anthropology as the effort to "explain human universals" while also explaining "cultural particulars."[1] Anthropology asks theoretical questions while insisting on social reference and diversity. Anthropological models thus address overarching patterns while also arguing for the embeddedness of human behavior and its meanings within specific cultural systems.

Ortner proposed one such overarching pattern. She posited the foundational contrast between nature and culture to be gendered, with women consistently associated with nature—as body and the care of body, as disorder and requiring rule—and men associated with culture and its corollaries of order and command. Her seminal essay appeared in the groundbreaking collection, *Women, Culture and Society*, alongside other foundational essays in feminist theory, including Nancy Chodorow's "Family Structure and Feminine Personality," which proposed a relational model for girls' psychology and socialization as against male models of individuation and detachment; and Michelle Zimbalist Rosaldo's investigation of the public and private spheres as a cross-cultural enduring gender structure, constituting gender in social terms.[2]

In each case, these anthropologists were gendering anthropology itself, problemetizing the boundaries between nature and cultural arrangements as themselves gendered categories both in analyzing material and in the material analyzed. Anthropology examined gender at the "intersection of biology and culture."[3] In the words of Henrietta Moore, anthropology redefined gender as a symbolic category as well as a social relationship within interpenetrating boundaries between nature and culture. Biology takes on significance in "culturally defined value systems" as enacted in social interactions, and womanhood emerges as a constructed, cultural category.[4] Margaret Mead had early warned that sexuality is not a fixed category.[5] Gayle Rubin, reflecting on what she called "the oppression of women in its endless variety and monotonous similarity," then radically introduced the distinction between 'gender' as a social category, as against supposedly natural, biological 'sex.' The sex/gender distinction has been further destabilized as fixed categories in postmodern discussions, notably by Judith Butler, who has questioned the existence of 'nature' and gendered body as themselves cultural categories.[6] Anthropologists have persistently warned against confusing cultural categories with nature, including the distinctions between private and public, with gender not "biologically based differences which oppose women and men," but rather "the product of social relationships in concrete (and changeable) societies."[7] As Shirley Ardener warns, correlations between biological and social structures remain extremely difficult to gauge and deeply circular, where the perception and measure of so-called physical features are already cultural and gendered:

> Measurement itself is determined by an arbitrary set of distinctions [and may serve as] merely arbitrary markers which have been found useful for setting up social oppositions, and it is the opposition to men that is the basis of womanhood, however characterized in the world of events. Because of this opposition, women experience the world differently from men, regardless of whether or not innate differences are significant.[8]

Of particular relevance to literature are anthropological approaches to language. Language has emerged as both a field and an instrument of anthropological study. The social question of whether there is a 'women's language' distinct from men's has launched a series of behavioral studies investigating whether women have speech styles that differ from men's—whether "women and men use language in different ways," whether language "reflects and helps to constitute sexual inequality."[9] Robin Lakoff identifies in women expressive patterns of hesitation and apology, question-asking and qualification of what is said, and ambivalence as to their own authority when they speak.[10] The distinctions between formal and social/cultural interactions of language can be questioned. How things are said is deeply influenced and shaped by who is speaking and when and where something is spoken.[11] Studies have shown that female state legislators speak less than their male counterparts, and that when they do speak, they do so with more expressions of uncertainty. They are more often interrupted and ask questions rather than state opinions or initiate controversy.[12] Other work has focused on cases where women speak in special dialects or even different languages. Among certain tribes, marriageable women are captured from tribes that speak another language. Japanese women use not only other grammatical inflections (as is the case in many languages) but a distinctive vocabulary.[13] Natalie Zeman Davis describes Yiddish as a woman's language in seventeenth-century German-Ashkenaz communities.[14]

Especially interesting for literary study is the analysis of women's speech as explored by Edwin Ardener. In his essay on "Belief and the Problem of Women," Ardener reports a characteristic difficulty in obtaining anthropological accounts of women in their own words. Men and not women tend to provide the accounts both for men and for women, since it is men who regularly serve as native informants willing or able to communicate with anthropologists in terms that anthropologists recognize and systematize. Women thus enter ethnographic description as viewed from outside, "at the level of observation" provided by men but not in their own terms or through their own voices. They are, that is, only indirectly presented, as objects but not subjects: "The study of women is on a level little higher than the study of the ducks and fowls they commonly own—a mere birdwatching indeed."[15] To attempt to gain insight into women's culture and experiences, anthropologists therefore turn to symbols, rituals, artifacts, crafts, and other ethnographic but nonverbal representations. But while these do "uncover certain valuations of women," they do so without the interpretations and explanations of women themselves in their own voices. Women thus are seen but not seeing. But this also blocks them from view since they are 'seen' only through the eyes and words of male interpreters.

Ardener proposes a variety of explanations for this inaccessibility of women to the ethnographer. Even when anthropologists wish and attempt to approach women, men routinely prove to be more available to them: more willing to talk to anthropologists, more fluent in the anthropologist's foreign languages, and more able to work with the sorts of abstractions that anthropologists introduce for social schematization. Women, in contrast, have consistently been resistant to approach by anthropologists, whether male or female. Rather than responding to anthropological contact, they "giggle when young, snort when old, reject the question, laugh at the topic, etc." Women remain inaccessible, evasive in their speech, and inarticulate in terms recognizable to anthropologists and indeed to men in their own social settings.

Why should women's viewpoints and self-expression be so resistant to access? Why do women seem to lack or be unable to make available what Ardener calls a 'meta-language' of self-reflective explanation? To describe this inaccessibility of women's discourse, Ardener proposes a theory of 'dominant' and 'muted' models within a society. As Shirley Ardener elaborates, a 'model' represents the "underlying perceptual and symbolic systems" that organize the way a group understands itself and its world.[16] This organization is conscious but also unconscious, and it encompasses values and standards, categories and assumptions, measurements and assessments, all the substrata of constructing, assessing, and articulating one's world. What Ardener posits is that in any given society, there is in place a dominant model that operates according to the cultural understanding, paradigms, and values held by the dominant group. Through this dominant model, subgroups within the society must construe their world and indeed also themselves. But this requires translations and transformations from the subgroup experience into the discourse of the dominant group. A variety of 'rules' of transmutation through 'complex logical relationships' are necessary to connect the subgroup's expressions to the dominant group's ones. The nondominant or subgroup has perceptions, understandings, stances, and values of its own—its own subgroup or 'counterpart' models—that differ in varying degrees from the dominant one in which its members live. But to express themselves—perhaps even to themselves—they must conform to the terms set by the dominant group, which are what they learn or accept as valid. What results is a discrepancy between the subgroup model and the dominant one, making the subgroup inarticulate, what Ardener calls 'mute.' This is not to imply simple silence, but rather what can be called a 'veiled' speech that stands in complex relation to the dominant discourse through which it gains only partial and transmuted expression.

In these transformations, the subgroup viewpoints, although at variance with those of the dominant group, still have to negotiate and to some degree adopt the dominant terms. But as a result, even apparently familiar expressions may mean something quite different when used by the subgroup, as against its meanings for the dominant one. The subgroup finds ways to articulate its own counter-models but in disguised and indirect ways. In outward daily life and formal language expression, the muted group may conform to the modes of the dominant group, using the same words. Yet the way subgroup members use and mean these words may differ from their meaning in the dominant discourse.

Although it remains positioned as subordinate within the assessments and hierarchies of the dominant group, the subgroup embraces independent values, standards, and meanings for its own activities, which it also expresses. But, still functioning within the dominant model and discourse, it does so in "rickety or cumbersome" ways (xiv). The subgroup thus becomes a muted group: a group whose life views do not find direct or ready expression but are instead veiled for and by the dominant group, only expressible in transmuted ways still framed through the dominant discourses.

Ardener's theory of 'muted discourses,' where women's voices may be said to be 'veiled,' is distinct from accounts of women's language that have emerged in French feminist theory. Hélène Cixous's 'écriture feminine,' Luce Irigaray's 'parler femme,' and Julia Kristeva's pre-Oedipal, pre-Symbolic maternal language each variously claims to describe a language peculiar to women, derived in and expressing woman's body and psyche, as source and model of a specifically female creativity. These, however, are psychoanalytic theories, rather than socio-historical or for that matter expressly literary ones. What Cixous calls a 'counter-language' that "is never simple or linear or objectified," "generalized," a language of "mother's milk" written in "white ink," does not concretely describe actual women's literary writing. The same is the case for Irigaray's women's language as "continuous, compressible, dilatable, viscous, conductive, diffusible."[17] Nor does Kristeva's pre-Oedipal language specifically describe writing by women: Kristeva in fact has mainly modernist male writers in mind.[18] Such theories of women's language, while psychoanalytically interesting and provocative in feminist terms, ultimately serve to limit the kinds of expression ascribed to women. In terms of poetry, such theories tend to enclose poetic writing away from surrounding discourses, into substrata at once organic and psychic, apart from all ordinary discourse.[19]

The model of dominant as against subordinate groups in society also recalls Marxian analysis, where it has been applied to class. Antonio Gramsci's discusses hegemony as the process by which dominant groups win the consent of subordinate ones. These models do not, however, specifically consider gender, and, as has been much noted, class categories are not fully congruent with gendered ones.[20] Ardener's model of dominant and muted discourses is directed to gender and is especially apt for analyzing women's literature, as Elaine Showalter notes in her essay "Feminist Criticism in the Wilderness," although it also yields rich results in minority literatures other than those by women.[21] African-American and other cultural identities in American culture similarly deploy veiled and transformational language in relation to dominant Anglo-American models.

In terms of gender, the Ardener theory of models offers methods directly connecting literary language to the discourses surrounding them. Literature draws its words from those in general circulation. It uses these words in varied and complex response to the discourses of society, exposing or confirming but always intensifying resonance and implication. This is the case for poetry as for prose. Formalist notions of the poem as a self-referring, pure language enclosed in its own unitary composition, despite recent historicist critical trends, continue greatly to influence approaches to poetic texts, putting them at a remove from surrounding discourses.[22] Ardener's model suggests ways to interpret poetry as engaged with other discourses—indeed, as a particular site for such engagement and transformation among discourses, made visible in poetic textuality.

Within literary study, the notion of literary language as circulating and in dialogical exchange has been best developed in the work of Mikhail Bakhtin. Bakhtin denied the application of his dialogical theory to poetry, continuing to accept the formalist model that enclosed poetry in a pure idiom, remote from relationship to the surrounding discourses that he saw the novel to sustain. Novelistic discourses are "heteroglot, multi-voiced, multi-styled and often multi-languaged elements," but poetry is monological. Ardener's anthropological discussion, however, points ways to connect

Bakhtinian theory to poetry despite Bakhtin's own exclusion of it. Poetry is, in fact, albeit differently from fiction, a scene of linguistic collision and exchange deeply embedded as, in Bakhtin's terms, a "struggle among sociolinguistic points of view." It participates in the importation, contention, polemic, affirmation, intensification, assault, repression, and every other relation to surrounding socio-historical discourses from which it draws and in which it takes place.[23] Ardener's discussion further opens a gendered dimension in Bakhtin, from which it is largely absent.[24]

Gender is an interrelational and not isolated discourse, identity, or social group. Women, like all individuals, participate in a range of subgroups, which enter their poetry through forms of cross-discourse. Among American women poets, Frances Harper and Gwendolyn Brooks are African-American, Emma Lazarus and Muriel Rukeyser are Jewish-American, Elizabeth Bishop and Adrienne Rich are gay. Balances and exchanges between several muted or veiled discourses enter into their texts, each in complex relation with the others and with dominant forms. Poets may belong to the dominant group in socio-economic, regional, or religious senses but, as women, take up distinctive positions within those groups. Within their texts, relationships among the varied discourses can take the form of submission to and internalization of dominant models or rebellion and rejection of them. Other stances besides these extremes include partial identifications, selective appropriations, redirected implications, changed valences in which what is praiseworthy in one discourse becomes culpable in another and vice versa, with expansion of terms to include women, or inversion of terms to critique men. Elements that mean and reside within a dominant context in one way may mean and reside within the subgroup's model and expression differently. Images that have one significance within the dominant male tradition may take on other meanings and significance when deployed by women.

These sorts of conversions and transformations have been explored in women's uses of traditional female figures and of imagery. H. D. (Hilda Doolittle 1886–1961) rewrote female figures from past mythology. Her transformations of imagery to positive from negative valence, and vice versa, have been studied by Alicia Ostriker.[25] But these references and transfigurations also extend beyond literary history into social discourses. The poetic text emerges as fully permeable. Its words pick up and present anew, highlight and undercut, the words surrounding it. Through these and other techniques, women's poetry challenges the meanings of words as determined within the dominant models of male culture. Their poetry attempts, not always successfully, to wrest meanings away for their own purposes. The poetry invokes senses of words in the surrounding discourses, each carrying with it the dynamic interrelations with its other uses, histories, appearances, and circulations, and then may contend with or confirm, oppose or intensify, submit to or expose these words, redeploying them in concrete poetic events.

ARTS OF QUOTATION

In a theory of poetry as public and cultural discourse, Emily Dickinson provides a limit case. To all appearances—and in most interpretations—Dickinson's is a poetry of the most profound privacy, at the greatest remove from public discourse or affairs. Yet her writing is very much an arena in which cross-discourses confront each other, with dominant terms examined and reoriented through her own countering language. Such cross-discourse analysis helps release her from the gendered incarceration in which, until recently, she has been held.[26] Dickinson's poems are certainly formal objects, intricately etched into highly complex linguistic forms. But they equally address surrounding cultural languages and are alive with contest, claim, disclaimer, appeal, denial, and desire. They are a texture of voices answering and contending with each other. And they strongly pose a veiled female discourse against a dominant male one, contesting, transforming, or exposing normative voices of male social models.

Dickinson's series of 'wife' poems engage and counter surrounding discourses at a distance, since she of course never was one.[27] Obviously at issue are gender roles, where 'wife' becomes a term lifted from dominant discourses, which then undergo poetic examination, critique, and ultimately altered senses. Quotation marks often play a central role in handling these incorporated terms. What quotation marks signal is that the words inside them are not one's own. The words are instead both adopted and removed from their ordinary, which is to say assumed meanings. The quotations mark them exactly *as* someone else's words, exposing and then pulling them toward other significations. Reading a poem guided by quotation marks means carefully attending to and picking a path through these contested senses: how the words were used in their original settings and how they now are removed and mean differently from those settings. This poetic art of quotation can be compared to "mimicry" in the senses given that term by Homi Babha:

> The discourse of mimicry is constructed around an ambivalence; in order to be effective, mimicry must continually produce its slippage, its excess, its difference. The authority of that mode of colonial discourse that I have called mimicry is therefore stricken by an indeterminacy: mimicry emerges as the representation of a difference that is itself a process of disavowal.[28]

Mimicry at once adopts and disavows what is dictated to it by a dominant authority, in a mode of repetition that is also slippage. Luce Irigaray likewise speaks of mimicry in a specifically feminist and linguistic framework concerning "the articulation of the female sex in discourse." There is, she writes, perhaps only one "path," the one assigned to the feminine: that of *mimicry*. One must assume the feminine role deliberately. Which means already to convert a form of subordination into an affirmation, and thus to begin to thwart it. Whereas a direct feminine challenge to this condition means demanding to speak as a (masculine) "subject," that is, it means to postulate a relation to the intelligible that would maintain sexual indifference.[29]

As in mimicry, in poetry gendered words—words revealed as gendered—can be lifted out from social discourse and replaced in the mouth of a woman persona to mean differently, yet in reflective slippage against dominant usages.

In Dickinson, the poem I'm "wife"—"I've finished that—/ That other state—"(J 199/F 225) enacts just such a mimicry, displacement, exposure, and examination of the meaning of "wife" as lifted out of its ordinary and unreflected usages. Dickinson speaks here at an angle, since the "I" of the poem, speaking as a wife, can not be herself. In a sense, this poem's subject is not only becoming a wife but the word 'wife' and all that it imports. As is usual in Dickinson, severe syntactic obfuscations and tricky grammatical distributions make it difficult to discern how each word is meant and even what phrases and groupings belong together. The term 'wife' is strangely positioned between unclearly specified 'that's—which one is 'that' finished state, which one "that—/ That other state—"? 'Wife' presumably contrasts with maidenhood,. compared to which the speaker is, she goes on to say, fully ""Woman" now." The text in this reflects on how girlhood is usually taken to be an incomplete and unfulfilled state, while it is as 'wife' that one comes fully to be 'Woman,' only then achieving one's identity, at least according to ordinary social discourse: "I'm Czar—I'm 'Woman' now—/ It's safer so—."

Yet this configuration of terms creates a paradox. As the poet implies, to fulfill her estate as 'Woman,' she must also cede it as 'wife.' For to gain identity as 'wife' is also to lose it, since to be a wife by definition entails subordination of her self to her husband. The strain of this paradox is registered in the poem's strange declaration: "I'm Czar." 'Czar' seems another figure for 'wife' and 'Woman.' Yet 'Czar' offers a position of command that the speaker as 'wife' and 'Woman' cannot possess. As a cross-gendered term (Dickinson could have said 'Queen' if she'd wanted to), 'Czar' declares that accession to her so-called full estate is impossible to her, since wifehood entails also a loss of her own sovereignty. She cannot be 'Czar.' 'Czar' remains a male status—not to mention a foreign one, Dickinson being American and not Russian. Royal claim is in any case then retracted in the fourth line: "It's safer so." Being 'wife' is not a matter of fulfilled social accession but rather a retreat to security from the exposure and danger presumably of "that other state," i.e. "that" of being unmarried.

The poem thus opens in apparent accord with the official social code that sees being a 'wife' as being a true 'woman,' yet it introduces into this dominant discourse complications that allow a second voice, the countermodel voice, to intrude and be heard. The quotation marks show the official language to be not the speaker's own but someone else's. What she actually claims is not accession to but being barred from full status. To be 'wife' is a socially necessary but also a costly protection. The poem's second stanza keeps up this cross-discourse of official and unofficial, dominant and veiled voices. From the vantage point of her new married status, the 'Girl's life' looks 'odd.' But Dickinson's subtly caustic epithet for wifehood proves to be 'soft Eclipse': a cushioned or gentle state, perhaps, but no less an eclipsed one for all that. The imagery of 'Earth' and 'Heaven' which follows extends astronomical reference into a religious one that becomes implicated as well in the gender structures the poem is reweaving. But again alignments among terms remain unclear to say the least. When the speaker says: "I think that Earth feels so / To Folks in Heaven—now—," when is 'now'? And which term is in fact being preferred, heaven or earth? And does 'Earth' represent girl or wifehood? Which one is heavenly? Is heaven deliverance or death? Ambiguous syntax makes it difficult to tell whether the poem is following an official line or undercutting it.

The final stanza pretends to a conclusion it does not in fact offer: in the lines "This being comfort—then / That other kind—was pain—," 'This' and 'that' become, if anything, less clearly assigned. Which estate, girl or wife, refers to "This being comfort," which to "That other kind," which is 'pain'? There is no clear decision of privilege. Indeed, just posing the question is subversive. The poem's ending, "But why compare?" already demurs from the clear social preference toward wifehood, since in fact this is what she has been doing. The last line at once suggests a muting of such questioning and defiance of it. "I'm 'Wife'! Stop there!" To 'Stop' here registers not so much satisfaction with her state as society's injunction to silence. It seems to consent to her position of 'Wife' in accordance with social versions of what this word may mean. Yet 'Wife' remains quoted as represented speech. It is thus distanced from the poet's own language, as not her own words, not her own senses. And the discourse of the poem is not stopped. Even while apparently conforming to official meanings, it opens up within them other voices: of doubt, of dissent, of judgment from a variant viewpoint that is veiled but not eclipsed.

A similar strategy of citation, ascription, recirculation, and contest of words is pursued in another Dickinson poem concerned with the roles of wife and their evaluation:

> A solemn thing—it was—I said—
> A woman—white—to be—
> And wear—if God should count me fit—
> Her blameless mystery—(*J* 271/*F* 307)

This poem opens with speech quoted, as it were, from the speaker herself, who says that she "said" that it is a "solemn thing" to be a "woman—white." This gesture of citation serves to place these words at one remove from Dickinson herself. The phrase "Blameless mystery" sums up a whole attitude of female positioning, but here it is in the conditional: "If God should count me fit." Is this speaker accepting and defining herself in the dominant imagery of white purity (and Dickinson herself dressed in white)? Or is she examining it as prescription and language that surround her but about which she is doubtful? The conditional tense is sustained in the poem. The next stanza wonders, "I pondered how the bliss would look—And would it feel as big." Whether as bride or simply pure, to be 'white' and 'blameless' is a 'bliss' according to social norms. But the speaker ponders rather than expressing this position, wondering how it conditionally 'would look' or 'feel.' Whose words then are these? To what extent does the speaker own or mean them?

The poem thus remains poised between voicing acquiescence to normative meanings of words in gendered social orders and questioning these meanings by suggesting they have other, oblique senses. Such doubly assigned linguistic encoding becomes dramatized as quotation in the final stanza, which marks what is said as sites of struggle over whose words they are and what they will mean in the poet's mouth. Thus, the poem concludes around quoted forms of the word 'small,' repeated three times in the final four lines. "And then—the size of this "small" life—The Sages—call it small—." But just what 'small' refers to and by what it is measured remains unclear. The (male) 'Sages' call 'this' a "small life." But despite their male authority and prerogative, the quotations around 'small' keep questionable what makes 'this' 'small' and which life it is. Is it the life of the 'blameless' white woman as defined by dominant society? Or is a defiant life what is intended, which would then be 'small' only by conventional standards? This might be the life the poem describes as one that "Swelled—like Horizons—in my vest—." The "small" is now large as "Horizons." (Does swelled vest imply pregnancy, perhaps in a sense of literary creativity?) This notion is confirmed by the poem's final rejoinder, which requotes the Sages but dismissively: "And I sneered—softly—'small!'" The poet here in effect doubles the quotations, quoting the Sages, and in this she further distances herself from their words and judgment.

This poem enacts the challenges of directing and intending our words, as these remain embedded in dominant languages that set standards and establish norms. In the poem's course, each word and image pulls at once toward the normative meanings of society's dominant codes but also toward subgroup meanings in veiled terms. But these are difficult to bring to expression while using language already established through dominant usage. It is as if one discourse glimmers through the other, speaking through its words but with an opposite, qualifying, or dissenting intention.

CHARLOTTE GILMAN'S COUNTER-RHETORIC

At the opposite pole from Dickinson's privacy is Charlotte Gilman's resolutely public feminist address. Dickinson's poems remained almost entirely unpublished in her lifetime, although about a third of them circulated through letters. As lecturer, journalist, and writer of fiction and verse, Gilman launched her words into direct circulation. One of the nineteenth century's most radical feminist activists, Gilman makes rhetorical counter-determinations, exposures, and resistances between discourses the central drama of her verse.

Gilman's biography (1860–1935) offers its own feminist plot, from her nervous breakdown in the face of standard wife and mother roles to her subsequent recovery only on separating from and finally divorcing her husband. Relinquishing her daughter to her former husband, newly married at her encouragement to her own best friend, caused scandal, which was followed at last by a happy, unconventional second marriage six years later. Her nervous collapse and 'rest-cure,' which she said almost drove her to insanity, became the basis for her autobiographical "The Yellow Wallpaper," now an American classic but at the time of its publication viewed as merely a gothic tale. Her utopian novel *Herland* and its sequel *With Her in Ourland* imagine a society made up only of women and their transformative powers. Her prose, journalism, lectures, and fiction are all devoted to her feminist commitments. Her poetry joins with these other of Gilman's writings as pointedly ideological. As she writes in "Lecture Verse 1," "To all you friends who've gathered here tonight, / And paid for this address with solid money, / I want to say—don't look for wild delight" (*LP* 151).

Although ideological, Gilman's poetry can be highly artful (although it can also be simply programmatic), especially when seen as a rhetorical battleground, where she sets out to command, expose, denounce, and resist dominant discourses regarding women. Gilman in fact has a coherent schema for this rhetorical engagement, although she does not always succeed in fulfilling it. Her stances can be analyzed into component points. First, Gilman asserts that there exists a distinctive women's experience, grounded in historical and social strata. Women, she shows, inhabit a counter-model different from the dominant, male one. Second, she sets out to give voice or expression to this counter- model, to rescue women's voices and viewpoints from muteness. Third, she brings this counter-model into direct confrontation with the dominant model in order to expose and challenge the dominant model in its role of suppressing the voices of women. Last, she attempts to replace the dominant model (and in effect the muted, veiled one as well) with a newly constructed egalitarian and utopian discourse. For Gilman, this reconstruction would require reconstructing the economic and social orders at large. To restructure the male/female, dominant/muted groups and the discourses that now obtain would require embracing a different idea of community as a whole.

In actual verse practice, Gilman is at her best when she does not directly exhort her reformist program but rather indirectly implicates and awakens her readers to recognize the dominant discourses as deeply ideological ones. To do this, she employs satire and irony, often through rhetorical citation and exposure, which demands recognition, challenge, and response. Typically she recirculates in her verse dominant discourses—common sayings or assumptions—that direct and determine, consciously or not, women's sense of themselves, of their place in the world, and of their possibilities. Hers becomes a voice of quotation or citation, of lifting out of general discourse phrases and formulae that operate with uncontested power but that her recirculation of them exposes as to what they claim and how they claim it. Gilman's poetry is thus continuous with her political activism and takes part in it. In her verse, Gilman sets out to contest gender norms in recognizable scenes and above all in normative language. One of her first published poems, for example, sets out to raise and address the "Unmentionable" topic (as she calls it in another poem) of prostitution (*World* 118). Gilman wishes to expose the double standard that condemns women to prostitution and ultimately death. In "One Girl of Many," she recounts the social history of poverty and the lack of options to escape from it as what launches girls into sexual misconduct. In this way, Gilman shifts the ground of discussion from moral condemnation to economic analysis. But she does this by mouthing the sorts of things people say about fallen women, showing how self-serving, hypocritical, and dooming these platitudes are:

> One Girl of Many. Tis a need
> Of man's existence to repeat the deed.
> Social necessity. Men cannot live
> Without what these disgraceful creatures give.
>
> Black shame. Dishonor. Misery & Sin.
> And men find needed health & life therein. (*LP* 115)

Here, Gilman strings together common phrases, which is to say dominant wisdom that at once condemns and underwrites prostitution. Yet in doing so she twists or displaces terms to force them to be heard differently. "One girl of many" becomes not platitude but accusation. The assumed "need of man's existence" or "Social necessity" are not matter-of-fact justifications but rather a shifting of responsibility from the "fallen" women to the men who seduce them and make seduction pay. Yet in the end, the cost is borne by the women, who are called "disgraceful creatures" by these same men. The poem, in counteraction, transfers the disgrace to the "men" who "cannot live without" these women and whose actions create them as "creatures." "Black shame" and "Dishonor" become uncoupled and transferred terms. In dominant discourse, they are directed against the women. But here they are turned back on the men, as is the "Sin," which normatively is cast at the women but is directed here against the men.

As in the case of "Sin" here, religion offers another discourse that Gilman exposes and contests. Gilman is infuriated by the use of religion for the purpose of control and repression of women, against religion's presumed commitment to respect the dignity of persons. In her poem "To the Preacher," Gilman presents the preacher's own rhetoric in order to counter it:

> You must not steal nor take man's life
> You must not covet your neighbor's wife,
> And woman must cling at every cost
> To her one virtue, or she is lost. (*World* 19)

The commandments are here shown to be economic and gendered. Women are among the properties that men must not steal from each other. Women's "one virtue" is chastity, which is a commodity in the exchange of property that marriage so often involves.[30] Without such chastity, the woman is nothing.

Another Gilman poem, "An Old Proverb," similarly recites the sorts of truisms that are in fact 'true' because the dominant voice of society asserts them to be so. This text directly cites dominant discourses in all their crushing weight of authority.

> No escape, little creature! The earth hath no place
> For the woman who seeketh to fly from her race.
> Poor, ignorant, timid, too helpless to roam,
> The woman must bear what befalls her, at home.
> Bear bravely, bear dumbly—it is but the same
> That all others endure who live under the name.
> No escape, little creature!
>
> No escape under heaven! Can man treat you worse
> After God has laid on you his infinite curse?
> The heaviest burden of sorrow you win
> Cannot weigh with the load of original sin;
> No shame be too black for the cowering face
> Of her who brought shame to the whole human race!
> No escape under heaven! (*World* 137)

"An Old Proverb" examines and dramatizes the ordinary circulation of language and its power. Proverbs are common knowledge, words in everyone's mouth. Yet they do much to create the situations they sum up. Not least, the proverb penetrates into those it epitomizes and defines. It shapes the views we have of ourselves, influencing internal definitions as well as reflecting external situations. Here, Gilman is not directly speaking but rather is representing someone else's language—the language of the dominant norms of society. She invokes, imitates, and imports directly into her text the proverbial language of conventional wisdom as it acts to create the conditions it announces. That women must "Bear bravely, bear dumbly" what befalls them, with "no escape," is not descriptive but directive. It assigns women to a status they are meant to adopt and obey. Religious discourse here is cast as founding and enforcing dominant models. "Can man treat you worse," the poem asks, "After God has laid on you his infinite curse?" Women's suffering, the proverb tells us, is deserved and sanctioned as divine decree.

Gilman's hope is that in dramatizing these voices of society, she will be able to extricate women from them. Although there are no overt markers within the text as to the poet's stance toward the language she is reporting, she displays the proverbial language in an act of exposure. The reader is meant to recognize and reject the phrases and comments that, in general circulation, are uncritically accepted. Sometimes it is difficult to gauge the status of Gilman's reported language, to distinguish irony from assertion. But most often Gilman provides signals so as to be able to identify what is meant as quoted speech, speech widely circulated but then lifted out and resituated in the poem, in order to make its implications visible and to counter them.

One way that Gilman makes otherwise ordinary claims seem outrageous and ridiculous is through hyperbolic exaggeration. In "More Females of the Species" (*LP*, 59), the poem repeats throughout as its refrain: "For the female of the species is deadlier than the male." This misogynist commonplace comes to seem more and more absurd as it is applied to a "milch cow" as against the "he-bull," a "Nag" as against a "raging stallion," squaws as against Indian warriors, and a "Mrs. Genghis Khan," as if it were the cow, nag, squaws, and Mrs. who attack. Finally, "Atilla" is declared "a female of the species and more deadly than the male."

In Bakhtinian terms, Gilman proposes her words as sites in which multiple usages, senses, and intentions collide and jostle. Her language approaches what Bakhtin calls dialogic relationship, not in terms of the character viewpoints that he emphasizes but as variant meanings or implications of specific words whose uses change depending on ideological contexts. Such dialogical collisions can occur not only in longer utterances but also, Bakhtin proposes, in individual words, "if that word is perceived not as the impersonal word of language but as a sign of someone else's semantic position, as the representative of another person's utterance."[31] Just so, in Gilman, the word is not an "impersonal word of language" but signifies a "semantic position," that of dominant discourses as these fail to represent, and in fact deny or restrict, women's meanings and models of understanding. Each word thus becomes part not only of the utterance of the poem but is directed toward other usages of the word in other utterances outside the poetic text. In this way, Gilman is trying to bring into the open the muted or veiled meanings of women's discourses that ordinarily do not even appear within the arena of exchanges.

Gilman's most concerted image and site for this struggle of viewpoints and voices is domestic space. The nineteenth century made explicit women's assignment to the domestic sphere, although the home has been assigned as feminine place in various guises throughout history and across societies, as anthropologists have explored. In Gilman, domesticity is both a central topos and a powerful rhetoric. Many poems are devoted to identifying and presenting familiar appeals to the domestic norm and to exposing what these appeals entail. In "The Housewife," for example, the apparently innocent opening plays on and progressively complicates and darkens the traditional marital vows of having and holding:

> Here is the House to hold me—cradle of all the race;
> Here is my lord and my love, here are my children dear—
> Here is the House enclosing, the dear-loved dwelling place;
> Why should I ever weary for aught that I find not here? (*LP* 73)

As often in Gilman, questions that appear ingenuous emerge as in fact rhetorical. Why, indeed, at least according to the official line, ought not the wife find all within the "enclosing" house? As the poem continues, such enclosure becomes increasingly an image of an imprisonment called "Duty," expressed suspiciously in language recalling a corset:

> Here for the hours of the day and the hours of the night;
> Bound with the bands of Duty, riveted tight;
> Duty older than Adam—Duty that saw
> Acceptance utter and hopeless in the eyes of the serving squaw.

Gilman was incensed that, despite claims of progress, the lives of modern American women have changed little, leaving them in the same roles, with the same constricted experience and duties, as through the centuries before. Religion joins with social invocations to "Duty" that devolve, as the poem proceeds, into slavish repetitive performance—"Food and the serving of food," "soiling and cleaning of things" until the "mind is trodden in circles."

In the poem "Two Callings" (*LP* 75), a veritable battle of rhetorics takes place, with one voice (apparently sweet and warm) affirming "Home," "Duty," "Love," and "Mother" but meaning by it, in another voice, "Allegiance in an idleness abhorred—I am the squaw—the slave—the harem beauty—I serve and serve, the handmaid of the world." Gilman does not reject the notion of service. On the contrary, like many nineteenth-century women activists, she urges devoted service. But she wishes her service to be directed toward the world, in public domains and for the public and common good. What she unmasks here in fact is how in the dominant voice 'service' for women means servitude, although the poem goes on to counter-propose a meaning of "Duty," which is not a disguise for subordination but rather for venture into "high" and "noble deed."

"Homes: A Sestina" (*World* 7) is one of Gilman's most accomplished pieces. In it the cult of domesticity seems to be speaking but in a complex rhetorical strategy that undermines the claims it would make. On the one hand, the text is made up of almost a series of stereotyped clichés. On the other hand, the poem takes these ordinary sayings and pulls them toward critical and self-exposing meanings.

> We are the smiling comfortable homes
> With happy families enthroned therein,
> Where baby souls are brought to meet the world,
> Where women end their duties and desires,
> For which men labor as the goal of life,
> That people worship now instead of God.

The sacred "Homes" of the domestic ideal speak here for themselves, in a text that, on one level, sustains and is conducted in the official language and approved discourses of the dominant domestic culture. On another level, however, every word and every line is self-betraying. Each utterance thus becomes a struggle between meanings, as the dominant assertion collides with a second meaning that unmasks and contests it. It thus becomes transformed, its direction and import turned through the second, although still muted and indirect voice of woman's protest and assertion of a contrasting set of values. Thus, the "homes" regard and declare themselves to be "comfortable," "happy," and even royal, where families are "enthroned." Yet when the poem continues, "Where women end their duties and desires," double and contested meanings enter in. In the dominant discourse, "end" means achieved fulfillment. But in the second, veiled discourse, "end" means not fulfillment but its opposite: the death and burial of larger duties and desires.

These contending senses are carried over into the next line, "for which men labor as the goal of life." The dominant voice declares labor for the home to be life's goal, but the second, veiled voice throws doubt on whether this is the case. "Labor" becomes an excuse that takes men from their attachments to others while restricting women's attachments to the home alone. The last line of the stanza moves into more open irony. "That people worship now instead of God." The bourgeois home has become the object of worship, and it is for economic status and comfort that men truly labor.

It is the art of the sestina as a verse form to recirculate its words from stanza to stanza, in a complex reordering of the same end words through six stanzas of six lines each and then a final three-line conclusion (envoy) in which all six key words are then interwoven for a final time. The sestina thus is an examination of relationships between its six key words. This makes the sestina an especially suitable form for Gilman's poetic intention, which is precisely to repeat core words and in doing so expose their meanings. The second stanza picks up the already compromised meaning of "God" from the first stanza and then traces how the child's soul is "bounded" by the home, "constrained to serve the wants therein, / Domestic needs and personal desires." One of Gilman's original ideas was day care, so that child care could be shared, leaving women free to work. Confining women to the home, Gilman insisted, confines the mind and narrows not only their world, but their children's as well, to a constricted, walled-in selfhood. The third stanza presents a rhetoric of social normalization through religious complicity. The woman's "perfect" world of domesticity is "Prescribed by nature and ordained by God." Nature and God indeed are the authorities that have been marshaled to cement women into their places and to insist that beyond these domestic spaces "she can have no right desires" or any other "service."

The dominant discourse entraps women. But it is part of Gilman's egalitarianism that she feels it also narrows the lives of men, entrapping them as well. Women confined to the home cannot make good educators for children or good companions to husbands, not to mention full members of society. Conversely, men who ascribe to the cult of (female) domesticity deprive not only their women, but themselves, of life's fuller resources and larger meanings.

> And man? What other need hath he in life
> Than to go forth and labor in the world,
> And struggle sore with other men therein?
> Not to serve other men, nor yet his God,
> But to maintain these comfortable homes,—
> The end of all a normal man's desires.

Official discourse declares that man has no "other need" in life than to "go forth and labor in the world." But the poem's veiled voice sees this as "struggle sore with other men." The question of "What other need" man has in life becomes a forceful rather than an empty question. The "homes" provide the wrong answer, as if maintaining "comfortable homes" trumps all other values. Again, Gilman exploits the pun on "end," taken in the dominant voice as goal, but in the veiled voice as constricting closure and dead end. As the poem's concluding three-line envoy ironically sums up, the homes "Wring dry the world to meet our wide desires." Against its own claims, the cult of domesticity reduces the world to our narrowest selves.

AFRICAN-AMERICAN WOMEN POETS

African-American women poets represent a crossing or combination of subgroup identities, each in tension against the dominant discourses and ruling powers surrounding them. In their work, a number of veiled or muted discourses emerge in different balances, with different strains against the normative languages each contests.[32] At times the pressure of the dominant language can seem overwhelming, drowning out the subgroup voice, thickening its veil until what it would say becomes barely audible. This seems painfully the case in some of the writings of Phyllis Wheatley (1753–1784), such as "On Being Brought from Africa to America":

> 'Twas mercy brought me from my Pagan Land
> Taught my benighted soul to understand
> That there's a God, that there's a Saviour too
> Once I redemption neither sought nor knew.
> Some view our sable race with scornful eye,
> "Their colour is a diabolic dye."
> Remember, Christians, Negroes, black as Cain,
> May be refined, and join th' angelic train.

W. W. B. DuBois cites Wheatley in *The Souls of Black Folks* as an exemplar of the more or less delusive eighteenth-century desire of African-Americans to achieve "ultimate adjustment and assimilation."[33] Taken from Africa in 1760 at a young age and sold to a Boston family that recognized her abilities and provided her with an education, Wheatley in this verse seems to have been stolen not only into slavery but into the dominant discourse of her enslavers. In this text, she renames abduction as "mercy." Her native Africa becomes "my Pagan Land." She adopts the white account and justification for slavery as a salvation and rescue from heathen darkness. Even the poem's color-semiotics follows white codes, her unsaved soul "benighted" and African-Americans "black as Cain" who still might be "refined."

Yet the poem also resists and contests this dominated language. Wheatley's metaphors of dark and light can be seen to urge against and not only toward confusing sin with skin color.[34] And while she embraces Christian religion, she speaks against white Christians who remain racists. They betray their own Christianity. Her voice is as critical as it is complicit, with the words pointing both ways. Wheatley demands that the redemption of her soul be recognized and embraced—even if she does so in imagery of angelic refinement that demands the bleaching of her color and language.

Wheatley's text enacts a severe overvoicing of her own cultural identity by another one to which it is subordinate. Her own voice remains veiled, evident only indirectly. She seems nearly pirated by dominant discourses. Frances Harper, a nineteenth-century African-American poet, offers a stronger and more audible voice for her cultural affiliations. Born a free African-American in Baltimore in 1825, Harper was active in the Underground Railroad, abolition, and women's suffrage, lecturing widely. After the Civil War, she devoted herself to education of the freedmen.[35] A devout Christian, she claims her African-American religion to be Christianity's true form against white distortions and betrayal. Like Frederick Douglass, she writes mainly in Standard English, the language of the white masters, but she does so to her own purposes, in clear dissent and critique of the values of white slave ownership. She also experiments with African-American dialect through the voice of an elderly freed slave woman, Chloe.

In Harper, every textual moment becomes a battle, a struggle, to wrest and resist, to refuse and to rename. This struggle extends to the English she uses. In African-American writing, dominant language is a political site of contested identities. The slaves imported to the South were systematically sold out of their own linguistic tribal groups to prevent solidarity. Therefore, they did not share a common language, and, needless to say, they were not instructed in English, with literacy illegal and teaching it punishable from early on in the Black Code slave laws. The dialect forms that grew up were therefore at once cultural expressions and signs of oppression. For the African-American poet, language therefore presents particular dilemmas. Dialect offers in some senses a more authentic expression of subgroup experience but one also deeply marked by its persecutions. Standard American English is theirs as Americans and gives both acceptability and accessibility to their work for a larger, white audience. But it poses at the same time the problem of conformity to dominant norms and expression.

The challenge of negotiating between dialect and Standard English poems was central to the poetry of Paul Laurence Dunbar.[36] Frances Harper antedates him in experimenting with African-American dialect poetry. Her "Aunt Chloe" series (*CP* 117–230) marks a daring entry into the viewpoint and speech of a freedwoman. In the voice of Aunt Chloe, Harper challenges and opposes dominant discourses. Aunt Chloe starkly and indignantly reports how she remembers "That dark and dreadful day, / When they whispered to me, 'Chloe, / Your children's sold away'" (*CP* 117). She recounts the resistance to literacy by masters, how "some of us would try to steal / A little from the book," and how she "longed to read my Bible" despite a long life kept from doing so (*CP* 127–128). The image of the Bible is a crucial one for Harper. Religion to her is a form of self-confirmation, rather than, as in Phyllis Wheatley's verse, almost a kind of possession by others. Christianity becomes for Harper a powerful resource for the discovery and assertion of equality, identity, and her own voice. In Harper, religion is a battleground between dominant and subgroup discourses and claims. Harper opposes a falsified and self-betraying religious discourse associated with the dominant whites, against Christianity's true call, as seen in African-American religion. Writing of Aunt Chloe's suffering at the sale of her children confutes the dominant slave society's denial of her humanity and repression of her voice, and it exposes white society's betrayal of its own supposedly Christian principles. When Aunt Chloe, "wasted to a shadow" in her sorrow, turns to the divine "blessed Master's feet," this is cast against false human masters who sell children.

What happens in the Aunt Chloe poems, as elsewhere, is a split vision or voicing in which standard white positions are countered by Harper's African-American ones. As Aunt Chloe recounts her own experience of the Civil War, this split structures the poems, in contest against the white slave-owning point of view. Chloe's subordinated voice emerges into its own expression. As this occurs, the meaning of basic terms pulls apart. When, for example, the son of the white owners goes off to fight, prayer takes on different and opposing meanings for mistress and slave.

> Mistus prayed up in the parlor
> That the Secesh all might win;
> We were praying in the cabins,
> Wanting freedom to begin.

Both sides pray to the same God, as Lincoln said in his Second Inaugural, but the prayers of both are quite at variance. They face different ways: If the "old Mistus' face . . . looked quite long," then "My heart would fairly skip." In the end, the positions of mistress and slave reverse. Aunt Chloe's now freed son finds her, and "Old Mistus got no power now / To tear us both apart."

> Indeed, I'm richer now than Mistus,
> Because I have got my son;
> And Mister Thomas he is dead
> And she's nary one.

The meaning of "richer" has altered from possession—including possession of persons—to family reunion. For both poet and speaker, there is justice in these outcomes.

Slave women, and women in general, emerge in Harper's work as voices she will unveil. As with Gilman and many other nineteenth-century women writers, including Alice Carey (1820–1871) ("The Spectre Woman"), Phoebe Carey (1824–1871) ("The Outcast), and Julia Ward Howe (1819–1910) (Outside the Party), Harper returns repeatedly to the double standard as a compelling issue. In terms of discourse analysis, the double standard can be approached through discrepancies between dominant and muted voices. In a series of poems, Harper shows the double standard to be that of dominant male norms against women who are subordinate to and silenced by them. The supposedly moral claims regarding sexual virtue—hypocritical in any case as they do not apply to men—she reveals to be essentially questions of economy and power. Yet it is difficult for women to voice their own standpoints within this system. Harper's poems enact this difficulty of expressing women's meanings in the language and social structures that rule over them, as she opens words to doubled, which is to say dominant and veiled meanings.

In the poem "A Double Standard" (*CP* 176), the meanings of "sinning" and "fall" come under contest, with dominant and submerged senses at issue and at odds:

> They scorned her for her sinning,
> Spoke harshly of her fall,
> Nor let the hand of mercy
> To break her hated thrall.
>
> The dews of meek repentance
> Stood in her downcast eye:
> Would no one heed her anguish?
> All pass her coldly by?

The woman here is caught in a net of words that Harper shows to be gravely distorted. "Sinning" and "fall" prove not to be measures of purity or goodness but of conformity and power. Nor is there "mercy" despite the 'fallen' woman's "repentance," but only social scorn and continued economic exploitation to which she is in "thrall." As to the seducer whose deception put her into this outcast state:

> Through the halls of wealth and fashion
> In gaiety and pride
> He was leading to the Altar
> A fair and lovely bride.
>
> None scorned him for his sinning,
> Few saw it through his gold;
> His crimes were only foibles,
> And these were gently told.

"Sinning" applies only to the woman, not to the man. It is therefore a term of gendered and economic, not moral meanings. The man's "pride" is similarly not a negative but an admired attribute. His acts, no less "crimes" than hers (and indeed far more so, in his act of abandonment), are shrugged off as "foibles" and are "gently told." The imagery of language is telling. The double standard becomes a double discourse of wealth and poverty, male and female, dominant and subordinated. But Harper here speaks the truer and more moral language that the dominant group supposedly, but only falsely, pretends to.

It is interesting to consider Gwendolyn Brooks (1917–2000) in this context. Writing a century after Harper, she records not only the contest against dominating language but its continued power. In fact, in some ways, there is less optimism or confidence in Brooks than in Harper. Harper believes in the power of the word to reveal and bring to redemptive recognition. Brooks grapples with a deeper sense of language as compromised, as dominated in ways that are enormously difficult to counter. The poem "A Bronzeville Mother Loiters in Mississippi. Meanwhile, A Mississippi Mother Burns Bacon" involves a particularly complex set of voice-exchanges (B 333–339). It is a poetic rendering of the murder of Emmet Till, an African-American boy who, while visiting Mississippi from Bronzeville, Chicago, was lynched for allegedly approaching or addressing a white woman. Brooks, astonishingly, makes the white woman the speaker in the poem. This woman, whose husband is the murderer of Emmet Till, speaks in words layered through her gendered powerlessness as wife. As mother, the role the poem's title emphasizes, she tries to care for her own children against incipient violence from their father while haunted by the image of the African-American child he murdered. Her counterpart, the African-American mother of the murdered child, appears only in the title, but her shadow is cast over the text in a solidarity that links her to the white mother, a gendered bond against but also vulnerable to violence.

These grids of gender, race, and economy, since the woman is financially dependent on her husband, are further textured through dominating paradigms that are cultural and indeed literary. These, too, deploy dominating structures, with literature serving dominant models.[37] The poem's opening lines declare: "From the first it had been like a Ballad. / It had the beat inevitable. It had the blood." The speaker's sense of herself and her life, her paradigms for self-understanding, are shown to be shaped by paradigmatic texts of her culture such as ballads. But the poem goes on to explore the misfit between the ballad conventions—the roles they assign and the plot they enact—and the woman's own life. Toward the beginning of the poem, the mother reflects on herself in comparison to the ballad model of the "maid mild" and the plot and characters that this projects:

> Herself: the milk-white maid, the "maid mild"
> Of the ballad. Pursued
> By the Dark Villain. Rescued by the Fine Prince.
> The Happiness-Ever-After
> That was worth anything.
> It was good to be a "maid mild."
> That made the breath go fast.

But the ballad's conventional "maid mild" and her "milk white" imagery don't match the events of this woman's life. Her husband is no "Fine Prince"; the little boy he murdered is no "Dark Villain," and her "Happiness-Ever-After" turns into the terror and pressure of marital intimidation. "The fun was disturbed, then all but nullified / When the Dark Villain was a blackish child of fourteen." In light of the events in which she is caught, these ballad figures, which "she had never quite understood," become not explanatory but distorting lenses that serve to warp and disguise what is happening. They are not only suspicious as false paradigms but in fact are violent, with "beat inevitable" and "blood,"(does this pun on both poetic and physical beating?)

The woman is largely represented through the language of the kitchen and cooking—"She set out a jar / Of her new quince preserve"—or of the female body—"before calling Him, she hurried / To the mirror with her comb and lipstick." Both put her in a position of vulnerability and stealth. "Her bacon burned," she must "hide it in the step-on can" lest her husband discover it. Her husband's "Hand," after slapping the "older baby," then comes to grip her as sexual body, while he "whispered something to her, did the Fine Prince, something about love." But these romance images do not accord with her experience. "She heard no hoof-beat of the horse and saw no flash of shining steel." They instead are exposed as modes of coercion:

> She, their mother,
> Could not protect them. She looked at her shoulders, still
> Gripped in the claim of his hands. She tried, but could not resist the idea
> That a red ooze was seeping, spreading darkly, thickly, slowly,
> Over her white shoulders, her own shoulders,
> And over all of Earth and Mars.

"She, their mother, / Could not protect them." When her husband grips her shoulders, what she sees is a bloody "red ooze" from his violation of the other unpresent black child, seeping and spreading over "white shoulders" and ultimately "over all of Earth and Mars."

In this text, dominant paradigms of marriage, of male chivalry and female protection, of racial superiority and legal justice, are gradually stripped to reveal their concealed violence, power, and injustice. The words of ballad and romance are exposed and reassigned. The ballad's language does not apply. Indeed, its model only underscores the gap between official versions of love and marriage and what is actually the case. In this text, however, no alternatives to official language and dominant structures are offered. The woman remains entrapped in them. No escape from this marriage is imagined or available, or from the Mississippi that, as the husband declares, "Nothing and nothing could stop." Yet the patterns of this woman's world are coming apart:

The one thing in the world that she did know and knew

> With terrifying clarity was that her composition
> Had disintegrated. That, although the pattern prevailed,
> The breaks were everywhere. That she could think
> Of no thread capable of the necessary
> Sew-work.

"Composition" here carries a multiple burden, of the woman's social world, its political and racial paradigms, the literature that reaffirms them, and the language she has available to formulate it. These increasingly stand in dispute with the official versions of them, leaving her with "breaks everywhere." But her woman's world lacks the power to either stand independent or heal its breach with the life she has, "no thread capable of the necessary / Sew work." The white Mississippi mother comes to feel increasing "sickness" and "hatred" of her own social world and comes closer and closer to the viewpoint of "that Other Woman's eyes," the mother of the murdered boy.[38] But this does not free her. She remains caught between the breakdown of her given guidelines and any other possible ones, in a domestic language that offers at once an assertion of her counter-model and of her continued subordination. Here Brooks writes a language of both woman and African-American that contests against dominant patterns and claims, but in ways that also confirm their continued power of domination.

3 Recovering Women's Voices
Feminist Psychology

Women today seem increasingly divided not only among various kinds of feminism but regarding feminism itself. Critical of traditional women's roles, feminism of different kinds seems to make its own demands and assign its own prescriptive images of who and what women should be. Postfeminism disclaims what it takes to be feminism's image of womanhood, mainly based on Second Wave feminism's liberal project of advancing individual women as liberal autonomous selves. This project certainly contributed immensely to the advancement of women's rights but has come to be viewed as a narrow version of womanhood, one that is remote from women's historical commitments—commitments that remain for many women today positive aspects of their lives. 'Feminism' has come to seem antagonistic to attachments, activities, and values that women have traditionally upheld.[1] In response, 'postfeminist' women feel they need to resist feminism in order to be true to what remains a fundamental part of their identities—as if feminism opposes women's worlds, values, and choices.

In this context, Carol Gilligan's *In a Different Voice* has struck a deep chord, giving voice and confirmation to values and viewpoints with which many women identify. Drawing on psychological work that investigates and reassesses women's psychological development, Gilligan's theories challenge traditional moral theory. Autonomy, independence, and the ability to judge individual rights against each other have been the normative measures of moral development. Judged by these standards, women have rated poorly. Their senses of responsibility, commitment to others, and care have been regarded as lower moral stages, signaling a lack of detachment and independence—the character traits that are valued most highly. Instead Gilligan claims that responsibility is indeed a high moral value, rather oddly in challenge to traditional ethics.

In focusing on the moral force of care and responsibility, Gilligan has in fact been criticized as recasting in new terms what really are just traditional and limiting women's roles. Other questions are directed at her methods and records of quantifiable results regarding the gender differences she claims to see in surveys and questionnaires. However, Gilligan's work can be seen for present purposes as interpretive, analyzing ways in which women have expressed themselves, and her greatest impact has been through the ethical questions she raises. She examines women's self-understanding in terms of the psychological, social, and moral norms and experiences that have framed women's development. As to the critical concern about Gilligan's regendering of women's virtues, Linda Kerber, for example, warns that Gilligan has found a new vocabulary for old gender stereotypes, in which men think and women feel, men compete and women nurture.[2] As Catherine MacKinnon puts it, Gilligan gives more dignity to gender difference than one could ever imagine it having.[3] As such, Gilligan is suspected of reconfirming social roles from which women need to be freed.[4]

Gilligan insists that her work addresses not women but rather both genders and is therefore a social and moral critique, not a biological prescription.[5] She points out that her goal is to describe a 'different' voice from the dominant one, not an exclusively female gendered one. Yet she does approach the dominant model as a male one, claiming it to be constructed through assumptions and measures by which women's experiences are judged, by themselves and others, according to male standards that devalue them.

Gilligan's first claim is that women have been consistently interpreted and measured through models based on men, and that according to such scales, women turn out to be deviant and inferior. Originally working with Lawrence Kohlberg in his tests for assessing moral development, she found that his standards for measuring moral development resulted in women scoring lower than men.[6] Gilligan came to question measuring women by criteria established without reference to them, which take men as the basis for judgment and then judge women according to these male standards. In relation to psychological and moral development, her point was not only to question this bias but also the criteria themselves—the norms and values that governed them. Any developmental chart necessarily presumes values and achievements, which set and define how development is to be measured. What is seen to be the highest value will define the stages that move toward it. As Gilligan puts it, "A change in the definition of maturity does not simply alter the description of the highest stage but recasts the understanding of development, changing the entire account" (*DV* 19).

Gilligan claims that in the Kohlberg tests of moral development, the highest developmental achievements are individuation, independence, and autonomy. But this is not only a psychological configuration. It is also a moral one. If autonomy is accepted as the highest stage of development, then morality becomes the ability to adjudicate among autonomous individuals, weighing each one's rights against the others. Psychological development thus implies ethical models, with maturity equated with autonomy and ethics as the ability to judge among individuals, each of whom possesses competing rights. But Gilligan found that women, as expressed in the accounts they gave her of their own moral thinking, worked in terms of a different ethical model, implying a different course of psychological development. Rather than weighing one person's rights against those of others, women approached moral dilemmas in terms of sustaining ties between people and responsibilities toward them. Difficult choices between courses of action were understood in terms of "conflicting responsibilities rather than from competing rights." Rather than posing right against right, girls attempted to find solutions that would mediate between and answer to the needs of each and each other. To them, what was of first importance was to defuse conflict in order to maintain relationships, by responding to the claims of each of those involved. Sustaining relationships, and mutual participation in them, took precedence over assessments of fairness and assignments of rights. This is a 'different' ethic that "centers moral development around the understanding of responsibility and relationships." Gilligan describes these two concepts of morality as a "morality of rights" and a "morality of responsibility," where the first places its "emphasis on separation rather than connection, in its consideration of the individual rather than the relationship as primary." The second, however, bases moral understanding "not on the primacy and universality of individual rights," which conceives of the person as a self-defined, self-sufficient individual negotiating with other individuals, but instead as defined through relationships to others and feeling responsibility to them, thus attempting to find resolutions to conflict that will maintain the relationships and connections between them (*DV* 19, 21).

What Gilligan proposes is not only a different developmental chart, both psychologically and morally, but a different model of the self. Moral norms and fundamental senses of what a self is come to redefinition. In Gilligan's 'different' model, the self is not an independent self-defining unit but an embedded person, born out of relationships with others and continuously defined through these relationships. Morality becomes a mode of responding to others and sustaining them within a network of ties that extend beyond the self and in which each is inscribed. Responsibility becomes as high a moral value as are individual rights and justice.

Gilligan's work takes its place within a wide range of investigation and argument across many feminist fields. The question of models taken as normative, but that are in fact based on men and then applied to women, has been an increasingly recognized issue in medicine, where men's bodies have served as standards for women's despite the obvious differences in weight, size, physiology, and reproductive organs.[7] A whole body of work in moral and political theory has in turn become directed toward investigating the ethic of responsibility that Gilligan formulated. Gilligan's theory of the embedded self joins with current political theories that critique pure liberal individualism as assuming a model of autonomy while overlooking other aspects of the self. The sense of one moral paradigm eclipsing others accords with analysis of dominant as against muted voices in anthropology and social theory. In psychology, Gilligan exposes a similar incorporation of female into male and then extends this challenge to moral standards. Psychological models have overlooked and absorbed women's viewpoints and voices into supposedly universal models that prove to be male, correlating these with ethical positions that are then taken to be universally valid. "Men's experience," as Gilligan puts it, typically "stands for all human experience."[8] But this is to "eclipse the lives of women and shut out women's voices" (*DV* xiii).

This eclipse of women's voices in judgments that discount and are prejudicial against them has, feminist psychologists show, been deeply entrenched in psychological tradition, from Freud through Erikson to Kohlberg. That Freud's is a male model has been recognized and critiqued through several generations of feminist psychologists.[9] The Oedipal complex presumes a male son who desires his mother in rivalry against his father. How this may serve as a model for poetic creativity, but may differ when applied to a female rather than a male poet, is explored by feminist Bloomian theory, as discussed in Chapter 1. Freud's own attempts to consider how Oedipal structures do or do not apply to daughters remained late and incomplete.[10] Gender structures on the whole in classic psychoanalytic theory continue to be asymmetrical, with the girl's relation to her mother never parallel to the rivalry the boy experiences toward his father and her relation to the Oedipal complex unstable—a psychological imbalance that profoundly affects the understanding of female development, not least in moral senses. Indeed, in Freud, the Oedipal complex shapes not only psychological but moral judgment. For Freud, fear of castration by the father is what impels the formation of a superego in boys, the internalized conscience that both prompts obedience to the father as the voice of social authority and promises autonomy as the boy becomes an adult male. But girls do not fear the father's threat of castration since, in Freud's terms, they already are. Nor do they identify with the father in promise to someday take his authoritative place, since this is something socially forbidden to them. They instead persist in 'pre-Oedipal' attachment to the mother, achieving neither the separation that impels autonomy nor the objectivity that structures moral judgment. "For women," writes Freud, "the level of what is ethically normal is different from what it is in men." More emotional and less rational, women "show less sense of justice than men," are "less ready to submit to the great exigencies of life," and "are more often influenced in their judgments by feelings of affection or hostility" (*DV* 7).

It is not only that identity formation is different for girls than for boys. Girls are seen as less mature or inferior in their development, both psychologically and morally. This implicit valuation can be seen in Erik Erikson's model of psychological development. Erikson charts development as stages of increasing autonomy and individuation, rather than in terms of intimate attachments as defining who the person is and his or her level of maturity. Erikson's paradigm in *Childhood and Society* thus moves from "autonomy vs. shame" to "initiative vs. guilt" to "industry vs. inferiority," with each first term consistently defining maturity as increased self-definition and separation.[11] Only the "initial stage of trust versus mistrust," Gilligan comments, "suggests the type of mutuality" that she argues continues to have formative power in human lives. There is thus little preparation for intimacy. The main course that Erikson traces is instead one of "separateness, with the result that development itself comes to be identified with separation, and attachments appear to be developmental impediments, as is repeatedly the case in the assessment of women." This trajectory of increased self-sufficiency as the mark of development is further schematized in Lawrence Kohlberg. Kohlberg demarcates six stages that describe the development of moral judgment from childhood to adulthood. Females, however, seem fixed at the third stage, where "morality is conceived in interpersonal terms and goodness is equated with helping and pleasing others." It is men who reach the higher stages "where relationships are subordinated to rules (stage four) and rules to universal principles of justice (stages five and six)" (*DV* 12–13, 18).

In these models, self-sufficiency signals and defines the higher moral norms of objective and detached judgment. Lack of self-sufficiency through attachments to others, in contrast, is taken to show problematic development, weak identity, and a compromised psychological and moral selfhood: dependence, emotionalism, and lack of sense of justice. These undermine moral judgment, defined as objective detachment judging between the rights of autonomous subjects.

But work by women psychologists has questioned self-sufficiency as either an accurate or ideal definition of the self and has challenged the notion that connection to others is a form of dependent weakness, seeing it instead as a resource of strength. Thus, Jean Baker Miller, whose *Toward a New Psychology of Women* raises many issues that Gilligan then explores, notes that "psychologists use such terms as 'merger,' 'fusion,' 'attachment,' or dependence to characterize the child's early relationship with its mother, as a sign of immaturity. Terms such as 'separation,' 'independence,' 'autonomy,' indicate maturity and the achievement of higher states of development."[12] Yet none of these terms, neither 'fusion' nor 'autonomy,' captures the experience of interaction that defines selves dynamically in relation to each other. Such interaction, however, is precisely the way in which human development and indeed experience takes place: "For everyone—men as well as women—individual development proceeds only by means of connection." Men, no less than women, develop through and require these attachments. But they deny and repress this need and its importance even while they benefit from and depend on them. "We all begin life deeply attached to the people around us. Men, or boys, are encouraged to move out of this state of existence—in which they and their fate are intimately intertwined in the lives and fate of other people." Women thus become the "carriers" of this "basic necessity for human communion," even while their very doing so is denied by the men whom such "communion" supports and further marks the women "carriers" as inferior according to the psychological and societal models that privilege male values and evaluations.[13] In a discussion that recalls Ardener's analysis that women's models do not correspond with the dominant one based on men, Miller argues that our notions of selfhood do not "fit" women's experience. The dominant model assumes separating the self out from the matrix of others. The goal is separation and not greater capacity for connection or interchange. Yet most men actually, if not consciously, continue to depend on the support their model of selfhood denies.[14]

This question of attachment and its denial and demotion has also been a subject of psychoanalytic theory. Dorothy Dinnerstein's *The Mermaid and the Minotaur* attributes the anxieties and subsequent repression of the need for and value of relationship and attachment to the infant's experience as one of utter dependence on the mother who seems overwhelmingly powerful. Feelings toward the mother become ambivalent: desire and its inevitable frustration, anger and fear of loss, bliss when satisfied and hostility when interrupted or disappointed, and fear at the threat to selfhood when the mother is inattentive or ineffective or absent, or too overwhelmingly present and overpowering. For boy babies, the outcome is unease about dependence, as well as later possessiveness and desire to control women. Girls, according to Dinnerstein, similarly harbor these ambivalent feelings toward their mothers but also identify with them.[15]

One possible way out of these dead-ends of mother dependence and its resentment is to share primary child care equally between men and women. This is a path proposed and developed in the psychoanalytic work of Nancy Chodorow. Chodorow approaches the different developmental and psychological structures of girls and boys as derived in their differently gendered positioning relative to their earliest primary caregivers, who tend to be women. Girls identify with the women who raise them, whereas boys see themselves as different from their caregivers, and hence as achieving their distinctive sexual identity through separation from them. Boys follow a path of individuation and separation, girls one of continued relationship with their primary caregivers and objects of love. In psychoanalytic terms, the girl remains pre-Oedipal for a longer time. The girl's sense of self remains closely tied to those who care for her and for whom she cares:

> Girls emerge with a stronger basis for experiencing another's needs or feelings as one's own. . . . From very early, then, because they are parented by a person of the same gender . . . girls come to experience themselves as less differentiated than boys. . . . Growing girls come to define and experience themselves as continuous with others; their experience of self contains more flexible or permeable ego boundaries. Boys come to define themselves as more separate and distinct, with a greater sense of rigid ego boundaries and differentiation. The basic feminine sense of self is connected to the world, the basic masculine sense of self is separate.[16]

Girls develop a sense of identification with others, of sympathy and connection with them, rather than learning detachment, independence, and autonomy as the very construction of identity. In a negative description, girls may be said to have 'weaker' ego boundaries. But in a positive sense, girls develop greater empathy with others. Expanding on Freud's view of narcissistic neurosis as the inability to feel connection to others, Chodorow shifts emphasis from the structures that constitute the Freudian self to an emphasis on the self as "fundamentally implicated in relations with others," as "intrinsically social, constructed in a relational matrix and includes aspects of others."[17]

Gilligan, building on these discussions, schematizes distinctive psychological definitions of masculinity through separation and of femininity through attachment. Accordingly, male identity becomes threatened by relationships, whereas female identity is threatened by separation. Yet Gilligan insists that in fact both genders encompass both aspects of psychological experience. For both genders the self is relational, embedded in and emerging from attachments, which become for both the basis, not the antithesis, of individual identity. What she claims is that in each gender, the relational aspect has been denied, repressed, or undervalued in a psychological scale that reflects the dominant norm of self-defined independence. Gilligan's is not an essentialized gendering assigning qualities to one gender as opposed to the other. Gilligan sees the self as multiple and dynamic, changing in time, not a unitary and fixed identity but a continual negotiation among tendencies, within and between selves. The relational self is not a metaphysical or atemporal identity. Instead, selfhood emerges as temporalized, historicized, responsive, and negotiating. Yet this rejection of a fixed or an essential self is not a negation of self, not a dissolving of all selfhood into coercive historical or ideological constructions as determining them. Gilligan's work shows how recognition of the self in time and multiplicity need not entail the destruction of self and its dissolution—a dissolution which presents enormous problems not only for feminist agency but for moral action altogether.

Selves are not fixed by gender or other determinations. The study of women, Gilligan writes, "calls attention to a different way of constituting the self and morality." While she explores the "dissonance between psychological theory and women's experiences," she reduces neither to "how much are women like men" nor to how much "women deviate from the male standard." Instead, she examines how much has been missed by leaving women's experiences out of models of selfhood and what new interpretive frameworks are opened by including them.[18]

These involve imagining development not only along one trajectory but "across two dimensions of relationship," with what Gilligan describes as a "straight line that leads towards equality and increased authority" and also an "elaborating line that follows the development of attachment."[19] It is indeed part of her critique of the commonly accepted psychological models that they pursue only one of these dimensions. Yet within the economy of these traditional (male) models, profound inconsistency exists. In fact, the economy of 'self-sufficiency' is erected on the unacknowledged care given to the self in interaction and affiliation with others, obviously in infancy and early life, but also continuously through the entire human experience. The attainment of (male) autonomy and independence in fact depends on the attachment and responsibility of others, an attachment and responsibility, however, largely denied or experienced as threatening. This recognition of the actuality and need of relationships is avoided, indeed repressed, in both psychological theory and the dominant gender models that underwrite it. In the economy of male-based definitions of the self, such relational selfhood appears weak and flawed. The model defines achieving autonomy as denying attachment. In this process, the sources of social life, of human life, are devalued and regarded as deficient morally rather than as forming the basis of ethics. As Gilligan writes, "herein lies a paradox, for the very traits that traditionally have defined the "goodness" of women, their care for and sensitivity to the needs of others, are those that mark them as deficient in moral development" (*DV* 18).

RECOVERING VOICES

Gilligan's work is of immediate and direct interest for the interpretation of literature on several planes. First, she attunes us to women's voices, to their expression of experiences and viewpoints different from those that prevail in a society whose values are largely determined by men. She shows how what women express may be according to and in the name of different measures and standards of value. Second, her work suggests new assessments of the poetic selfhood of women. From the perspective of dominant poetics as from the norms of dominant psychology, women's poetic selfhood often looks weak, lacking subjectivity, lacking authority, and lacking strong senses of self which may seem muted or silenced in a negative sense. But from a different viewpoint, women's selfhood emerges not as weak but as defined through structures and premises other than those that idealize and fantasize radical autonomy. Women poets instead express their own distinctive senses of self, their own senses of values and stances, different from and often critical of dominant ones. From this different perspective, women poets would not lack authoritative selves but rather base their authority in a structure of poetic selfhood different from what has been assumed by (male) poets and poetics, one that is focused on address and context rather than personal self-reflection. What seems lacking in selfhood from one perspective may be strongly expressive of selfhood in a different sense.

Gilligan's theories of psychological-moral patterns is, from a literary viewpoint, foremostly a theory of voices. She insists that her focus in fact is not on gender as such but on "two modes of thought," which she traces as "the interplay of these voices within each sex" (*DV* 2). She is seeking to hear voices that are different from the dominant model, a difference that, however, is historically and psychologically associated with women. Listening to such different voices involves a number of techniques. One is noticing and analyzing in ways that recall Ardener's anthropological work, different meanings within words, according not only to their normative senses but as they mean within the experiences and models common to women. Thus, in her essay "Remapping the Moral Domain: New Images of Self in Relationship," Gilligan explores how basic terms of value mean differently according to different notions of self and relationship. There are, she observes, "two meanings of the word 'responsibility'—commitment to obligations and responsiveness in relationships." These

> two conceptions of responsibility reflect[ ] different images of the self in relationship, [and] correct an individualism that has been centered within a single interpretive framework. At the same time, the identification of attachment or interdependence as a primary dimension of human experience ties the psychology of love to the representation of moral growth and self-development.[20]

Similarly, two senses to the word 'dependence' come into view when dependence is seen in terms of its contrasting opposites: "the opposition between dependence and autonomy," where dependence becomes an obstacle to development according to the normative (aka male) charts that do not take account of the experience of girls and women; and "the opposition of dependence to isolation," where dependence means recognizing the "human capacity to move others and to be moved by them."

Being dependent, then, need not mean being helpless, powerless, and without control. Rather, it may signify embracing attachment to others, a conviction that one is able to have an effect on others, as well as the recognition that interdependence empowers both the self and the other, rather than being viewed as one person gaining at the other's expense. "The activities of care—being there, listening, the willingness to help, and the ability to understand—take on a moral dimension. . . . In this active construction, dependence, rather than signifying a failure of individuation, denotes a decision on the part of the individual to enact a vision of love."[21] Human bonds and attachments become not failures of self-definition but modes of the self's participation. What is a self at all if not the multiple, mutual interactions, through myriad events and activities, with the selves that surround it?

But since the male model is dominant, the woman's model becomes muted, with women's voices lost in two senses. First, they are inaudible or invalid in terms of the dominant models. Deviating from the norm, they are neither visible nor recognizable in its terms. This inaudibility penetrates into women themselves. They, too, adopt normative models against which their own experiences are measured as lesser—less independent, less strong, less objective—and therefore are repressed or devalued.

But a second loss of voice in women is not due only to the eclipsing of women's senses of experience by normative standards or to women's internalizing these standards. Girls and women, Gilligan argues, lose their voices as a result of their own psychological and moral commitments. If relationship is so impelling for girls and women, then preserving relationship may take priority over expressing one's own feelings, thoughts, and needs. This is a dilemma. What if expressing desires or thoughts seems to threaten relationship—either because they conflict with the roles or images expected of women or because their own thoughts or feelings disagree with those around them? In either case, women fear that expressing themselves will threaten relationship. Yet to suppress their voices will also make relationship impossible because the women will not be participating in the relationship in a genuine way, as themselves. The desire for relationship paradoxically defeats relationship. The self is at an 'impasse,' faced with the option either of "feeling abandoned by others or feeling one should abandon oneself for others."[22] What results is a form of dissociation, what Gilligan calls "knowing and not knowing," as if we disown or don't know what we know. In terms of voice, such a "mechanism of disconnection" involves using one's own voice to "cover rather than to convey thoughts and feelings, and thus to close rather than to open a channel of connection between people." As they become adolescents, young girls begin to repress feelings that may contradict what is expected of them or whose expression threatens the relationships they value. But this also empties those relationships of genuine connection, and it comes at the cost of self-knowledge and psychological development.[23]

To mitigate or recast this dilemma, the sharp opposition between self-definition and responsibility, autonomy and dependence, self-assertion and self-denial, of being either "selfish" or "selfless" must be called into question.[24] Embracing the notion of the self-in-relation can instead affirm both the self and its relationships, neither sacrificing oneself for others nor defining the self through detachment from others. Responsibility would extend to the self as well as to others, so that women can be both "responsive to themselves without losing connection with others" yet also "respond to others without abandoning themselves."[25]

This challenge to what has been accepted as normative, questioning basic values and moral assumptions of our society in light of women's psychological and moral experience, exposes the suppression and self-suppression of women's voices and points to ways to attend to and make possible their expression. This can take the form of critique of the dominant model and its moral standards, commitments, and psychological understanding or of direct and indirect expression of dissenting views. But it first involves detecting the forms of suppression themselves.

MISSED DIALOGUES

In literary terms, feminist psychology opens striking ways of analyzing how women's voices express values and viewpoints that differ from those that prevail in a society largely defined by men. It also opens different understandings of structures of poetic selfhood for women. The apparent weakness of women's poetic selfhood from the viewpoint of self-assertive claims to authority based on autonomous vision from a different viewpoint can be seen as expressing distinctive senses of authority based on a different construction of the self in relation to others. From this different perspective, women poets would not lack authoritative selves but rather would redefine what constitutes authority and selfhood.

Voices and silencing emerge in women's poetry as persistent and characteristic topics and topoi. They register the anxiety women have as to not being heard, and their ambivalence about being heard as well, of raising their voices and acknowledging their desire to do so. As with modesty, women's attunement to the feelings of others may indeed give rise to a deference that is silencing. It can represent conformity, complicity, and internalization of the need to efface their own voices. The challenge is to be able to articulate one's voice in ways that still express and strengthen ties to and concern for others, making room for the voices of others while still affirming one's own. This, however, often proves a difficult challenge to meet. Many poems register, even as they expose, a sense of lack of voice, swallowed by internal concerns for sustaining relationships as much as by external conventions and roles.

One literary mode in which the loss of women's voices is a defining structure can be called a *missed dialogue*. In such dialogue, women speak or report their speaking to men, who, however, do not hear or listen to them. Women and men instead talk past each other, as if each were speaking a different language. Such missed speech acts can take explicit dialogue form; or they can be the record of unspoken thoughts that the woman does not say to the man; or a third-person account may be cast through these gendered viewpoints in explicit or implicit misunderstanding with each other. Whatever the speaking and nonspeaking roles, lack of communication is represented, with women not being heard and/or failing to express themselves, knowing that what they say will not be understood or will only increase the distance between themselves and their men. Thus, women's voices become veiled, often in the attempt to maintain relationship, but then cost both relationship and selfhood. In such missed dialogues, women evade expressing themselves and yet register that this is what they are doing, albeit in veiled ways. The representation of such submerged voices is a powerful mode in women's poetry.

Such missed dialogue can be found in the work of Helen Hunt Jackson (1830–1885). An immediate contemporary of Emily Dickinson, also born in Amherst, Jackson turned to writing in order to earn her living after the death of her husband in an army accident. In her poem "Two Truths" (*CP* 32), a man and a woman talk completely past each other:

"Darling," he said, "I never meant
To hurt you;" and his eyes were wet.
"I would not hurt you for the world:
Am I to blame if I forget?"

"Forgive my selfish tears!" she cried,
"Forgive! I knew that it was not
Because you meant to hurt me, sweet,—
I knew it was that you forgot!"

But all the same, deep in her heart
Rankled this thought, and rankles yet,—
"When love is at its best, one loves
So much that he cannot forget."

Two truths, two viewpoints, two voices. A man speaks, apparently to declare his consideration of his (presumably) wife: "I would not hurt you for the world." Yet what he actually offers is a justification of himself and a dismissal of the hurt he is supposed to be regretting. He in fact is denying, not acknowledging, that he is at fault. "Am I to blame if I forget" in effect places the blame not on himself but on her. He is blaming her for blaming him for forgetting.

The woman, in turn, accepts this blame. In doing so, she renounces her own feelings as "selfish," so that her sense of being hurt is silenced. It becomes reversed into concern for the man at the expense of herself. She becomes the one apologizing to him, asking twice for him to "Forgive her" that she has even mentioned the fact that he has hurt her. Maintaining her relationship with him requires that she efface herself, that she lose relationship with herself and silence her own voice, and that she instead experience and accede to his: "I knew it was that you forgot."

The poem, however, displays but does not enact this silencing. Its final stanza gives the woman a last word. Here the woman's "truths" are voiced, although it is unclear whether it is she, or the poet, who recovers them. "Deep in her heart" she contests her husband's denial of her feelings and his justifications of it. She reasserts her hurt and anger that he not only does not listen to her but denies her the right to feel hurt by it. This is shown to be a double forgetting of her: the original neglect and then its dismissal. In the third stanza, "she" seems to regain her own voice, against the forgetting of herself that her relationship required in the second stanza. Yet the voice remains one that "he" does not hear, for it is never spoken. Her questioning of his justification—"When love is at its best, one loves / So much that he cannot forget"—she in fact keeps to herself. It remains what she does not say. But in this she disowns her own voice and strengthens her dissociation from both him and herself—a disowning the text, however, displays.

Another poem by Jackson, "A Woman's Battle" (*CP* 179), reenacts such gendered self-silencing, again as a form of missed dialogue. Here the woman speaker addresses the man only silently. She keeps all her words to herself and from him so that the dialogue is in fact never voiced but remains as a whole a muted discourse:

> Dear foe, I know thou'lt win the fight.
> I know thou hast the stronger bark,
> And thou art sailing in the light,
> While I am creeping in the dark.
> Thou dost not dream that I am crying,
> As I come up with colors flying.
>
> I clear away my wounded, slain,
> With strength like frenzy, strong and swift;
> I do not feel the tug and strain,
> Though dead are heavy, hard to lift.
> If I looked in their faces dying,
> I could not keep my colors flying.
>
> Dear foe, it will be short,—our fight,—
> Though lazily thou train'st thy guns;
> Fate steers us,—me to deeper night,
> And thee to brighter seas and suns;
> But thou'lt not dream that I am dying,
> As I sail by with colors flying!

The poem opens with an oxymoron. "Dear foe" asserts at once the deep tie and yet no less profound contest between the speaker and the person (presumably male since the poem underscores gender in its title) whom she does and does not address. What the poem offers is precisely an anatomy of these distances and connections, these silences and their hidden voices. The "woman's battle" is with him but also within herself.

What the woman says, or rather doesn't say, is that the man has the advantage of her in the situation from the start, indeed setting the terms for both of them. He is "stronger" and sails in the "light," while she creeps in the "dark." This darkness is both inside and outside her. The poem traces not only all that the woman keeps from the man in this silent speech but also all that she feels she must keep from herself. He must not suspect that she is "crying" but must only be allowed to see her "colors flying" as she puts on the appearance she feels is required. Yet she also hides her tears from herself.

The second stanza is one of profound inner dissociation, where she does not "feel" the pain of this battle and its wounded, does not look it in the face, for fear that she would then show her own face, show herself to herself other than with "colors flying." This is an effort, a battle, which she must finally lose. "Fate," which is gender, "steers" herself into still "deeper night," which will enclose her more and more profoundly as she continues to conceal herself to prevent him from seeing that she is "dying" to herself and to him, into a silence that ultimately costs herself.

Poems such as these, posing women's voices against men's, or rather tracing the submerging of women's voices in the face of men who do not hear them, recur throughout the nineteenth and twentieth centuries. Some poets make this an occasion for irony or humor, as do Lucy Larcom, Phoebe Carey, and Charlotte Gilman. Their comic texts inscribe the pressure of concealment. Humor, in fact, like quotation, is at once a way of owning and disowning one's own voice, a way of both saying and not saying at once. Such poems seem on one level to be telling open secrets, at least among women. Yet on another level, the secrets seem to be kept even from themselves. This is the case in "Getting Along" (*PW* 25), a poem by Lucy Larcom (1824–1893). Larcom worked at the Lowell Mills—one of the first textile factories in America, established in the 1830s as a 'homelike' setting for a labor force of girls and young women. Larcom wrote for the "Lowell Offerings" newspaper organized by the girl factory workers. She then went West to teach and marry but returned back East alone. After years of onerous teaching, she eventually collaborated with Whittier in editing abolitionist writing.

Larcom's poem "Getting Along" offers a woman's account of marriage, spoken to herself while husband and wife trudge together down a dusty road.

> We trudge on together, my good man and I.
> Our steps growing slow as the years hasten by
> Our children are healthy, our neighbors are kind,
> And with the world round us we've no fault to find.

It turns out, however, that the two are walking quite different paths. Each stanza tells of this double way but only indirectly and implicitly. The woman never openly says what she feels or how she sees her husband and marriage, speaking always in conformity with the dominant model and the socially normal voice, to both herself and her husband. The man, as the woman portrays him, is non-communicative, indifferent, and dominating. But this she never directly states, covering it over instead through what becomes the poem's refrain of cliché and denial. As she later concedes, "We're different, sure; still, we're getting along." Thus, from the normative viewpoint, all is well: "Our children are healthy, our neighbors are kind, / And with the world round us we've no fault to find." But this conformist declaration is followed by qualification:

Recovering Women's Voices 61

> T'is true that he sometimes will choose the worst way
> For sore feet to walk in, a weary hot day;
> But then my wise husband can scarcely go wrong
> And, somehow or other, we're getting along.

Thus, the poem's overt rhetoric consists of the woman's justification of her married life—what she says to her husband or herself about him and them. Yet in its course, it also strongly asserts what she is not saying—what she suppresses, even to herself, even though she deeply knows what she refuses to acknowledge. Thus, she calls her husband "wise" but then concedes "T'is true that he sometimes will choose the worst way," on which she, however, must follow him. In ensuing verses, she says that he speaks "No harsh word" to her, but this is due to the fact that he barely speaks to her at all—"He seems not to know what I eat, drink, or wear. . . . I wouldn't mind scolding,—so seldom he talks." And if she insists she does not "care" as long as he is "trim and hearty," it is a paradoxical caring and not caring, and one that goes all one way.

The joke of the poem is in the disparity between the rhetoric of love and marriage—"He only has promised to love and protect"—and the reality of alienation, indifference, and silence. The vows of marriage emerge as empty clichés, a dominant language that covers over the woman's voice. This veiling of voice is something the woman participates in, adopting the dominant discourse as her own. "We're getting along" is a form of normative language, as is calling her husband a "good man" who has vowed to "love and protect." Like quotation and proverb, such phrases emerge in the text as not the woman's own words but alien sounds in her mouth, not expressing what she feels and thinks but rather veiling and disguising it. As she goes along in the poem, the more she insists they are "Getting Along," the more we understand that they are not; or rather, they are only at the cost of her own self-suppression and inner dissociation. Her silence is the price she pays in order to sustain and continue in the marriage. Yet the poet does name what the woman cannot, including the acute pressure of woman's muting by convention and conventional words. It is the poet, and the reader, who recognize the ironic contrast between the refrain of "Getting Along" and the detachment and suppression it would deny. The woman speaker remains in effect as silent as the man. His lack of recognition of her needs, his disconnection from her, she reenacts in her own inability to directly express them.

This mode of women and men talking past each other, of women in a way talking past themselves, is a poetic form that endures from the nineteenth into the twentieth century. Many H. D. (Hilda Doolittle, 1886–1961) texts are structured around revisiting and revoicing women's positions that have been omitted in traditional mythologies, where they languish as uninvestigated, almost invisible backdrops for the actions and speeches of men. H. D.'s poem "Eurydice" offers her account of the failed rescue from Hades by

Orpheus. This heretofore silent figure now speaks in a voice of anger, viewing Orpheus's actions as a selfish betrayal of her. "So for your arrogance . . . I am swept back / where dead lichens drip" (*CP* 51). H. D.'s Electra and Orestes, Calypso and Odysseus, engage in extended dialogues that only underscore how blind and deaf each one is to the other's world, but where the woman's version has been omitted from the cultural record.

Elizabeth Bishop's (1911–1979) "Songs for a Colored Singer I and II" (*CP* 53) likewise feature modes of veiled discourses, of women speaking their own silences, their own failures to communicate or be heard. These poems, like Larcom's "Getting Along," are constructed around refrains, repeatedly restated in each poem's course but not out loud to the male (non) interlocutor, thus defeating any possibility of actual dialogue. In "Songs I," the husband's competitive restlessness drives and consumes him so that the life he leads points away from the speaker/wife's. She feels herself left in a depleted home-world. "What have we got for all his dollars and cents?—A pile of bottles by the fence." The wife's repeated lament, "Le Roy, you're earning too much money now," reflects back on herself critically as well. Are her desires for a bourgeois home more legitimate or more authentic than his restlessness, always thinking of getting "a job in the next town?" Perhaps she is betraying her own "inquiring mind" in complaining about him, so that Bishop is also critiquing the woman's critique of her husband as her own narrowed gender role. Bishop both traveled and inquired in ways that are here attributed to the man. In "Songs II," the refrain the woman repeats to herself is, "The time has come to call a halt." This, however, is not spoken to her husband, and its very repetition shows that the woman has not in fact taken this step. In the texts, there is no actual exchange or conversation as a means of maintaining relationship. The woman's words to herself mark her impotence and failure of communication. The poem continues, "Now I'm pursuing my own way. . . . I'll ride and ride and not come back." But this is a plan never acted on. Although she repeats that she'll "ride and ride," there is no sense of real pathways going anywhere, certainly not to repaired relationships and selves reciprocally engaged.

Muriel Rukeyser's (1913–1980) "Waiting for Icarus" likewise returns to a classical site to voice the woman's viewpoint omitted in the traditional mythologies. Rukeyser uses a pointedly contemporary, natural language in revisiting this classical scene. The phrases are ones you could hear anywhere, in empty, conventional nonconversations: "He said he would be back and we'd drink wine together / He said that everything would be better than before / He said we were on the edge of a new relation. . . . He said he would never again cringe before his father / He said that he was going to invent full-time" (*CP* 495). Repetition in the form of the anaphora "He said" at the start of each line becomes incantatory—an incantation that is all in the woman's head and yet not in her own voice. It is only the woman's report of what Icarus has said, with nothing of what she has said to him. The poem's title already gives his words an ironic cast, as a record of failed promises, registering not reassurance but strategic evasion on his part, to allow him to leave the woman as he wants to do. Thus the woman speaks, but in his voice only, transmitted by her while she herself says nothing: He said, He said, He said.

The poem, then, is constructed through two voices, but they are not in dialogue with each other, the woman repeating what the man says and the man essentially speaking to deceive rather than communicate while dreading the voice of the woman: "He said Just don't cry." In this relationship, which is not one, the man's language is one of empty phrases—"everything would be better than before"—that function neither to imagine future ties nor to confirm present ones but to disengage the man from the woman. These platitudes extricate him from bonds potentially holding him back from his desire to penetrate the sky as he penetrates her: "He said he loved me that going into me /. He said was going into the world and the sky." The failure of bonds, however, is what eventually destroys him. "He said the wax was the best wax." But the wax melts, the buckles open, and Icarus falls to his death.

The woman is then left, in a second stanza, talking to herself through a sequence of anaphoric lines that start with "I remember, I remember, I remember." This voice, in a dialogue that never happened, is situated on the beach where he has instructed her to wait, attesting to the deception of what "he said" in the first stanza, since she is still waiting and he has not returned. The man's assurances have come to nothing, and the woman is left abandoned. Yet it is she who is blamed. The second stanza is filled with the remembered voices of other women, but only as they restate the dominant power structures of gender: "I remember they said he only wanted to get away from me / I remember mother saying: Inventors are like poets, a trashy lot." These women's voices express the dominant culture's views of gender and class stereotypes. The "girls laughing" blame the woman as unable to keep a man; her mother reproves her in terms of bourgeois roles and values. The poem's conclusion does, however, take a turn toward the woman's own and present voice: "I have been waiting all day, or perhaps longer. / I would have liked to try those wings myself. / It would have been better than this." The waiting has been long indeed since the myth of Icarus was first recounted. But only now, in this modern text, does the woman—if only in the conditional tense and not directly to the missing lover—voice the possibility of her own desire and her own adventure.

Poems of missed dialogues enact gendered experiences and the difficulty of communicating across their divide. To some extent, they are therefore poems of complaint, but they are also poems of critique, and project, often indirectly through the muting of women's voices, an alternate set of values and approach to experience. In a poet such as Adrienne Rich, both critique and alternative views shift from muffled voices to explosive ones. Rich makes the silencing of women a central concern in poetry and in prose such as her collection of essays *On Lies, Secrets, and Silence*. In her work, the

64 Feminist Theory across Disciplines

difficulty for women to find their voices is a pervasive social scene between women and men and between women themselves. Rich's poems "Snapshots of a Daughter-in-Law" (1963) and "Mother-in-Law" portray women struggling to address each other out of layers of social roles instituted within and without them. The language barriers stand between woman and woman as well as between woman and man. "*Tell me something.* . . . Some secret we both know and have never spoken? Some sentence that could flood with light your life and mine?" the mother-in-law tells the daughter-in-law (*Fact* 290). In the early poem "An Unsaid Word," Rich names this silencing as the idealized condition of women, in the figure of an as yet imaginary woman "who has power to call her man / From that estranged intensity / Where his mind forages alone, / Yet keeps her peace and leaves him free" (*P* 6). In this idealized relationship, the woman would penetrate the man's isolation without being intrusive while she herself could be in "peace." But this possibility relies on what the title calls "an unsaid word," that is, silence. The woman is left passive and muted, waiting "where he left her" until he decides to "return" to her.

Rich moves through her career from indirect to increasingly direct vocalizations of scenes that normatively depend on women not speaking. "Aunt Jennifer's Tigers" portray the silent Aunt who speaks only through the feminized medium of needlework, where her art enacts her own silencing in its fantasy of the potent tigers she has embroidered. "Living in Sin" depicts a consciousness by day of resentment at gender roles in the poem's female figure, but that is then erased by night: "By evening she is back in love again." This capitulation is the "sin" in which the woman lives, not traditional sexual morality (*P* 19). "Novella" (*P* 65) presents gendered missed discourses and women's silencing in the form of archetypal plot.

> Two people in a room, speaking harshly.
> One gets up, goes out to walk.
> (That is the man.)
> The other goes into the next room
> And washes the dishes, cracking one.
> (That is the woman.)

This woman's distress is directly expressed by the poem if not by the woman herself. The gestures are characteristic. The man walks out, severing connection. The woman remains tied to her household tasks, her misery expressed only via the cracked dish. Although the man, returning later, hears her "sobbing on the stairs," there is no further exchange between them. The poem alone says what the woman does not.

Feminist psychological approaches, whether developmental or psychoanalytic, even as they have importantly opened paths into women's viewpoints, do pose a danger of confining concern to private experience and interior responses. Indeed, just how or whether a psychology of attachment and its ethics of responsibility may be applied to public social and political structures remains controversial. Efforts to extend a feminist psychology to political and social life have been pursued in arguments for motherhood as a public and not only a private model of behavior and values. Sarah Ruddick's *Maternal Thinking*, Nel Noddings's *Care*, writings by Virginia Held, and others propose the mother/child relationship as a model for social life, as against the paradigm of autonomous individuals in both psychological and social terms, who would adjudicate rights in detached, impersonal ways.[26] Yet such maternal models have also been critiqued as an inappropriate confusion of public and private. Hannah Arendt in *On Revolution* excludes empathy from the political arena, as eliminating the "distance" necessary to public deliberation and also as "incapable of establishing lasting institutions."[27] Maternity, moreover, is culturally variable rather than some unified form of femininity, and therefore cannot simply be invoked as a model for either public or private life.[28] Maternal models, it has been argued, confuse intimate with public structures. "Many feminists have moved," writes Elizabeth Fox-Genovese, "from naming their personal experience as political to naming established political norms and practices as personal."[29] Susan Moller Okin has protested idealizations of the family that, in proposing it as a model of care, omit its traditional hierarchies in which women are not granted equal respect or status or just treatment.[30] As Mary Dietz sums up, "Women are not uniquely identified by maternal thinking, nor does maternal thinking necessarily promote . . . democratic politics." The attempt to extend into the public sphere "private" virtues overlooks how much family structures are themselves "open to political control and may be politically determined" (the primary meaning of "the personal is political").[31]

The ethic of relationship and responsibility as introduced through feminist psychology offers, then, only a partial direction for public and political conduct. The self-in-relation of interactional feminist psychology would have to be extended to what might be called a broader self-in-community, recognizing the formation of the self not only in psychological and personal relationships but also as constituted through cultural and community histories, traditions, and contexts. In this framework, not only the extension of psychological insights into the public arena is at issue, but also the penetration of public structures into the private domain in terms of models of selfhood as well. Of course, a core feminist recognition has been "the personal is the political," one of whose claims is that social, political, and economic structures penetrate the privacy of relationship. The converse would be to extend an ethic of relationship into the public sphere, with a redefined self at the crux of both directions.

Such pressure from socio-economic spheres into private ones is forcefully confronted in Gwendolyn Brooks's poetry, which refracts scenes of motherhood, care, and responsibility through the power structures in

66 Feminist Theory across Disciplines

which they reside. She shows how women's voices are at risk, with the difficulties of their being heard systemic to both public and private scenes of gender. Thus, Brooks's much anthologized poem "The Mother" explores the voice of a woman as she probes the deep ambivalence she feels about an abortion. This focus on abortion resonates with Carol Gilligan's original project of interviews with women about abortion as a contested and deeply overdetermined site where women's senses of themselves, of their obligations to themselves and others, come dramatically into the arena of political and moral concerns. What is at stake and in conflict are not only issues of autonomy as against obligation but also how to sustain and fulfill different sorts of obligations. Brooks's poem resists rigid positions, showing instead an ongoing, fragile balancing between different sorts of ties. As Barbara Johnson argues, the poem offers both the woman's decision to abort and her right to mourn.[32] "The children you got that you did not get" exist together with those she has borne, in an intense web of memory, failure, anxiety, responsibility, and love. Above all, the poem allows the mother to speak in a field where her voice has been drowned out and appropriated by political and religious organizational struggles for power. The self-address of the text takes back to herself this decision made in her own moral struggle between obligations to herself and her living family in relation to unrealized children. Here the dialogue is between the mother and herself, as well as her children, born and unborn. Her voice(s) come to a clearing of audibility.

In Brooks's poem "Mrs. Small" (B 341), the scene returns to a kind of missed dialogue but one that is not circumscribed to personal relationship.[33] Rather, the poem shows how motherhood is a social institution inscribed in other social strata, including racial and economic ones. The mother's voice is seriously curtailed by these circumstances. Yet in the poem, it also resounds, with its strength to confront social hardship grounded in her role and responsibilities.

In the poem, Mrs. Small faces an "insurance man" whose demands are closer to extortion than to security.

> Mrs. Small went to the kitchen for her pocketbook
> And came back to the living room with a peculiar look
> And the coffee pot.
> Pocketbook. Pot.
> Pot. Pocketbook.
>
> The insurance man was waiting there
> With superb and cared-for hair.
> His face did not have much time.
> He did not glance with sublime
> Love upon the little plump tan woman
> With the half-open mouth and the half-mad eyes

And the smile half-human
Who stood in the middle of the living-room floor planning apple pies
And graciously offering him a steaming coffee pot.
Pocketbook. Pot.

To the insurance man, Mrs. Small is invisible: "He did not glance with sublime / Love upon the little plump tan woman." What screens her from his view is his stereotyped image of her as grotesque, as a "half-open mouth and the half-mad eyes / And the smile half-human." To him she is also trivial, standing "in the middle of the living-room floor planning apple pies." His voice and viewpoint reduces her to metonymic objects of cookery and monetary exploitations: "Pocketbook. Pot. Pot. Pocketbook."

But the poem also registers Mrs. Small's viewpoint, which sees the insurance man as mechanical like a clock: "His face did not have much time;" and as reduced to his business regimen, his "shirt on its morning run."

"Oh!" Mrs. Small came to her senses,
Peered earnestly through thick lenses,
Jumped terribly. This, too, was a mistake,
Unforgiveable no matter how much she had to bake.
For there can be no whiter whiteness than this one:
An insurance man's shirt on its morning run.
This Mrs. Small now soiled
With a pair of brown
Spurts (just recently boiled)
Of the "very best coffee in town."

The man's laundered "whiter whiteness" is an image of both race and bureaucratic and economic power, as well as gendered authority. Against all of this, in an apparent "mistake," Mrs. Small spurts "the very best coffee in town" over the white shirt. This phrase, "the very best coffee," in a further gendered and dialogical turn is her husband's, who in his own way casts a shadow of power over her. "No bandier of words at all," he "was likely to give you a good swat." Mrs. Small, then, is even within her domesticity inscribed in a gender hierarchy, as she is in ways more hostile from outside as well.

The very name of Mrs. Small is in itself a site of contest between how the world sees her and her own moral stature and sense of selfhood. In one sense, her small rebellion of the spurting coffee is ineffectual. It does not offset the power the insurance man holds over her, which she cannot escape: "she paid him." But she does withstand his viewpoint and his voice, refusing to subordinate herself to him. She thus scorns "Apologies! / For there was so much / For which to apologize! Oh such / Mountains of things, she'd never get anything done / If she begged forgiveness for each one." The poem in the end turns back toward her concerns, of caring for her children and carrying on in tasks that give foundation to their and her world, and without which there is no public one: "Continuing her part / Of the world's business."

Carol Gilligan observes that the self is not only psychological and moral but cultural and historical:

> Within the context of U.S. society, the values of separation, independence, and autonomy are so historically grounded ... that they are often taken as facts: that people are by nature separate, independent from one another, and self-governing. To call these "facts" into question is seemingly to question the value of freedom. And yet this is not at all the case. The questioning of separation has nothing to do with questioning freedom but rather with seeing and speaking about relationships. (*DV* xiv)

Gilligan's model strives not to repudiate individual selfhood but to redefine it in terms of the relationships that inevitably shape it and whose connections enlarge it. This "self-in-relation" attempts to overcome the dichotomy between egotism and altruism, serving self or serving others, by acknowledging oneself also as a person with whom one is in relationship. It can be extended into a self-in-community, with implications for the self as inscribed and acting in public life. As Nancy Hirschmann pursues,

> this ideal recognizes that individuals cannot exist without relationship and community, and that we get our unique and individual traits and characteristics only through relationships. But at the same time, relationships cannot exist without selves, without individuals. Relationships require mutual and reciprocal participation, which in turn requires selfhood among participants.[34]

Brooks's Mrs. Small is large, weaving her world out of ties and obligations that are rarely heard in traditional literary and psychological writing: of her own plight and strengths, expressed in the voice of the mother, as well as her limitations and her responsibilities. The devotion to others is then presented not as a moral weakness but rather as strength, extending beyond herself into her social world.

4 Separate Spheres
Feminist History

There are, no doubt, many entries into feminist recognitions. History, however, offers something of a special invitation. In reading history, what appears to be merely personal experience, isolated and idiosyncratic, suddenly finds place in a sequence of events clearly not of one's own making. Learning about the legal, social, political, and cultural contexts of women in the past serves as a powerful frame for assessing our own freedoms and continued constraints, even while raising questions about our goals in terms of aspects of the past we may wish to continue, if in transformed ways.

In his essay "The Poet," Ralph Waldo Emerson declared that "the poet is representative. He stands among partial men for the complete man, and apprises us not of his wealth, but of the commonwealth." American women in these terms are 'partial men.' For according to the norms in Emerson's time, women did not have access to, address, or take part in the 'commonwealth.' Instead, women and men were thought to inhabit what came in the nineteenth century to be called separate spheres, with women assigned to the home and men to the public realm. As De Toqueville puts it in *Democracy in America*, American women led their lives within the "narrow circle of domestic interests and duties," whereas men found there places in what was simply called the "world."[1] For poets, this has meant the denial to women of Emerson's representative status. In her circumscribed state, the woman poet seems cut off from history, more or less excluded from public issues and discourses. Hers is therefore a double failure: she is unworthy to command attention as speaking for anyone beyond herself, while also lacking the strong sense of identity that makes the poet's words represent his world.

The private and public as a gendered division, while explicitly adopted within nineteenth-century America's discourses as separate spheres, has been in place in differing ways throughout history and also, as anthropologists have observed, across societies. Yet recent work has begun seriously to complicate these traditional assignments. The very notions of public and private are in fact complex and far from clearly demarcated. Historical investigation increasingly reveals the boundaries of the public and private realms to be highly unstable, with women far less contained in the one and

70 Feminist Theory across Disciplines

excluded from the other than at first appears. The circumstances, activities, commitments, and even geographies of women reveal that their lives are often called private even when they are not, thus using the terms in ideological senses that are already gendered. The very distinction of domestic/nondomestic as private/public emerges not as descriptive but proscriptive, not an assessment of what women do but a way of a priori categorizing women's activities. When activities are performed by women, they are often called private, but when the same activities are performed by men they are called public and then valued more highly. Michelle Zimbalist Rosaldo identifies the sexual assignment of women to private spaces as the basis of female devaluation.[2] But in fact it may not be that women's activities, because private, are devalued, but rather that they are called private, and hence devalued, because they are undertaken by women. The very terms, one comes to feel, are gendered and in this sense tautological. It is not simply that women do private things. It is that what women do is by definition private.[3]

Literary studies have tended to adopt the historical terms of public and private, with women's verse characteristically described as domestic. This has implied a limit to its reach and stature, both in the subjects it is thought to address and in the poet's interest and accomplishment. Yet study of the verse reveals domesticity to be at best an incomplete description of women's poetry. To a significant extent, women's poetry instead addresses topics that are directly public and not private. This goes beyond the recent rethinking of domesticity as a political strategy. Jane Tompkin's discussions of sentimental fiction have opened it to political readings, where domestic scenes are seen not only to elicit personal and emotive responses, but rather emerge as modes for critiquing America's dominant social norms, offering its own distinctive ideological vision.[4] This is the case in poetry as well. Yet the sentimental too remains a restricted category and is only one form of the political, ideological, and ethical reach of women's poetry. Other kinds of women's writing are located in and reach outside both sentimentality and domesticity. These record and reflect core aspects of women's historical experience.[5] Women in America were involved in a wide range of activisms that projected their specific vision of society. While domesticity, as has been increasingly investigated, was incorporated into ideological projects such as American expansion, in what Amy Kaplan calls "Manifest Domesticity,"[6] not all women's writing was domestic, and not all domestic literature was complicitous politically.[7] In general, I will argue, in the American context, conservative and progressive impulses are often inextricably intertwined. Conservative intentions repeatedly prove unable to control progressive outcomes, whereas radical impulses may oddly intercross with conservative commitments.

Literature, including poetry, was a primary form of women's entry into public discourse. Publication is a public form, and literature was one of the few avenues women had to public expression altogether. Women did not hold political office. They were neither ministers nor journalists, lawyers nor judges, professors nor lyceum lecturers, nor elected officials: the main forums for public address. Women nonetheless did engage in public affairs through a range of practices political, civic, religious, and social. Both poetry and fiction were important parts of this activism. Women wrote poems directly addressed to a wide range of women's political and social activities. These poems are a rich resource for women's history, providing direct documentation of women's own voices. They express and explore women's points of view on historical events and movements, as well as on paradigms of historical understanding and the values these reflect. These viewpoints and values, needless to say, vary widely among different women and the worlds they inhabited. But in this very diversity they are a vital form of public engagement and public address, reflecting on the whole the relationship between public and private spheres from the women's own viewpoints.

HOME AND OTHER WORK

In America, the ideology of the separate spheres emerged explicitly and centrally in the nineteenth century. Public/private divisions in fact are longstanding, but gendered spheres as public and private acquired new shape in the contexts of industrialization and the social transformations it brought: urban demographic shifts of agrarian populations, new technologies of distribution and communication as well as manufacture, the radical reorganization of work and its locations, and new sociologies of the middle class. New city directories offer for the first time listings distinguishing between residence and business addresses, separating work from home. On the farm or in the craftsmen's shop prior to industrialization, boundaries between work and home were permeable, with shared or largely overlapping spaces. This is not to invite nostalgic fantasies about pre-industrial gender equality.[8] Gendered divisions of labor have pretty much always been in place, even when home and work were not so sharply demarcated. On the farm, men were more involved in fieldwork and production of marketable goods, whereas women were occupied with goods for domestic consumption and domestic chores.[9] Already through the eighteenth century, commercial activity and prosperity sharpened the divisions between men and women, with women increasingly excluded from systems of trade.[10]

The decisive removal in the nineteenth century of the workplace from the home to factories, offices, and commercial sites more officially and ideologically relegated women to a domestic space defined in opposition to the nondomestic one. But this spatial imagery, as Linda Kerber has shown, proves highly obfuscating.[11] Neither in their activities nor in their locations were women fully confined to private spaces. This is not to deny that the lives of women, in the nineteenth century as at other times, were highly restricted legally, politically, and economically. They could not act in court as judge, lawyer, witness, or plaintiff. They could not sign contracts, bring suits, or even stand for certain criminal charges.[12] They could not vote or hold office, and their very status as citizens was unclear, with women's nationality often determined by their husband's.[13] Upon marrying, all personal property came under the ownership and control of their husbands, who could take it at will for any purpose. Women's rights to bequeath, as to inherit, were highly restricted. The first law granting women the power to control their own property was passed in New York in 1848, introduced by irate fathers who wished to prevent the property intended for their daughters from passing into the hands of their sons-in-law. Married women could not hold bank accounts or sign checks; hence, the first treasurers of women's organizations were unmarried or widows. As the English Common Law tradition summed up, to be married was to enter what Blackstone called "Civil Death," becoming a "covered women" (femme couvert) whose entire legal status was absorbed into her husband's—as signaled in the taking on of the husband's name.[14] Marital status for women meant being subsumed under the authority of the heads of households, moving from their father's to their husband's proprietary ownership.

As to domestic norms, although the ideology of the separate spheres dictated that women did not work outside the home, many nineteenth-century women of course did so: as domestic servants in the homes of others, as factory girls, as shop girls; as piece-workers sewing on assignments for textile industries, as prostitutes, and as slaves.[15] Even middle-class women in different stages of their lives worked for pay outside the home. An estimated 20% of women in Massachusetts before 1860 were employed at some time in the course of their lives in teaching positions.[16] Widows might conduct businesses left to them by their husbands or branch off into millenary or other textile-related work. But pay was low, and women both unmarried and married owed their wages to their fathers or husbands. The paradigm of women's place, despite geographic locations, remained domesticity. Middle-class ideology of the woman at home influenced even the working classes. Domesticity further dictated a wide range of social behaviors, governing how and whether women could travel or even walk in public, where the norm was that she be accompanied.[17] It was considered improper to speak in public, especially in mixed 'promiscuous' company. It is interesting to note that one of the first venues that it was respectable for women to visit unaccompanied by a man were department stores.[18]

Yet despite these many constraints, women were, as more and more research makes clear, not entirely defined by domestic roles. In American practice, severities and enforcements of femme couverture were in various ways circumvented or eased. Attempts to protect women's dower rights, powers to bequeath and inherit, to be consulted on sale of property that she had brought into marriage, to conduct business, administer land, and enter into contracts, especially in the absences of husbands: these and other restrictions of English law underwent modification in the New World.[19] Such contextual transformation gained ideological force in the Revolutionary period. Linda Kerber and Mary Beth Norton have portrayed women's responses to Revolutionary experience, when, despite their limitations in juridical, economic, and political terms, women were drawn into the public events swirling around them. They undertook boycotts and other modes of economic pressure as a way of participating in the momentous events and Revolutionary concerns of the times. They also participated in political debate.[20] Nor could they fail to notice the implications of Revolutionary commitment to equality, self-determination, and the right to representation.[21] As Abigail Adams famously wrote to her husband John, then at work on "the new Code of Laws" at the Continental Congress: "Remember the Ladies. . . . If particular care and attention is not paid to the Ladies we are determined to foment a Rebellion, and will not hold ourselves bound by any Laws in which we have no voice, or Representation."[22]

In the event, he did not. Women were not granted in the new Constitution significant changes in public status in terms of official roles in the exercise of political power. Indeed, the nineteenth century intensified ideologies of gender boundary. Nonetheless, the Revolutionary era inaugurated trends that ultimately and radically altered women's positions in the American polity. The first of these was education. Education in America had included both boys and girls from the Puritan settlements, out of the commitment to Bible reading by all Christians, even female ones. Actual attendance at primary schools varied widely, with girls kept home for seasonal work, and records show a considerable evasion of the law. Secondary schools and Harvard College were, moreover, reserved for boys preparing for public careers, mainly as ministers.[23] Nonetheless, literacy rates in New England for girls were the highest in the world.[24] The Revolution then opened higher education to girls, with the establishment of the first secondary school for girls in history, at the Philadelphia Young Ladies Academy in 1787. The experiment in self-government required a literate citizenry, informed in public affairs, and able to participate in public debate. Franklin, Jefferson, Adams, Benjamin Rush, and Noah Webster each designed curricula, wrote treatises, and delivered speeches toward this civic purpose of education.[25] Although this education to active citizenship was intended for boys, girls were also implicated. Locke's view of school as a training ground in civic participation greatly influenced the founding fathers. Locke had also written that education begins in earliest childhood, forming habits and manners as well as laying foundations of knowledge. The duty of childrearing fell to women. If women were not meant to be directly active in the political process or fully to be citizens, they were still the wives and mothers to Americans who were. So-called Republican Motherhood was born.[26] As Benjamin Rush put it in his 1787 address to the first Philadelphia Young Ladies Academy:

The equal share that every citizen has in the liberty and the possible share he may have in the government of our country make it necessary that our ladies should be qualified to a certain degree, by a peculiar and suitable education, to concur in instructing their sons in the principles of liberty and government.[27]

Historians have emphasized that Republican Motherhood remained, however, a structure of ambivalence. On the one hand, it denied women roles as direct participants in self-government; on the other, their roles as mothers took on civic and public importance. Women's traditional activities acquired public and political significance; at the same time, their political activity remained within the orbit of gendered norms.[28] This balance has been variously argued: as to whether conservative impulses outweighed progressive ones, restrictions controlled opportunities, and concessions vitiated gains.[29] Yet with education as with many of the shifts in American women's history, conservative and radical, restrictive and expansive impulses merge, collide, coincide, and even amplify each other in often unpredictable and ultimately uncontrollable ways. In education, conservative intentions failed to limit or fully direct the energies they set free. Launched for delimited purposes, the American education of women was shaped and yet also failed to be contained by its initial conservative intentions. Thus, although women's education was initially justified and established with only limited roles in mind, these proved unable to control the forces they then unleashed. Schools burgeoned. The Philadelphia Young Ladies Academy was rapidly followed by Emma Willard's Seminary at Troy in 1821; Catherine Beecher's Female Seminary in 1823 at Hartford, where her sister Harriet first learned and then taught English; and Mary Lyon's Mount Holyoke Seminary in 1837, where Emily Dickinson went to school after attending co-educational Amherst Academy, and finally becoming a college in 1870.[30] Co-educational university education was opened to women at Oberlin in 1837, followed by women's colleges, beginning with Vasser in 1865.

The first unforeseen consequences of these educational advances were professional ones: women gained admittance to medicine, law, journalism, teaching, and literature on a new, if still limited, scale. Women rapidly became not only students but teachers. Noah Webster, imagining American education as a great project in civic learning, lamented the shortage of men willing to carry it forward. "From a strange inversion of the order of nature," as he remarks, "the most important business in civil society is in many parts of America committed to the most worthless characters." By the mid-nineteenth century, four-fifths of teachers were women making up this slack. In Webster's terms, women had taken on the task to "implant in the tender mind such sentiments of virtue, propriety, and dignity as are suited to the freedom of our governments."[31] The sphere of education also provided training in civic rhetoric, which women then deployed, participating in debate that was foundational to the Republican experiment.[32] Education in this sense, and women's roles as educators, is a public and not a private venture.[33]

PUBLIC ACTION

Teaching was one arena of women's public service, but there were many others. Women took on the tasks of coping with the new urban boom in population, with its new immigrants, new conditions of labor, and new challenges to health and sanitation.[34] Throughout the nineteenth century, women organized, raised funds for, and (wo)manned services for the poor, the orphans, the aged, and the sick. For these needs, newly intensified in nineteenth-century American cities, official or governmental programs had not yet been designed.

This public activism of women has been increasingly researched and documented. Yet there remains a strong tendency to interpret and assimilate it according to gendered public/private ascriptions. This tendency to privatized interpretation applies to nineteenth-century women, as well as men, and also to later historians. Women in the nineteenth century characteristically justified, to both themselves and others, their activities not as a break from the 'domestic sphere' but only as its 'extension.' To some degree, this is true. In many cases, women were doing outside the home the sorts of things they did inside them. Inside the house, they cared for children, and so they did outside, in schools and orphanages. Inside the house, they cared for the sick and aged, and so they did outside, in hospitals and hospices. Inside the house, they fed and sewed, and so they did outside, in poor relief. Temperance and the attack on prostitution of the moral reform movements likewise had domestic reference. They were undertaken to protect the home from alcoholic violence and deprivation, and to protect prostitutes from disease and exploitation, and wives and families from betrayal and abuse.[35]

Other activities, however, are not really like what women did at home. Yet they are still described as 'domestic.' Abolition, although it too was associated with protecting the integrity of the family against assault, both sexual and through the breakup of parents from each other and their children at auction, remains a public, civic, and political activism. Other activities have little tie to domesticity and cannot properly be seen as its extension. While women remained barred from electoral politics, many sorts of political activities were open to them, including petition writing, fundraising, lobbying, letter writing, demonstrations, marches—an impressive array of political interventions.[36] Other civic activities were not specifically related to either domestic or 'women's' issues. Paula Baker, for example, describes women's involvements in employment services, libraries, water and sewage plans, and establishing city parks. Specifically, women's initiatives include clubs for women journalists, for literary activities, besides the movements for suffrage and women's rights.[37]

Many women's activities can thus only with strain be seen as extensions of domesticity. Nor does 'privacy' accurately describe them, even when they do recall women's traditional roles. What makes these undertakings 'private'? Not location as it turns out since they were conducted in the streets, buildings, and institutions of cities, such as schools and hospitals. The whole term 'domestic' in spatial, geographic senses is questionable. Activities that are neither like those in the home nor located there involve churches, meeting halls, club houses, government offices, and legislatures. Women went into the cities to demonstrate and heckle, march and canvas, circulating through public spaces, as Mary Ryan has traced in *Women in Public*.[38] In many cases, neither purpose, nor interest, nor commitment, nor arena can be called private. In fact, it begins to seem that neither geography nor the nature of the activities, but only the fact that women are performing them, causes them to be ascribed to the private sphere. Even in cases such as abolition, trade organization, temperance, and moral reform, which are not prima facia 'women's' concerns, these continued to be called private only because or when women were doing them. Men involved in these activities were not considered 'domestic.' It is not location, but the fact that women undertake these activities that makes them be described as 'private.'

Thus, calling women's activism 'domestic' is a strange distortion of language. What it does is presuppose a paradigm in which women are 'private' and then forces events to conform to this model: a saving of 'domestic' appearances for the sake of the paradigm. Indeed, this tendency can still be felt. As Sara Evans sums up, feminists continue to describe women's lives as 'private sphere' and see women's more visible activities only as "expressions of private concerns in public life."[39] How to assess women's activism thus remains controversial. The First Wave feminism of nineteenth-century women's initiatives is often suspected as limiting women's positions as much as furthering them. To the extent that women adopted the notion of a woman's sphere as the justification for public action, they confirmed its boundaries in ways that may have prevented them from more fully breaking through its limitations. Yet describing or conceiving their projects as continuous or concordant with domestic values also allowed women to secure entry into new arenas and expand their scope of activity. On the one hand, adopting or invoking women's traditional roles continued to define women's activities within its terms, keeping women within the bounds of dominant images and standards rather than challenging them. On the other hand, through these means women ventured into terrain well beyond the traditional home. Conversely, women could do more things and go more places, but only as long as these actions and sites accorded with their traditional conceptions and self-conceptions.

This balance continues to be argued: as to whether working within the ideology of the spheres ultimately strengthened or challenged women's confinement in traditional roles. Women's worlds were certainly expanded. But defining new activities in old terms ultimately may have limited their transformative power. Reform activities have been seen as doing the ideological work of the bourgeoisie in ways that confirm hierarchical class strata. Reform activism then becomes a mode of social control, what Gayatry Spivak calls "the imperialist project cathected as civil society through social mission."[40] Yet reform also opened public space to a wider range of voices acting in diverse and contentious ways, as Mary Ryan argues.[41] Similar arguments concern African-American women. As Hazel Carby, Claudia Tate, and others argue, genteel values, while reflecting white society, were also drafted toward achieving equality and strengthening both self and African-American community.[42] For white women, too, domesticity performed various and often conflicting functions.

The fight for suffrage is exemplary in this debate. Suffrage was in many ways the least successful political campaign of the nineteenth century. Its assertion of women's independent right to vote challenged the definition of women as members of a household, thereby directly confronting women's sphere and the question of women as independent individuals. This challenge to the accepted definition of the self kept suffrage from attracting large numbers of women (temperance had a much larger following), with its goals not achieved until the twentieth century. Indeed, it was only when suffrage, instead of challenging the definitions of women as members of a household, changed its rhetoric from claims to individual rights to the argument that women voters would promote women's values in the public sphere that the vote was finally obtained.[43] Thus, suffrage duplicated the ambivalences of First Wave feminism, of working within and yet against nineteenth-century gender norms as to means of entry and action in the public world. At issue were women's values: was the goal to free women to enter the public world as defined by men? Or would women's entry into the pubic world redirect public life and the individual's place in it, which in nineteenth-century America was rapidly being defined in terms of economic selfhood and interests rather than civic community?

THE SPHERES OF POETRY

Rufus Griswold, in his landmark 1848 anthology of *Female Writers in America*, cautioned readers to beware of mistaking

> for the efflorescent energy of creative intelligence, that which is only the exuberance of personal "feelings unemployed." We may confound the vivid dreamings of an unsatisfied heart, with the aspirations of a mind impatient of the fetters of time, and matter, and mortality. That

may seem to us the abstract imagining of a soul rapt into sympathy with a purer beauty and a higher truth than earth and space exhibit, which in fact shall be only the natural craving of affections, undefined and wandering.[44]

In Griswold's view, women's poetry, unlike men's, is made of "feelings unemployed," "dreamings of the unsatisfied heart," not "abstract imaginings" of "pure beauty" and "higher truth" but "natural craving of affections." Placing women's poetry under the shadow of the separate sphere in fact continues well into the twentieth century. For fiction, the circle of privacy has been increasingly punctured, with more and more attention given to the public dimensions of women's writing. Much has been written on the fact of publication itself: an emergence into print that was enormously consequential, not only in publicizing women's words beyond the home but in bringing, through print, public experience into the home. Here, however, 'public' often has meant publication itself, the bringing to view of the private lives of women in the domestic sphere—'private woman' made visible on the 'public stage' of circulating texts.[45] Further research has pressed more directly into the public world. The 'sentimental' novel has been rightly and powerfully linked to its address to and influence on public affairs.[46] Seeing the fictional representation of women's voices as cultural constructions, and also more direct analysis of civic rhetoric in writings by women, have contested and complicated the literary separation of spheres.[47]

Discussions of women's poetry have, however, tended to keep to the confines of domestic ideology, although this has also been changing recently.[48] Feminist literary criticism has focused on uncovering the obstacles to writing and publishing by women poets, underscoring the difficulties of entering into and finding place in a male literary tradition; of countering reductive representations of women within it; of confined experience and senses of the self as undermining women's senses of their own poetic authority; and, hence, the difficulty of fashioning a poetic self or 'subjectivity' to ground the creative power and personal authority necessary to becoming a poet at all.[49] But the emphasis on these constraints paradoxically keeps the portrait of women's poetry essentially domestic, private, and of limited scope—even as it shows women as failing to achieve a true subjectivity necessary to great lyric. Women, that is, are seen as both too private and not private enough—too private in their domestic enclosure but not private enough in the sense of strong senses of selfhood.

But this is a partial account of American women's poetry—as much derived in the paradigm of privacy as evidence for it. A review of the poetic work by nineteenth-century women proves it neither to be concerned mainly with domestic worlds nor to present only a failed attainment of selfhood. Instead, the poetry—like the women's lives it represents and indeed many activities of the poets themselves—addresses public concerns: a public involvement that in turn informs senses of the self and representations of the poet's role.

Women's poetry has a profound historical dimension and address, engaging public issues and also helping to define what these are. Indeed, they offer what amounts to a contemporary analysis from the point of view of women of transformations taking place in nineteenth-century America, and of the conflicts of values and interests this involved, with the separation between private selves and public commitment a major concern. The poetry negotiates and reflects the definitions of the self, of individual identity within American society and culture, as this was taking complex shape through the century. This public involvement of women, however, casts the role of the poet and of poetry in ways that importantly distinguish women's self-representation from that of the Emersonian Poet as Self-Reliant (which is in any case a simplified and flattened version of Emerson's own "Poet").[50]

Emily Dickinson is the paradigmatic case of how gendered assumptions about women's privacy prejudice historical interpretation. Dickinson's reclusion in her Amherst home, which she barely left from the age of around thirty, certainly establishes her as a dramatic case of domesticity. Refusing to meet visitors, declining to address letters, dressing only in white and, momentously, choosing not to publish the nearly 1800 poems, many sewn in fascicle booklets or arranged in sheets, that she left in her bureau drawer at her death. Dickinson epitomizes almost to the point of parody the gender expectations of her society: that women remain domestic, modest, and hidden.

Yet a number of Dickinson's male-writer contemporaries were also remote from direct historical experience. Emerson and Thoreau remained resolutely in Concord, Hawthorne in his Salem attic and then his Liverpool consulship, and Melville in his custom house in New York. Whitman alone can be said to have roamed and ventured. And regardless of locations, Dickinson, no less than her great male contemporaries, illuminates, addresses, and critiques broad cultural trends and registers historical events. This includes the momentous and traumatic Civil War that coincided with the onset of her reclusion and during which she wrote more than half of her poems.[51] Whatever her personal eccentricities, what emerges from Dickinson's work are senses of womanhood, notions of manhood, and the cultural and historical contexts in which each took shape.

Despite her reclusion, Dickinson was positioned in close contact with American events. Her family was one of active civic involvement. Her father, after assuming prominent roles in town meetings, in Amherst College, in the Home Mission Society, and in the railroad project, was elected representative to the General Court of Massachusetts in 1838; was elected to the Massachusetts State Senate (1842–1843); served as delegate to the National Whig Convention in 1852; and in the same year was elected to the U.S. Congress. His term in the Congress spanned the period of the Kansas-Nebraska Act, the Fugitive Slave Act, and the first attempts to found the new Republican Party (with meetings to discuss this issue taking place in rooms he shared with Thomas D. Eliot, granduncle to later poet Thomas Stearnes).

Dickinson's father and brother were both active recruiters and outfitters of Amherst soldiers in the Civil War, involved in raising both funds and morale. Many of Dickinson's close correspondents were directly involved in political reporting and public affairs: Samuel Bowles, who was editor of the *Springfield Republican*—which published soldiers' letters home and a column on "Piety and Patriotism"; and Dr. Josiah Holland, columnist for the *Springfield Republican*, editor of *Scribner's Magazine*, and one of the first biographers of Lincoln. Thomas Wentworth Higginson, central in the drama of Dickinson's failure to publish, was a radical abolitionist (even to the point of supporting the John Brown conspiracy), an activist in women's rights, and Colonel to the first black regiment of the Union army when Dickinson first wrote to him. The trauma of war, cultural tensions, and social questions all penetrate Dickinson's work. Numerous poems as well as letters record her response to war on many levels. These are being steadily uncovered in Dickinsonscholarship. Some poems intersect with Dickinson's contemporary history by echoed words, oblique references, or sudden images.[52] There are also a number of specific elegies for Amherst dead. "My Triumph Lasted till the Drums" imagines the poet herself on the battlefield, witnessing "the finished Faces" that new technologies of photographing were transmitting from the war to the home front. Home and war fronts are blurred in a more specifically gendered way when Dickinson describes life in war as "dissolved. . . . In Battle's—horrid Bowl," bringing imagery of the kitchen into the war zone (probably the battle of Antietam) (J 444/Fr 524). The problem of justifying death—always traumatic in Dickinson—takes on broad cultural and historical challenge in war. As she writes, to be "Robbed by death" is "easy / To the Failing Eye" (J 971/ Fr 838). Dickinson generally sees death as robbery: the taking from her and the world what is rightfully theirs. Even so, Dickinson, in a sentimental tradition turned macabre, hovers in many poems at deathbeds watching the "failing Eye" to detect what it may be seeing or whether it is indeed, as the poem goes on to say, at its "latest Glowing." But then she adds: "Robbed by Liberty." This oxymoron involves historical complication. How can liberty rob the self when it exactly is the pledge to protect self-interest? In the context of war, citizens can be called to defend liberty—a context indicated by the words that follow, which are associated with battle and sacrifice: "Hint of Glory—it afforded—/ For the Brave Beloved." Nonetheless, the poem underscores that death in defense of "Liberty" is strangely paradoxical. "Liberty" was a central word in American discourse and in the Civil War conflict itself, its meanings as divided as the country. In the South, it denoted the right to private property, including slaves. In the North, it was taken as an ideology of freedom in the sense of each individual's right to self-determination, which was beginning, for some, to extend to slaves as well.[53] Dickinson's text shows these and other strains in the term. Being called to fight by country is to be "Robbed" not only *of* liberty but "by Liberty," which is to say in the name of it. Dickinson is characteristically skeptical of abstract claims that require immediate sacrifice. Personal liberty can radically clash with civic obligation, even in its own name. The conclusion of the poem confronts liberty's economic senses and rights, meanings that project painful uncertainties and blank unpredictability of outcomes: "Staking our entire Possession / On a Hair's result."

Despite (or through) their cryptic and riddling forms, Dickinson's words are drawn from, and address, public events, often in subtle ways. In this she is continuous with other women poets despite the extremity of her practices. Other women poets have also been categorized—and dismissed—as remote from the world. Yet they also often engage, address, and represent historical concerns.

HISTORICAL POETRY

One such case is Lydia Sigourney. Extremely popular in her lifetime, she was dropped with her death from literary historical view. Scorned as the "sweet singer of Hartford," Sigourney was conservative, indeed an ideologue of the separate spheres, authoring advice books on domesticity for young girls and brides. Her poems paint intensive domestic scenes, including, notoriously, endless consolations on dead babies. But as Nina Baym has shown, even Sigourney's sentimental poems of mourning join with other elegies and commemorative poems that are historically concerned. Domestic scenes also have their historicity, registering changes in family size and shifts in gender roles in the nineteenth century, including increased authority for women at least within the domain of the household.[54] Sigourney's poems further address a wide range of topics beyond the home, offering a form of women's American history. Poems describe the then new experience of girls going off to school (Sigourney, as so commonly in New England, had been a schoolteacher and then, successfully, a school headmistress). These texts often feature tragic deaths either away at school or among those left behind, registering what must have been considerable anxiety and conflict over these new opportunities and roles away from home.

Sigourney also portrays women's lives in terms of national undertakings, such as westward expansion, and of specifically women's projects in the new urban environments and their social and economic ills, such as care of poverty, illness, drunkenness, and disability. Sigourney's senses of gender became the basis rather than the barrier to her social and political projects. In a yet wider political involvement are poems on Revolutionary history, national heroes, territorial expansion, and incorporation, largely cast in feminine imagery and drawing on what Sigourney took to be woman's nature.[55]

Sigourney's own strongest social commitment was opposing Indian Removal, against which she continuously and unsuccessfully campaigned. Her most anthologized poem is "Indian Names" (*SP* 258), which stands as an elegiac but angry protest and exposure against an imperialism she portrays and identifies in linguistic terms: "Ye say, they all have passed away, / That noble race and brave." But, she adds, "their name is on your waters, / Ye may not wash it out." The importance of naming, and poetry's power to do so, becomes a mode of national formation, even as America is presented here as a linguistic event. In exposing the erasure of Native Americans from both land and language, Sigourney is giving voice to a muted group whose very words have been appropriated by a dominant discourse.

Other Sigourney poems on Native Americans follow more sentimental conventions, focusing on family ties. This keeps to the language of emotional bonds familiar to domestic verse. Domesticity could be enlisted as a rhetoric to promote American expansionism, but this is not Sigourney's case.[56] "The Indian's Welcome to the Pilgrim Fathers" (*SP* 146) undermines and contests the normative American narrative of settlement: Sigourney shows the Native American's welcome to the settlers to be unreciprocated and self-destructive. Their good will turns against them to become "a blast and ban / Upon thy race unborn." Sigourney's poem is a discordant and dissenting version of Thanksgiving Day.

When Joan Kelly-Gadol famously questioned what the Renaissance was for women, her answer was: not the same one as for men.[57] Nineteenth-century women's poetry asks: what was westward expansion for women? The response is similar: a different one from men's history. The poet's representations of women's experience in fact provide access to a history that has been largely overlooked until recently.[58] These omissions of women and their lives from history reflect paradigms as to what constitutes history itself and what counts in its accounts. History traditionally is the history of public life, itself narrowly defined as the exercise of political power—an arena in which women have rarely directed events. Women's lives thus had remained unrecorded and invisible to history, as trivial, private, and without public consequence, with few leaving their own records through the centuries due to lack of literacy. Women's delimiting to a private sphere has thus blocked approaches to their actual doings, excluding them from investigation. A broader historical interest in the conduct of life, and new senses of what constitutes the public, tears the veil that has kept women's worlds from view while reconstituting not only historiography but our very senses of the categories through which history is examined and understood.

Some poems of the westward movement take the form of missed dialogues, as husbands invest all their energy and attention in settling and developing new land, while the women experience dislocation and mourn for the connections they have left behind. In Lydia Sigourney's "The Western Emigrant" (*SP* 63), the homesteader asks his wife: "Did I see thee brush away a tear? / Say, was it so? Thy heart was with the halls of thy nativity." Alice Cary's "The West Country" (*P* 208) conjures both the hard work and the lost ties of western settlement:

> Have you seen the women forget their wheels
> As they sat at the door to spin—
> Have you seen the darning fall away
> From their fingers worn and thin

Cary ends this text by endorsing the woman's toil in a vision of American success, where her son at last "Strips off his ragged coat, and makes / Men clothe him with their praise." But in "The Emigrants," the prospect of going west, so long looked forward to, in the end casts "shadows . . . on the heart and brow / From the home we are leaving here." In "Growing Rich" (*P* 97), Cary is still more pessimistic. When the husband asks his wife, "Why are you pale, my Nora? . . . The black ewe had twin lambs to-day, / And we shall be rich folk yet," he doesn't really listen to her answer, which is posed in entirely different terms. While she "know[s] we are growing rich," her own mind is on "my little brother Phil . . . down / In the dismal coal-pit yet," on "my father's eyes, / That are going blind, they say," and "darling Molly's hand, last year / cut off in the mill." Here is a portrait of woman's isolation in her life out west, as well as the industrial cost to those who do not share the wealth they help to produce; of opportunity as against obligation to those who are aging or injured. Frances Harper similarly tells the gendered story of western migration in "Going East" in terms not only of cut personal ties but of bifurcated experiences, measured by wealth and its costs. ""Golden Grain" (itself a reductive pun) comes to block out every other experience for the man: "nor music . . . nor brooks, nor bees / was as sweet as the dollar's chime." But the woman

> Toiled and waited through weary years
> For the fortune that came at length;
> But toil and care and hope deferred,
> Had stolen and wasted her strength.

These women poets contest the divisions between domesticity and history, the existence of any separate sphere at all except as ideological construct. The socio-economic order both establishes and penetrates domesticity. Charlotte Gilman presents this as a direct ideological challenge. Gilman's groundbreaking *Women and Economics* analyzes the economic dependence of women on men as a profoundly distorting and determining substructure of all their interrelations. It is this dependence, she argues, that defines and distorts socio-economic life both within and outside the home. Merely private life is to her an evasion of the way in which domesticity is shaped by economics and also of the obligation to public engagement. In a poem called "Exiles" (*CP* 74), for example, Gilman portrays the experience of women immigrants who have become American domestic workers. They are displaced in terms of both country and home, which becomes a scene of work rather than of personal relationships:

Exiled from home. The far sea rolls
Between them and the country of their birth;
The childhood-turning impulse of their souls
Pulls half across the earth.

Exiled from home. No mother to take care
That they work not too hard, grieve not too sore;
No older brother nor small sister fair;
No father any more . . . .

Blinded with homesick tears the exile stands;
To toil for alien household gods she comes;
A servant and a stranger in our lands,
Homeless within our homes.

Immigration to America is portrayed here not as redemptive liberation but as exile, not only from homeland but from family. Nor is family only a matter of personal comfort. It is a support network committed to care, a vital resource, as opposed to the households that are now only a place of labor. The 'alien gods' whose altars these girls tend is money. The distinction between public and private blurs when alienated work is in the home, where the domestic servant is paradoxically 'homeless' in terms of interrelationships regardless of location.

A number of studies on sentimental writing have noted its complex mix of the progressive and restrictive. Domesticity, it has been claimed, made a space within print culture for women's voices, even if conceived as a separate sphere.[59] While domesticity conformed with patriarchal structure, it cannot necessarily be entirely reduced to it.[60] In women's poetry, domesticity both defines and breaks boundaries. This takes a special turn in the work of Frances Harper. Harper has been criticized as adopting genteel styles, seen in part as complicitous with white audiences and values but is also interpreted as radicalizing these values toward furthering racial equality and gendered power. Harper in fact enacts a tension and an ambivalence often faced in black literature: what Bruce Dickson describes as embracing or assimilating to dominant culture as a means of asserting black cultural values.[61] Representing African-American women as modest and virtuous, for example, contests association with illicit sexuality and was part, according to Hazel Carby, of the battle for sexual autonomy.[62] Claudia Tate particularly traces how domesticity and genteel values serve within its own historical context as a vital means of contesting prejudice by showing African-American women and men as able to advance themselves through virtue and hard work. "The idealized domestic mask is not a denial or erasure of black people's political desire," she writes, "but an image for their acquisition and the full exercise of that desire." Within the norms of nineteenth-century gendered life, Harper's heroines have authority and serve as models of initiative "within the roles of wife, mother, and teacher," dedicated as they are to advancing education and civil rights within their communities.[63]

In Harper's work, domesticity interpenetrates with socio-economic-political structure. In fact, domesticity has a distinctive meaning within African-American culture. Slavery deeply challenged notions of private spheres as separate from historical forces. Harper's anti-slavery poetry is often sentimental, but in this way it appeals to human ties in order to protest and oppose the degradations of slavery. "The Slave Auction," "The Slave Mother," "Eliza Harris" (dramatizing the scene of escape from *Uncle Tom's Cabin*), "The Fugitive's Wife," and Harper's Aunt Chloe sequence all show slavery's assault on family in order to arouse moral outrage and awaken political conscience. This of course was a vital impulse and tactic within abolitionism, not least among the women supporters who made up the great number of its activists. Abolitionist ideology was grounded in moral and indeed religious senses of the horrors of slavery in ethical terms, as destructive to families and violating sexual and moral norms.[64] As Harriet Beecher Stowe more than demonstrated, this tactic of personal moral appeal had enormous political effect. *Uncle Tom's Cabin* turned out to be, as Lincoln put it, "the little book that started this big war," proving a significant force in mobilizing the Northern Civil War effort.

In the case of slavery, domesticity had a unique status in that homes, family ties, and personal commitments were modes of resistance against efforts to destroy them. Sentiment emerges as a militant claim for those whose humanity has been refused acknowledgment. Harper's domesticity is therefore radical. It grants to slaves the family relationships and emotional attachments that the slave institutions foundationally denied them. To represent the slave family as a site of domestic attachments was to contest the slave system's assertions and procedures, which denied to slaves just such personal humanity.[65] Thus, in "The Slave Auction" (CP 10),

> Mothers stood with streaming eyes,
> And saw their dearest children sold;
> Unheeded rose their bitter cries,
> While tyrants bartered them for gold.

"Gold" rhymes with "sold," in harsh contrast against the streaming "eyes" and bitter "cries" of children and mothers separated by sale. Americans claim to stand for freedom when in fact they are "tyrants." If this is sentimental, the issues it addresses are pressingly institutional—the South's "peculiar institution" itself, which defined many of the South's institutional and cultural life as well as its economy.

In Harper's poem "A Fairer Hope, A Brighter Morn" (CP 199), the speaker becomes a personification of slave history:

86 *Feminist Theory across Disciplines*

>From the peaceful heights of a higher life
>I heard your maddening cry of strife;
>It quivered with anguish, wrath and pain,
>Like a demon struggling with his chain.
>
>A chain of evil, heavy and strong,
>Rusted with ages of fearful wrong,
>Encrusted with blood and burning tears,
>The chain I had worn and dragged for years.

At the start, the speaker is clearly identified with slavery, herself wearing its chains: "The chain I had worn and dragged for years." But the "maddening cry of strife" that the speaker hears and compares to a "demon struggling with his chain" turns out not to be those of the slave but rather of the slave owner. The "you" she addresses are in fact not African-Americans but whites. They too are implicated and enmeshed in slavery's "chain," and it is their story she is telling as well.

>It clasped my limbs, but it bound your heart,
>And formed of your life a fearful part;
>You sowed the wind, but could not control
>The tempest wild of a guilty soul.

"It clasped my limbs, but it bound your heart." Slavery ultimately binds together African-Americans and whites in one American history, inseparably biracial. If the African-American has suffered from slavery's abominations, the white has been horribly corrupted by it. But part of the American story is the repression of this fact. The poem goes on, in something like an incantation, to uncover these repressed memories and knowledge and bring them to light: "you saw," "you remembered," "You thought of," "you thought of," recalling "rice swamps," children bought and sold, beatings and anguish.

>You saw me stand with my broken chain
>Forged in the furnace of fiery pain,
>You saw my children around me stand
>Lovingly clasping my unbound hand.
>
>But you remembered my blood and tears
>Mid the weary wasting flight of years,
>You thought of the rice swamps, lone and dank,
>When my heart in hopeless anguish shrank,
>
>You wove from your fears a fearful fate
>To spring from your seeds of scorn and hate

You imagined, the saddest, wildest thing,
That time, with revenges fierce, could bring.

The white Americans view the now "broken chain" of slavery with fear and project a future of "fearful fate / To spring from your seeds of scorn and hate." But repression of the past can only create a dark future. It breeds fear of "revenges fierce," which can only be avoided by bringing this dark and hidden past to light.

Harper's poems are rhythmically and syntactically simple, in keeping with her desire for her verse to be a mode of public address. Indeed, she often read her verse as part of her public lectures on abolition, freedman's education, and women's rights, tying it to both the hymnal and preaching traditions. Yet this poem is not simple in its figural construction. This is especially so in the constitution of its speaking voice and its address. The poem, as often in Harper, sets out to create a community of listeners who will see and hear each other in a conscious and committed response. The "I" who speaks here speaks not only for herself, nor even only to her people, the former slaves, but also to the former enslavers, as she calls them all against a false America and toward its transformation. As the poem goes on to declare and envision:

> Beyond the mist of your gloomy fears
> I see the promise of brighter years,
> Through the dark I see their golden hem
> And my heart gives out its glad amen.

Again, it is white America she addresses, under the dark shadow of the past now clouding the future as well with "gloomy fears." To them as well as to African-Americans, the poet promises a future historical redemption.

GENDERED MODERNISM

In the twentieth century, one might expect that the presumed quarantine of women and women poets from history would have vanished. But this is not the case. Twentieth-century women poets indeed do often address history, weaving their texts out of or directing them toward historical references and materials. Yet there has been a widespread interpretive resistance to such historical dimensions. H. D., a founder of the Imagist movement, remains anthologized mainly through her early writings of isolated, concentrated poetic moments. Her later, long meditations set against backgrounds of war have failed to gain a foothold in literary history. Marianne Moore and Elizabeth Bishop have been widely regarded as poets of intricate description, suspended in time, as if recording their world while themselves remaining invisible and inaudible. Plath and Sexton are treated as confessional poets.

Recent feminist investigations emphasize how discussions of modernism have largely defined it in terms of select male practitioners.[66] Such male High Modernism pursued an aesthetic of formal closure and self-reference, an aesthetic from which women modernist practices often however diverge. Modernist women writers may share the formal self-consciousness of High Modernism, although in women even these shared modernist techniques tend to be interpreted in gendered ways, as a reticent, precious, and narrow frame in which to weave a limited art. But central women modernists also continue forms of self-representation that recall earlier women poets, as against the assertion of personal authority characteristic of Eliot, Pound, and Yeats, each of whom puts himself forward as speaking for, indeed defining, cultural worlds that each claims to represent and further. Of most significance, in my view, is how the entry of women modernists into discussion challenges the main understanding of modernism as a formal investment that subsumes history, with theoretical issues of construction displacing historical ones. Gender makes such segregation impossible. Gender inevitably raises issues of history, politics, and culture as these in turn shape art. Therefore, taking gender into account forces reconsideration of aesthetics. The formalist tradition, strongly associated with modernism, cast art as a kind of separate sphere, removed from contexts, speakers, and audiences. Poetic form, seen in the light of gender, instead intensifies just such interactions among different areas, making the text a site of interchange and resonance among the different fields of its cultural situation.[67] Intensity of form, far from isolating the artwork, brings into it divergent domains of experience, with an accompanying greater burden on and consciousness of language. This is the case for women modernists, whose historical engagements and public address are, however, often ignored, in their case in ways that compound women's assignments to personal privacies.

Elizabeth Bishop, for example, was long admired for her meticulous craftsmanship, seen as rendering detached portraits of often exotic places. But Bishop inscribes selfhood deeply and thickly in social histories, shaped by and also responsible to them. The self is a sort of map, to invoke one of Bishop's own core images, of cultural/historical/social strata in which the self is embedded. Often enough Bishop does place figures of the self in domestic scenes, while, however, distancing her tone from the sentimental and representing social and political forces. These multiple foci structure her own poetic voice. This voice is not so much neutral as composite, made up of the different voices and viewpoints her texts cross between and among, as in "Squatter's Children" (*CP* 110). The portrait of home life in "Squatter's Children" registers an extended and intrusive socio-economic world, in which the home is precarious, illegal, and vulnerable. As characteristically in Bishop, the poem establishes a site at once domestic and alien, homelike and strange, but also private and public—private as public.[68] To do so, it shifts among varying perspectives, introducing, recognizing, and acknowledging different experiences. The poem begins at a distance, seeing the girl and boy as "specklike" near a "specklike house." But the text then plunges into the children's viewpoint. It is they who see the light as "gigantic waves of light and shade." To them, too, the storm in the second stanza is something to be ignored. "Their laughter spreads / effulgence in the thunderheads." It hardly disturbs their play. That play, in contrast, is constrained in ways they themselves are not aware of. Their toys are their father's broken tools, in hard ground. Above all, the house that should shelter them is an "unwarrantable ark." Illegal, it is no Noah's ark to carry them through the storm and flood, which the poem reveals as being economic and social in ways that deeply impinge on their lives, defining their very domesticity. But this larger view is implied from outside the children's viewpoints in a voice that registers the poet's without its being personalized to her.

Another voice is the "Mother's." This distressed voice compulsively intrudes on the children's play but is impotent to protect them: "Mother's voice, ugly as sin, / keeps calling to them to come in." If "Mother's Voice" is "ugly as sin," then the sin is economic and not religious, and not of her making. The "storm" accrues wider and wider meaning as, in the last stanza, it comes to stand for the children's social and legal rather than meteorological world. Storm invades and defines their place in the world, marking a "threshold" for their social homelessness. In the end, the poet addresses the squatter children:

> wet and beguiled, you stand among
> the mansions you may choose
> out of a bigger house than yours

The children's ability to choose "mansions" is constrained and not a matter of free invention or imagination since they are ever situated in the "bigger house" of society, one in which their "rights" are no more than "soggy documents . . . in rooms of falling rain."

None of the voices in this poem is fully independent of the others. They are bound together and also with the poet's. Bishop does not restrict herself to one viewpoint identified as hers. Her role is to bring forth, into public light, these experiences and, ultimately, the responsibility to and for them. The poet is not dramatized, and she does not openly locate the poem's speaking within her own poetic persona. Yet she is there as a committed figure who sees and speaks the network of relations in which people find their home and their place. That place is at once intimate, social, and political, defined by legal "rights," or rather the lack of them, in "rooms of falling rain."

Sylvia Plath is a striking case where women's poetry has been seen as an interior confessional and aesthetically formal affair, even when poems are radically engaged in historicity. Plath's biography, like Dickinson's, is almost seductive in its distraction. Her strained daughterhood, her obsession with her father, her betrayed marriage, and her suicidal attempts and final success act to encircle her work into biographical and psychological spaces. To the extent that she is seen as representative, it is of the duress of women's private incarcerations, away from public life. This of course is true, although even as psycho-gendered, her work can be viewed as a public record of women's experience in the 1950s and 1960s. But Plath's poetry repeatedly blurs such boundaries of inward life and historical experience. Hers is a powerful woman's voice describing, registering, and exposing the culture and history around her. "Daddy" is famous for controversially adopting Nazi rhetoric and the suffering of the Jews as apparent metaphors for Plath's own personal anger and anguish over her father.[69] Plath, however, in this poem is also exploring the psychology of mass-sadism.[70] In "Getting There" (*CP* 247), a Holocaust war scene is vividly elaborated through, but also defining, personal metaphor: "It is Russia I have to get across, it is some war or other. / I am dragging my body / Quietly through the straw of the boxcars." "The Thin People" portrays how historical experience shadows ordinary and private life (*CP* 64).[71] Registering the almost invisible yet explosive presence of Holocaust survivors in the lives of those living around them, the poem works against efforts to suppress disturbances in a defensive normalcy. "They are always with us, the thin people / Meager of dimension as the gray people / On a movie-screen. . . . In a war making evil headlines." The poem is an early exploration of how mass media shapes experience, as war-reels make visible the historical shadows of daily scenes. Thus, the "thin people" on the streets are images of the "gray people / on the movie screen" that brings war to the home front.[72] After the war, the thin limbs remain "stalky," haunting as they are haunted in the postwar world, continuing to "famish" and "grow lean" in the hunger—not least for acknowledgment—they cannot shake off. Their thinness marks their continued erasure in the world around them, which thereby is reduced into a "thin silence."

"The Thin People" is an early portrait of the Holocaust, exposing the 1950s silences about it. This silence spreads through each of the poem's scenes, almost as a subtraction, like a leak of color and substance, "Making the world go thin as a wasp's nest." It is part of the poem's power not to give any direct historical account, just as no direct account was given of or by the thin people hidden in the midst of militant normalcy. The cause is repressed, but the effect is everywhere. The half-looked-at people cast their shadow into "The sunlit room" whose "wallpaper / Frieze of cabbage-roses and cornflowers" bespeak the most intent household gentility but that nevertheless "pales / Under their thin-lipped smiles." Their "menace" is not "guns, not abuses," but rather a thinning of our very sense of where we are. The very fact that "The Thin People" is not set in war but at home, on the streets of peace in the course of ordinary days, only intensifies its historicity.

Anne Sexton, like Plath, has been mainly categorized as a "confessional poet," a kind of twentieth-century version of sentimentality, only more hysterical.[73] But Sexton's personal voices are often pointedly social and historical. She too evokes and introduces Holocaust imagery, often in conjunction or intersection with aspects of women's lives, as in "Uses," where the speaker herself turns to ash, "gray—hair, eyes, nose, mouth, face" (*CP* 610). In Sexton, this can seem to absorb the historical into the personal. But domesticity comes to be treated as a historical phenomenon, not a natural or fixed place.

Sexton's much anthologized poem, "Her Kind" (*CP* 15), is an explicitly historical treatment of the witch-crazes during which hundreds of thousands of women were put to death, a women's history contemporaneous with what is periodized as the Renaissance for men.[74] The poem's points of views are in fact quite unstable. Sometimes the speaker takes on the voices of society as they have been internalized by the witches, in self-alienation. Or the speaker seems to be citing dominant social voices as a way of opposing and exposing their intention: "A woman like that is not a woman, quite." Sometimes the speaker seems to be speaking in the witch's own voice, identifying with her. At other times, she is indirectly accusatory of social norms that treat odd women as witches. The poem is a play of dominant voices and muted ones, which can be difficult at times to sort out from each other, distinguishing women's versions of themselves from the official versions that tell the women/witches who they are.

Throughout, the speaker(s) approach the witch-figure in anthropological, social, and historical senses. At the opening, the speaker declares herself a "possessed witch." But this description reflects the images others have of her. It is the images in fact that can be said to possess her. If she is "haunting the black air," she does so through the fears and hostilities that others project onto her. In this sense, they, not she, are "dreaming evil." These opening voices are at once those of an outside speaker, the witch herself, and the voices of social norms, which is to say of hostility and exclusion towards her. The different voices come at the end of each stanza to rest, however, in a refrain, where the speaker's voice radically merges with the witch's: "I have been her kind." This identification becomes domestic in the middle stanza, where the home becomes the uncanny, suspect scene, and finally deadly, as in the last stanza, when the witch/poet speaker rides in a cart toward execution by burning. The "nude arms" and flame-bitten "thigh" conjures the prurience, indeed the pornographic sexualization of the witch's body, both in the inquisitorial inspections imposed on her and in public exposures of her body at execution. At the last, the poet again directly adopts the witch's voice in defiance: "A woman like that is not ashamed to die." Indeed, the shame is her killer's. Thus, the poet joins her voice with that of the witch-figure that haunts our culture and our history, challenging norms and giving voice to those historically silenced.

But the history of violence does not require mythologies of witchcraft. It is in fact quite mundane and present. Sexton's subjects, far from being merely personal, are shown as part of a social structure, social history, which situates and in Sexton largely entraps the individual. Sexton's "Buying the Whore" (*CP* 581) harks back to earlier exposures of double standards and prostitution, as integral to gendered society and economies. Indeed, the erasure of agency and voice of the woman is enacted by the poet's speaking voice, which is a man's: "You are a roast beef I have purchased / and I stuff you with my very own onion . . . You are the grate I warm my trembling hands on, Searing the flesh until it is so nice and juicy." The woman is object, in domestic imagery of cooking and of the hearth, here exposed as sexualized and violent.

Sexton's "The Housewife" (*CP* 77) similarly offers a twentieth-century reflection on domesticity: "Some women marry houses. / It's another kind of skin." "Housewife" is wife as married to the domicile and reduced to it. The woman's body becomes the house and the house her body, including, as the poem goes on to list, all the organs and bodily functions that women have had the task of attending and have therefore been defined through: "it has a heart, / A mouth, a liver and bowel movements." Yet housewife as house-body also must conceal herself, exhibiting only as "walls" that are "permanent and pink." She is thus physical and yet pristine; or, as in the next lines, abject—"on her knees all day" in household tasks yet (or therefore?) highly sexualized: "Men enter by force." What finally emerges is the domicile as a site of contradiction, a condition the poem concludes in deeply psychoanalytical terms. To the husband, the housewife is at once wife and mother: "A woman is her mother," who he sexually penetrates: "into their fleshy mothers." The private domain is situated in a chain of generational reproduction, socialized as well as psychological, and therefore ultimately political.

5 Public Women, Private Men
Feminist Political Theory

It is telling that 'public woman' remains a compromised phrase, suggesting illicit sexuality, improper conduct, or indecent exposure.[1] The 'woman of the street' has little in common with the canny city-cruiser in Baudelaire or Walter Benjamin. This asymmetry belongs to a long history that feminist critics have begun to trace, in which the terms 'public' and 'private' have held a central place not only in historical discussions and the literary criticism often corollary to them but also in political theory, philosophy, and anthropology. A fair amount of feminist political writing can in fact be described as attempting to review, expose, and challenge the configurations of public and private as these have placed women both culturally and materially. Yet the terms are far from stable. Their meanings are instead shifting and often contradictory. From discipline to discipline, the terms in fact deploy a series of quite distinct assignations and valuations. This lack of alignment has blunted full recognition as to just how suspicious the terms public and private are and how their usages have both obscured and strengthened distortions in understanding and interpreting women's lives and writings. Assembling and investigating the variant usages from a number of different disciplines can bring to light how their inconsistencies and outright contradictions have distorted the understanding of women, and not least appreciation of the values women have historically represented. In political terms, what is involved are different meanings deployed in parallel systems: private and public as understood in historical discourses; then also, but differently, in liberal theory, with its emphasis on the autonomous individual; and, with special relevance to women, in the republican tradition and its commitment to the common good.

SLIPPED DISCOURSES

In history and in literary discussions corollary to it, public and private have largely meant, as we have seen, the 'separate spheres,' which placed women in the home and men outside it. Here, public/private means essentially domestic/nondomestic. In this case, private as domestic denotes a sphere that is limited, confined, enclosed, material—and female. This, however, is a meaning altogether distinct from the sense of 'privacy' in what has been the dominant modern political discourse in the West, the discourse of liberalism. In liberal discourse, 'private,' far from meaning narrow, confined, limited, or secondary, instead denotes autonomy, self-determination, rights, or property—in C. P. McPherson's phrase, possessive individualism.[2] This is profoundly inconsistent with the meaning of 'privacy' in the discourse of the separate spheres, especially when seen from the angle of gender. In the discourse of the spheres, privacy applies to women as limitation, constraint, and enclosure. In liberal discourse, privacy applies to men as self-determination and self-ownership. This male right to property actually incorporates rather than applying to women. Women are not private in the liberal sense. Far from being autonomous, self-determining individuals, women are instead subsumed into the private rights of men. They are part of what possessive individuals possess; part of the 'private' realm of the 'family,' which autonomous men head and command. Women are not possessive individuals but possessed ones. They do not have 'privacy' and the rights to liberty, property, and self-government that this confers. They fall under the private jurisdiction of male rights, into which arena the 'public' world, notably as the state, cannot interfere. In this sense, as Linda Kerber has particularly shown, women are not 'individuals' at all; they do not command the basic rights—legal, political, economic—that constitute liberal individualism.[3]

This failure to extend liberal privacy to women is one of the central feminist critiques of liberalism. That is, some feminists criticize not liberal individualism as such, but its failure to grant to women the same status that male liberal individuals enjoy. Women, it is argued, are not, but should be, accorded the same rights and privacy that men have. The failure of liberalism is thus its failure to be liberal enough, to extend to all, women and men alike, the protections and privileges of individual self-determination in a just, equal, and genuine fashion. Women should be treated not as entailed in male privacy but as themselves private individuals and justly accorded the legally protected rights that every (male) autonomous individual enjoys.[4]

There is thus almost an incommensurate set of meanings with regard to 'privacy'—it really can be called a catachresis—between liberal discourse as against the discourse of the historical separate spheres. But this is not the only case of linguistic slippage. Almost as striking an inconsistency subsists with regard to the meanings of 'public' as well—something that emerges when yet another discourse is brought to bear, the discourse of republicanism. Here again, apparent similarity of terms disguises genuine differences, by which public and private are used not merely descriptively, but normatively and ideologically, with the result of serious distortion. For although in republican discourses 'privacy' means something close to what it means in the discourse of the separate spheres—a domestic world conceived as limited, narrow, material, and secondary—and that is consistently assigned to women; this is not the case for the republican term 'public,' which has a quite distinctive meaning.[5]

'Public' through republican tradition has a specific and positive content. It is essentially defined as commitment and contribution to the common good. In liberal discourses, privacy as self-ownership and self-determination is prior to, and the ground of, the public realm, which exists as a space ceded by autonomous individuals for their greater protection and prosperity. In an important sense, the private founds the public since it is the consent among private, autonomous, propertied, and self-owning individuals which establishes a public sphere for their own better advancement and security and constrains public life to this priority. In the republican tradition, however, the public realm has priority as the ultimate end of human activity. This is the case despite the variety of distinct republican trends—classical, Renaissance, American, modern—which encompass significant differences.[6] But whether in the classical sense articulated by Hannah Arendt's reading of Aristotle; in the Renaissance and then American senses of republican commitment to virtue as described by J. G. A. Pocock, Joyce Appleby, and others; or, lastly, in accordance with the discourse model of the public sphere constructed by Jürgen Habermas, the public realm is more than a realm ceded from private rights for their greater protection. In Hannah Arendt's formula, the public realm is where the citizen is "concerned with the world and the public welfare rather than with his own well being." The 'public sphere' comes into being wherever citizens come together to negotiate, debate, acknowledge, and promote 'what is communal.' It is "a community of things which gathers men together and relates them to each other."[7] J. G. A. Pocock similarly describes Renaissance civic republicanism as the view of a public life where "citizenship was a universal activity, the polis a universal community," and "the individual as citizen, engaged in the universal activity of pursuing and distributing the common good."[8] In Habermas's discussion, "A portion of the public sphere comes into being in every conversation in which private individuals assemble to form a public body . . . about matters of general interest."[9]

But such a republican sphere entails a startling reversal of the meaning of the terms 'public' and 'private' from those of liberal discourses, where privacy has priority. Republican traditions instead give priority to the public realm. As Joan Landes points out, "liberals associate privacy with freedom: they value the private sphere and defend the individual's right to privacy against interference by other persons or the state. In contrast, republicans . . . associate the public with freedom, or acting in concert with others on behalf of the common good."[10] There are further striking implications and inconsistencies for the uses of private and public in the 'historical' terminology of the separate spheres. In all the discourses—liberal, republican, and historical—women are assigned or subsumed into the 'private' realm of domesticity, as the realm of necessity, restriction, and unfreedom. However, if the meaning of 'public' is taken in the republican sense, then it can be argued that it is women in nineteenth-century America who are in effect committed to the public realm.[11] The areas of women's involvement in the nineteenth century, their activities and their writings—including also their poetry—reveal women to be pursuing and involved in the public good, devoted to and responsible for 'public' affairs in the republican sense of concern for the common good—a public dimension denied and veiled by the variant uses of the terms public and private.

If women, however, were engaged in the public world of community activities, we may go on to ask, what world did men inhabit? The gendered paradigms that describe whatever women do as private, regardless of their actual engagements, tend to describe whatever men do as 'public.' Yet what is the nature of most nineteenth-century men's activities and interests? In the discourse of the separate spheres, assigning men to the public sphere adopts geographic terms of definition. In the ideology of the spheres, women remained at home, whereas men did not. But if the 'geographic' definition of private and public is discarded and, in its stead, what is considered is not the location of activities but the activities themselves, with their specific interests and aims, then women were to a significant degree engaged in public affairs in the republican sense, that is, those that pertain to the common good. In contrast, what men were largely pursuing was not community interests but what, despite being located outside the home, can best be described as private interests: making a living or profit.

This is not to deny that in the nineteenth century men were engaged in public life. In the sense of holding office and of voting, only men were 'public.' Few men, however, then as now, were actual officeholders; government was generally quite limited, with few men employed in it. If we look at nineteenth-century American civic life, one striking feature is the extreme smallness of the governmental bureaucracies and offices. As Theodore Lowi notes in "The Public Philosophy," "Until astonishingly recent times American national government played a marginal role in the life of the nation. ... In 1800 there was less than one-half a federal bureaucrat per 1,000 citizens, and by 1900 that ratio had climbed to 2.7. This compares with 7 per 1,000 in 1940, and 13 per 1,000 in 1962."[12] Even regarding electoral politics, there were periods when relatively few men actually voted.[13] If the public life of men is intended to mean their active work in political organizations or public policy organs, then few men were in fact engaged in public life. Instead, then as now, most men were occupied with working for money, whether as laborers or owners, whether for wages or for increasing wealth, in the realm of private enterprise.

At issue fundamentally is how one assigns the sphere of economics: a terrain that floats through the various assignments of public/private, further complicated by gendering. In the classical republican tradition, economics is decidedly private: the *oikos* was the household, as the private realm of necessity and material provision. As Arendt observes, this is the realm of necessity, of lack of freedom, private in the sense of privation: "To live an

Public Women, Private Men 97

entirely private life means above all to be deprived of things essential to a truly human life" lived in relation to others in a common world. Of course, as Jean Bethke Elshtain elaborates, this was the sphere of women, who were enclosed in this private economy by nature whereas men, although partaking in the *oikos* as material base and source of status, could also participate together in a public sphere beyond it.[14]

Thus, in the classical republican tradition, economy is labeled private but is gendered female, designating women's limitation and confinement to material needs. In the later republican tradition, in contrast, economy is gendered male. However, it then remains private—and, as such, becomes suspicious as undermining higher devotion to the public good. The fear was that "the jarring interests of individuals, regarding themselves only, and indifferent to the welfare of others . . . would end in the ruin and subversion of the state."[15] In liberal discourses, the terms become even shiftier. There, economy is gendered male, but its status is radically altered from the republican ones. In one sense, the economy is public, as the nondomestic space where women aren't allowed. But in another, economy is foundationally private. It is the ground of the private rights and individual autonomy, the life, liberty, and property, in Locke's terms, that public life, as the state, is bound to protect. Private rights, granted only to males, thus ground the possibility of participation in public spheres. As Carole Pateman and Susan Moller Okin have explored, the economic realm thus shifts between public—as nondomestic—and private, as 'civil society,' where autonomous men pursue private ends; as against and protected from interference by the 'public' state.[16]

But this configuration contrasts, again startlingly, with the place of economy in the discourse of the separate spheres, where it is seen as public as against female privacy, even to the denial of female labor in the home.[17] Economy is then 'public' in its geographic rather than substantive meanings, as whatever falls outside the domestic sphere, although remaining 'private' when posed against 'public' state regulation. Frances Olsen has charted these vacillations:

> Although the woman's sphere has been described as "private" and contrasted with the "public sphere of the marketplace and government," such a characterization can be misleading. There are two different dichotomies involved in this contrast: on the one hand, a dichotomy between the state, considered public, and civil society, considered private. Both the market and the family are thought of as part of "private" civil society in opposition to the "public" state. Calling both the marketplace and the state "public" can thus confuse our thinking about the two dichotomies.[18]

One begins to suspect that 'public,' like 'private,' does not simply mean what it says. Neither location (domestic or not) nor interest (private or not) stabilizes its usage. Instead, 'public' seems to denote, first, gender, as male; and, second, power itself. In this sense, 'political' and 'public' are not simply identical terms. While politics may be conducted in the public sphere—as the policy of the polis—what it registers above all is the power to affect that policy, whatever interests it may serve.[19] The liberal public sphere, as Marxists have long contested, can be deeply penetrated by private interests.[20] Of course power structures are not confined to the public sphere. This sense of the 'political' as power is one of the meanings deployed in the slogan "the personal is political," which declares among other things (the phrase is an intensely complex site of intersecting discourses and critiques) that power structures general to society operate no less in the so-called 'privacy' of the family, which is 'political' in this sense.

Of course, as Foucault has shown, many kinds of power exist, concentrated and diffused across societies in many ways.[21] If, however, power is taken to mean decision making over public policy, then women have rarely wielded it. What becomes increasingly evident is that the dissociation of women from the 'public sphere' is not due to the lack of women's 'public' activity but rather to their lack of power over political decisions and allocations. As Carole Pateman puts it, the one area of social welfare from which women have been largely excluded is that of "legislation, policymaking, and higher-level administration."[22] To say that women's activities aren't 'public' is then to say that they are not 1) powerful, and 2) important and valued. The public nature of women's community services is denied, not because these were indeed 'private' and 'domestic' but first, because of women's lack of power in decision making on governmental levels, and, second, by the lack of value increasingly accorded to such contributive activities within American life.

CONFLICTING AMERICAN SELVES

Here in fact questions of gender become inextricable from questions of the American polity itself. Strains between public and private interests were inherent from the outset in the Puritan founding and then continued in different ways into Revolutionary America. J. G. A. Pocock writes of the republican ethos, "There were tensions in conceptualizing the individual as citizen and member of this structure. On the one hand, it was his pursuit of particular goods as an individual that made him a citizen; on the other, it was only in his concern for and awareness of the common universal good that his citizenship could be expressed; and there was always the possibility of conflict between the two."[23] This conflict within republican ideology intensified, as Joyce Appleby shows, through the eighteenth and nineteenth centuries, registered in the increasing displacement of the common good from American life.[24] In effect at issue, and also in various degrees of tension, were (and are) the American commitment to the individual as authority and center of decision making, as a private self; as against obligations as well as self-formation through relationships the individual may have to his or her surrounding society.

In American ideology, the individual remains the site of initiative and accountability. Society arises out of the association of individuals. Rather than seeing the individual as largely defined by, obedient to, and under the authority of a collective, American priority is granted to the self, who then enters into association. But even granting such priority to individual selfhood, just how the self is seen to be constituted, and the relationship to the society he or she is part of, can be seen in a number of different ways—differences that the term 'individualism' obscures. The self that is seen to be embedded in and responsible to society, culture, and community—the civic republican self—differs from the liberal individual who is defined as autonomous and independent, Macpherson's possessive or economic individual. In the civic tradition, selfhood shapes but is also shaped by community, which, as in Arendt's Aristotelian model, remains the arena for the fullest realization of selfhood.[25] In America, then, the individual has precedence over a collectivist ideal that grants authority to the group rather than to its members. But the priority of privacy as constituting autonomous selfhood is just one kind of individualism, implying a liberal public in which each self retains and exercises his own self-definition, whereas civic republicanism constitutes the self through public responsibility and not only or primarily in terms of private rights. This republican selfhood then is shaped by and shapes neither authoritative collective nor liberal association but community in a sense that is in-between: the mutual responsibility of free individuals who, however, see their selfhood as expressed exactly in this mutual responsibility.[26]

What is striking from a feminist perspective is the gendering of these distinct kinds of selves. Joyce Appleby writes about the gender ideology of American individuals:

> Dependency, lack of ambition, attachment to place and person—these qualities were stripped from the masculine carrier of inalienable rights and conferred upon women. In this ideological division of labor women became the exemplifiers of the personal and intimate, maintainers of family cohesion, and repositories of romantic fantasies about the past. This allowed the unsentimental, self-improving, restlessly ambitious, free and independent man to hold sway as a universal hero.[27]

As the centuries proceed, women may be said—contra stereotypes of their privacy—to be committed to common interests. Such female public life, however, coincides with the decline in importance of civic life as private interests came into increasing dominance. This public investment stands despite the obvious exclusion of women from political office and elections. What Sidney Verba says of later periods is true of earlier ones as well:

100 Feminist Theory across Disciplines

women's contributions to organizational and charitable activity have been long overlooked due to emphasis on voting and other electoral activities.[28] Elizabeth Fox-Genovese emphasizes that "women contributed not merely their share of the time and skills required to build [community], but frequently the decisive commitment as well . . . a civilized existence grounded in responsible human networks." Feminist historians recognize that "most of women's earlier activities outside their own households are exercises in community building." But "women's distinct activities, from charity and social work through the education of children and the sustenance of families to the support of culture and churches, have remained dissociated from, or in sufferance to, the world of men, understood as the world of real power."[29] Jane Mansbridge points out that the very notions of duty and the possibility of common interests in democratic politics are "sissified," "hampered by female connotations."[30] Power becomes divorced from the sorts of public services that women performed. Devotion, commitment, and service become associated with women and their sphere whereas the (private) male domain of economics, competition, and self-interest gained greater and greater centrality, importance, and value. Even within the parlance of the separate spheres, if women's sphere becomes a haven, a 'moral' enclave, this presumably posits the male world as 'immoral' political power and economic competition, as Jean Bethke Elshtain suggests.[31] Civic virtue, once the foundational republican value as "the willingness of citizens to engage actively in civic life and to sacrifice individual interests to the common good," becomes, as Ruth Bloch argues, the inheritance of women.[32]

As feminized, civic values come to be seen as private—confined to the home and the women who inhabit it. But this is primarily a sign of the loss of central importance and the emptying of civic values from the public sphere: a coding that signals feminization, not privacy except in its negative, trivializing sense. Civic virtue as inherited by women is disinherited. As Rosemary Ruether observes, "moral virtues were sentimentalized and privatized, so they ceased to have serious public power." Or as Ruth Bloch writes, Revolutionary civic virtue became a matter of "private benevolence, personal manners, and female sexual propriety" and "an extension of maternal virtue."[33] 'Privacy' here carries the historicist sense of losing public support and funding (although in fact large sums of money were raised and distributed by these volunteer women, and state funding was also often involved).[34] But it also records the devaluation of the activities of public concern, which women assumed. At work in fact is a strong rhetorical sleight of hand. The public activities of women are devalued to private matters whereas the private pursuits of economic men are dubbed 'public' because they are outside the home. As Anne Douglas comments:

> Many nineteenth-century Americans in the Northeast acted every day as if they believed that economic expansion, urbanization, and industrialization represented the greatest good. It is to their credit that they

indirectly acknowledged that the pursuit of these "masculine" goals meant damaging, perhaps losing, another good, one they increasingly included under the "feminine" ideal. Yet the fact remains that their regret was calculated not to interfere with their actions.[35]

At work here is less the feminization of American culture and more the feminization of American communal life. Despite a continued rhetoric praising public values, Americans became increasingly committed to private ones. The continued association of the male world of work with the 'public' sphere effectively disguises the increasingly dominant value of private pursuit under the rhetoric of public importance. Women's doings, in contrast, become private: both as lacking in public power and as involvements of lesser value.

Disputes among feminists have arisen over assessing and interpreting this association of women with virtue, devotion, and commitment. For some feminists, the devaluation of these qualities has resulted in an impoverishment of both the public and private worlds. Here a second critique of liberalism emerges: not, as before, on the grounds (only) of the failure to extend to women the right to be liberal individuals, but rather as a critique of liberal individualism itself. The liberal notion of the individual is seen as problematic on several grounds. It is problematic in the way it ignores the sources of individuality in family and community life—ignores the fact that people don't just spring up full grown out of nowhere but come into the world as infants requiring care and are shaped by the family and community into which they are born and in which they grow.[36] Liberal individualism is problematic in the way it fails to address areas of common social concern and mutual responsibility—in its lack of a positive vision of a common public world.[37] These feminist critiques of liberalism join with republican and communitarian critiques, albeit with an added sense of how gender has played a central role in both constructing and sustaining the liberal private sphere.[38]

To other feminists, however, an emphasis on service and responsibility threatens to entrap women in stereotypes of femininity, assigning to women a fixed nature that confines them to traditional roles. These commitments are defended but also attacked as 'maternal values,' criticized as stereotypically gendered and continuing to undermine women's autonomy and self-determination.[39] The point, however, is not that women alone should sacrifice autonomy to the needs of others and certainly not that women essentially are, or must be, mothers. The mother here, as so often, is something of a straw woman. At issue is the value of the activities that are undertaken and also, for all feminists, the issue of their gendering. In civic feminism, autonomy and self-determination are seen as partial values derived in other values of relationship and commitment that require continued, one might say constant, exercise in order to uphold a common world of shared lives and interests. The work of responsibility, which the ideal of unadulterated autonomy would keep invisible even while depending on it, must be brought to light, named, and acknowledged for its full and necessary value—by men as well as women, to be shared by men as well as women. This is a civic implication of Carol Gilligan's work, where an ethic of moral responsibility is urged alongside, rather than as subordinate to, an ethic of rights—and not only for women but equally for men.[40]

Yet even among those who wish to speak for the values which women have historically upheld and realized, there is a tendency to speak of them as 'private values' in a public devoid of them.[41] To some extent, this simply reflects liberal usage, where 'public' means state funding and regulation, making 'voluntary' activities 'private' because they are neither supported nor regulated by the state. The usage, however, also implies a continuity with the 'domestic' space of the separate spheres, where domesticity remains a limiting and devaluing term.

Here, however, I will venture a still more radical proposal: that the activities of service by their nature (rather than their geography or their funding) are public not private, and that this is the case wherever they take place, including inside the home. It is not only outside the home that women undertake public responsibilities. They also undertake them inside the home. Inside the home, women too are pursuing not private interests (as Charlotte Gilman writes, "In the home, who has any privacy?"[42]) but rather services—to children, to the sick, to the aged, and, of course, to men and family—without which no community can even exist, without which society is not even possible. That is, women in these roles, inside the home as outside it, serve the common good and are devoted to the general interest. This recognition runs exactly counter to Hegel, who denounces women as nontranscendental, shrunken, lesser beings because of their confinement to the 'family' as against a greater public investment.[43] It is only too true that it is difficult for women in traditional family roles to achieve the independence and freedom of economic or cultural man, even as women's housework makes it possible for men to do so, which is, however, also to say that such 'independence' is not really autonomous but, on the contrary, dependent on just such support. But this is exactly the point. The traditional lives of women, far from being 'private,' are exactly public: devoted to others in the family and community. Calling them 'private' is a way of keeping the essential and humane work that women have traditionally performed merely the concern of women, rather than recognizing it to be for the good of society and hence a general social responsibility—in whatever variety of institutions, regulations, or supports this might call for. Arguing, as I certainly would, that a fair distribution of both supportive and independent activities among men and women should be instituted, still first requires recognizing the value and priority of civic and community service, whether in the home or outside it: that it exists, that it is being performed invisibly, and that it is necessary.

This recognition of the value of women's service and responsibility is not meant to define the essence of womanhood as natural to women alone or to urge that women alone be responsible for these tasks, rather than sharing them equally with men. Rather, it is to insist that women's work and its value be recognized. It is to rescue women's contribution first, from invisibility, the invisibility that (conveniently) blocks from awareness the existence of this labor and the necessary work it performs. Without such recognition, without bringing this work from the 'privacy' that keeps it hidden from view to full visibility, the work of women remains unacknowledged, unaddressed, and unvalued. Recognizing its public contribution would be a step towards regendering the work of responsibility and towards reaffirming core values of community service and civic commitment—of which childrearing is surely an important instance. But neither must this necessarily betray the individuality, and the rights, women have also striven to achieve. Civic feminism should not be seen in stark opposition against liberal feminism.[44] Both affirm the integrity and authority of the individual. But civic feminism, along with feminist moral psychology, envisions individuals as living in relationship to each other and in communities, relationships that mutually require and support each other.[45] Civic feminism would specifically affirm the values of public service, community commitment, social relationships, and the general good that women have traditionally supported and undertaken—affirm that it is indeed women who have performed this work and embodied these common values, but which should be shared by men. It would demand the 1) recognition of this contribution; 2) importance of these values; and 3) reaffirmation and recommitment to these values in the common lives of both men and women, shared equally by both, toward the common good of both.

CIVIC POETRY

American women's poetry offers a compelling anatomy and register of the different structures of selfhood in the American context and of how these situate women as well as men. It is not just that American women's poetry addresses historical concerns or engages with public events. Both in address and self-representation, much poetry also offers counter and critique against the increasing trend through the nineteenth century of American selfhood as an isolated economic individualism. Commercialism and the ascendancy of economic self-interest as against senses of obligation to the community are exposed and opposed in the name of definitions of the self in terms of community. Women's poetry thus emerges as a voice for community social values in the American polity, as against their increasing displacement by the trend of individual economic calculation. It affirms both positive responsibility and protests against reduction of life to monetary and material measures. This critique of commercialism is, in the nineteenth century, mainly rooted in a tradition of Christian spirituality rather than a secular economic consciousness. Socialist critique of individual ownership does emerge in Gilman and also in the twentieth century, in Rukeyser. In either case, women become speakers for the common good, with a vision of selfhood that runs counter to narrow definitions of the self in terms of self-interest and achievement of material prosperity.

In light of civic involvements and the selfhood it entails, other topics in women's verse take on an added social extension in meaning. Double standards then represent not only a sexual but social division, posing human relationship against economic reduction and objectification of women's bodies for material exploitation. The failed exchanges of 'missed dialogues' prove to be rooted in separate and nonintersecting discourses of commitment and attachment as against private interests and assertions. What emerges in missed dialogues are confrontations and failures of understanding between economic interests and the selfhood this constructs, as against a self that is embedded in relationships and community. This correlates with a sharp sense of gender as it situates each sex in what amounts to different social worlds and selves who inhabit them: a male world increasingly defined by business and money and a female world of personal relationships, moral obligations, and community commitments.

This sense of women and men as inhabiting different worlds pervades Ella Wheeler Wilcox's verse (1850–1919). To Wilcox, the important distinction is not women's worlds as private and men's as public but rather that the former is relational and the latter is monetary and calculated. The poem "A Holiday" (*PProg* 23), for example, is a missed dialogue in which the wife and husband talk past each other, each from a separate world. The wife pleads with the husband to leave the office and join the family for Christmas dinner, assuring him that his presence means more than his presents. But the husband replies, "You women do not know / The toil it takes to make a business grow." To him, all questions are rendered in economic terms:

> Of course I love you, and the children too;
> Be sensible, my dear; it is for you
> I work so hard to make my business pay.
> There now, run home; enjoy your holiday.

As in other missed dialogues where women lose their voices rather than threaten relationship, the wife assures herself: "He does not mean to wound me / I know his heart is kind." But she then adds, if only to herself, "Alas that men can love us / And be so blind, so blind." The husband in turn partly excuses the wife, but within the act of dismissing her as failing to understand the meaning of business. "She has not meant to wound me or to vex. . . . I've housed and gowned her like a very queen, / Yet there she goes with discontented mien." Each ultimately remains unable to reach or understand the other in their separate orientations, paradigms, values, and goals.

This division of values is dramatized in Wilcox's poem "The Cost" (*PProg* 58) in ways that point to the kinds of selfhood each sphere implies and creates. The poem's speaker begins in domesticity, in "unrest" and anguish at "her great wrong" of domestic confinement. In response, she rebels. She decides to "let brain Rule now" instead of "heart" and to venture out into the man's world of ambition, economy, and success:

> She wept no more. By new ambition stirred
> Her ways led out, to regions strange and vast.
> Men stood aside and watched, dismayed, aghast,
>   And all the world demurred
>   Misjudged her and demurred.

Gender prejudice at first dismay the men whose world she enters, who are "aghast." But this does not prevent her from overcoming barriers to her success and achieving eventual acclaim:

> Still on and up, from sphere to widening sphere,
> Till thorny paths bloomed with the rose of fame.
> Who once demurred, now followed with acclaim:
>   The hiss died in the cheer—
>   The loud applauding cheer.

The woman leaves her own separate "sphere" to join the male "widening sphere." She does achieve the success she sought. Nevertheless, the final outcome is ambivalent:

> She stood triumphant in that radiant hour,
> Man's mental equal, and competitor.
> But ah! The cost! From out the heart of her
>   Had gone love's motive power—
>   Love's all-compelling power.

In this text, the woman successfully takes her place with (and against) men in their competitive world. Yet she questions not her ability to achieve but the value of this achievement. This has, she discovers, a 'cost,' as the poem title's economic pun emphasizes, in her relationships to others.

Wilcox has irritated some twentieth-century commentators as being too conformist to nineteenth-century gender ideologies. After the initial scandal and notoriety of her sexually concerned *Poems of Passion*, she in fact went on to marry and live "a highly respectable life" in conformity with "rather conventional views on gender roles."[46] Much of her work (she published forty-six books of poetry) in fact engages in social and cultural issues, including many reflections on gender. But Wilcox remains "First Wave" in her feminist values, loyal to traditional women's values. Yet she is also caught up in the image of the "New Woman" that emerges in the late nineteenth century—not unlike today's ambivalence among many women coming out of Second Wave feminism and into Third Wave critiques of it as we face continuing conflicts between work and home. Wilcox's texts register this experience of ambivalence. The poem "Sisters of Mine" queries women activists: "As we gain something big do we lose something sweet? In the growth of our might is our grace lost to sight?" But the poem written in "Answer" sides with activism (*PProb* 15–18):

> We have toiled and saved, for the masters, and helped them to power and place;
> And when we asked for a pittance, they gave it with grudging grace.

Even here, women's rebellion is carried on in the name of women's virtues but with an egalitarian twist. Women have served men who turn out to be "masters" seeking "power and place" and who then are treated unkindly and in fact unjustly. The social world proves to be one that has sold itself, and human relationships, to the "dollar":

> On the bold bright face of the dollar all the evils of earth are shown.
> We are weary of love that is barter, and of virtue that pines alone;
> We are out in the world with the masters: we are finding and claiming our own.

For women here to claim "our own" is not simply to claim their "dollar" but to challenge the standard of "barter" that has reduced "virtue" to money and power.

Wilcox's "love that is barter" refers to marriage. Marriage has never been exclusively a personal affair. As Nancy Cott reminds in *Public Vows*, marital structures are part of public order, as important to one's standing in the community as it is to self-understanding.[47] Nor is marriage as an economic arrangement new to the nineteenth century. Stephanie Coontz traces a long history of marriage as a political and economic institution.[48] The sexual double standard is rooted in concerns for the transference of property to the proper male heir.[49] But in the nineteenth century, the sexual double standard became an intense focus for women's activism, beginning in the 1830's Social Purity movement and emerging with renewed effort and outrage after the Civil War. These campaigns organized the energies of thousands of women. One issue was prostitution, which had burgeoned with urban growth and immigration. Women's "Purity" and moral reform movements sought to criminalize not the prostitutes but the gentlemen who made the business pay. These campaigns had a singular lack of success: the 1848 New York Seduction Law led to at most one or two arrests a year.[50]

Yet the movement marked important steps into political and legislative activity by women. Albeit in the name of conservative sexual standards, Purity campaigns still represented a drive toward gender equality by challenging the double standard of sexual conduct that punished women and not men. The double standard comes to represent not only unequal and punitive sexual strictures for women, nor only the economic power that this unequal gender structure reflects and establishes, but the whole split between economic self-interest as against social responsibility and community involvement. The ultimate instance of the double standard is prostitution: the complete reduction of sexuality, and therefore of women, to an economic object. Yet Charlotte Gilman's *Women and Economics* analyzes prostitution on a continuum with marriage as sexual sale of women who have no other means of support.

> Women's economic profit comes through the power of sex-attraction. When we confront this fact boldly and plainly in the open market of vice, we are sick with horror. When we see the same economic relation made permanent, established by law, sanctioned and sanctified by religion, covered with flowers and incense and all accumulated sentiment, we think it innocent, lovely, and right. The transient trade we think evil. The bargain for life we think good.[51]

Gilman's is a direct and ideological analysis of gender in economic terms. But the overlap between economic values and the commodification of women can be seen in verse as well. Helen Hunt Jackson's "The Money-Seekers," for example, calls the double standard an "Unreckoned shame, of which he feels no stain," but sees it not only in terms of gender and sexuality. Rather, it is one instance of a general selling out of man's life for money: "What has he in this glorious world's domain / [But] Unreckoned loss which he counts up for gain." Julia Ward Howe's (1819–1910) "Save the Old South" similarly charts a masculine as against a feminine America, associating men with consuming ambition and women, stereotypically yet suggestively, with patience and love. For the love has "high command," and its venue is the political "councils of the land":

> Manhood in its zeal and haste
> Leaves cruel overthrow and waste
> Upon its pathway, roughly traced.
>
> Then woman comes with patient hand,
> With loving heart of high command,
> To save the councils of the land. (*SR* 129)

Women poets, of course, are not alone in critiquing the economic pursuits increasingly driving American life. It is in fact a major impulse in American

108 *Feminist Theory across Disciplines*

Renaissance literature. Thoreau in *Walden* sees farmers as imprisoning themselves as "serfs of the soil," whose "farms, houses, barns, cattle, and farming tools; for these are more easily acquired than got rid of." As he asks, "How many a poor immortal soul have I met well nigh crushed and smothered under its load, creeping down the road of life." Laboring as if condemned to a life sentence, owned by their own property, and struggling under the weight of the burden of its hold over them, men in this image of America waste their lives rather than making their livings. Emerson, too, denounces "the reliance on Property, including the reliance on governments which protect it [as] the want of self-reliance." Emersonian self-reliance never simply means atomized selves but rather activist ones.[52] Yet there remains a distinction in the picture of the self these men draw from the ones drawn by women. Thoreau's sojourn at Walden, if not completely solitary (there was plenty of visiting with Concord), is still meant to be exemplary of a truly independent individual as the foundation of an ideal society. In Emerson, similarly, the image of the self as "self-evolving circle" rushes "on all sides outwards to new and larger circles" at the cost of undoing its ties to others:

> The continual effort to raise himself above himself, to work a pitch above his last height, betrays itself in a man's relations. . . . Men cease to interest us when we find their limitations. The only sin is limitation. As soon as you once come up with a man's limitations, it is all over with. . . . Infinitely alluring and attractive was he to you yesterday, a great hope, a sea to swim in; now, you have found his shores, found it a pond, and you care not if you never see it again.[53]

In Emerson's quite masculine language, the ever-erasing circles of self-expansion "betrays itself in man's relations," which is to say requires their abandonment.[54] This vision of "sin" as "limitation" peculiarly pertains to women, who are indeed limited by social convention as a constraint. But women formulate their lives in terms of obligations and attachments to others—not only as constraint in a negative sense but as its own kind of enlargement of the self as enmeshed in a joint life.

Phoebe Cary's "Homes for All" (*P* 376) speaks for such an enlarged vision of the self in social terms. It imagines America as a feminized, quite sentimental, "queenly" mother "Nursing the cherub Peace upon thy breast" and with an immense "heritage" in land, forests, rivers, prairies, and lakes. But then the poem takes a critical turn:

> In populous cities do men live and die,
> That never breathe the pure and liberal air:
> Down where the damp and desolate rice swamps lie,
> Wearying the ear of Heaven with constant prayer,
> Are souls that never yet have learned to raise

Under God's equal slay the psalm of praise.
Turn not, Columbia! from their pleading eyes;
Give to thy sons that ask of thee a home;
So shall they gather round thee, not with sighs,
But as young children to their mother come;
And brightly to the centuries shall go down
The glory that thou wearest like a crown.

Pastoral scenes give way to cities whose inhabitants are denied "liberal" participation and to slavery's "rice swamps." The poem at the end tries to redefine and redirect "glory" from the country's prosperity and natural bounty to its ethical and moral life, figured (again sentimentally) as "young children to their mother come," where "mother" represents "Columbia" itself in a restored social vision. But this call to a glory that is not prosperity but is charity registers the betrayal of this vision in actual America. In this, the poem recalls Emma Lazarus's Statue of Liberty poem, which is perhaps above all a vision of a feminized public America. The Statue's invitation to "Send me your tired and your poor" casts America in the image of Hostess-Mother, welcoming the needy to a caring society. Lazarus's "mighty woman with a torch" personifies the efforts of countless women's benevolent societies dedicated to public service giving welfare to the waves of immigrants arriving in America.[55]

Charlotte Gilman's poem named "Nationalism" (World 197) after Bellamy's utopian movement similarly affirms devotion to the public sphere as a framework for individual endeavor:

> The nation is a unit. That which makes
> You an American of our today
> Requires the nation and its history,
> Requires the sum of all our citizens,
> Requires the product of our common toil,
> Requires the freedom of our common laws,
> The common heart of our humanity . . . .
> Our liberty belongs to each of us;
> The nation guarantees it; in return
> We serve the nation, serving so ourselves.

Gilman's feminism was directed toward transforming society into a common effort rather than offering visions of personal freedom. She rejected liberty as liberty from obligation to others. Associated with Jane Addams's Hull House experiment, Gilman identified with its attention to material support, educational opportunity, restructuring of gender roles, and social welfare. Hers was a sense of the public sphere and participation in it as defining and shaping human endeavor beyond narrow self-interest. Gilman was truly radical in imagining ways to rearrange family life so as to release women and men from its monotonous duplications in order to free time and energy for community life. Her early twentieth-century writings outline programs of day care; of pooled domestic duties such as cooking, shopping, and cleaning among groups of families sharing resources; as well as sweeping egalitarianism between genders. Still, Gilman's vision includes many of the traditional virtues assigned to women. What she rejects is the assignment of these virtues only to women in private spheres, something that worked to devalue them as mere women's concerns and left public life bereft of common commitments. Service, for Gilman, should be neither gendered nor privatized. It should be a general ethos undertaken for the sake of building a shared public world. What she unmasks in her poetry is the way "service," as it has been assigned to women, means servitude. The poem "Nationalism" accordingly defends liberty of the self while insisting that the self is at the same time defined as participating in community. The individual retains a "liberty that belongs to each of us," even as the nation and its history form the individual. How to balance these pulls between society and the individual remains in Gilman as difficult as it is today. But hers is an ethos derived in republican norms, which contests the assumptions and commitments of ascending and rampant individualist interests. Women's texts such as hers defend an American civic heritage that was, in the nineteenth century, dramatically being pressed aside by increasingly dominant economic individualist impulses.

RELATIONAL VOICES

Twentieth-century poetry is most often thought to depart from the feminized values of the nineteenth century, with comparisons between the two centuries mostly posed in terms of aesthetics. Indeed, there are strong aesthetic shifts from the one to the other, both in women's poetry and in men's. Above all there is a new self-consciousness of form, making the text more apparently self-referring to artistic questions. This difference can certainly be felt in the writings of Marianne Moore, Elizabeth Bishop, H. D., and Sylvia Plath as against most nineteenth-century poets, with Dickinson, as usual, the exceptional case. Interpretive trends emerged that put more attention on formal textual composition, with art increasingly distanced not only from history but from enterprise in social and economic senses, at least in America (the Frankfurt School, and Adorno in particular, did intend to link art to society, but ultimately even he regards art as interruption). The change in period is also marked by an increased feminist interest in private liberal freedoms. As Nancy Cott traces in *The Grounding of Modern Feminism*, the passage of suffrage, a movement that implied women had individual rights and could act independently of family and household, marked a turn from earlier feminism of the woman's sphere to more liberal and economic individualism.[56] Tensions emerge between an earlier feminist identity, grounded in the roles and activities of service that women characteristically undertook, as against a twentieth-century focus on self, liberation, self-development, and, indeed, self-interest as the goals of political as well as personal action. This can be felt, for example, in the writings of Adrienne Rich (1929–2012). Rich is an interesting combination of radical feminism, emphasizing the solidarity among women as a distinct group centered in their sexuality and bodily experience, but also a feminism of liberation and self-expression that shares much with emancipatory liberal politics. The result in poetic terms is strangely confessional. Poetry becomes a vehicle of self-exploration and an avenue of self-realization, in protest against constrictions women continue to experience. Rich's poems directly protest and defy obstacles to accomplishing such self-realization. She exposes how many political institutions, including marriage as a heterosexual arrangement, foreclose possibilities of women's sexuality and other choices.[57] Rich offers vignettes of entrapped wives in the prison house of marriage. "The Prisoners" depicts a man and woman as seeking "in hopeless war each others' blood / Though suffering in one identity" (*Facts* 187). "Moving in Winter" presents man and wife "collapsed like unplayed cards," whose bed canopy, in their death or death-like life together, will "smother her once more" (*P* 131). "The Loser" (*P* 46) presents a woman from the viewpoint of her unsuccessful suitor ten years after her marriage to another man. The poem registers the cost to the woman of married life: "I turn my head and wish him well / Who chafed your beauty into use / And lives forever in a house." The woman is here assimilated to the "house," her ""beauty" roughened and reduced to "use"—Rich's term for the domestic world and its work. Just so, in "Snapshots of a Daughter-in-Law" (*P* 47) written in the looser forms of Rich's later work, the housewife's "mind" takes on the shapes of the kitchen that encloses her, "moldering like wedding-cake," "crumbling to pieces under the knife-edge / of mere fact." In a kind of reification, the daughter-in-law becomes the moldering cake of her falsely romantic paradigms. Daily life here is represented as decay in a kind of feminized *memento mori*. Rich's goal is release: release from gender roles and confinement as such. Longings for escape are figured through imagined voices of women as they muse and meditate, remember and explode. The promise they are pursuing is a kind of self-sovereignty that society has denied to them. Rich explicitly distinguishes her vision from the nineteenth-century one, as in the poem "Heroines," which pays tribute to the past century's women but as caught within a restrictive and racist culture, which it is imperative to break out of. Rich thus speaks for a certain kind of twentieth-century feminist liberatory vision, which sees current society as a nightmare from which women must awake.

Rich's work stands in interesting comparison with the poetry of Muriel Rukeyser (1913–1980). This is as radical as anyone's but points in different directions from the kind of liberation Rich calls for. Rukeyser's is a socialized vision closer to Charlotte Gilman's communitarianism than to late twentieth-century liberatory feminism. Rukeyser has largely been excluded from the modernist canon, whose formalist aesthetics, at least in the academy, discounted her. Emerging as a writer when the New Criticism was taking hold, Rukeyser rejected the New Critical idealization of poetry as a chiseled and iconic language referring to itself; New Criticism in turn rejected her. Instead, she approached writing as a direct activism in cultural, political, and social concerns.[58] She considered poetic language to be not a self-referring enclosure but a permeable boundary with other kinds of language and social practices. These include practices of war. Her 1944 sequence "Letter to the Front" opens with the home front as another battlefield of war: "Women and poets see the truth arrive / Then it is acted out, The lives are lost, and all the newsboys shout" (*CP* 239). This "truth" that "women and poets see" even before it explodes in war and in war-reporting penetrates the private spaces of the "heart that comes to know its war," a war of "gambling powers" that commandeer "every human care" (*CP* 240). But war itself for Rukeyser is just one force betraying both the individual and society, alongside and complicitous with reduction to business and commercial exchange. As Rukeyser writes in *The Life of Poetry*, "We are a people tending toward democracy at the level of hope; on another level, the economy of the nation, the empire of business within the republic, both include in their basic premise the concept of perpetual warfare."

At issue in Rukeyser are blurred boundaries between home and war, domestic and nondomestic worlds. Domesticity is, on the one hand, a place of women's exclusion; on the other, it is vulnerable to social forces and complicitous with a variety of coercions. Family in Rukeyser is more allied with community than with privacy, and selfhood becomes a value that can be claimed in the name of commitments beyond the self. But it is also then threatened by social forces that penetrate them and each other. Rukeyser's much circulated "Poem," starting "I lived in the first century of the world wars," comments, "The news would pour out of various devices / Interrupted by attempts to sell products to the unseen." The unseen are as reified as the products; the news is inextricable from commercial interests, which Rukeyser, as a socialist, sees as no less destructive, and of course as implicated, in war itself.

Rukeyser's 1938 poem "Boy With His Hair Cut Short" (*CP* 119) offers a poignant portrait of a home during the depression, with the brother and sister who live there invaded by economic structures in both their relationship and their bodies. "The boy . . . sits at the table, head down, the young clear neck exposed." "The girl's thin hands [are] above his head," poised so she can give him the haircut they hope will help him find work. Gender is marked by the boy being the one who must go out day after day, while his sister at home assures him: "You'll surely find something, they can't keep turning you down." But both are objects in a commercial culture. The boy's eye is "tattoo[ed]" by the "neon . . . drugstore sign" that flashes across the street. He is the target of its "arrow's electric red," his "forehead . . . bleached against the lamplight," making him part of, or defined by, the advertising technology that surrounds him and penetrates his domicile. The sister is likewise exposed beneath the "impersonal sign" of the neon advertisement across from them, its blue matching the sister's "blue vein."

There is no self completely independent of circumstances, contexts, and environment. Yet this does not lessen for Rukeyser the strength of moral and personal commitment between brother and sister. This is moral strength evoked in archetypal and mythological imagery that Rukeyser introduces into the poem, in characteristic modernist technique. The boy, his "young clear neck exposed," is sacrificial lamb to the implacable economic god:

> He lets his head fall, meeting
> her earnest hopeless look, seeing the sharp blades splitting,
> the darkened room, the impersonal sign, her motion,
> the blue vein, bright on her temple, pitifully beating.

The brother is finally imaged as a lamb "pitifully bleating," a sacrifice to a cruel god of Mammon. The sister does the shearing, but she, like her brother, appears from between the split light of the "sharp blades." The last phrase, "pitifully beating," brings brother and sister into a joint condition, with "beating" suggesting "bleating" of the boy-lamb, as well as the girl's fragile life blood and struggle. Yet Rukeyser, for all her socio-economic conscience, also portrays here a deep sense of the individual selves as each attempts to withstand the economic world whose tremendous pressure they register on their very bodies. On the one hand, there is no merely pre-political individual free of such economic pressures. Rukeyser nevertheless celebrates in the poem the integrity and commitment of sister and brother to each other, in a selfhood strengthened by their mutual devotion.

Senses of community and mutual commitment thus endure in twentieth-century feminist discourses and poetics, perhaps becoming even more pronounced as the Second Wave of feminism moves into a Third. bell hooks describes her feminism as one not seeking an equality in the liberal individualist sense but as the "struggle for a new society based on new values of mutual respect, cooperation and social responsibility . . . eradicating domination and transforming society." She critiques individualist, liberatory programs as seeking a "freedom to decide one's own destiny as almost apolitical in tone." Instead, she works to replace "unjust authoritarian rule . . . with an ethic of communalism and shared responsibility," including "transformed family relationships," which have been among the central sources of women's strength and sites of women's social and community activism.[59] Audre Lorde's much quoted injunction that "the master's tools will never dismantle the master's house" intends among other things the notions of individualism as opposed to community, although she too supports differences among selves rather than conformity to collective norms.

"Without community there is no liberation, only the most vulnerable and temporary armistice between an individual and her oppression. But community must not mean a shedding of our differences, nor the pathetic pretense that these differences do not exist."[60]

The late twentieth-century woman poet Judy Grahn likewise consciously rejects isolated poetics in the name of community, which she calls "commonality."[61] Grahn's work recalls Muriel Rukeyser in particular, who rejected New Critical formalism and saw poetry as an intensely public space. Grahn's "The Work of a Common Woman" has circulated widely on the internet. Part of the "feminist poetry movement," Grahn's is a poetics of participation, offering figures of women that are not representative in any unitary sense but are concretely recognizable. "Commonality," she writes, evokes "the commons of England and of Boston where people could meet together and assert themselves." She wishes to indicate "what we have in common, which is a cross connection between us all" in a "many-centered multiverse" poetics.[62] Her sequence on the "Common Woman" includes a critical portrait of a woman absorbed into economic individualism:

> Her ambition is to be more shiny
> And metallic, black and purple as a thief
> At midday, trying to make it in
> a male form, she's become
> as stiff as possible.
> Wearing trim suits and high heels
> she says "bust" instead of breast
> somewhere underneath she misses
> love and trust but she feels that
> spite and malice are the prices
> of success.

This woman (named Helen in one of Grahn's rewritings of the great beauty-figure) has turned into a piece of office furniture, "shiny," "metallic," become "stiff." She has followed a path of what the poem calls "male form," meaning here a "success" that poses isolated individual against isolated individual and is measured in economic terms by price. Her body is alien to her, in word—she will not say "breast"—and in the "trim suit and high heels," which is the fashion correlate of office regimen.

There is also a portrait of a woman, Nadine, as a builder of community. She upholds, protects, and resists the world's incursions into home life without which no one can survive: "She holds things together, collects bail, / makes the landlord patch the largest holes." Located "on her neighbor's stoop," Nadine, on the one hand, is what keeps her community going: "The neighborhood would burn itself out / without her." But the fire imagery is also potentially incendiary, her anger at the materialist forces that condition the lives held in its possession. "One of these days she'll strike the spark herself." Is Nadine, who is "made of grease and metal," defiant of gender or reified and reduced to the (male) world's economic terms? Each section of the poem's sequence ends with variations on a refrain. "Helen" is "common woman is as common / as the common crow," a figure of omnivorous consumption. "Nadine" as the "common woman" is "as common as a nail," hard metal and almost invisible but holding her world together.

Literature was in the nineteenth century, and remains in the twentieth, a major form of women's participation and expression in public life. Civic selfhood strikingly characterizes their poetic roles and address. These are particularly concerned with both recording and protesting the increasing dominance of economic sphere and relationships as against other American political and cultural traditions. Women's poetry is therefore far from exclusively or even predominantly domestic, as a complicit "haven" from but also support for economic individualism.[63] Instead, women's poetry aligns with the civic realm, its concerns, its values, its structures of the self, and their modes of interrelationship. These are affirmed in a poetry not constructed only as self-expression, but rather as a voice within a community, addressing others and speaking through contexts and for commitments.

6 Civic Feminism and Religious Association

Feminism and religion tend to be regarded as if on opposite sides of a barricade.[1] When the question of religion is raised in feminist discussion, it is usually seen as complicit or oppressive in the construction of gender relations. Progressive trends are viewed only as rooted in liberal traditions remote from religious life.[2] Conversely, general discussions of religious history often barely mention women—something striking in the American context, where women have been the majority of church members since the mid-1600s.[3]

Mere opposition between feminism and religion is not, however, adequate to American culture. Within the histories of American Protestantism, religion in fact provides one central framework for women's activism in both social and literary terms. In this religious context, conservative and liberal trends mix in complex fashion. In the American context, democratizing movements do not only originate outside religious life, in political, ideological, and philosophical liberalism that then subsequently influence or are imposed on religious organization and activity. Rather, elements within religious Protestantism generated and influenced democratic trends in American life at large. This is not to claim that American religion is essentially or exclusively liberal. There are strong conservative tendencies, prominent in different ways at different times. But in America, religion can be said to have made available resources of strong selfhood for women, which supported their emergence into public life and became expressed in different arenas, including women's writing and women's poetry.

The importance of religious experience and contexts for women's political and social activities has been increasingly documented, although in ways that are not often integrated into wider discussions of either religion or gender.[4] Especially the religious backgrounds of abolitionism are widely cited. Yet even then women's activism is often described as private and sentimental, with religion a feminized and marginalized sphere.[5] To call religion 'private' is in a sense already to mark it as feminized, with privacy a gendered term. Such usage partly reflects women's disproportionate involvement in religion compared with men, who were already in the late seventeenth century increasingly taken up with work, which sphere, however, because nondomestic, is classified as 'public.' It also reflects a general demotion of community concerns, as these were increasingly pressed to the side by emerging and intensifying economic individualism in the contexts of urbanization and industrialization as against other kinds of selfhood.[6] But religion, however much based in interior experience, is not simply private. It functions as a central site of community life and of women's activism within it. As Barbara Welter writes, women become displaced into religion as a repository for feminine values when nation building no longer required or respected them.[7]

Instead of seeing religion as privatized, American religion can be seen as a central social institution in which women could participate in public affairs, alongside, and closely related to, education and literature. Religion contests the separation of the spheres of traditional gender ideology. It cannot be simply relegated to either the public or the private. Rather, it foundationally belongs to both. In one sense, American Protestant religious experience is grounded as private and interior. Yet its religious life is no less traditionally conducted within communities. While it is individuals who are 'called,' they then mutually covenant to each other in 'gathered' churches and together pursue a joint course as a community in history.[8] What emerges is a double construction of selfhood involving a mutual invocation and balance between inner and outer, private and public, self and community.[9]

This dual dimension of religious experience as at once private and public, inward and outward, historically shapes American women's senses of selfhood. It remains one backdrop and basis for women's poetry throughout the nineteenth century, persisting as well into the twentieth. Almost all women's poetry through the nineteenth century engages with religious discourses, although this takes a wide variety of forms. The Bible, its interpretation and revision, is a fundamental poetic genre.[10] Hymnal forms, which are the basis of poetic form in Emily Dickinson's and other women's poetry, tie women's writing to public poetry, whether as devotion, critique, or transformation. Most crucially, women's poetry invokes prophetic models in which the self acts for and draws authority from some larger purpose, directed through public address. Throughout, the self-representation of women's poetic selfhood reflects a complex constitution of the self in relation to community that draws on, while it also can transform, the construction of religious selfhood.

Such religious modes and constructions of the self are foundational for women's poetic voices and poetic selfhood, in ways that suggest differences from men's in the claim to and structure of authority, voice, and self. Women's writing focuses much less on a romantic poetics of originality, of the creative self drawing on its own resources. Nor is there a sense of the poet as instituting and defining culture, as is the case in Longfellow and the New England poets, as well as Whitman; or of art and artist as autonomous authorities in senses that begin to develop in turn of the century aestheticism, then emerging in twentieth-century High Modernism.[11] These notions of the artist are all largely missing from nineteenth-century women's writing. Their absence, however, registers not only what Sandra Gilbert calls an anxiety of authorship as a lack of strong or autonomous poetic selfhood.[12] What emerges instead is a specific construction of selfhood in which self is strengthened by drawing on authorities beyond the self, represented in poetry as a distinctive poetic voice.

AMERICAN WOMEN'S RELIGION

Puritan America inaugurated new contexts for women in a New World. Just how Protestantism affected women as compared with Catholic norms has been variously argued. On one side, the convent was lost as an alternative life-world for women, one that had released them from traditional family roles and the authority of husband and father. The convent made available education in ways otherwise impossible for women and created an environment of mutual support and a context for a women's culture. In contrast, Protestantism strengthened nuclear, patriarchal family structures, eclipsing and eliminating other forms of religious as well as social vocation.[13] Yet Protestantism reevaluated sexuality, elevated the family's religious status, and opened new roles for women within it, with a shared if still inferior authority in household prayer, teaching, and supervision.[14]

The impact on women of Protestantism greatly intensified in America, where the Protestant religious imagination could unfold far from the constraints of European histories, institutions, and norms. Although the first settlers of course brought with them European expectations and assumptions, these altered in the radically different circumstances of the New World, and the settlers, especially the Puritan ones, were among the most radical dissenters of Europe. This introduced unpredictable elements into social and religious proceedings, with Puritan innovations and commitments leading to significant and often unintended consequences for women.

The first of these, certainly from the viewpoint of women's writing, was the extension of basic literacy to girls. To write literature, women had to be literate. Protestant contexts created new impetus for girls' schooling.[15] Calvin pledged himself to general education, insisting that "Everyone be educated to God."[16] He instituted public schooling for all children, including girls, in 1536. Natalie Zemon Davis describes how, against Catholic practices, Calvinist women read and discussed the Bible.[17] In America, Massachusetts Bay Colony passed literacy laws in the 1630s, followed by the "Old Seducer Satan" laws of 1647 requiring all towns of 50 to have a schoolmaster for both boys and girls (towns of 100 were mandated a Latin schoolmaster for boys only) at the primary school level, although secondary schools and college remained reserved for men, above all those studying for the ministry. Records of literacy rates and school attendance are difficult to obtain, but by the end of the century in Puritan New England, 95% of women could write their names, and around two-thirds of middle-class women could read with fluency.[18]

The Puritan churches also shifted norms for women's participation in church government. The rejection of the priesthood opened much greater lay activism that included women, who participated in calling and electing ministers, as well as in the admission, dismissal, admonition, and excommunication of both male and female church members.[19] Regardless of the status of their husbands, women could join churches of their choice.[20] An official grant allowing women to vote was established for the first time at the Brattle Street Church in Boston, whose 1699 Manifesto declared: "We cannot confine the right of chusing a minister to the Male communicants alone."[21] Church practices of lay participation carried over into civil government of town meetings, which took place in the same meeting houses and followed similar voluntarist forms, connecting religious to civic activities in both governmental structure and activist attitudes.[22] New Haven records of 1674 show women attending meetings, writing petitions, and possibly voting.

The Quakers of course went the furthest in championing female equality in church participation and governance. Doctrines of spiritual rebirth, direct inspiration by the divine light in continuing revelation, and lay ministries all embraced women and opened active roles to them, triumphing over the curse of Eve. Women participated in lay ministry and missions, had their own meetings (in America from 1681), influenced doctrine, and took part in the discipline and control of membership.[23] Baptists in America likewise allowed women to participate in church governance, electing and dismissing pastors, admitting and excommunicating members, and taking part in theological debate. Ezra Stiles reports, "It is a usage practiced among the Baptists of this colony to admit sisters to equal votes in the church meetings."[24] But practices among such 'sectaries' extended to varying degrees into other more mainstream churches.[25] Spiritualist, prophetic impulses penetrated Congregational Churches and indeed were fundamental to the conversion experiences requisite for membership. Puritan orthodoxy had to constantly compromise between the workings of the Holy Spirit and institutional emphases on behavior.[26]

Protestantism in America generally balanced between anti-institutional energies and the impulse for direction and control.[27] In general, when institutions consolidate, women's leadership and equality tend to be increasingly restricted. Yet women activists were not necessarily sectarian and heretical.[28] The emergence of women is visible in a range of religious contexts. Laurel Thatcher Ulrich emphasizes the way in which providential history made it possible for any believer, male or female, to think of him or herself as affecting larger society, even if, for women, such greater involvement retained the language of modesty. Thus, Cotton Mather's call to "Handmaids of the Lord, who though they lie very much concealed from the world may be called the 'hidden ones' yet have no little share in the beauty and defense of the land."[29] Another democratizing influence that embraced women was increased engagement with the Bible for lay women and men. In the move Christopher Hill describes as from altar to pulpit, focus in the Protestant service shifted to preaching, including close biblical commentary that then could be carried into the home as Bible discussions.[30] The practice in England of 'gadding' from church to church in order to hear inspiring preachers loosened the parish framework and substituted for it voluntary participation, weakening the authority of the appointed Anglican minister. Bible reading and discussion were central to 'conventicle' meetings of small numbers of mutually committed members, with women participating. These practices carried over into American 'gathered' churches and prayer meetings, with women's prayer and discussion groups serving as the context, for example, for Anne Hutchinson's subversions.[31] Both women and men had exposure to political, communal issues articulated through sermons, with clergy traditionally speaking at public events.[32] Religion further entered public discourse, reaching a wide audience, in published sermons and political speeches using a populist biblical hermeneutics via common language. Public discourse in newspapers, sermons, and political speeches drew widely on a populist hermeneutic of the Bible.[33] Thus, public discussion became an arena partly generated by biblical interpretation and religious discourse.

Religious public discourse spread still more widely during the First and then the Second Great Awakenings, along with other democratizing trends. In just what ways and to what extent the First Great Awakening influenced Revolutionary principles are major topics in American historiography. Certainly the clergy were among the most effective supporters of the Revolution.[34] Within the Awakening, the breakdown of hierarchy and church controls, the uses of a common rhetoric accessible to all, and the lay call to preach all transformed American religion toward popular appeal through persuasion.[35] Revivals introduced a new mode of communication that redefined the social context in which public address took place. As Harry Stout describes, they opened religious expression to new leadership outside traditional church jurisdictions, creating new modes of organization and authority that challenged the established ministry.[36] Lay preachers multiplied as, among other factors, expanded settlements moved beyond the reach of fixed churches and far outstripped professionally trained ministers available to serve them. Religion can thus be seen to contribute toward establishing a public sphere in the Habermasian sense, as David Zaret argues. Besides any specific doctrinal forms, religion can be linked to "rising republicanism," leading "to an unintended democratization of knowledge and critical reason in religious life."[37]

Women were among the called and also among those doing the calling. No less than men, women were potential converts, whose voices could be heard in testimony, witness, and praying aloud. The line between these personal expressions and public address through teaching and exhortation could be blurry, even if first restricted to their own and others' homes. Women's prayer groups formed. Women even began to preach, joining their voices to others in the public sphere.[38] In this, they were authorized by religion. As one Baptist church record book reports, a woman in 1772 attested, "Therefore I say that I have free liberty by the rules of the Gospel and the natural rights of mankind to think and judge for myself without being accountable to any but God."[39]

WOMEN'S SELFHOOD AND POETIC VOCATION

The religious sphere, then, offered an intermediary space between private and public experience and expression, acting as an avenue through which women moved to participate in and address their communities. They saw their authorization as rooted in forces around and beyond themselves, very much including religious ones, which in fundamental ways shaped their senses of who a self is. This is also the case for many women writers. Topics they address and the audience they address them to, their very definition of selfhood and of poetic selfhood, mirrors as well as incorporates the religious self as intensely interior but also, equally, intensively communal. Indeed, religious and civic selfhood form parallels to each other, as well as having a kind of causal link in the way gathered churches became participatory town meetings.[40] In both arenas, the religious and the civic, women tend to understand themselves within a framework of community investment, with their senses of self tied to some larger purpose of which they are a part. The individual does not precede as an established entity in its social existence. The self is rather constituted through relationships within social and institutional life, which conversely are shaped through initiatives by individuals. In this duplex fashioning and agency of the self, religious selfhood thus overlaps with the forms of civic selfhood in which individual and community each mutually constitute each other.[41] The self remains the site of initiative, as conscience, divine image, and agent center, but agency is directed both from and toward community values and common vision. A duplex public/private religious selfhood gave rise to and then overlapped with a duplex public/private civic selfhood. What thus emerge in religious as in civic contexts, and ultimately in literary ones as well, are structures of self-in-community.

As with other attempts to weigh conservative against progressive trends in women's history, there is disagreement about whether the religious context ultimately furthered or limited feminist possibility. Religious affiliation is often seen to restrain women within the orbit of conservative values and roles. Genuine advancement is understood to derive from enlightenment and liberal sources as opposed to religious ones.[42] This is largely the position taken in Elizabeth Cady Stanton and Susan Antony's history of women's suffrage, which ignores origins of feminist work in churches. But Stanton, the Grimké sisters, Lucy Stone, and Antoinette Brown all came from revivalist backgrounds and attended Oberlin College under Charles Finney. The first women's rights convention was held in a Wesleyan Methodist church, the second in a Baptist church. Suffrage meetings always invited women ministers and opened with prayer. Point seventeen in the Seneca Falls Declaration of Sentiments contests, but also claims, religious sources, declaring that man "has usurped the prerogative of Jehovah himself, claiming it as his right to assign for her a sphere of action, when that belongs to her conscience and to her God." Angelina Grimké similarly wrote, "Women's rights are an integral part of her moral being, created by and responsible to God alone."[43] Lydia Maria Child pointed out that "the sects called evangelical were the first agitators of the woman question."[44]

Feminism, then, even suffragist, political, and enlightened feminism, did not draw its resources or strength only from Enlightenment sources. Indeed, Enlightenment feminists, according to Alice Rossi, mainly engaged in theoretical writing. It was moral reform and church activism that provided the "social roots of the women's movement" and the "moral crusader feminists" who organized "public meetings for protest and discussion" that impelled feminism forward.[45] Carolyn Haynes similarly describes a "Christian feminism" in which evangelical women forged public roles, underscoring Stanton's own use of Protestant rhetoric and resources. In this mode, women reinterpreted evangelical gender roles in ways that disarmed opposition while contesting the church's conservative authority. Although largely using the language of the separate spheres, Christian feminists challenged anti-feminist norms and specific abuses, initiating, for example, legislation against wife beating. They did so within the framework of church, doctrines, and sacred texts.[46]

Religion played a duplex role not only in defining the self as at once private and invested in community, but in women's sense of authorization to act in public altogether. On the one hand, religion definitely endorsed modesty for women. But appeal to religion also directed women to public roles in its name. This is not merely a question of strategy in order to get past social guards, nor only self-assertion disguised as a call from the Spirit.[47] Women often had to overcome deep-seated reluctance to accept authority against their accepted social roles. Maria Stewart, an African-American and the first woman to speak before mixed audiences in order to chastise America, insisted, "It is the divine influence of the Holy Spirit operating on my heart that could possibly induce me to make the feeble and unworthy efforts that I have."[48] Such prophetic authorization is repeatedly invoked in other prominent African-American women preachers, such as Zilpha Elaw, who, when asked about "contention over ministry of females," replied, "No ambition of mine, but the special appointment of God, had put me into the ministry; and therefore I had no option in the matter." Julia Foote similarly describes "severe mental and spiritual conflicts" and a profound "resistance to the call: I lay weeping and beseeching the dear Lord to remove this burden from me, but there appeared the same angel, and on his breast were these words: you are lost unless you obey God's righteous commands."[49] Even Angelina Grimké writes in her "Letter on Equality" that "Nothing can strengthen [woman] in the character of a preacher of righteousness, but a call from Jehovah himself."

This question of authorization profoundly informs women's poetry. Most American women poets until the twentieth century wrote within religious contexts and discourses. In the twentieth century, religion is a less pervasive framework and is no longer the outstanding public institution in which women can participate. Nonetheless, twentieth-century women poets also regularly situate themselves in terms of religious cultural discourses, in ways that can be critical and contentious yet still invoke religious paradigms, and also positively. For women poets, religious reference characteristically revolves around two axes: *biblical citation* and *prophetic call*. In both the nineteenth and twentieth centuries, biblical commentary and revision form a distinctive subgenre of women's poetry, acting as a scene of interpretive authority and witness, which can in turn be allied with prophetic gifts.[50] The structure of prophesy is itself duplex. It gives voice to the individual but not in her own name, nor as an assertion of her own power. It is thus at once personal and public, the self's voice and yet speaking to and for wider commitments than the self's own.

The Bible, or rather access to and discussion of it, has been a democratizing and egalitarian influence in America. American freedoms of speech, of assembly, and of religion of course derive in Enlightenment principles of rationalism based on theories of individual rights. Yet Enlightenment teachings drew on biblical ones, of man in God's image and the equality of souls.[51] The republican implications of biblical teaching, not least for women, is visible in the English Civil War, when women Levelers crossed from religious to political egalitarianism, petitioning Parliament for their liberty on religious grounds: "That since we are assured of our creation in the image of God . . . have we not equal interest with the men of this nation in those liberties and securities contained in the *Petition of Right*?"[52] Biblical discussion groups invited different voices to participate, while the Bible was persistently invoked and cited through public discussion. The Bible in fact presents another arena where progressive and conservative forces intercross. The traditional assumption remained that the biblical message was a unitary one that everyone seeing the light would see in the same light and biblical interpretation was conducted within frameworks of church understandings and teachings: *Sola Scriptura* never really assumed or anointed solitary individuals.[53] Yet once discussions were opened, variant interpretations bore fruit and multiplied. In this sense, the Bible cannot be simply opposed against prophetic impulses.[54] Both prophetic and hermeneutic events involve tensions between community authority and the individuals who comprise it and who also claim authority of conscience and call.[55]

Within the community of activist women, there is profound appeal to personal calling and spiritual illumination, also expressed as biblical interpretation and prooftexting. Biblical texts are invoked to ground authority, a resource even Elizabeth Cady Stanton—herself early in life a convert through a Finney revival—did not dismiss. Women on the left as on the right (although in the latter case implicitly undermining conservative beliefs in hierarchized chains of authority) anchored their activism in religious experience and biblical appeal, including Stanton and Lucretia Mott, various Beechers, Antoinette Brown, and the Grimké sisters.[56] Frances Willard, the charismatic and intensely popular and powerful leader of the in many ways conservative Temperance movement, likewise came from a revivalist evangelical background: her family moved to join Finney at Oberlin College in 1841, there acting as a station for the Underground Railroad. Willard's *Women in the Pulpit* defends and explains her own deep commitment to active roles for women in the church via biblical prooftexts for women's equality.[57]

In the decades preceding the Civil War, the Bible was split between opposing ideologies, marshaled as prooftexts for both sides.[58] As Lincoln stated in the Second Inaugural of both North and South, "Both read the same Bible and pray to the same God, and each invokes His aid against the other." The South invoked the Bible in defense of hierarchy, defining its core of teachings to be obedience within providentially instituted orders of masters over slaves and, as feminists contended, of men over women. In the North, a more liberal reading emphasized equality before God, supporting progressive religious movements such as Universalism and Unitarianism—although abolition was equally rooted in evangelicalism. These abolitionist arguments inspired feminist ones, with biblical interpretation again supporting violently opposing causes, confirming its individualization while also its public import. Sara Grimké's "Letters on the Equality of the Sexes and the Condition of Women," for example, were written in response to an 1837 Pastoral Letter condemning women's public speaking. Grimke declared:

> I shall depend solely on the Bible to designate the sphere of woman . . . and I also claim to judge for myself what is the meaning of the inspired writers, because I believe it to be the solemn duty of every individual to search the Scriptures for themselves, with the aid of the Holy Spirit, and not be governed by the views of any man or set of men.[59]

To Catherine Beecher, Angelina Grimké wrote:

> Human beings have *rights*, because they are *moral* beings: the rights of all men grow out of their moral nature; and as all men have the same moral nature, they have essentially the same rights. . . . Now if rights are founded in the nature of our moral being, then the mere

Civic Feminism and Religious Association   125

circumstance of sex does not give to man higher rights and responsibilities than to woman. . . . My doctrine then is, that whatever is morally right for man to do, it is morally right for woman to do.[60]

Women poets actively participated in the practices of biblical interpretation and authorization in ways that grounded and gave structure to poetic voice. Biblical engagement was one way that women spoke out of, and to, contexts beyond the self, granting them authority to address public issues. The most famous poetic case is Julia Ward Howe's Civil War "Battle Hymn of the Republic." Howe's "Battle Hymn" offers a highly elaborated set of biblical typological parallels, matching immediate events to scriptural images, from Old Testament to New, all seen to be fulfilled in America's immediate destiny. The "Grapes of Wrath" of Daniel shadow forth the 'terrible swift sword' of Revelations, finding immediate realization in the 'watch-fires' of Civil War encampments. In an intense revelation of American civil religion, religious vision is then translated into civic devotion: "As he died to make men holy / let us die to make men free." America's sacrifice for liberty is conflated with Christ's sacrifice for salvation, making freedom sacred.

In this hymn, the vision seen is not more striking than the visionary seer. The poet remains at the center of the historical-providential-soteriological drama, as its witness and announcer. Each stanza opens with an act of vision: "Mine eyes have seen," "I have seen," "I have seen." In one sense, the vision, not the seer, is emphasized. Yet the seer is a present and potent figure, constituted through the vision she reports yet would remain invisible and unheard without her. This witness, although unstated, is a woman's. She is the prophetess, announcing her reading of historical event, grounded in the Bible and delivered by her, but also to her (as she claimed) by a power greater than her own and that she only serves.

Rosemary Ruether describes nineteenth-century women's as a "radical obedience" in which women appropriate orthodoxy for "radical ends."[61] Indeed, the radical and the orthodox enter into strange combinations and interchanges. Women could feel called to speak and write not just in defiance of, but also in accordance with, religious traditions that remained in many ways conservative.[62] Lydia Sigourney, for example, the first popular woman poet of the century, was a traditional Christian who ideologically supported gendered separate spheres, often in profitable advice books and albums such as her annual "Religious Souvenir" editions. Yet religious commitment grounded her poetic voice in ways that affirmed her own right to speak, to some extent at cross-purposes with her own conservative ideology. The voice that emerges in her verse is at one and the same time veiled and assertive. Thus, Sigourney's poem "A Name" offers her commentary on the story of the tower of Babel and warns her largely female audience against a "fame that vaunts." Yet the poem's repeated refrain is to "Make to Thyself a Name," warning against improper ways for doing so while nonetheless asserting and enacting that possibility.

Emily Dickinson most intensely represents cross-currents in which religious appeal remains fundamental but in ways that question and undermine, even as it draws on religious resources. Raised in the revivalist and conservative evangelism of Amherst and educated at Mary Lyon's Mount Holyoke Seminary for missionaries, Dickinson structures her poems through repeated biblical references and religious engagement and contention. Her texts, based in hymnal forms and permeated with biblical citations, are never merely secular.[63] God is a major, perhaps the central, figure in her poetry, with his authority, and her own, a constant site of contention. His silence and her own, his power and her own, and his justice and her own are constantly tested and contested, with gender at issue in ways that prefigure much twentieth-century feminist theology. Just how far gender structures the relation of God to man, as against his relation to woman, is something that Dickinson's texts repeatedly explore and expose. The Bible in turn poses questions regarding a woman's interpretive stances and rights. She challenges its male exemplary figures as both sources of authority and moral models, so that biblical citation becomes a complex scene of invocation as revocation. "I took my Power in my Hand," for example, offers a biblical commentary on David and Goliath:

> I took my Power in my Hand
> And went against the World
> 'Twas not so much as David had
> But I was twice as bold—
>
> I aimed my Pebble—but Myself
> Was all the one that fell—
> Was it Goliah—was too large—
> Or was myself—too small? (J 540/Fr 660)

The poet's attempt to take power in her hand, which can also suggest her writing, goes "against the World," which restricts the propriety of women taking power in this way or at all. Here she is like but also unlike David, who, though facing an enemy (whereas she goes against the entire "world"), did so sanctioned by the people and presumably by God. Her own act of assertion requires her to be twice bold, then, since she does so against norms and, as the second stanza shows, against herself as she has internalized her gender position. The second stanza registers a profound self-division, where to go forth into the world is to betray her woman's role. In the end, then, David cannot be for her a biblical model since she, as a woman, cannot really identify with him. Her position is not his. Nor can she directly represent or act for God except by way of a cross-gendering that withholds from her full authorization. Her state thus is inevitably one of conflict: with herself, with her society, and with the religious forms available to her. To appeal to them is to divide and finally defeat herself. "I aimed my Pebble—but Myself—Was all the one that fell."

AFRICAN-AMERICAN RELIGIOUS COMMUNITY

For Dickinson, the Bible, and religious discourse and experience in general, is a major source of poetic energy almost despite itself. For Frances Harper, closely contemporary with Dickinson but writing out of African-American experience, biblical engagement converges into prophetic call as her core source of poetic power and vocation. Frances Harper is both devout and radical. Religion remains a crucial reference for her understanding of both history and ethics and, urgently, the conflict between them set before her. Continuing to embrace a providential and sacral history, she must nonetheless account for the American world's defiance and defilement of the sacred dignity of the person. In her prophetic voice, she sets out to denounce history's failure but also to recall history to its truer course. This is possible because she draws clear lines between true and false religious vision, true and false religious sanction. Hers is not a relativist or skeptical position, nor a concession to religious schism. False religion betrays whereas true religion provides her with her own authority and voice.

Harper's stances are firmly rooted in African-American church culture. Religion has been for African-Americans one of the core institutions of community solidarity and the pursuit of equality. Women, moreover, have been traditionally activist within the African-American church. As Jualyne E. Dodson and Cheryl Townsend Gilkes write, "the black church is the organizational and expressive core of black culture and community," with an "overwhelming importance and pivotal position of black women in all aspects of community organization." The extent to which African-American women have exercised leadership roles has varied, with a larger direct authority granted to them in the later nineteenth century and then a retraction or resistance to women's leadership in the twentieth, as often occurs with consolidation and formalization of institutions. But leadership by women has always had its boundaries. Thus, women have been permitted to speak and teach, but only men could be officially ordained as preachers. Yet African-American women have regarded their participation in religious life as "an extension of their individual sense of regeneration, release, redemption and spiritual liberation to a collective ethos of struggle for and with the entire black community." As often in women's religion, there is a 'paradox' of the conservative and the liberatory. "The maintenance of community integrity has an inherently conservative role," but "political struggles to eliminate suffering and to 'crusade for justice' are expressions of a radical thrust."[64] Women in the African-American community have been "some of the most enterprising agents of tradition," where "religion and religious activity are the most important spheres for this creation and maintenance of tradition." They have struggled to maintain "cherished values, providing a context for distinctive ethnic identity and group consciousness."[65] Religious selfhood has thus been closely tied to identity, to preserving a heritage that frames and links private conscience and spirituality to public act and responsibility. As Ellen Brooks Higgenbotham underscores, religion is seen as "not just a private sphere of spiritual experience but a public discourse of the church as historically linked to slavery and joining social regeneration with spiritual regeneration, in the name of human freedom and equality before God."[66] African-American tradition connects equality to religion; liberation thereby emerges not as pure liberal individualism but as freedom that affirms community solidarity through social activism.

Frances Harper was raised and educated by her uncle William Watkins in his religious school for free blacks in Baltimore, and she became a member of the African Methodist Episcopal Church, which was founded in 1816 and in which her uncle was a preacher. She also later joined a Philadelphia Unitarian Church affiliated with abolitionism.[67] In this sense, Harper represents an intersection between evangelical and rationalist religious trends. Politically, Harper was active in abolition and the Underground Railroad before the Civil War, and freedman's education after it, as well as women's rights. Her poetry is closely tied to these projects, grounding them in acts of biblical interpretation and related prophetic gifts. Unlike feminists such as Elizabeth Cady Stanton, Harper did not turn to Higher Criticism and a critique of the institutions of biblical interpretation. She doubts neither the truth of Scripture nor the power to recognize that truth. Contest with the Bible is not over its truth but rather toward recognizing what constitutes genuine interpretation of it. Thus, Harper is committed to biblical authority as textually given but also to the validity of her own interpretative conscience, authorized by religion. This conscience is expressed in her selection of texts and her treatments of them, with individual interpretation guided by set principles. To her, the Bible teaches not submission to hierarchical authority but an egalitarian message granting each person absolute dignity and calling each to witness. If Augustine's interpretive rule is charity, Harper's is equality. At the same time, or rather through this egalitarianism, Harper's prophetic authorization remains directed toward and derived not simply through individual liberation or private claim to rights, but in the name of historical justice as fulfillment of the divine will.

Harper's "Bible Defense of Slavery" (*CP* 5) directly dramatizes the contradictions of biblical hermeneutic. The poem attacks a book of that title published in 1851, as the ideological need to defend slavery intensified in the face of abolition. The poem, structured through a rhetoric of reversal, shows this Southern reading to turn the Bible on its head.

> A reverend man, whose light should be
> The guide of age and youth,
> Brings to the shrine of slavery
> The sacrifice of truth!
>
> For the direst wrong of man imposed,
> Since Sodom's fearful cry,

> The word of life has been enclosed,
> To give your God the lie.

The "reverend man" who should bring light and truth instead sacrifices truth. To use the Bible to defend slavery is to exchange "light" for darkness. But the poet reveals and corrects this inversion. Naming what is wrong, she reclaims the "word of life" that the false reading has "enclosed" in the sense of hiding it, but that the text truly contains when approached through proper understanding. In a complex play on "truth" and "lie," Harper's true reading will give "the lie" to overturn the Southern false God. In a further reversal, the poem declares the African-American community to be the true Christian one, which the white American church betrays:

> Let sorrow breathe in every tone,
> In every strain ye raise;
> Insult not God's majestic throne
> With th' mockery of praise.

It is the slaves' spiritual "sorrow" songs that truly praise "God's throne," opposing "th' mockery of praise" offered by the white Christians. Harper's own voice speaks for them. Through her the truth is revealed despite the distribution of power in the world, in a rebuke against those who claim to be her masters, but over whom she has, in delivering these truths, greater authority.

This prophetic voice is characteristic of Harper. In her poem "Deliverance" (CP 76), Harper effectively writes her own spiritual, interpreting, as the spirituals do, biblical history in a complex orchestration of past, present, and future.[68] This is history in the light of providential promise. The poem, following traditional typology, forecasts the past redemption from Egypt as pointing to a future glorious deliverance, experienced in the present as faith. The poet's own voice delivers this prophetic biblical typology. The poet pronounces the opening summons based on Isaiah: "Rise up, rise up! Oh Israel." Her visionary cross-temporal prophecy unites past to present travail and future hope. Passover feast becomes Jubilee. What stands in the center is the release from slavery, as yet awaited but inscribed in divine pattern, now revealed by the poet and experienced within the text itself.

> And ye shall hold in unborn years
> A feast to mark this day,
> When joyfully the fathers rose
> And cast their chains away.

"This day" is the present of the text, partaking in the "unborn years" yet to come, but experienced in the present voice of promise delivered by the poet.

130   *Feminist Theory across Disciplines*

This prophetic/poetic power, interwoven through an Exodus pattern, implicitly allies the figure of the poet to Moses. He is her anti-type. Moses in the poem is described as "A leader" in the sense of being "friend and guide," roles she takes on in continuation of his redemptive model. Moses in fact is a recurrent figure in Harper, as he is in the spirituals tradition. Harper's long narrative poem "Moses: A Story of the Nile" translates Exodus to the American South, focusing through a series of women characters, Pharaoh's daughter and Moses's mother and sister, whose viewpoints mediate the story. It becomes a story of refused passing. Moses declines to identify with his Egyptian family to remain in solidarity with his Hebrew people. In the poem "Bury Me in a Free Land" (*CP* 93), Moses is again a central if oblique figure. This poem dramatically enacts prophetic voice as retracted and directed selfhood, as was the case for Moses.

> Make me a grave where'er you will,
> In a lowly plain, or a lofty hill,
> Make it among earth's humblest graves,
> But not in a land where men are slaves . . . .
>
> I could not rest if around my grave
> I heard the steps of a trembling slave:
> His shadow above my silent tomb
> Would make it a place of fearful gloom . . . .
>
> I could not rest if I heard the tread
> Of a coffle gang to the shambles led,
> And the mother's shriek of wild despair
> Rise like a curse on the trembling air . . . .
>
> I ask no monument, proud and high
> To arrest the gaze of the passers-by;
> All that my yearning spirit craves
> Is bury me not in a land of slaves.

This poem, like "Bible Defense," is conducted through a sequence of disturbing reversals. The American land of the free and home of the brave is exposed instead as the land of slaves.[69] The grave becomes a site of restlessness, not rest. The living slave haunts the dead, who alone are free. The poet speaks as if out of a silent tomb. What she says is urgent, but she speaks not only of herself. Rather, her act is to put herself to the side, asking for herself "no monument, proud and high," but rather to be buried "where'er you will." Yet this retraction of the self affirms her prophetic vocation since it is Moses who is recalled, who was buried with "no monument" but "where'er you will" on a "lofty hill." Harper here epitomizes her poetic role: a biblical voice that is also prophetic, speaking to serve rather than to assert her own visible presence.

Civic Feminism and Religious Association 131

In these poems, the accent is not on gender, although Harper's work includes poems on Mary Magdelena as first witness to Christ's resurrection, Ruth and Naomi, Rizpah and Hagar. But gendered representation is implicit in Harper's poetic voice, and she is firm in her role as biblical interpreter with its prophetic power. The full implication of the prophetic role for women emerges here. The prophet speaks not for herself, but for an authority that works through her, to a purpose beyond her. She exercises power but without herself becoming the subject. Although she is strenuously active, at issue is not her private personhood except as an enactment of her public role.

The poem "A Fairer Hope, A Brighter Morn" (*CP* 199), discussed earlier in Chapter 4, particularly dramatizes structures of poetic selfhood as both personal and authorized by a truth beyond the self. The speaker is personified history but in a prophetic vision that looks backward, toward reconstituting a redeemed present and future. History and prophecy, however, remain in severe tension against each other. Historical interpretation struggles with prophetic vision, in a clash between false Southern religious claims and Harper's true prophetic voice:

> Oh prophet of evil, could not your voice
> In our new hopes and freedom rejoice?
> 'Mid the light which streams around our way
> Was there naught to see but an evil day? . . .
>
> The banner of Christ was your sacred trust,
> But you trailed that banner in the dust,
> And mockingly told us amid our pain
> The hand of your God had forged our chain.

White Christianity had claimed that slavery was divinely willed: that "God had forged our chain." But this is an evil prophecy. Against it Harper poses her own prophetic voice, rejecting this version of both religion and history to declare not "an evil day," but, as the poem concludes, "the hope of a brighter, fairer morn." To do this she feels called. "God," she writes, "has not sent us to walk with aimless feet, / To cower and couch with bated breath." It is hers not to cower but to speak. She does so with divine sanction through prophetic gift.

Rosemary Ruether notes that the "close identification between progressive feminism and progressive Christianity typical of America in the nineteenth century collapse[d] in the 1920s." By the time of the Second Wave, feminism emerged as "more secular and more suspicious of the positive character of Christianity," largely assuming "that the Christian churches are inherently antiwoman."[70] But as she notes, this is not the same case for African-American feminism. In the work of Gwendolyn Brooks, the tradition of African-American women's public and community activism with its ties to black religion is strongly evident, if also strongly tested. Both of Brooks's memoirs, *Report from Part I* and *Report from Part II*, portray the church as a mainstay of family life, particularly associated with her mother.[71] "Beulah at Church," a "children's" poem she included in *Bronzeville Boys and Girls*, she describes in *Part II* (14) as a direct account of her own feelings as a child. These are dual. Church is disciplinary—"big people closing you in"—and yet "I do not want to stay away. . . . Something there surprises me."

Brooks's later poetry is more openly activist than her earlier, and it moves into an increasingly prophetic voice, although in an interview with George Stavros Brooks is cautious: "I don't want to be 'a prophet.'" She calls her "Sermons on the Warpland" "tiny speeches to black people" (*Report Part I* 153). In contrast, in a 1971 interview with Ida Lewis, she speaks of her desire to "write poems that will somehow successfully 'call' all black people. . . . I wish to reach black people in pulpits, black people in mines, on farms, on thrones."[72] Preaching tradition and rhythms becomes the central organizing trope in Brooks's "Sermon on the Warpland" sequence (*B* 451–456). "Warpland" seems a complex pun: suggesting both warp-land and war-planned, which in either case announces urgent address to a disturbed American state.

The first "Sermon" bids to "Build now your Church, my brothers, sisters. . . . Prepare to meet . . . the brash and terrible weather." The "Second Sermon on the Warpland" summons to face the "whirlwind," as the condition that has to be met in order to move forward: "This is the urgency: Live! / and have your blooming in the noise of the whirlwind." Life, in the dramatic imagery of the poem, is a place of storm, with "whirlwind" an apocalyptic trope. But the poem insists on being able to "salvage in the spin" even if facing a "malign or failing light." This rescue is also political: the poem calls on its readers to "know the whirlwind is our commonwealth." Shared polity is the framework in which individuals act. However, leadership in this "commonwealth" is not arrogance, "not the easy man, who rides above them all." Nor is it economic, "not the jumbo brigand." Art, the "sweetest sonnet," is not a "pet bird," not remote beauty. Instead, the poet, like and as leader, must "straddle the whirlwind." Political engagement and artistic venture become figures of each other.[73]

DISSENT AND CONSENT

To say that women poets remain embedded within religious matrixes does not mean that they are orthodox and uncritical, allowing traditional versions to determine theirs. Women's poetic voices have been launched from religion but also against it. In either case, religion remains a discourse context, and the authority of the writer continues to have religious reference and resonance, at times with a visionary fervor rivaling traditional religious ones.

By the turn of the twentieth century, religious experimentation had become common among women poets. Religious norms are not simply accepted or necessarily simply rejected, but they may be radically recast. Ella Wheeler Wilcox's poem "The Cost" (*PProg* 53), for example, opens with a commentary on Genesis that presents a resonant anatomy of gender roles as well as their wider cultural implications and determinations. She assigns to women the highly conventional one of motherhood, "With love the motive power." But in doing so she also critiques the cultural model of economic man, in creating whom, the poem declares, God himself erred and "marred His own great plan."

> But God neglected, when He fashioned man,
> To fuse the molten splendor of his mind
> With that sixth sense He gave to womankind.
> And so He marred His plan—
> Aye, marred His own great plan.

God here is mistaken or faulty, having divided the genders and neglected to instill in man the values and sensibilities that women have. Yet woman too is at fault for acceding to these gender divisions:

> She asked so little, and so much she gave,
> That man grew selfish: and she soon became,
> To God's great sorrow and the whole world's shame,
>   Man's sweet and patient slave—
>   His uncomplaining slave.

To be only selfless is to betray your personhood. A balance between self and selflessness seems instead to be urged for both men and women, who ought not only to give, but also to ask, in an acknowledgment of selfhood with rich interior and unnoticed power. But this is not just a personal problem or question. It is a cultural critique, about what sort of society these gender roles build.

In another extended venture into biblical commentary, Wilcox, along with Harper and Helen Hunt Jackson, rewrote the *Book of Esther*. Wilcox's "The Revolt of Vashti" casts Ahasverosh's first Queen, Vashti, as the heroine for her defiance of his summons to her to display herself before his court. Instead, she declares, "I will loose my veil and loose my tongue!" (*PProg* 49). Vashti becomes an icon of defiance, although in Harper's version, this remains combined with a modesty that stands against a male objectifying gaze. Harper's Vashti would rather lose her crown than expose her "shrinking eyes. . . . Before their rude and careless gaze" (*CP* 49).

Charlotte Gilman's *His Religion and Hers*, written at the turn of the century, offers a sustained theological inquiry, radically critiquing traditional religion, which Gilman sees as male, and outlining a transformed woman's religion. Gilman strikingly anticipates core issues in twentieth-century feminist theology. Male religion she sees as "death based" in its focus on the afterworld rather than the earthly one, acting out a "limitless individualism" of "eternal extension of personality." In contrast, she proposes a "Birth based" feminized religion that involves "love and labor into a widening range of family, state, and world." These contrasts and claims are encoded in her poem "The Real Religion" (*LP* 83).

> Man, the hunter, Man, the warrior;
> Slew for gain and slew for safety,
> Slew for rage, for sport, for glory—
> Slaughter was his breath:
> So the man's mind, searching inward,
> Saw in all one red reflection,
> Filled the world with dark religions
> Built on Death.

"Man the hunter, Man the warrior" institutes a religion of red "inward" reflection—a prioritizing of interiority that is dualistic and deadly. "Built on Death," it, in "searching inward," institutes and reflects isolation, with its goal a self-seeking personal immortality, what she calls "posthumous egotism" in *His Religion and Hers*.[74] In this dualist religion, "The soul [is] from the body dissevered" while the body cowers in fear of loss of its potency in "the withering failure of age." The soul, bound up with its own limitations and preoccupied by its own ultimate fate, goes "forth on its journey, alone, / To eternity, fearful, unknown."

Feminine religion, in stark contrast, binds self to others.

> Birth, and the Growth of the Soul;—
> The Soul, in the body established;
> In the ever-new beauty of childhood,
> In the wonder of opening power,
> Still learning, improving, achieving;
> In hope, new knowledge and light,
> Sure faith in the world's fresh Spring,—
> Together we live, we grow,
> On the earth that we love and know—
> Birth, and the Growth of the Soul.

In its programmatic writing, this is closer to preaching than to poetry. Still, its points are emphatic. Nondualist, with "The Soul, in the body established," the self is not cut off as an interiority opposed to body and world. Rather than a solitary voyage to the next world, this religion is an earthly one, its "faith in the world's fresh Spring." Rather than static, it is in motion, written in verbs in the present progressive. Power is not claimed for the self but is rather a source of "wonder" for what is beyond. But the poem also calls on the self to contribute. The singular "man" becomes a plural, ungendered "we." This religion is based on "Birth" and the earthly "Growth of the Soul" in the world, rather than on an afterlife that involves death to this world and is, to Gilman, ultimately self-seeking and self-preoccupied. In Gilman, the religious impulse becomes utopian in a this-worldly reconstruction of community.

The twentieth-century emergence of modernist poetics signaled a crisis of relation to community and tradition. The shift to formal experiment and anti-mimesis, with its increased indecipherability, to some extent created, but also reflected, a loss of sense of the place of art in cultural participation, as well as a lack of common cultural forms. In this context of cultural atomization, biblical and other religious discourses continued to offer some degree of shared cultural terrain, even if for personal or anti-traditional purposes. They provide, for H. D., Sylvia Plath, Anne Sexton, Muriel Rukeyser, and other subversive poets, a forum for revising, and indeed assaulting, traditional narratives. For example, in her earlier work, H. D. specifically explored images and relationships to Greek goddesses. Her later long narrative poem *Trilogy* was launched under the stress of the bombings of London from 1942 to 1944. This poem addresses three areas common to feminist theology: a deathly male religion as against a feminized one; the syncretic expansion of divine imagery to include female as well as male goddesses drawn from Greek, Egyptian, Christian, and other sources; and a recovery of women figures from the Bible and in the history of Christianity, as in the concentrated sequence of the "Lady" in *Trilogy* II and the rewriting of Mary Magdalena's narrative in *Trilogy* III—a figure of intense contemporary interest in reconsiderations of female disciples of Christ.[75]

Thus, on one side is a masculine religion "of pain-worship and death-symbol" (I 18, 525), fulfilled in apocalyptic imaginings that have come true as "the world's burning" (I 17, 524). The war-world of "bitter fire of destruction" and "smouldering cities below" is "The-place-of-the-skull" and should be left "to those who have fashioned it" (I, II 1; III 2, 578–579). As in the "battle of the Titans," "Zeus' thunderbolts in action" fall from "giant hands, / the lightning shattered earth/ and splintered sky" (II 6, 550).

Against this deadly religion, H. D. pursues a women's lore, in which "we are the keepers of the secret ... of the rare intangible thread / that binds all humanity / to ancient wisdom" (I 15, 523). This emerges as an esoteric devotion to resurrection rather than destruction, represented throughout the poem by ancient goddesses and gods, eclectically resurfacing in Christian mythologies by rites of myrrh, balm, incense, and incantation (III 7), and by core feminized images such as shell, jar, butterfly, and tree, which come together throughout the text in variously rewoven configurations. *Trilogy* Part II (23, 560) introduces the resurrection image of "the flowering of the rood" that becomes the title of Part III, evoking an earth-cult associated with Demeter as well as "Aset, Isis ... the original great-mother" (cf. III 25, 596) and "De-meter, earth-mother, or Venus, in a star" (I 34, 536). Christian figures, in a highly syncretic vision, are seen as ongoing manifestations of ancient resurrection cults. Visions of the Lady (II 29–41) present her in contest against the *Revelation* of John's destructive apocalyptism, substituting for his a feminized "Book of Life" (II 36, 569) with "blank pages/ of the unwritten volume of the new but without Bridegroom or Child" (II 39, 571).

In Plath, poems such as "Magi," "Mary's Song," and "Brasilia" recast scenes of Christ's birth, retaining the mother's tenderness but in resistance against the uses to which society and religion have put it. "Magi" pictures the wise men's visit to the holy crib as an evasion of the bodily life and of the earthly infant, who is a girl here. "Their whiteness bears no relation to laundry," religious purity is remote from the daily care and labor of child and mother. Indeed, the poem challenges the Magi and the whole male tradition they represent, defiantly asking at the end, "What girl ever flourished in their company?" "Mary's Song" places Mary in a mundane kitchen and a murderous history. In one of Plath's controversial holocaust references, she sees Christ as a child the world consumes, "O golden child the world will kill and eat." "Brasilia" places mother and child again in a scene of apocalyptic destruction and betrayal. "my baby a nail / Driven, driven in. / He shrieks in his grease" in a world where "power" and "glory" are manifested "By the dove's annihilation."[76] In ways that recall Emily Dickinson, religion remains a powerful experience of image, event, and word, but through its betrayal in history, as also its own betrayal of history in its violent imagery of ends of time and world.

In women's modernism, both biblical reference and earlier prophetic traditions continue to be called on as a means of addressing, sustaining, assaulting, and reshaping a shared world. This is the case in Anne Sexton, who has many poems devoted to Mary; in Muriel Rukeyser, who draws on Hebrew tradition, rewriting legends of Rabbi Akiva as well as a surprising number of poems on Jewish history and community[77]; and very much so in Marianne Moore. Radically experimental in form, Moore nonetheless draws on biblical and prophetic traditions in a poetry with a strong public vocation. As Cristanne Miller argues, Hebrew prophecy served as a model for Moore's stance as "ethical speaker addressing issues of public concern," as well as for her poetics.[78] Moore thus claims the authority of a tradition of socially responsible poetic speech, although also insisting, in ways characteristic of women's writing, on the limits of this power and of herself as wielding it. Moore's prophetic stance allows her to signal firm commitment without explicit self-assertion or self-dramatization. In this she can be distinguished from male high modernists. They of course also draw on cultural traditions, literary, philosophical, mythological, and, also notably in Eliot's case, religious. Yet they do so in authoritative, imperious, and dictatorial ways that dramatize themselves. Moore's is a more modest, less self-dramatizing voice, one that, however, addresses her world, its events, and its ethics.

Expressly prophetic references are especially visible in Moore's earlier work. "Feed Me, Also, River God" is a kind of commentary on verses from Isaiah. In Isaiah 8:7, God brings up "the waters of the River, mighty and many." Isaiah is reprimanding the Northern Kingdom of Israel as overconfident in its power to overcome any obstacle, who say, "The bricks are fallen down, We will Build them with hewn stone, the sycamores are cut down we will change to Cedars" (Isaiah 9:9–10). Such boasts are, Isaiah warns, a "pride and arrogance of heart" (Isaiah 9:8).

The "River God" in Moore's poem is a syncretist image, invoking both the Egyptian Nile and the notion of God as Lord of creation. In the poem, Moore contrasts the "Israelites who said / In pride / And stoniness of heart, The bricks are fallen down, / We will / Build them with hewn stone" against herself as not ambitious to dress stones

> To renew
> Forts, nor to match
> My value in action against their ability to catch
>
> Up with arrested prosperity. I am not like
>   Them, indefatigable.[79]

The speaker in this poem avoids the pride and arrogance against which Isaiah warns. She underscores not her own capability but rather her distrust of it. She is "not ambitious" in demonstrations of power such as attempting to "To renew Forts." Nor is she invested in competitions that "match / My value in action against their ability to catch / Up with arrested prosperity." The strength the poet seeks is neither military nor moneyed. Nor does she claim for herself unusual power: "I am not, like them, indefatigable." Hers is, then, a call not to self-sufficiency but, as the poem's opening underscores, to a sense of petition and gratitude: "Feed me, also, River God." And yet neither does Moore simply ascribe to pregiven religious formulae:

> But if you are a god you will
> Not discriminate against me. Yet—if you may fulfill
> None but prayers dressed
> As gifts in return for your own gifts—disregard
> the request.

Moore here is refusing to bargain with God or a God of bargaining. She will not exchange gifts for gifts, which defeats the notion of gift and grace. Refusing the power of "forts" or "property," she specifies a God who will "not discriminate against me" (can she also mean gender discrimination?). Her pressing question is what is meant by God. In any case, Moore's voice, without being explicitly feminized, pursues patterns often characteristic of women poets' religious voices: limiting its own claims to power or competitive force, not trying to "match / My value in action against their ability." Instead, she offers a call to act with values of nondiscrimination and free gifts, as against exchange, ambition, and the assertion of power.

7 The Subject of the Body
Foucault and Culture Studies

Reading Foucault can seem like the revenge of arcane theological disputes on free will and determinism.[1] Here, however, the determiner is not God but octapoid microforces of social apparatus. These reach in endlessly penetrating tendrils into every gesture that makes up selves in societies. Foucault's vision is of society as the site of multiple intersections of systemic powers, institutionalized through the disciplines, social structures, and discourses in which subjects are ensnared.

A core locus of such social apparatus is the body, "in the grip," as Foucault describes it in *Discipline and Punish*, "of very strict powers, which imposed on it constraints, prohibitions, or obligations." This encompassing "micro-physics" operates as a more or less constant "mechanics of power" whose "coercions . . . act upon the body, [as] a calculated manipulation of its elements, its gestures, its behavior." Executed through the varied and central institutions of modern life, these methods of coercion are exercised via "the meticulous control of the operations of the body which assured the constant subjection of its forces and imposed upon them a relation of docility-utility"; methods, Foucault sums up, "which might be called "disciplines.""[2]

Foucault shows rather little interest in women within these disciplinary micropractices (his viewpoints overall remain male; when asked in a 1977 interview about the implications of his work for the "women's question," he is content to consign such applications to others: "It is not up to me").[3] Nevertheless, the power of Foucauldian analysis for feminist interpretation is great and has been powerfully deployed in feminist discussion. Especially central are Foucauldian approaches to the female body as a disciplinary site through which multiple institutions intersect, with gender emerging as itself a foundational institution and disciplinary matrix.

Gender and the body take their place within Foucault's genealogical project of investigating terms long accepted as a 'natural' ground for historical processes, as instead themselves products of history to be subjected to historical analysis and critique. The body and gender emerge not as nature, nor as unchanging metaphysical constants, but as cultural and historical products. Foucault here pursues a Nietzschean critique of essential metaphysical being, substituting historical, cultural construction in its stead. The same is true of the self itself, who emerges in Foucault as a 'subject,' which is no longer a fixed and stable center. "I wanted to see how these problems of constitution could be resolved within a historical framework, instead of referring them back to a constituent object . . . [but not just to] fabricate a subject that evolves through the course of history. One has to dispense with the constituent subject, to get rid of the subject itself, that's to say, to arrive at an analysis which can account for the constitution of the subject within a historical framework" (P/K 117).

For Foucault, to be historical is to be dissolved into conditions, to lose stable contours to changeable, shifting forces. Yet Foucauldian theory has its own substratum to which history is referred, which is power. Power seems to underlay all forms of historical processes, defining and conducting human interactions.[4] Such power analysis extends to definitions of selfhood as well. It is one of Foucault's most compelling gestures to investigate the pun implicit in the word 'subject,' which signifies selfhood but also or as selfhood emerges from being subjected to disciplinary institutional practices. "There are two meanings of the word *subject*: subject to someone else by control and dependence, and tied to his own identity by a conscience or self-knowledge. Both meanings suggest a form of power which subjugates and makes subject to."[5] The self is produced not just by social forces but by its own subjection to power, exercised through a discipline that is above all punishing. Selfhood thus emerges as an "effect of subjugation" (DP 30) through myriad disciplinary practices and power strategies. But power is instituted rather than agent; not "conscious intention or decision," not "what is the aim of someone who possesses power," but rather an "on-going subjugation, at the level of those continuous and uninterrupted processes which subject our bodies, govern our gestures, dictate our behaviors, . . . subjection in its material instance as a constitution of subjects" (P/K 97).

The problems in accounting for political agency or processes in this Foucauldian construction have been discussed by political theorists such as Michael Walzer, Charles Taylor, and Jürgen Habermas.[6] Its negative implications for feminism, as depriving women of the very categories of selfhood, agency, and political initiative just as they begin to claim them, have been discussed by Susan Bordo and others.[7] Just how Foucault's own independent and critical view can be accounted for within his theory of subjection has also been queried: if power is so pervasive and so dominating, how can any self act autonomously or agently or, also, critically, as Foucault is able to do? In feminist terms, what avenues remain for women to negotiate and initiate creative activities and transformative practices if the self is so thoroughly subjected to socializing discipline? Foucault, further, fails to analyze women as situated in the deployments of power differently from the ways men are.[8] As Sandra Lee Bartky puts it, "Foucault treats the body throughout as if it were one, as if the bodily experiences of men and women

The Subject of the Body 141

did not differ and as if men and women bore the same relationship to the characteristic institutions of modern life. Where is the account of the disciplinary practices that engender the docile bodies, bodies more docile than the bodies of men?"[9] Foucault writes in *The History of Sexuality I*, power does not result "from the choice or decision of an individual subject" but within "the manifold relationships of force that take shape and come into play . . . that run through the social body as a whole" (94–95). Even granting that not all exploitation is consciously intentional or ideological—some is sheer convenience;—nor ignoring that how something is situated may have an historical origin in an accidental sense (although history is one kind of reason); it is still ethically important to distinguish how hierarchical privilege carries with it advantages and the exercise of power over those who remain subordinate to them.

Nonetheless, Foucault's work has great analytical power, if also limitations, especially in terms of ethics. Both its strengths and limitations emerge with peculiar clarity when brought to bear on the historical and social horizons of women. Above all, Foucault fails to imagine a community from which selves can draw strength and creativity, not only in resistance but also in solidarity, and not only as disciplinary punishment but as positive resource and contribution.

FOUCAULDIAN POETICS: SYLVIA PLATH

Various social and cultural practices—advertising, pornography, philosophy, and theory—have provided rich fields of Foucauldian investigation. Poetry, however, in that it is often viewed as a self-enclosed, formal language, has not been fully considered in historicist, Culture Studies discussions. But poetic texts engage and register, mark and are marked by the discourses surrounding them—indeed, poetry offers an extreme self-consciousness to cultural practices exactly as discourses, that is, in their linguistic conduct and its effects. As linguistic self-reflection, poetry engages Foucault at several central sites. First, women's poetry offers women's own representations of the image of woman and specifically of women's bodies, often in self-conscious and critical ways. Such poetry exposes how the body is constructed through a variety of cultural practices and specifically how these take place in linguistic forms. Poetry by women can thus display the intersection of discourses and practices as they take women into their grasp in Foucauldian senses, with special reflection on language as an institutional and a disciplinary force. Poetic representation reveals the body as a site of practices and language as itself a central practice instituting selves in social processes.

However, women's poetry also can offer responses to the Foucauldian challenge to notions of personal agency in his analysis of the disciplined subject. One response concerns aesthetic creation itself, not as a separate and self-enclosed domain of activity but rather as an engaged activity that probes and revises its own claims and those of other experiences. Further, women's poetry proposes and explores a number of avenues for asserting possibilities of agent selfhood, free creativity, and constructive power that Foucault's work has made so problematic, not least for women and for feminism. Thus, poetry can demonstrate and explore Foucauldian coercions, but it also challenges them in the very acts of artistic creation, critical reflection, and linguistic power that the poems perform and affirm. Lastly, the specific forms of women's poetic self-representation as embedded within and committed to wider social networks raises questions about Foucault's anti-institutionalism. Foucault views social structures resolutely as forces of erasive disciplinary coercion. Women's poetry, even from the standpoint of historical and cultural situation, often embed the self in society and community (not to mention the investment in poetic form itself) in ways seen to support and strengthen, not only to determine and discipline the self.

American women's poetry provides a dramatic space displaying the disciplinary forces in society inscribed on women's bodies and discourses that enmesh it. Such a poetry of women's bodies is already present in the nineteenth century. There is Emily Dickinson's profound ambivalence about being in a (gendered) body, in such poems as "I Am Afraid to Own a Body," "Publication," and "It Would Have Starved a Gnat." Charlotte Gilman and others satirize women's dress and household postures while many poems describe prostitution, double standards, and silencing. In twentieth-century writing, the focus on the body intensifies, with a greater consciousness of language as a formative force, whose shaping power, however, in being so exposed, may also be recognized and redirected. Anne Sexton's "Woman With Girdle" (*CP* 70) is written from the viewpoint of the woman looking down at her own body, who sees a "midriff sags toward your knees," while the girdle "hides your genius from your patron." Her "Snow White and the Seven Dwarfs" traces the deadly force of the mirror for both older and younger women. Being told "Snow White is fairer than you," the queen "saw brown spots on her hand/ and four whiskers over her lip / so she condemned Snow White / to be hacked to death" (*CP* 224). Thus, women are taught to regard themselves as a bodily spectacle, seen from the eye of reduction to social standards defined as beauty. This same disciplinary force of fairy tales is exposed in Audre Lorde's "The One Who Got Away," imagining "The youngest sister" for whom "never a woman / peeks out from the folds / of her bed-scented mirror / to whisper you are the fairest / daughter" (*CP* 438).

Sylvia Plath may be said to enter into the discourses of bodily regime with special visionary violence. She explicitly situates the poetic text as an intense intersection of institutions gripping/penetrating the female body. Plath's poetry, in one of its tasks, takes hold of contemporary discourses and displays them as a coercive technology of women's selves. This becomes

The Subject of the Body 143

in her poetry a matter of language taking on, in ways she shows, disciplinary roles. Language is shown to be a technique of coercion—and yet also, in this recognition and exposure, an ethical power of possible resistance, transformation, and redefinition.

One exemplary text is Plath's "Face Lift" (*CP* 155), a poem written in 1961, well before cosmetic surgery (not to mention Botox) became a billion dollar worldwide industry.[10] Plath has an almost uncannily Foucauldian eye and ear. Her poems cruelly represent cultural practices at their most malicious, in their hidden coercive powers and coercive languages. In "Face Lift," the woman's body is exposed as institutional site and intersection of interests and rhetorics: commercial, medical, aesthetic, and political. All of these collude, but the first is the most insidious. The coercion of women into a narrowly defined bodily process and product is billed as voluntary choice, indeed as self-realization and self-fulfillment. The remaking of the female body is advertised as a woman's free effort to become her better self. A number of feminist writers have analyzed how these notions of liberty and selfhood are deeply complicitous in what is a highly aggressive industry of feminine products and procedures. A penetrating discipline, it promises and on some levels delivers control, but in a much greater degree, it excruciatingly determines the women in its grasp.[11] There are counterarguments. Some recent discussions of the beauty industry have contested this coercive reading as too one-sided, arguing that beauty can be practiced not only as the Foucauldian regulation of female bodily appearance and behavior, but as a "tactical" resistance tied to the "pursuit of pleasure and frivolity within feminine culture." In such case, it articulates a feminine experience that runs counter to the determinations by gender and money that fashion and beauty impose.[12] However, the question of resistance and its limits as liberative action, and whether pleasure as a privatized experience can exert cultural transformation in a public sphere, are questions that Plath's poetry raises.

The institutional location of "Face Lift" is at the junction of commerce and medicine. The opening announcement—"You bring me good news from the clinic"—may evoke the gospel or, at first, a birth. The voice of the poem then switches to that of the woman who has returned from her cosmetic surgery and then dominates the text. Birth imagery does in fact abound, but in a macabre re/unmaking of the woman's own body. "Whipping off your silk scarf," the post-operative woman exhibits "the tight white / Mummy-cloths, smiling: I'm all right." These "Mummy-cloths" confuse birth and death, motherhood and reification. Delivery becomes self-deformation, a being delivered to forces that disguise defiguration as rebirth. The anesthesia for the operation, which becomes a core image throughout, is first presented through child-memory—"When I was nine, a lime-green anesthetist / Fed me banana gas through a frog-mask"—to become a larger and larger obliteration as the poem proceeds. The hospital in this memory takes on mythical proportions.

To the child's eye, "Jovian" (male) surgeons do magisterial and inexplicable things to her body, alongside her mother, who she remembers as complicitous, holding the "tin basin" for the child's nausea in cahoots with the doctors whose actions—presumably the removal of tonsils—are never made clear to her or given her consent. Now, however:

> They've changed all that. Traveling
> Nude as Cleopatra in my well-boiled hospital shift,
> Fizzy with sedatives and unusually humorous,
> I roll to an anteroom where a kind man
> Fists my fingers for me. He makes me feel something precious
> Is leaking from the finger-vents. At the count of two
> Darkness wipes me out like chalk on a blackboard . . .
> I don't know a thing.

Medical progress has repackaged the anesthetic as an upper class "fizzy" cocktail, while the strategy of the clinic reproduces her as a heroic-mythological "Cleopatra," carried on her litter-stretcher. "Nude" evokes an age-old aesthetic of the female body—art, that is, as male erotics. Yet this is doubly delusive since, in "my well-boiled hospital shift," the woman is not queenly but instead bureaucratically encased. As to the doctor, he at first is said to be "a kind man" who "makes me feel something precious." But this turns out, by way of a radical line break, to be not a giving but a taking. "Something precious / Is leaking from the finger-vents." All this apparent self-possession proves to be a self-draining mechanization. The crucial image is again anesthesia. The man "fists my fingers for me. . . . At the count of two / Darkness wipes me out like chalk on a blackboard. . . . / I don't know a thing." What the adult woman parades as conscious choice translates into images of lost consciousness. First she leaks and then she is wiped out "like chalk on a blackboard." Two interlocking figural systems emerge here. One involves the body in time—the face lift is born out of the aging body. But this is also a figure of writing, as the poem unmasks the effort to halt, to reverse human time, as instead a mode of erasure. To the self as text, the face lift is disfiguration, an effacement of the inscription that is one's life.

What is achieved is not agency but deletion and infantilization. The "kind man / Fists my fingers for me" in a passive and infantile reflex of the hand. A womb-like initiation rite—"For five days I lie in secret"—instead traces a loss of self, as drainage:

> For five days I lie in secret,
> Tapped like a cask, the years draining into my pillow.
> Even my best friend thinks I'm in the country.
> Skin doesn't have roots, it peels away easy as paper.
> When I grin, the stitches tauten. I grow backward. I'm twenty . . . .

Reification, objectification, and reduction—"Tapped like a cask, the years draining into my pillow"—leads to retractive oxymoron: "I grow backward. I'm twenty." Imagery of (un)birth again joins with imagery of (un)writing while the question of selfhood as natural or cultural is dreadfully posed through organic as against textual imagery: "Skin doesn't have roots, it peels away easy as paper." The earlier "Mummy-cloths" intercross swaddling clothes with embalmment. In the last stanza, the speaker would be "Mother to myself," at once rejecting, displacing, and incorporating that earlier feared mother-power, to give birth to herself with skin "Pink and smooth as a baby." Here the fantasy of autochthonous birth joins with that of autonomy and self-determination. Yet the poem, in a textuality that works against the woman's own account, reveals this to be instead an unraveling of the self as writing, both as body and text:

> Now she's done for, the dewlapped lady
> I watched settle, line by line, in my mirror—
> Old sock-face, sagged on a darning egg.
> They've trapped her in some laboratory jar.
> Let her die there, or wither incessantly for the next fifty years,
> Nodding and rocking and fingering her thin hair.
> Mother to myself, I wake swaddled in gauze,
> Pink and smooth as a baby.

The marks of time on the woman's body are the registry of her self's own history. They are now gone. Who then is left? The pursuit of beauty is a flight from, not a realization, of her self, not a command of institutions but a determination by them, not an accession to self-definition but a retreat from selfhood as it has taken shape through a life. What she is left with is not personal self-expression but a fixed image within a set of cultural norms, inscribed on or as the woman's own body.

The very fantasy of autonomous birth into self-creation proves to be derived, imposed, the product of a commercial system, now made interior in the most intimate, physical sense. It is a fantasy of enormous social power. Plath proleptically projects an industry of immense proportions; in Foucauldian terms, a technology and apparatus whose effects can be traced in the moneys made and the rigors undergone by untold numbers of women (and increasingly also men). Analyses of the regimens of women's beauty and its close shadow in body disorders such as anorexia uncannily gloss the poem.

> The very expressions of her face can subvert the disciplinary project of bodily perfection. An expressive face lines and creases more readily than an inexpressive one. Hence, if women are unable to suppress strong emotions, they can at least learn to inhibit the tendency of the face to register them.

The requirement that a woman maintain a smooth and hairless skin carries further the theme of inexperience, for an infantalized face must accompany her infantalized [thin] body, a face that never ages or furrows its brow in thought. The face of the ideally feminine woman must never display the marks of character, wisdom, and experience that we so admire in men.[13]

Female beauty is not an aesthetic category but a disciplinary one. More than any objective or visual category or pleasure, it is a rigorous regimen for directing and constraining the female person. In the poem, beauty operates as disdain for the woman's own body. Her fantasy to be "Pink and smooth as a baby," which combines imagery of regression with written erasure, is not simply her own. It is a cultural ideal that women be without experience, without history, and without a formed self, pliant and blank. The woman, in and as her body, thus registers forces that direct her identity, her very desire. But these are paradoxical since what she desires entails her own negation, denying any life history that she can claim as her own. This is the history that, through her life's time, she has "watched settle, line by line, in my mirror," the writing she would dissolve in what comes through, in the final stanza of "Face Lift," to be extraordinary self-hatred. "Old sock-face, sagged on a darning egg. . . . Let her die there." The woman's dreadful split into a third person that refers to herself shows her language to be invaded by disciplinary, effacing viewpoints, dividing and overwriting her with estranged locution. Birth here is burial. Her own head is repudiated: "They've trapped her in some laboratory jar" like formaldehyde embryos. To evade aging is to lose and betray your own history. The disciplined self costs your selfhood.

Bodily regimens of beauty are one major practice for disciplining women. Plath in other poems exhibits other practices that render the female body, as Susan Bordo elaborates, marginal, contracted, unobtrusive, and invisible.[14] "Tulips," "In Plaster," and "Fever 103" treat, as does "Face Lift," the medicalized female body, entrapped in its own self-consuming. "The Applicant" and "Death & Co." enter into bureaucratic process and the business office as places where the self is deformed by fixed structures and structured languages. "The Applicant" (*CP* 221) converts the apparently most intimate, most volitional events—love and marriage—into an alienated exchange in some service-office, where the self takes shape as an application form. "First, are you our sort of a person?" The applicant is reduced to a set of terms to match some other set, in this case, as it turns out, of a wife-function (this is well before online dating services), part of whose function is not only to fulfill any need but to be entirely pliant. In imagery again of writing, she is offered as "Naked as paper to start," with the promise that "in twenty-five years she'll be silver, / in fifty gold." The woman becomes inscribed as anniversary registers, which just happen to correspond to stock certificates or precious metals. "Will you marry me"

The Subject of the Body 147

becomes "will you marry it," the "suit" of courtship becomes a uniform "Black and stiff, but not a bad fit," and the prospective bride-commodity "A living doll wherever you look," "guaranteed" to sew, cook, and "talk, talk, talk."

In "Face Lift," the woman is so disciplined as to embrace her own erasure as rebirth. She is caught in the procedures worked on her. Yet Plath's is also a venture of critique, writing the lines the face lift would efface. In this the poet appeals beyond the woman in the poem. She speaks to readers who can form a newly conscious and newly critical community. This is the work and the hope of the poem. It is a difficult hope. Plath can record this cultural inscription but not necessarily be free of it: just look at her photographs of dyed-blond hair carefully arranged over a necklace of pearls.[15] Yet fury at her world, as woman and poet, foments and seethes in explosive texts that may impel the reader to outrage and revulsion, and to an effort to repossess ourselves and our language for our own purposes.

INDUSTRIAL-MEDICAL DISCOURSES: MURIEL RUKEYSER

Muriel Rukeyser is a poet overtly engaged in political-poetic practices, with a pointed concern with how institutional structures both define and confine individual selves. Socialist and feminist, Rukeyser allies her poetry with the journalism she also pursued. Her *Book of the Dead in U.S.1* (1938) emerged from her coverage of the first major industrial disaster in America, at Gauley Bridge in West Virginia. There, thousands of migrants, mainly African-American workers who had been employed to construct a hydraulic dam, began to die of suffocation from inhaling the almost pure silicon through which they were drilling and which, after its discovery, they then also were assigned to mine.

For Rukeyser, the Gauley Bridge disaster was not only a major journalistic venture but also a poetic one. Drawing on personal accounts and interviews, medical reports, legal proceedings, and even legislative hearings, Rukeyser created a documentary poetics far from the New Critical formalism that reigned for most of her writing life. In these poems, she detects and exposes not only the complicities between medical and industrial-legal institutions but the ways in which these take place through specific modes of language: discourses that penetrate, disperse, absorb, and direct experiences through the institutional interests of those who deploy them. In this, she looks forward to a Foucauldian recognition of the enormous disciplinary power of institutions in their mutual complicity—legal, medical, industrial, legislative—and their power specifically as discourses. Rukeyser's texts become Foucauldian sites where institutional disciplines occur in their discourse deployments, flattening, shaping, and processing all who circulate through their disciplinary linguistic systems. She represents how these discourses penetrate and grasp, assimilate and process the individuals caught within them. Rukeyser draws on a Marxist critique of liberal institutions and liberal definitions of the self as autonomous individual. Against claims of the self's and society's autonomy from economic and social contexts, Rukeyser understands and portrays the self as embedded within and shaped by social, historical, and material conditions, with their various discourses competing and aligning, augmenting and also resisting each other, in ways that poetry can expose and examine. Yet Rukeyser remains fully committed to agent selfhood. Against Marxism's insistence on the priority of the collective, and even given Rukeyser's own sense of the force of institutional powers and discourses such as Foucault anatomizes, Rukeyser's texts speak in and for the individual voice as it, both against and within social context, asserts its own sense of self and world. Indeed, she offers poetry as a model for such individual expression. Poetry is a unique and individual creation. The self and its expression is framed and even penetrated by social forces, which inevitably and both positively and negatively shape it. But they do not simply determine poetic or individual assertion. The self remains a unique site, where intersecting forces find distinctive formation, and which poetry can express and affirm in a unique creative voice.

As poet, then, it is for Rukeyser to represent individuals and their situations as linguistic configurations—on the one hand as discourses that frame and conduct institutional power, yet on the other in the possibility and power of personal vision and expression. As poet, she asserts or explores possible modes of language other than, although always within the contexts of, disciplinary discourses. In this project, she does not work in what might be called a liberal tradition of aesthetics, where the poet is a unique and vatic seer affirming his own originality. Hers is a different model of poetry and also of the poet. Her poetic draws on, affirms, and serves the words of others, in a fully Bakhtinian dialogics. In Rukeyser's *Book of the Dead*, many passages are constructed out of testimony and documentary record, personal interview or letter. She thus offers a vision of poetry in stark opposition against what was just then emerging as the defining model in the American academy as a rigorous formalism freed from context.[16] Rukeyser instead sees the concern of poetry to be the representation of languages drawn from many spheres and contexts. Ultimately her goal is to bring language's claims and force, modes and implications to heightened consciousness and ultimately to ethical action.

To Rukeyser, poetry is never merely "aesthetic," if this is taken to mean removed from other norms and human engagements. Indeed, Rukeyser's work raises questions of the purposes of poetry, their social function and place. *The Book of the Dead* attests to the immense force of institutional norms and languages as these situate and penetrate the humans caught up in their procedures. Yet the poet is a self who reflects and represents this. In doing so, she points to a selfhood not only as subjected to intersecting and often complicitous institutional powers but one that, through devotion to others and as a member of a social community, can recover the voices of protest, of resistance, and also of affirmation in terms other than the disciplinary ones that are so admittedly potent. In and through her words, as reflection as well as intensification of those of others, these diverse and unique selves find voice.

In *The Book of the Dead*, quoted speech is interwoven with Rukeyser's own descriptions, observations, images, and techniques. Even when her textual materials are most documentary, literary techniques of transposition and formatting, quotation and rupture, lineation and interposition, perform tasks of exposure and critique, involvement and indignation, claim and contest, in an activist poetics. The title of the sequence, *The Book of the Dead*, introduces a mythic dimension into the otherwise technological and social-realist documentary modes, in a high modernist technique of arranging material through archetypal or mythic correlations. Through these literary strategies, the enormous force of institutional and bureaucratic languages is made to be felt, but so are the efforts and speech of persons who are not agents of the technologies of bureaucracy. The poems incorporate the words of those who are inexpert in institutional procedures, who lack the professional training in them necessary to be able to answer to them. Individuals instead speak from within their own experiences and commitments, which the poetry renders vocal. What emerges is how humans are caught up in procedures and the threat of their assimilation into impersonal discourses. Yet Rukeyser also poses against these instituted discourses personal voices that attest to and bring to the light of language agent selfhood. This in turn is rooted in webs of relationship that support and attend to the self, and to which the self is tied, as to a lifeline.

The poem "The Disease" (*CP* 83), for example, is mainly conducted through a discourse of medical presentation and its legal cross-examination:

> This is a lung disease. Silica dust makes it.
> The dust causing the growth of.

Documentary reportage becomes poetry through grammatical abruptness and interruption, with the oxymoron of "growth" linked to "dust" and "disease." What follows is the assimilation of the afflicted miner into a medicalized body, rendered as "X-ray picture" via the pointer of the examiner: "This is the heart (a wide white shadow filled with blood.) . . . Spaces between the lungs." Two-dimensional, black and white, "white shadow filled with blood," the self is defined as technological image just as it is penetrated by the industrial substance of the silica that is filling his lungs and suffocating him to death.[17] Investigative questions punctuate stanza breaks—"What stage?"—eliciting information, clarifying points, but also poetically echoing and calling into question such a representation of a person and its consequences. The poem becomes the chart of this discourse body, this body as medical chart and industrial waste. Both time and space

150 *Feminist Theory across Disciplines*

become functions of medical representation. The body is tracked from stage to stage as a manifestation of symptoms. "Third stage. Each time I place my pencil point: There and there and there, there, there." What the poem ultimately documents is how the body is rendered as medical affidavit, within juridical procedures that follow its own institutional norms, all converging into this brief to be filed against indemnities. When the medical technician refers to the crystalline lung formations as a "Model conglomeration," this ironically and painfully applies both to this body and to the corporation that has possessed it.

But then the living voice cuts in: "It is growing worse every day. At night / I get up to catch my breath." A missed dialogue of its own sort goes back and forth between examiner and experiencer:

> It gradually chokes off the air cells in the lungs?
> I am trying to say it the best I can.
> That is what happens isn't it?
> A choking-off in the air cells?

Perspectives reverse but do not connect between the person suffering, going from seen to seer, from spoken about to speaker, as against the requirements of medical evidence. "Catch my breath" must register as "choking-off in the air-cells." He protests, "I am trying to say it the best I can." Official discourse confronts personal account. One has a sense of pushing boulders uphill. Personal experience is subordinated to medical language as legal procedure directed by interests while the legal framework for uncovering truth and achieving justice are deeply compromised by their own formats and rules. Just so, in the poem "The Doctors" (*CP* 86), different voices both collude and work at cross-purposes. The poem renders a medical-legal conversion of experience into a presentation in court. A "Dr. Goldwater" insists that "Medicine has no hundred percent / We speak of possibilities, have opinions" and "avoid dogmatic statements." But then the prosecuting lawyer insists that "Doctors testify answering 'yes' and 'no.'" And when the defense lawyer asks: "—I wish you would tell the jury whether or not those lungs were silicotic" the court dialogue continues:

> —*We object.*
> —*Objection overruled.*
> —*They were.*

Thus, testimony takes shape as regulated through legal exchange. Medical discourses claim their own integrity but also are complicitous with legal ones. The doctors at Gauley Bridge were mostly employed by Union Carbide. Their desire to "avoid dogmatic statements" may have to do with their own liability as much as any scientific scruple or medical ethics. As one company doctor reports in a prose passage within the poem, "I warned

The Subject of the Body 151

many of them of the dust hazard and advised them that continued work under these conditions would result in serious lung disease. Disregarding this warning many of the men continued at this work and later brought suit against their employer for damages." Even if the medical implications were clear and the law entirely devoted to justice, what choices and chances had these men to refuse employment in a depression era? Economic pressures and necessities compromise liberal promises of choice and equality. As to establishing medical facts, these must emerge as best they can while embedded within litigious practices and interests.

Drawing on yet another discourse event, the "The Disease: After-Effects" (*CP* 98) inscribes a congressional hearing on silica poisoning and industrial responsibility. While in the poem "The Disease" the mineral material of the landscape penetrates the body, suffocating it, now the American landscape becomes deformed with disease, scarred and suffocating. As if from the viewpoint of a plane high above land, "map and X-ray seem / Resemblant pictures of one living breath." Scar-scape becomes landscape:

> It sets up a gradual scar formation;
> This increases, blocking all drainage from the lung,
> Eventually scars, blocking the blood supply,
> And then they block the air passageways.

Representation by X-ray now is redistributed as the country's map. The "air passageways" of the diseased lungs are like air passageways of planes over land. The "gradual scar formation" configures an aerial photograph of the land below, the formation of the interior spaces of the diseased bodies of those who worked the land, and finally also the body politic and its processes of governing the land with which the poem concludes: "Bill blocked; investigation blocked." Like a silicotic lung, the bills and investigations of industrial disaster are "blocked."

This poem is followed in the sequence by "The Bill" (*CP* 100), which addresses the industrial disaster in the language of a motion to be voted on the Congressional floor: "We recommend./ Bring them. Their books and records. / Investigate. Require." Again, truncation, reduction, and juxtaposition transform documentary into poetic exposure.

The formal terms of the congressional motion become shocking in its contrast against the horror of the disease it formally addresses:

> THAT the effects are well known.
>   Disease incurable.
>   Physical incapacity, cases fatal.

Rendering institutional, disciplinary languages as poetic text opens a rupture in them, a reflective distance from their operation that unmasks them, culminating in parodic conclusion: "The subcommittee subcommits."

Rukeyser thus mobilizes poetry as political activism, projecting an anatomy of social forces as they construct and are constructed by the individuals within them. The notion of the self as penetrated by and implicating institutional systems already distinguishes her vision from libertarian understandings, which fantasizes a self-determined self that is free of social contexts. Her poetry stands in critique of such reductive notions of the self without regard for the institutional settings and overarching powers within which any individual resides and in terms of which we are not merely self-determining.

But is there a language event besides these instituted discourses? In her poetic weave, Rukeyser interposes and counter-poses other voices against disciplinary ones. In the poem "Absalom" (CP 81), Rukeyser represents the voice of the mother who was "the first of the line of lawsuits." It was she who first provided the medical evidence, after begging on the highway for the money to pay for X-rays. As the poem recounts, the official company doctor would not examine her last dying son Shirley. But with X-rays came evidence that the deaths of her husband and three sons had been caused by silicosis. The poem "Absalom" is at once an official report and personal account, further interwoven with lyrical cries as if from the Egyptian "Book of the Dead," as of course also biblical lament through the poem's title "Absalom," and haunted by the dead son's voice: "He said, 'Mother, I cannot get my breath' . . . I would carry him from his bed to the table, / from his bed to the porch, in my arms." The back and forth of repeated care becomes the back and forth of the poetic line. The mother retells her son's words, then gives her factual report, and then utters her cry of personal devotion, in which her voice merges with her son's:

My heart is mine in the place of hearts,
They gave me back my heart, it lies in me.

This lyric voice evokes a funeral scarab displayed at a New York Metropolitan Museum Egypt exhibit during 1935–1937 called the "Heart Amulet of Hatnofer."[18] A black stone marked with white hieroglyphs, it is one of the amulets inserted into the chests of embalmed kings and queens, seen as vital to their final judgment. Its white markings on black recall the reductions of X-ray and photograph, of race and writing, of silica dust and American society. In its image, this mother will claim her own heart, in her mission to carry her boy's words, as she did his body, against the worlds and words that destroyed him.

I shall journey over the earth among the living.

He shall not be diminished, never;
I shall give a mouth to my son.

The mother's voice, part mythological, part historical, answers back the voices of power, giving "mouth to my son," at least in the poem.

The poem "Arthur Peyton" (*CP* 90) is spoken in his voice and in strong strain against the pressure of legal, medical, technological, and business languages. The opening passage records a letter announcing his compensation: "Dear Sir, . . . pleasure . . . enclosing herewith our check . . . / payable to you, for $21.59 . . . after collecting all we could, we find this balance due you." This death letter, with its devaluation of the person to $21.59, is embedded in a love letter that Arthur Peyton is writing to his fiancé, in the knowledge that they will never marry, since he is dying of silicosis (O love tell the committee that I know:/ never repeat you mean to marry me . . . two years O love two years he said he gave). The letter's opening, "Consumed. Eaten away. And love across the street," refers firstly to himself, consumed by the industrial disease silicosis, and also by the commercial-legal procedures that no less consume him; and also to the love that must forever remain "across the street." But it is not only Arthur Peyton who is being consumed. Everything in the poem turns into glass—landscape, city, persons. The romantic-like image, "the moon blows glassy over our native river," in fact is a physical, industrial product and takes on a new unnatural, inorganic meaning. The city is one "long glass street," and as to Peyton himself, whose lungs have filled with the silica glass:

> my face becoming glass
> strong challenged time making me win immortal
> our street our river a deadly glass to hold.
> now they are feeding me into a steel mill furnace
> O love the stream of glass a stream of living fire.

Street and self, inner world and landscape, public and private, become a deadly mirror to industrial practices. The individual turns at last into ore fed into the "steel mill furnace," smelted into "the stream of glass a stream of living fire"—not only in his labor but in his very body.

Arthur Peyton is to a painful degree defeated by the procedures that engulf him. Yet his voice in the poem remains unsilenced and powerful. It is a voice of clarity, a voice of love, a voice of judgment: "O love tell the committee that I know" bids his beloved to go on to confirm the accusations he leaves behind. His address is to her; and through her, to the committee of investigation; and perhaps above all, to this poetry that continues to carry his words. In this verse, he can say: "Strong challenged time making me win immortal."

Rukeyser, writing out of a leftist context in the 1930s, is supremely aware that any self is not freely self-formed, not autonomously defined, not independently 'private' as in the image of classical liberalism. Selves are situated in the many social and economic structures that open possibilities and also close them. Yet she also remains within an American tradition

154 Feminist Theory across Disciplines

of 'individuality' if not strict liberal individualism, emphasizing individual integrity, personal relationships, and vision as a precious and hope-inspiring resource.[19] Rukeyser's poetic does not accept stark division between 'private' and 'public' but rather insists on their mutual implication. While she disputes a notion of autonomous self as self-defined, without contexts or relationships, she is committed to an agent selfhood, not reductively determined by contexts but rather drawing definition and strength from them. The self in her verse remains situated within social orders—inscribed in the world of relationships, both social and personal. It is constituted not out of its own self-reliance and self-definition, but from the myriad relations and histories in which each self inevitably partakes. Institutional life is thus not utterly condemned. Some institutions, such as family, community, love and devotion provide other models and possibilities. And in the poems, the impersonal force and indifferent procedures of institutions are called to account. The poems register voices threading through and against the depersonalized institutions that humans construct and inhabit. Indeed, the poems call them to account. This marks, for Rukeyser, the possibility, indeed the urgency, of activism, both poetic and political. The voices in her texts are meant to affirm the power of the individual voice, to demand response from the institutions that Rukeyser exposes. Poetry is a model and enactment for such individual assertion, activism, and challenge. The voice of her poetry is thus a register of the voices circulating around her, yet in their unique formation, they attest to the human voice as it emerges from, but also responds to and creates within, the contexts and institutions that shape and demand responsibility.

GWENDOLYN BROOKS AND THE RESOURCES OF COMMUNITY

In his later work, Foucault became increasingly interested in an account of an 'ethical' self that, without renouncing Foucault's vision of intricate and intimate social discipline, could retain a space of freedom for the subject. Foucault describes his own development as moving from the "history of power to the history of the self" (E 225–226). Such free space of the self takes shape primarily in Foucault in terms of resistance as an anti- or counter-disciplinary force. Slippage, conflicts, and gaps among multiple modes of power make resistance to them possible. As he remarks in one interview, in that power is always "dispersed, heteromorphous, localized, . . . accompanied by numerous phenomena of inertia, displacement, and resistance . . . there are no relations of power without resistances" (P/K 142). Power produces resistance; indeed, resistances "can only exist in the strategic field of power relations," although this does not necessitate "that they are only a reaction or rebound . . . always passive and always doomed to defeat."[20]

The Subject of the Body 155

The power of resistance has been emphasized by some Foucauldian feminists, notably Sawicki. In Foucault's own discourses, however, just how far this pathway can travel remains unclear. While Foucault sees "an insubordination and a certain essential obstinacy on the part of the principles of freedom," they remain bound to the powers they resist, with the two convertible into each other in an ever "possible reversal" (SP 225–226). Foucault increasingly in his later remarks is also committed to the possibility of self-creation. For him, the self, as part of its definition, always remains inside power relations, in the "situation" of resistance. "We cannot jump outside the situation, and there is no point where you are free from all power relations." Yet he also wishes to claim that "you can always change it . . . we are always free—well, anyway, there is always the possibility of changing" (E 167; cf. E 292). As to disciplinary structure, Foucault's later notion of the "care of the self" and a "cultivation of the self" posits constructive technologies or techniques that would remain coercive but also self-forming practices of freedom (E 282).[21] Foucault, in one late interview, even mentions, although he does not specify, the possibility of "consensual disciplines."[22] While the care of the self remains a practice of self-construction, Foucault also invokes "reciprocity" with others in an "intensification of social relations" (HS II, 54, 149). "The care of the self," he remarks, "is ethical in itself; but it implies complex relationships with others insofar as this ethos of freedom is also a way of caring for others" (E 287).

Nevertheless, despite these suggestions, Foucault's ethics remain in many ways incomplete. For one thing, he finds it hard to project, at least in his rhetoric, a relation of the self to social formations that would be genuinely positive. Freedom and transformation for him work less within, than against, existing social structures. These remain essentially disciplinary and punitive. Government is surveillance (E 67, 81) and education is subjection (E 327). The "strategy of struggle" is a "free play of antagonistic reactions," whose danger, yet fatality, is to convert into "stable mechanisms" that become power relations (E 225). As his pivotal essay on "What Is Enlightenment" shows, Foucault remains engaged in the Enlightenment project of autonomy, even if, consistent with much postmetaphysical thinking, he rejects notions of the self as a transcendental essence, metaphysical or natural, insisting instead on its cultural-historical formation. In some sense, the depth of his vision of disciplinary power is exactly the measure of his sense of its threat. His genius at analyzing institutional powers remains an image of his sense of their tentacular extent. Like Atlas, like Sisyphus, like some mythological hero at some Herculean task, Foucault attempts to open space for the self against the crushing weight of the norm and its institutions. Liberty strains against any "moral or religious imperative" (E 148). Relationship takes place "outside of institutional relations, family, profession, and obligatory camaraderie" (E 136). "Army, bureaucracy, administration, universities, schools, and so on" all work against "intense friendships" (E 17). Nor is his goal to launch new institutions (E 160,

171–172). Rather, it is "to create an empty space" for endless "new relational possibilities" (E 160), a utopia of ongoing improvisation and "mobility" of selves and relations (E 283, 292).[23]

With regard to this strangely unhistorical and unsocialized vision of a self—surprisingly at odds with Foucault's own historicist commitments—feminist writing and women's poetry has a particular contribution to make. In the poetry of women, as we have seen in Plath, the dangers of institutionalized selfhood can be urgent and severe. Yet, for example, in the expressly political and ethical poetry of Muriel Rukeyser and Gwendolyn Brooks, the woman's voice situates itself deeply in terms of surrounding community: a community she speaks for and speaks to, whose audience and activity she is trying to mobilize and awaken. Senses of selfhood are fundamentally enmeshed in just this communal engagement. In Plath's "Face Lift" and other poems, women are almost violently disciplined by their surrounding worlds. Yet even here, the poetic voice is one of address to others: a call, an invocation, to the reader to see, recognize, and act. Muriel Rukeyser's appeal to political consciousness and activism is direct and fierce. In Gwendolyn Brooks, the sense of selfhood as drawing on and acting for and within community is paramount. In her work, the disciplinary self emerges as a sustained construction, where institutions of race, economy, religion, and gender mutually intersect and amplify each other. Her poetry is intensively scened. The composition of human figures, their parameters and their interactions, proceed in terms of the materiality of their social existences, as this presses on them and as they press back. This is the case throughout her writing, despite changes in both aesthetic and political modes from her earliest to her latest work, which are in this way more continuous than is often claimed. The poems of (the early) *A Street in Bronzeville* inscribe a profound embedding of the African-American self into the social conditions of her and his life. In the opening poem, "Kitchenette Building" (*B* 20), tenement life seizes its inhabitants and their relationships, penetrating them through material conditions. "We are things of dry hours and the involuntary plan." The involuntary disguised as the voluntary is what this socio-economic space offers. Indeed, what would "voluntary" mean in this coercive environment, where ""Dream" makes a giddy sound, not strong / Like "rent," "feeding a wife," "satisfying a man."" Yet the poem insists on "dream" even "through onion fumes." Constraints are real but not all defining. The self witnesses and transforms the realities that constitute it. Brooks—who lived in such a kitchenette building—asks how it is possible to "sing an aria" there, yet she does so herself, not apart from, but "down these rooms."

Brooks thus at once registers the force of Foucauldian disciplinary vision and also offers terms for possible responses to its challenges. Nor does she propose or project only a resistant self but also a deeply embedded self, drawing her strength, indeed critique, from her indelible commitment to and attachment within her social communities. Resistance alone cannot constitute either freedom or personhood. This has an aesthetic dimension. Within Brooks's texts, disciplinary life is inscribed as well in steady, rigorous, formal demands. The poems as construction reside in specified genres: Brooks is, for example, a great writer of sonnets. Texts, both formally and in their creative conduct, are figures for investment in institutional structures as a basis for invention. This includes the figure of the poet herself, in her critical distance but also in her firm attachment to the worlds she at once draws from and participates in; which she judges and refuses, but also to which she is passionately committed and wills to transform.

Brooks's men and women are subjected to racist hatred and distortion, economic pressure and exploitation, gendered assignments, and sexualized power. Racial hierarchies pervade sexuality and define bodily self in poems such as "The Ballad of Chocolate Mabbie" and "The Anniad," as African-American men measure African-American women against deadly fantasies of white women. In "Jessie Mitchell's Mother," the ties of mother and daughter are distorted as each grades the other by a hierarchy of color. "The Sundays of Satin-Legs Smith" (*B* 17) constructs the bodies of African-American men through practices of the white bourgeois world they can never really enter; men who then, in turn, construct African-American women through social practices, bodily regimens, and sexual function.

> Squires his lady to dinner at Joe's Eats.
> His lady alters as to leg and eye,
> Thickness and height, such minor points as these,
> From Sunday to Sunday. But no matter what
> Her name or body positively she's
> In Queen Lace stockings with ambitious heels
> That strain to kiss the calves, and vivid shoes
> Frontless and backless, Chinese fingernails,
> Earrings, three layers of lipstick, intense hat
> Dripping with the most voluble of veils. (17)

"Squire," a word drawn from an older (if no less suspicious) courtly code, here is a sordid and deceiving role. As to the "lady," she is not one, but many and any, interchangeable from Sunday to Sunday. Differing in "Thickness and height," she/they are defined through conforming bodily practices. "No matter what her name of body . . . she's / In Queen Lace stockings with ambitious heels, . . . Earrings, three layers of lipstick." In something like a parodic blason , the interchangeable woman's body appears in pieces: leg and eye, height and weight and shape, ears and lips, with "Queen" a kind of lace stockings. This is who each of them is: measurements, dress styles, and make-up in the double sense of mask and composition. The parts are metonyms for the ladies, determined as they are by fashion: by "ambitious" shoes, "frontless and backless," who, like the woman herself, is caught in contradictions as she stumbles along in the styles of women's footwear in which no one can walk. Just so, disciplined "Chinese fingernails" immobilize women's hands. Cosmetic colors conceal skin and features. All is covered by an "intense hat / Dripping with the most voluble of veils." "Veils" are a recurrent trope for women's concealments, here imposed not by tradition but by commercial interest. Similarly, the "name," so crucial in women's poetry, is here emptied: "No matter what her name or body."

After such coercion, what autonomy? Brooks is suspicious of autonomy itself as a category. "Strong Men, Riding Horses" (B 71) exposes self-reliance as an image produced by the entertainment industry in its "Western" genre. "Bronzeville Man with a Belt in the Back" deploys the self-protective clichés of masculine bravado: "In such an armor he may rise and raid / The dark cave after midnight, unafraid / And slice the shadows with his able sword / Of good broad nonchalance" (B 100). The armor is inward as well as outward, a "nonchalance" of detachment. But it cannot finally accomplish its purpose. The "shadows" remain. The poem's conclusion, spoken indirectly as the man's own voice, is false: "In such an armor he cannot be slain."

Autonomy as armored disconnection emerges as delusive. Transgression, too, proves to be a limited strategy. "We Real Cool," one of Brooks's most widely anthologized poems, traces a course of rebellion not as free choice but as alienated destruction. "We / Lurk late. We / Strike straight. We / Sing sin. . . . We / Die soon" (B 73). Nonconformity in fact here conforms to a cultural masculine toughness, radicalized yet also reproduced in African-American rebellion that becomes deadly. In the case of women, the binds are similarly multiple. Approval is a tremendous disciplinary force in the lives of women. Yet so may be transgression. For "Sadie and Maud," either course—disdaining approval or seeking it—proves destructive. The good girl who "went to college" is left to live alone in a deserted house. But the other girl's resistance to "front yard" propriety, instead going to "peek at the back" where women are "bad," leads her into disciplines as reductive as is the norm: to "wear the brave stockings of night-black lace / And strut down the streets with paint on my face" (B 6). In "Gang Girls: A Rangerette" (B 449)—the third and last poem in the sequence "The Blackstone Rangers" on African-American urban Gang life—the Gang Girls are no more than "sweet exotics" for "Bowery Boys, Disciples, Whip-Birds" and other gangs. For the women, the transgressive structure of the Gang is exploitative and consuming.

In Brooks, protest, transgression, and exposure constitute critical strategies, indeed moral imperatives, in both act and art. Yet both act and art are also embedded within the social structures that situate the self and to which the self remains committed. The self only exists in terms of the cultural histories and instituted relationships that give it rise and that are not, therefore, starkly antithetical to selfhood. Indeed, devotion to community—in both critique and support—is in Brooks an impelling mode of activism, to which art is central as both mode and image, and in which the artist

The Subject of the Body 159

becomes a representative figure. In Foucault, the artist is also a pivotal figure, one that focuses his ethics as well as his aesthetics—marking what becomes their strange convergence. Even in his last writings, ethics remains a structure outside and opposed to social institution, "without any relation with the juridical per se . . . [nor] with a disciplinary structure" (*E* 260). Foucauldian care of the self turns back toward the self, in what emerges as an "ethics of control," but now self-directed. Technology of the self is a means to become "master of oneself" (*E* 260), to permit individuals "to effect, by their own means, a certain number of operations on their own bodies, their own souls, their own thoughts, their own conduct, and this in a manner so as to transform themselves" (*E* 177; *HS II* 67). Although the care of the self "will be beneficial to others," it remains "centered entirely on oneself, on what one does, on the place one occupies among others" (*E* 289). At its heart is "askesis"—the ascetic-like training of the self by the self in order "to seek the object within the self in relation to oneself, . . . to escape dependence and enslavements, . . . to turn away from preoccupations of the external world" (*HS II* 64–66). Ethics are thus "relations with oneself" (*E* 263, 318), in a rhetoric that emerges as decisively aesthetic, where aesthetics are closely linked to asceticism. Thus, Foucault speaks of an "art of governing" (*E* 287; cf. *HS I* 149), an "art of existence (*HS II* 43). Self-mastery is the "art of man" (*HS II* 144), and ascetic self-training is an "art of living" (*E* 208). The effort "to create ourselves as a work of art" (*E* 261–262), an "art of the self" within a "general practice of self-control and self-enjoyment" (*HS II* 238). Baudelaire becomes Foucault's hero of modernity, in the "dandyisme" that "makes of his body, his behavior . . . his very existence, a work of art" (*E* 311–312). "Baudelaire does not imagine that these have any place in society itself or in the body politic," but "can only be produced in another, a different place, which Baudelaire calls art" (*E* 312). On this model, Foucault extends dandyism from art to self and society. The aesthetic, the ethical, and the political are superimposed, with art a kind of exclusionary self-reference that is embraced as the ultimate model. Opposed to society, art is conceived as anti-institutional, "anarchic,"[24] closely akin to madness (*A* 339–340) and to the abnormals (*E* 51) of Foucault's earliest work.

Brooks opens other directions for both ethics and art, even within her recognition of disciplinary force and critique of it. As in Foucauldian discourses, freedom of the self occurs through interstices, intersections, the multiplicity of social participation, and the variety of the interrelations in which each self is involved. Such multiplicity is emphasized by Foucauldian feminists,[25] although Foucault associates multiplicity with the coercive multiplication of power strategies as well as with resistances to them (*DP* 138, 209; *HS I* 30; *P/K* 142). But a more ethically relational model of multiplicity can be constructed. Each self is inevitably multiply inscribed in varied relationships, and in multiple stances between and also within selves: confrontational and confirming, antagonistic and augmenting,

160   *Feminist Theory across Disciplines*

amplifying and refining. This does not dissolve the self but rather constitutes it in constant negotiations, continuities, and conflicts. The lack of a fixed or an essential self does not give rise to pure performativity in Judith Butler's sense, as a free self-construction from moment to moment. What is crucial is not a unity, but a uniqueness of the self. Out of many intersections, each self uniquely arises. This is what makes possible critical stances toward experiences, including instituted and disciplined ones, both in the self's relation to itself and in the self's relation to others. Yet critique itself, in Brooks, proceeds from devotion, engagement, attachment, and forms of relation that strengthen and positively define, and not only confine, the self uniquely and changingly negotiating among his and her complex situation. These are linked to creativity in art. In Brooks, the self is foundationally a self-in-community. The focus is not on self-determination as self-mastery, but selfhood as defined and acted through, and in relation to, a myriad of commitments and relations out of which the self has grown and which in turn she can shape. Brooks recalls core movements in feminist moral theory, whose central concern has been a reimagining of the self in relational terms.[26] It is a self that is inscribed within relationships, which in turn then extends into community. Self-definition emerges as intimately linked to and through others, situated within attachments, commitments, and obligations in concrete historical and cultural life: as coercion, as well as critique, creation, and assertion.

Art in Brooks is a pivotal image for this creative commitment/transformation—an art that, especially in Brooks's early work, was deeply immersed in traditional poetic forms that she both employed and transformed. As we have seen in Brooks as in other poets, this image of art is closely linked to that of motherhood—a figure of creativity and also constraint. Motherhood is not a universal category in Brooks but is rather specifically situated in her historical and African-American contexts, where, as Patricia Hill Collins discusses, motherhood is less privatized, more communal and seen as a basis of political self-definition and not only as exploitative and restrictive.[27] Brooks's "Sonnet-Ballad" (*B* 112) dramatizes the situatedness of motherhood in the severest circumstances of war:

> Oh mother, mother, where is happiness?
> They took my lover's tallness off to war,
> Left me lamenting. Now I cannot guess
> What I can use an empty heart-cup for.
> He won't be coming back here any more.
> Some day the war will end, but, oh, I knew
> When he went walking grandly out that door
> That my sweet love would have to be untrue.
> Would have to be untrue. Would have to court
> Coquettish death, whose impudent and strange
> Possessive arms and beauty (of a sort)

Can make a hard man hesitate—and change.
And he will be the one to stammer, "Yes."
Oh mother, mother, where is happiness?

The appeal to the mother frames this poem in something like a refrain, making the sonnet a kind of chiasm with the first and last lines the outward frame and the "would have to be untrue / would have to be untrue" at the center, as the pivot around which the sonnet turns. Brooks's extreme formal mastery is evident here. What the cry to the mother frames is, as in other historicist poems, the incursion of the battle front into the home. This is firstly psychological. The male lover is defined through "tallness," "walking grandly," and "hard," all images (metonyms) for a masculinity that seeks self-assertion and independence. His central action of going "off to war" is a further form of these drives, with the result of severing attachments. Masculine selfhood is a venture that cuts off ties to others. He goes off to "court" war's violence, personified and eroticized as "Coquettish death," making conquest fatal. The domestic image of the woman's world as a "heart-cup" links bodily emotion with the warmth of the kitchen. The cup stands for containment and shared commensibility, and perhaps also domestic sexuality. It is abandoned for public life as masculine combat and conquest, tall, grand, and (erotically) hard. The chiasmic cry to the mother at the opening and end cannot contain these masculine energies of the self, which break into the world of relationship as destructive of both love and selfhood.

Women's poetry can offer acute angles into the Foucauldian "question of the self: its dependence and independence" (*HS II* 238). Acknowledging the force of Foucaudian discipline, no one discipline or network of disciplines fully determines a self. Each self in fact has many affiliations. That is the self's uniqueness. This multiplicity may, as Foucault argues, leave open gaps between disciplinary coercions. They may also weave a unique web of positive identifications, with the self not merely resisting but negotiating among them. In Brooks, the poet figure represents such multiplicity as a possibility of agency that is not only negatively disciplinary or a resistance to institutional associations. Brooks ventures forthrightly into political activism and ethical terrain. Strongly protesting and resisting oppressive social institutions, Brooks still affirms the growth of the self out of, and not only against, the communities and commitments that situate it in ways that Foucault never really does. The poet-as-self reflects and addresses, pulls against and reaches toward, her surrounding historical and cultural exigencies. She imagines unique and agent selfhood as inscribed within and positively drawing strength from its social worlds, even as she seeks to transform them.

8 Feminist Poetics and Aesthetic Theory

Feminist poetics has meant, first, locating gender on the map of traditional literary concerns. How is gender represented? What are the places and possibilities of women authors and readers? But this introduction of gender also implies an altered aesthetics. The inclusion of gender propels different parameters for understanding textuality as such: what constitutes a literary artwork and analytic engagements with it. Recognizing gender as a dimension that must be considered in textual encounter, as fundamental to textual constitution and experience, has aesthetic consequences.

The aesthetic assumptions that dominated poetics in the twentieth century have been largely formalist.[1] Roman Jakobson can be taken as a presiding figure. His formalist distribution of constitutive textual structures defined the poetic as exactly what did not refer beyond its own composition.[2] Jakobson's systematic charting of the linguistic act as distributed among reference (context), addresser, addressee, contact, code, and then "message" as the compositional linguistic structure, defined the aesthetic proper as subordinating interests from all other functions, to focus on language alone within the text's own construction, ultimately pointing back to itself.

Such aesthetic self-reference has been challenged by a variety of contemporary approaches, notably Culture Studies. Yet Culture Studies tends to privilege ideological and historical formations, subordinating textual composition to these as their manifestation. Instead, however, of defining aesthetics in exclusionary terms—whether these are historicist or formalist—aesthetics can be seen as a domain of mutual interrelationship among the variable functions that go into its constitution and experience. In such a relational aesthetic theory, Jakobson's functions become mutually referring. The aesthetic dimension becomes defined not as the *exclusion* of every other function or element, to focus on the self-referring art object, but rather as the *inclusion* of multiple terms of speaker and audience, contact and context in its many aspects and dimensions. The aesthetic would not subordinate or detach from other references, interests, events, addresses, and receptions to the self-consciousness of the artwork's own composition but would exactly project the interrelationship among the various functions and the domains they address, engage, and concern as making up and marking the composition of the text. The artwork would not bracket out addresser and addressee, context, reference, contact, and code but would actively invoke each (although not always or equally all) of these dimensions, bringing them into interplay and interrelationship in a variety of connections and modes of interaction.

Considerations of gender impel and require such a relational aesthetic. Gender introduces a fundamental dimension into any art composition, implicating speaker and audience, imagery, and a wide range of representations: of the body, sexuality, gender-specified experiences, or locations, as these have been historically defined.[3] But gender also breaks the boundaries of experiential and disciplinary domains. Gender is a social, cultural, and historical category, with anthropological, psychological, and political dimensions. The text, in incorporating gender, necessarily incorporates material, historical, and social locations, cultural paradigms, as well as ethical and political norms and configurations. These conditions mark women's texts—as they also do men's in ways, however, that the attention to gender brings forward and underscores, and which may be (have been) overlooked or denied. Once gender is admitted as a constitutive element in textual formation, the text necessarily is seen to engage a wide range of domains.

This introduction of gender as a category of aesthetic analysis thus challenges the notion of aesthetics as a separate and self-defined sphere. The text instead emerges as an intersecting site of multiple domains and discourses. In fact, one can claim that this is the specific power of art: to bring into contact and mutual interrogation the variety of domains of experience and discourses: history, politics; philosophy, psychology; religion, as each may situate or enter into a text. Literature in this sense may be called a discourse of discourses, a language space in which different realms, positions, and their articulation are able to encounter conflict, dialogue, confrontation, disputation, and confirmation. The literary text offers a space for the encounter and interrelation among a wide range of domains. None of these can simply be reduced to any other, although the question of domination may be prominent in a given text and may be part of any textual encounter.

These diverse interests and references take their place in the artwork as compositional elements. Form does not counter or deny other constitutive aesthetic terms but rather becomes the scene of their contact or confrontation. The interrelationships into which they are drawn, moreover, take on in poetry a particular character, that of figural relationship: elements become figures for each other. The specific mode in poetics that governs the relationality among domains is the mode of figuration. Poetic language is figural language. Whatever enters a poetic text enters and performs as figures. In poetics, textual terms open into multiple, intersecting, and cross-cutting likenesses and unlikenesses, repetitions and contrasts, representations, augmentations, negations, and retractions. This is the way in which poetry brings diverse areas of experience into mutual interrogation, confirmation, and disputation; by bringing each term, drawn from a variety of positions and contexts, into figural relation to the others, each becoming a figure for—or against or with—the others, across various domains in their shifting relationships to each other.

Thus, contrary to defining aesthetics as a space of detachment enclosed within its own structures and compositional elements, poetry exactly brings varieties of elements into figural relationships with each other. The aesthetic experience offers a mutually referring, relational trajectory between and among its compositional elements, whose meanings open from and toward (and away from) each other, such that each term is a figure, in complex lines of connection and contest for and with each other.

This textuality as a relational and multi-dimensional encounter, interrogation, and renegotiation is both dramatized and impelled by feminist poetics. Gender emerges as deeply converse to enclosure. It opens the text into the different spaces that gender inhabits, bringing them in as textual elements and not only as references. Gender implicates psychology and history, politics and religion, anthropology and ideology. Its recognition as a textual constituent opens the text into these fields, with gender an ineradicable category of analysis. Such analysis extends through the domains engaged in the text and into the contexts of textual production and experience, the histories and cultures of its authorship, circulation, and audience. Feminist poetics thus opens a path between formalism and historicity, the divided ways of aesthetic theory.

Two strong critical trends can be drawn on toward developing such a relational aesthetics, which, rather than being split between formal and historicist interests, sees art as exactly their mutual address: the Bakhtinian and the Derridean theoretical discourses. Both Bakhtin and Derrida have been influential in feminist theory. But their critical implications can be further developed, both regarding gender, even where they do not address gender (as Bakhtin in fact does not[4]) and beyond the uses that have been made of them thus far. Bakhtinian discourse theory opens the text to multi-domainal encounters, whereas Derridean sign theory offers discussions of the figural status of language that clarify the specifically literary and aesthetic relationalities among different domains within textual composition.

The entry of gender into poetics alters the field of aesthetics. It also recasts the discussion of gender. Rigid lines that have been assigned to women, in both social and literary terms, are challenged when women's texts are approached and recognized as a relational field of multiple domains. Divisions especially between public and private fail to hold. The relegation of women to a private sphere separated from public ones has not only historical, anthropological, philosophical, political, and ethical implications, but also aesthetic ones, exactly in insisting on the interrelation among these diverse domains. Different arenas intercross within literary (as also other) aesthetics in ways that women's writing, exactly as it engages gender as a multi-domainal formation, underscores. In literature, traditional boundaries of gender are exposed and crossed, not least the boundary of public and private realms. Literature, including poetry, has been, as we have seen throughout this study, one of the central forums in which women have participated in public discourses as well as reflecting on them. A feminist poetic exposes gender as a social and public formation, with art among its most powerful representations. A feminist poetics self-consciously redraws lines between public and private as between other arenas whose boundaries become revised or challenged in the interrelationships that constitute art. This public discourse of poetry in its gendered and aesthetic implications can be examined and exemplified in the poetry of Marianne Moore.

CULTURE STUDIES

Culture Studies in particular has challenged the tenets of aestheticism as a formal, detached, and autonomous realm. Insisting on art as a cultural practice and not an autonomous formal object, cultural critics redraw lines between formalism and historicity. As Stephen Greenblatt describes it, a "poetics of culture" negotiates and exchanges among "contingent social practices," examining "how the boundaries were marked between cultural practices understood to be art forms and other, contiguous forms of expression."[5] This has been a major impulse in feminist criticism. Judith Lowder Newton sums up, New Historicism methodology involves the "juxtaposition of cultural texts" and the "reading of cultural codes . . . in a cross cultural montage [encompassing] academic disciplines, advertising, sex manuals, popular culture, diaries, political manifestoes, literature, and political movements and events." Lowder further underscores that feminist work in fact antedates New Historicism in often unacknowledged ways, in its interests in political, social, and historical construction, and feminism continues to overlap and intersect with New Historicist emphases and practices.[6]

Yet tensions remain strong between formal and political interests within cultural treatments of poetics. Raymond Williams's definition of "aesthetics" in *Keywords* emphasizes its sense of "isolated subjective sense-activity as the basis of art and beauty as distinct, for example, from social or cultural interpretations." Or, as he writes in *Marxism and Literature*, aesthetics and art "separate themselves, by ever more absolute abstraction, from the social processes within which they are still contained."[7] Terry Eagleton recounts how traditions of aesthetic theory, although grounded in the social-historical body, persistently tie aesthetics to an idealist, ahistorical formalism, tracing its course from what he calls Kant's "full-blown formalism" through Schiller, into symbolist poetry as being "in the presence of pure eidetic forms of language itself, purged of any determinate semantic substance." He concedes that, if not Marx, then Marxists tend to reduce "the internal complexity of the aesthetic to a direct set of ideological functions," a complexity he sets out to recover.[8] Yet Eagleton's account remains caught in the dualist construction that he seeks to overcome, with the formal remaining a mode of ahistorical abstraction complicit with "the subjectivism of bourgeois culture." Aesthetics emerges as the self-evasion of coercive ideology, "an isolated enclave within which the dominant social order can find an idealized refuge from its own actual values of competitiveness, exploitation and material possessiveness."[9] Social order is conceived as Foucaldian domination that art can only either reflect or evade. As form, art withdraws in either complicity or conformity to society's dominant modes.[10]

Thus, formalism continues association with aesthetic autonomy, whereas cultural aesthetics subordinates aesthetics to politics. As Winfried Fluck has argued, Cultural Studies tends to "erase the differences between politics and aesthetics so that literary texts can have a direct political function and the profession of literary criticism can be redefined as political work."[11] Priority is granted to the political domain, which is understood as Foucauldian domination and its resistance. Art is caught within dominant "institutional or disciplinary frameworks," which it resists by countering "hegemonic social formations" through withdrawal from them.[12] Literary structures are either assimilated to ideological ones or seen to be shaped through resistance to them. As one critic puts it, Foucauldian-based poetics sets out to explore "the possibilities for exchanges among disparate fields" in order to expose "the political interests masked by our ideas about order."[13]

But as Rita Felski argues about feminist aesthetics, which can be extended to aesthetics in general, "to simply read literary texts in terms of their fidelity to a pregiven notion of female experience or feminist ideology is in effect to deny any specificity to literary language and meaning, rendering literature redundant by reducing it to a purely documentary function as a more or less accurate reproduction of an already existing . . . political reality."[14] Max Weber's remark about religion also applies to literature: that it is mistaken to think it is "a simple 'function' of the social situation of the stratum which appears as its characteristic bearer, or that it represents the stratum's 'ideology,' or that it is a 'reflection' of a stratum's material or ideal interest-situation."[15]

BAKHTINIAN POETICS

Bakhtinian theory, including feminist discussions of it, has largely been pursued in Foucauldian directions. Bakhtinian feminist criticism often dualizes dialogics into opposing power relations of authority as against subversion, disciplinary order as against revolt, obedience as against resistance. To Dale Bauer, for example, society is a "hierarchical structure" like Foucault's "agencies of power." Participation requires "obeying community rules" while even "resistance can also be appropriated into the interpretive community, manipulated or reabsorbed into community." Resistance alone is creative, and even "resistance can be appropriated." Teresa De Lauretis too speaks of "strategies of writing and reading" as "forms of cultural resistance."[16] There is in fact a tendency to dualize language into a resistant, often anarchic "woman's language" as opposed to restrictive socialized discourses. This dualization can be especially seen in French Feminism's *écriture féminine*, identified with a pre-Oedipal nonrational language as against a structured masculine language of socialized coercion. *Écriture féminine* has been widely critiqued as unhistorical and also restrictive in its approach to women's writing.[17] As Rita Felski sums up, feminist theory threatens to "reduplicate existing disciplinary splits" between "an empirically based sociology or history on the one hand and a purely textualist literary theory on the other."[18]

This tendency to see "strategies of writing and reading" only as "forms of cultural resistance" ultimately narrows definitions of women's languages.[19] The model of a "split between the authoritative and the internally persuasive, between the desire to conform and the desire to resist," implies a dualistic opposition between an inner self as against an outer society.[20] But Bakhtin's work forcefully questions such dualism of inner against outer, self against society. Bakhtin's critique of Freud, for example, is based on just such suspicion of "subjectivity at the expense of community."[21] Much feminist criticism similarly posits a sense of voice as social and even "collective" rather than private and autonomous.[22] Yet the reassertion of social constitution often reverses into a problematic of the material determination of selfhood, leaving unclear how there can be any self at all: "The woman is likely to be at a loss to know whether she's using her own language or the language ascribed to her by culture." This formulation continues to assume an "own" language as against language in "culture."[23] It in effect retains what is a romanticist notion of the individual as self-constituted even while arguing for a socialized sense of the self. It is as if some self-determined "authentic" romantic voice has been betrayed by social coercion rather than emerging from complex interchanges that partly differ from and partly draw on social norms.

Especially theoretical arguments of a woman's counter-language as the avenue for feminist discourse threaten to restrict, prescribe, and proscribe the sorts of language that is feminine. Describing women's language as a "place of absence," which refuses to "assume the authority of logical discourse" in order to escape "the hierarchy of the official language" fails to address the works women have written and in many ways confines them to the silence that feminist discussion is protesting.[24] These arguments emerge in the writings of Jane Gallop, Alice Jardine, Luce Irigray, and Julia Kristeva.[25]

Julia Kristeva, educated in Bulgaria, is especially significant as being among the first writers to bring Bakhtin to the West and to introduce him into feminist discussion. In her treatment, the notion of a feminine counter-language as against "official" discourse takes, however, a psychoanalytic turn exactly away from Bakhtin's own social and political analysis. As against a

168 *Feminist Theory across Disciplines*

Laconian "Symbolic" father-language that in many way parallels Bakhtinian official discourse, Kristeva posits a pre-Oedipal mother-language. Antecedent to the logical structures of a 'masculine' discourse, this language is pre-logical and material, based in rhythm and sound in bodily ways.

This schema is troubling on many fronts. It ascribes an essential gendering to psychological structures and phases, rather than seeing gender as socially assigned. Gender here shapes selves into a priori structures that reflect gendered assumptions in circular ways. But gender is not only treated as if it were natural description rather than an assigned—and highly axiological—construction. In Kristeva, gendered characteristics remain restrictive and prejudicial. Kristeva defines the pre-Oedipal, feminine "semiotic" language as rhythmic, phonemic, material, repetitive, and alogical. This then is projected as poetic language. Semiotic language ruptures the communicative symbolic order, in an upsurge of drives, instincts, and the repressed. But this model is highly dualistic. It restricts as 'feminine' one sort of language use, reserving other kinds of language as not feminine. In this, Kristeva is both theoretically prescriptive and unempirical since many (most) women do not write *Écriture feminine*. Indeed, Kristeva's poetic models are largely men. The writers she privileges are Joyce and other male modernists.

Kristeva projects her poetics as a political one, of revolutionary incursion into the bourgeois social order (*Revolution* 15, 79). Ironically, however, she points back to an ahistorical formalism. Kristeva's semiotic, like Jakobson's poetic, "tends towards autonomy from meaning so as to maintain itself in a semiotic disposition near the instinctual drives' body" (*Desire* 135). In her application, Bakhtinian multi-voicedness becomes "intertextuality" as semiological system, "an intersection of textual surfaces" where "history and society" are "seen as texts read by the writer, and into which he inserts himself by rewriting them." As she puts it in *Revolution in Poetic Language*, "The term intertextuality denotes this transposition of one (or several) sign-systems into another. . . . Every signifying practice is a field of transpositions of various signifying systems (an intertextuality)."[26] Polysemy is reduced to relations among terms as transposed within "signifying systems," restoring the formalist closure Bakhtin had so powerfully opened.[27] In Kristeva, this is tied to a general ahistoricizing tendency, evident as well in her textual psychoanalytics. She sees the poetic text as "suspending the present moment," as an "upheaval of present place and meaning." Associated with the pre-Oedipal, alogical semiotic, the poetic "sign" is "deeply indicative of the instinctual drives' activity relative to the first structurations (constitution of the body as self) and identifications (with the mother)." Thus, poetic language "frees speech from historical constraint."[28] In terms of its political agency, Nancy Fraser argues that Kristeva's "structuralist model that treats language as a symbolic system or code" remains "static, unhistorical, and abstract," with Kristeva's ultimately a dualistic system that tends "to valorize transgression and innovation per se irrespective of social content." Thus, it cannot engage in the "reconstructive moment of feminist politics, a moment essential to social transformation."[29] In the end, Kristevan poetics uncannily reproduces Jakobsonian categories of poetic function as nontransparent, nonreferential, and against language in its communicative function.[30]

Écriture feminine has been widely critiqued as unhistorical and problematic for feminism.[31] Many question what political agency *Écriture feminine* makes possible.[32] Others warn against assuming direct linkage "between transgressive textual practices or experiments and feminist politics, or even women." As Rita Felski points out, an "abstract conception of a 'feminine' writing practice" hinders "adequate assessment" of contemporary feminist writing.[33] A split between feminine transgressive, as opposed to ordinary social discourses, reopens within feminist Bakhtinian theory as well. But Bakhtin's own writings are less dualized. He does not define individual linguistic acts in dualistic opposition against social discourse, as if this were unitary, but posits multiple linguistic events in multiple relationships. These include critique and rebellion, but also investment, affirmation, and intensification. "Within the arena of almost every utterance an intense interaction and struggle between one's own and another's word is being waged," he writes, but adds that this is "a process in which they oppose or dialogically interanimate each other" (*DI* 354). "Interanimation" in Bakhtin does not just mean opposition and struggle. There can also be dialogical "agreement, affirmation."[34] Language, as Bakhtin (with Saussure) emphasizes, is by definition social and inherited. No one merely invents the words he or she uses. Words are always embedded in contexts, situations, a history of usages. But this is not a barrier to personal creativity and expression. On the contrary, it is its ground: "Language is inherited: it becomes one's own only when the speaker populates it with his own intention, his own accent, when he appropriates the word, adapting it to his own semantic and expressive intention" (*DI* 293). Bakhtin does not see community as necessarily erasing selfhood but rather as the matrix out of which any self emerges. His work opens avenues into linguistic/social community, drawing on its resources as the energy of new creation. No voice is simply monological, however much it wishes to claim, achieve, or impose unitary meaning. But this lack of unity is the possibility, not the defeat, of aesthetic creativity.

As feminists argue, literature, discourse itself, is social, historical, and political. But that is not all it is. Bakhtin does not eliminate, nor does he reduce an aesthetic dimension to, culture or cultural conflict. Josephine Donovan, rightly associating Bakhtin with Marxist insistence that literature "exists in a political context and therefore literary devices reflect and refract the power differentials of the author's society," goes on to observe that "style is not innocent or neutral—i.e. purely aesthetic."[35] But the "aesthetic" need not be defined as "neutral." Nor does it entail eliminating or denying political context. At the same time, "literary devices" do not reflect and refract "power differentials" alone. Instead, the aesthetic brings the political into configuration with other dimensions, through both the interweaving and counter-weaving of its discourses with others.

Bakhtin's own theory opens the text to historical, social, and ideological engagements and does so in ways that sees the text in multi-relational rather than only politicized structures, introducing critical tools that define and examine the textual performance of these multiple terms. Bakhtin's discourse theory treats every word as drawing into the text its contextual settings and past usages, its political, ideological, and historical roles and senses, in the disputes and agreements, contests and redefinitions words have enacted in multiple exchanges. The relationships that emerge include not only domination and resistance but also investment, affirmation, intensification, modification, and transformation.

Bakhtin restricted his discourse theory to the novel, regarding poetry, as he repeatedly states, as a purely "extra-historical language, a language far removed from the petty rounds of everyday life, a language of the gods" (*DI* 331). For the novel, this formalist view combined in Bakhtin with Marxist historicism, transforming Jakobson's formalist categories into interactive events within concrete contexts and situations in open and unfinished exchanges. As Tzvetan Todorov explicates, Bakhtin's theories redirected formalist analysis of language as signs governed within systematic structural relationships, to regard texts instead as dynamic moments in exchanges situated in history and culture.[36] Bakhtin, however, never abandoned the formalist definition of poetry as a pure language dissociated from the everyday cultural exchanges he saw as constituting discourse in the novel. In the novel, words dialogically address, contest, invoke, and revoke each other across a range of usages and contexts. But the poetic "word is sufficient unto itself and does not presume alien utterances beyond its own boundaries. Poetic style is by convention suspended from any mutual interaction with alien discourse, any allusion to alien discourse" (*DI* 285).

But, contra Bakhtin, poetry is not "a unitary, monologically sealed-off utterance" that uses words so "they lose their link with concrete intentional levels of language and their connection with specific contexts" (*DI* 297–298). On the contrary, poetic language is heterogeneous, even while certain poetic periods, such as the neoclassical, tend to stylize language toward uniform registers. On the one hand, in poetry, words are excised from context, thrown onto the blankness of the page. On the other hand, the words bring into the text all the links, usages, and etymologies that interconnect them to general circulation. Words are at once released and tied, excised and reset, in ways that instead of erasing contexts can radicalize the text as a space of juxtaposition. Words become intensely inscribed in new combinations with other words, bringing their contexts and senses into radical recombinations that remain in many ways open-ended.

Bakhtin's term "microdialogue" points to such recombinatory poetics of the word: "relationships can permeate inside the utterance, even inside the individual word, as long as two voices collide within it dialogically (microdialogue)" (*Dost* 184). In microdialogue, even the individual poetic word becomes a dialogized site, such that, as in the novel, "each word tastes of the context and contexts in which it has lived its socially charged life; all words and forms are populated by intentions" (*DI* 293). The poetic word, too, imports "contexts" of the word's "socially charged life" into the text, in open and unfinalized conjunctions. Every word that enters a poem is drawn from some domain that it carries into the poem, where it resides alongside other words, likewise drawn from, and drawing with them, contexts of usage as well. These juxtapositions create dialogical relationships regardless of whether they are voiced through a character, although for Bakhtin, character is central to novelistic heteroglassia.[37] What creates poetic meaning is the relationships between the words, which includes sound, rhythm, and other material strata but also contexts and histories that situate and mark each word and are then imported through the word into the text.

Bakhtin's notion of speech genres extends the implications of microdialogue. He describes speech genres as a "diversity of generic forms of utterances in various spheres of human activity," such as "chronicles, contracts, texts of laws, clerical and other documents, various literary, scientific and commentarial genres, official and personal letters, rejoinders in everyday dialogue and so on."[38] Speech genres invoke the discourses of social groups (*DI* 289–290) as well as ideologies, world views, beliefs, and understandings—"the expressive planes of various belief systems." They include "bookish speech, popular speech, scientific, journalistic commercial, . . . as well as . . . stylistic subcategories: dialectical words, archaic words, occupational expressions" (*SG* 64–65). Words address and have addresses—places where they are characteristically encountered, where they historically, socially, and culturally are to be found, within the "particular real conditions of speech communication." The meaning of a word is then not fixed and given but always within "an active responsive position with respect to it (sympathy, agreement, stimulus to action)" (*SG* 86).

Bakhtinian aesthetics is thus invitational and not exclusionary of domains of experience and the languages of their conduct, in multiple responses including 'agreement' and 'sympathy' as well as contest and resistance. Audience and author, history and culture and politics, textual circulation and distribution all engage each other through the formal distributions of the words drawn from each domain, in ways that change in relation to each other as much as these positions do. Not detachment or self-enclosure, but such multiplication of its component relationships, constitutes the aesthetic.

Literature as discourse is social, historical, and political. But it shapes these in formal ways. Bakhtin does not eliminate or reduce an aesthetic dimension to politics, culture, or cultural conflict. The Bakhtinian aesthetic instead brings the political into configuration with other dimensions, through both the interweaving and counter-weaving of its discourses with others.

DERRIDA: FIGURAL THEORY AND HISTORICITY

If Bakhtinian theory is often aligned with historicist analysis as power relationships, deconstructive theory is characteristically seen as isolated from historicist, cultural, and political interests. Paul De Man, for example, argues for an unappeasable opposition between "trope" and "dialogism." "Trope" is "self-reflexive, autotelic," saying "something about language rather than about the world," whereas "dialogism" ventures to address the ideological, social, exterior, and heterogeneous world.[39] De Man specifically opposes deconstruction against Bakhtinian dialogics, seeing the first as positing unanchored signifiers, the second as engagement among discourses. This opposition is common. Bakhtin is political and social, whereas deconstructive signifiers, commonly associated with Derrida, point to each other in a linguistic world cut off from anything beyond or outside it.[40] As Allon White puts it, Bakhtin rescues literature from ahistoricism by placing it "in a sociological framework which thereby makes [it] responsive to an historical and social comprehension of literature," whereas Derrida's deconstruction is "purely metaphysical . . . insulated from the transformative and conflictual social arena of speech events."[41]

This aesthetic of enclosure reappears in feminist discussions, where Derrida's work is both enlisted and resisted in ways that can only be touched on here. The restaging in French feminism's *Écriture feminine* of the break between historicity and linguistic analysis involves not only a certain reading of psychoanalysis but also a certain application of deconstruction. French feminist theory not only isolates "woman's language" from culture and history but sees deconstruction, in Derrida and others, as placing it in a nonreferential intradiscourse, opposed to the logic of masculinity.

But deconstruction as a theory of signifiers is not necessarily disengaged and autotelic. It offers, rather, a theory of figures that redefines how signifiers mean both within the text and in relationship to contexts. In Derrida, the denial of the "signified" as "literal" does not deny signification, nor does it simply disjoin signifier from historicity, materiality, culture, or politics. Rather, Derridean sign theory points avenues toward linking historicity to textuality in ways that productively conjoin with Bakhtin's. In Bakhtin, compositional elements carry into the text the associations, contexts, and usages they have outside it. Yet what happens to them within the poetic textual frame is still distinctive in ways that Derridean theory illuminates: they take on figural meanings. Analysis of relationship among textual elements characteristically pulls toward textual isolation. Derridean theory of figuration, however, acts, like Bakhtin's, to link textual elements to the signifying chains of which they remain part.

Derrida's own writings cross a daunting range of disciplines: philosophy, psychology, law, politics, literature, and art. This cross-disciplinary practice also penetrates his sign theory and is intrinsic to his notions of signs and their meanings. Derrida educes historicist interpenetrations of signification. In his "Interview" in *Acts of Literature*, he insists that his notion of "iterability" is "historical through and through," is "the condition of historicity."[42] In *Speech and Phenomena*, he speaks of the sign as "always connecting empirical existents in the world," insisting that the "body of speech, in empirically determined language," is not "foreign to the nature of expression."[43]

Derrida's approach to the sign as diacritical inscription of likeness and difference, articulation and deferral, embeds meaning in processes of temporality, mutability, and multiplicity. These are the conditions of history as the site of meaning and the forms of historical process, and it is exactly such historicity of meaning that Derrida's sign theory formulates. The sign comes to mean through its changing relationships with signifiers before and after it, in an ongoing articulation of difference and connection. As trace, the sign only signifies within chains of displacement, deferral, and transference that at once differentiate and link and thus define signs in relation to each other. "The absence of the referent and even of the signified sense" entails not the collapse of sense but rather its relocation within "chains of differential marks," which extend into "all 'experience' in general."[44] As Diane Elam underscores, Derridean indeterminacy "is not the same thing as being condemned to the land of relativistic nihilism, where political action—or any action for that matter—becomes impossible."[45] Derrida insists on the importance of "context" in the title of his essay, "Signature, Event, Context," which projects a notion of situated signification: "identity can only determine or delimit itself through differential relations to other elements." Pre-given and fixed meaning is denied, but other meanings are opened through differential relations that multiply but also delimit signification, exactly as embedded in relationships within contexts. "The role of context is determinant . . . the contextual difference here may be fundamental and cannot be shunted aside." In his subsequent defense of "Signature Event Context," he reiterates that

> the written sytagma can always be detached from the chain in which it is inserted or given. . . . And in so doing, [the sign] can break with every context, engendering an infinity of new contexts in a manner which is absolutely illimitable. [But] this does not imply that the mark is valid outside of a context, but on the contrary that there are only contexts without any center or absolute anchoring.[46]

The signifier, emerging in various relations from and within a "chain" of signifiers, can always also be "detached" from one chain and "inserted" into others. This is in fact how language works, how the ability to create new utterances is possible ("without iterability there is no language at all") (*LTD* 244). Language only means in context, but these contexts are never final, and so meaning multiplies through new interreferences among the signifiers in the specific chains that repeatedly but differently locate them.

The result is multiple, although not unsituated, senses for signifiers. As Derrida writes in *Acts of Literature*:

> We have available contextual elements of great stability (not natural, universal and immutable but fairly stable, and thus also destabilizable) which . . . allow reading, transformation, transposition. There is possible play, with regulated gaps and interpretive transformations . . . [a] spacing between the pieces . . . which allows for movement and articulation, which is to say for history, for better or for worse. (*Acts* 64)

Rather than defeating, destroying, or even releasing meaning into endless indeterminacy, Derridian sign chains situate by linking words to each other to produce meanings. "Contextual elements" give "stability" to signs, although not fixed unity—signs are "also destabilizable." The "play" is "regulated" and not merely dissolved through "interpretive transformations." This not only "allows for movement and articulation" and for "history" but insists on it. The Derridean sign chains thus propose not the dissolution of meaning but models of signification through trajectories of signifiers. What is required is to elaborate "The value of context . . . by means of a new logic, of a graphematics of iterability" in which one "can't determine meaning univocally" but rather in and through the multiple relationships of signifiers (*LTD* 219, 215).

To say that there is no "determinate signified" fully and finally established by either "referent" or "intention" radically points to a figural theory, with immediate implications for poetics. In poetry, the signifier as figure is specifically cultivated and intensified, brought into configuration across many dimensions, including different histories in which the art is experienced, created, and received. There is no signified "behind the utterances," in that signification is enacted through them (*LTD* 212). Rather, signifiers signify as they interrefer with other signifiers, each as figures for the others. Signifiers signify signifiers and in this way mean. Signification occurs through relationships of signifiers to other signifiers in an open-ended chain. But to be a sign for something else is to act as a figure for it.

Derrida here verges toward Bakhtin: on the one side, in historicist implications of Derridean theory, and, on the other, as formal implications of Bakhtin. Bakhtin, too, speaks of traces, links, and chains:

> The longer this [dialogical] stratifying saturation goes on, the broader the social circle encompassed by it and consequently the more substantial the social force bringing about such a stratification of language, then the more sharply focused and stable will be those traces, the linguistic changes in the language markers (linguistic symbols) that are left behind in the language as a result of this social force's activity. (*DI* 293)

Dialogical interchange ties words to each other and their exchanges, even as it permits multiple participation and accepts ongoing alteration—not as arbitrary fiat but as emerging from social discourse. In this defense of multiplicity as "stable," Bakhtin interestingly speaks of "traces": "the more sharply focused and stable will be those traces." These relational meanings open out along multiple axes, as each word participates not only in the chain of signs of a particular utterance but brings into that chain its associations with other signs in other linkages: in text or by context, in discursive field or disciplinary usage, or ordinary language or traditional convention. This extension is further developed in Bakhtin's discussions of speech genres. These project signification through (differentiating) linkage, of signifying chains in which meaning inheres not in unique terms but in their unfolding in relation to each other. Thus, in "The Problem of Speech Genres," Bakhtin speaks of utterance as "a link in a very complexly organized chain of utterances" (*SG* 69), a "link in the chain of speech communication" (*SG* 84, 91, 93). "The utterance is related not only to preceding, but also to subsequent links in the chain of speech communion" (*SG* 94). Conversely, Derrida projects the reiterated signifier as carrying with it its usages, associations, and echoes from context to context: "The import of context can never be dissociated from the analysis of a text, and that despite or because of this a context is always transformative, transformable, exportative-exportable" (*LTD* 212, 220). The senses of the signifier are exported as well as imported.

What emerges is meaning not defined by reference to something pre-established outside the text, nor is the text established as closed framework, with meaning the product of its mutual, self-referring signs. As figural chains, signifiers do refer to other signifiers, but these chains extend beyond the text into their histories, their cultural usages, their ideological implications, and their personal meanings. Signs thus do not displace history, culture, or the contexts in which they take place—the notion of displacement that causes the split life, the schizophrenic poetics that pits history against theory, cultural experience against textual components. On the contrary, signs presuppose just such contexts, even as they also articulate them. The text emerges out of interrelation between signifiers, both within and without the text, drawn from different domains that it then draws in, opening up new possible relations among them. As Marjorie Perloff comments, the Derridean "signature" as an "identifying mark" counters the "closural, first person metaphoric model" of poetry. Signature marks the specific configuration of a given text, in its relation to authorship and also its distinctive trajectory of signifiers that link elements within the text to those in its contexts.[47] Derridean theory discloses how contextual relationships are drawn into texts through the signifiers, linking as chains that extend into usage, history, and discourse, and how each signifier stands as a figure for the others. But this is not a static structure. "Signifier" can connote not an inert sign, but *signers*, active speakers and writers, readers and audience who participate in the construction and interpretation of signs, always also in relation to each other in the trajectory of signifying chains and events.

FEMINIST POETICS: MARIANNE MOORE

Bakhtin and Derrida together point toward a relational aesthetic that feminist poetics particularly enacts and develops. Gender calls for a relational aesthetic, first, because gender emerges and is recognized as constituting a distinctive dimension in any textual event, bringing others into relationship with it; and second because considerations of gender necessarily introduce further domains that enter textual constitution. In Bakhtinian terms, women can be recognized as what Bakhtin describes as "different strata of society" who use specified discourses "of educational, professional, and class differences."[48] Such feminized discourses in historical, social, and political senses draw into the text women's distinctive social experience, roles, locations, activities, and so on. Within the contours of the text, they then enter as signifiers into multiple figural relations such as Derrida traces, representing other textual dimensions in specific ways. Bakhtinian discourse theory of interaddressing language confirms the multiple contextual links that enter into texts and that, in Derridean terms, act as mutually referring signifiers across any number of domains that are thus brought into figural relationship with each other. That gender, like other signifiers, is not grounded within pre-given "signified" meanings but rather emerges in what Derrida calls in "Choreographies" a "multiplicity of sexually marked voices" is part of the renegotiation of the very meaning of gender in its multiple connections that literature both explores and furthers. Such renegotiations of meaning should not be taken as indeterminacy that erases context and hence meaning.[49] In placing gender as a signifier in a chain of differentials, Derrida does not simply unanchor but rather situates gender within chains of signification. Even while denying a "signified" pre-given meaning, these enchained signifiers nonetheless define contexts within which meanings take place. "Indeterminacy" in this way remains, as Derrida writes, "always a determinate oscillation between possibilities . . . that are themselves highly determined in defined situations."[50]

These two critical trends of discourse theory and deconstruction, when considered in terms of each other, help to construct a feminist poetics: that is, a poetics that is engaged with gender and the multiple dimensions this entails. Situational and figural, textual and contextual, feminist poetics particularly performs and requires a relational aesthetic theory beyond the dualisms of historicity and formalism, instead insisting on their mutual reference across a range of domains. The text is cast as a space of multiple encounters, drawing in a variety of discourses, not in detachment from them but as interrogating and interrelating among them, opening relationships between them as figural levels of meaning toward and against each other. Such an aesthetics is especially apt and urgent for approaching women's poetry since multiple domains of social, historical, political, religious, and material concerns are obtrusively the conditions in terms of which women have been defined and situated. Recognizing this recasts as well the opposition between public and private as applied to gender and gendered poetics. Multiple engagements and interaddresses among different domains in poetry, including speaker and audience as each is historically and culturally situated; the contacts between them and the codes they share; and the historical, political, and religious contexts that are active as references and figures within texts all open women's writing to a public dimension beyond any gendered privacy. This public dimension is explicit in much of American women's poetry during the nineteenth century and in the twentieth century in poets such as Rukeyser, Levertov, Rich, Brooks, Lorde, and Grahn, for whom political activism is a fundamental poetic energy. But poetry's public address need not be a question of direct public performance or reference; nor can poetry be simply reduced to political action or address.[51] Rather, poetry brings political as other social, historical, cultural domains into configuration with each other in poetic, which is to say figural, ways, working through modes of address, presentation of speakers, material language and its conducts, and other many different methods of representation.

Marianne Moore's writing affords a powerful case of such indirect as well as direct multi-domainal poetics and its public engagements. Formally experimental and radically eclectic, Moore is distinctive for the heterogeneity of materials she introduces into her texts, drawn from truly far-flung sources and discourses, elite and popular, scientific and documentary, and also religious and ethical. Hers is a fully Bakhtinian multiple discourse. Diverse materials are inscribed into her texts in ways that force attention to questions of the interrelationships among them as figures within the poem and then, via the poem, into large cultural arenas. Moore's work offers an intense and particular nexus among aesthetic, cultural, political, religious, and gendered dimensions.

Moore's multiple discourses have been much discussed in terms of her practices of quotation, collage, and mosaic. Cristanne Miller underscores how Moore's citations differ from those of other (male) modernists in being drawn from ordinary rather than canonical sources, giving "no elevation to her verse." Miller explicates them as egalitarian and collaborative, and indeed as Bakhtinian heteroglossia in a specifically feminist sense.[52] Moore critics have additionally and variously discussed the many different arenas that the poetry addresses: Moore's historical references and contexts, her political interests, her religious affiliations, her gender, and, extensively, the poetic practices in which she treats these.

This variety of engagements can in turn be seen as constituting a relational poetics: the way Moore's citations and indications invoke and engage multiple domains, and the way Moore shapes these as figures for each other.

178 *Feminist Theory across Disciplines*

Gender emerges as a catalyst and also penetrating dimension: at the least because Moore is a woman poet and highly conscious of this, even if she characteristically brings gender into her texts quite obliquely. The question of gender enters inevitably with regard to her own right of entry into the multiple figural relationships she launches, reflecting on what this participation by women's words as signifiers implies.

To take one poem as a text case: Moore's "Blessed Is the Man" (*CP* 173) brings together into its discourse fields an extraordinary range of citations, voices, references, and domains:

BLESSED IS THE MAN

who does not sit in the seat of the scoffer—
    the man who does not denigrate, depreciate, denunciate;
    who is not "characteristically intemperate,"
who does not "excuse, retreat, equivocate; and will be heard."

(Ah, Giorgione! There are those who mongrelize
    and those who heighten anything they touch; although it
        may well be

    that if Giorgione's self-portrait were not said to be he,
it might not take my fancy. Blessed the geniuses who know
that egomania is not a duty.)
    "Diversity, controversy, tolerance"—in that "citadel
    of learning" we have a fort that ought to armor us well.
Blessed is the man who "takes the risk of a decision"—asks

himself the question: "Would it solve the problem?
    is it right as I see it? Is it in the best interests of all?"[53]

A full explication of this text would be lengthy and exacting. Even in these opening verses, the political, the aesthetic, the educational, the civic, the religious, and, implicitly (or is it explicitly?), gender are brought to bear. The poem's title and first line cite the first Psalm; this religious reference is then at once brought into the political arena. The first, expressly marked quotations, in the Notes that Moore attached to her poems, refer to contemporary politics involving Eisenhower ("characteristically intemperate") and, significantly, to Abraham Lincoln.

"Excuse, retreat, equivocate; and will be heard" were the words with which William Lloyd Garrison announced his abolitionist campaign, cited in turn by Lincoln (a citation then cited by Moore) on inviting Garrison to the White House. Projected here then are questions of political debate and public service, as these in turn intersect (or fail to) with moral commitment and religious injunction, religion having been a powerful motive in the abolitionist movement and in America's public discourses at large.

The next stanza, in an apparent aside, turns to a different domain. "Ah, Giorgione!" invokes aesthetics by way of the master painter about whom least is known, whose work balances self-expression with mystery, and whose self-portrait is highly unidealized, a representation of self without inflation. Here is a genius who knows "that egomania is not a duty." This gesture of modesty is among Moore's most characteristic and passionate principles, enacted in her poetry in myriad figures, serving as a moral norm while also placing Moore in a tradition of women's self-representation.[54] Modesty is one way in which gender is signaled in this text. Interestingly, the citation of the First Psalm launches gender as masculine, naming "the man" as one "who does not sit in the seat of the scoffer." But one might venture that this "man" is (also) a woman, not in the generic sense but as endowed and defined against "egomania." This would apply to Lincoln in the public sphere and to preferred artists in the aesthetic one, including Moore as a female poet.

The several realms of aesthetics, politics, and gender become mutually figuring in ways that transform each as well as the profile of gender. Moore's intercrossing discourses challenge at once divisions between disparate fields, the place of art among them, as well as geographies of gender as these have been assigned or, rather, largely excluded from many areas and domains. Her citations and invocations of the Eisenhower and Lincoln presidencies, of abolitionism with its political, moral, and religious involvements, firmly place her as addressing and participating in public discourses—as political, moral, religious, and, as the poem affirms, aesthetic as well. Neither women nor poetry prove as private as they are regularly assumed to be.[55]

The next citations pursue such intercrossing of public life and gender with civic policy and pedagogy. The phrase "Diversity, controversy, tolerance" is taken from the also cited "Citadel of Learning," a work by James Conant who, after serving as president of Harvard, went to Berlin as U.S. High Commissioner. A review of this work had been the source, the Notes tell us, for the Lincoln citation of William Lloyd Garrison, a pattern of citation and notation enacting a chain of embedded and circulated discourses. Conant's *The Citadel of Learning* expressly discusses the academy as involved in and reflecting public life and responsibility. The "citadel" is armed against an authoritarianism that betrays the energies and purposes of education. "No one uses the word 'unity,'" he writes, "more frequently than those who are attempting to force Stalinist ideology." In opposition, he affirms that "freedom and tolerance go hand in hand in matters of the spirit." The "absence of dissenters" is dangerous. Creativity in fact flowers when there is "dissension." In the passage that Moore cites, Conant asserts the necessity of "diversity, controversy, and

180 *Feminist Theory across Disciplines*

tolerance [in] an intellectual atmosphere where vital differences of opinion are not merely tolerated but encouraged."[56]

The poem thus proposes and also enacts a discourse of address among pluralist positions as at once political, educational, public, religious, gendered, and aesthetic. These domains are also interconnected, in some cases directly but always figurally. Being a public person is posited as, in some ways, like being a painter, which is like being a writer. A certain kind of man can be like a certain kind of woman, both representing a modest ethics. Political leadership can be informed by religious principles. Each of these domains here acts as figures for the others, with none, however, simply reduced to the other. The figural relation also respects difference. The poem pursues this complex contrapuntal music of distinctive spheres. In the political domain, it poses the classic republican question: "Is it in the best interests of all?" (quoting then President Eisenhower). But the phrase "who takes the risk of a decision" is quoted, as the Notes clarify, from a discussion of poetry: "Poetry . . . must . . . take the risk of decision," "to say what we know, loud and clear—and if necessary ugly." Both politics and art require decision but not willful self-assertion. Thus, both are betrayed when

> Ulysses' companions are now political—
> living self-indulgently until the moral sense is drowned,
>
> having lost all power of comparison,
> thinking license emancipates one, "slaves whom they
> themselves have bound."
> Brazen authors, downright soiled and downright spoiled, as
> If sound
> and exceptional, are the old quasi-modish counterfeit . . . .

Here is betrayal of aesthetic, public, and moral principle. "Brazen authors" figure the indulgent selves who, in a republican discourse, sacrifice public for private interest: "private lies and public shame." Moore here invokes the tradition of civic virtue, with its concern against placing private liberty before public commitment. This is, in the poem's rhetoric of the American Revolution, to become "slaves whom they themselves have bound." Yet to praise "liberty" is not to assume that "license emancipates." Liberty is not mere license; not just everything is to be tolerated. The poem's blessing finely balances restraint with affirmation.

> Blessed, the unaccommodating man.
> Blessed the man whose faith is different
> from possessiveness—of a kind not framed by "things which
> do appear"—
> who wsill not visualize defeat, too intent to cower;
> whose illumined eye has seen the shaft that gilds the sultan's tower.

The poem at the end collects together its variant domains in further and different interrelationship. Religious discourse is reaffirmed, although it insists that to have "faith is different from possessiveness," different from claiming any single discourse as truth, to the exclusion of others. Rather, religion, as Moore suggests in another inserted citation, points to "a kind not framed 'by things which appear'" (*Hebrews* 11:3). Religion, like literature, promises dimensions beyond the immediately apparent, always pointing to further possible meanings and engagements. This is one import of the poem's concluding lines. The "sultan's tower" may refer to the opening of the *Rubaiyat of Omar Khayyam* as a kind of poetic vision. But "Sultan" also recalls the poem's political contexts. In either case, the tower remains a beckoning vision, ever distant, never finally possessed.

This poem as both event and aesthetic draws together multiple domains brought into relationship(s); relationships that mutually interact and refer; relationships that are both figural and intercrossing, public and private, each distinct, yet variously and intricately linked. This is also the poem's compositional art. Gender emerges as a central and formative dimension extending across other experiential arenas, situating positions within them and relationships among them. It becomes one fundamental voice within a diversity that the poem at once proposes and performs: the arena of discourses in which none is necessarily excluded but allows each one to be heard and addressed. Moore's poetic becomes a public-discourse scene of negotiated meaning emerging among various texts and voices, opening aesthetics as the interrelational field of encounter and interrogation among distinctive domains. Her texts demonstrate the way the poem is a space in which multiple interests and endeavors confront and address each other, and into which women not only may venture but constitutively do so.

Notes

NOTES TO THE PREFACE

1. Discussions structured through ideological categories include: Toril Moi, *Sexual/Textual Politics*; Rosemary Tong. *Feminist Thought*; Alison Jaggar, *Feminist Politics*; and Josephine Donovan, *Feminist Theory*. Judith Grant's *Fundamental Feminism* takes these ideological divisions as her subject, even if she does so to critique them. An overview of such overviews is given by Elaine Showalter, "Feminism and Literature."
2. An early and exemplary case of true interdisciplinary effort is Gayle Greene and Coppelia Kahn, eds., *Making a Difference*.
3. Angela McRobbie, *Aftermath of Feminism*.
4. E.g. Clifford Geertz, *Interpretation of Cultures*.
5. One groundbreaking study of these divisions in philosophical history is Jean Bethke Elshtain, *Public Man*.
6. Hegel, *Philosophy of Right*, Third Part, Second Section, § 166, § 181. As Hegel remarks: "In the family the wife has her full substantive place, and in the feeling of family piety realizes her ethical disposition. The difference between man and woman is the same as that between animal and plant. The animal corresponds more closely to the character of the man, the plant to that of the woman. In woman there is a more peaceful unfolding of nature, a process, whose principle is the less clearly determined unity of feeling." § 166.
7. Carole Pateman, *Disorder of Women*, 118. Cf. Joan Kelly, "Doubled Vision of Feminist Theory" traces the public/private dichotomy through Marxist, Radical, and Liberal feminist treatments, arguing for a need to rethink this dichotomy by understanding the "systematic connections between them," 220.
8. Cf. Jane Flax's "Postmodernism and Gender Relations," 40.
9. See Michelle Zimbalist Rosaldo, "Woman, Culture and Society"; and Margaret Mead, *Male and Female*. Nancy Hirschmann sums up, "The idea of social construction is particularly important to feminism, for it is key to rejecting patriarchal arguments about men's and women's 'natures.' But she adds, "This construction of social behaviors and rules takes on a life of its own and becomes reality." Hirschmann, "Revisioning Freedom," 60.
10. Joan Kelly-Gadol, "Social Relations"; and Joan Scott, "Gender."
11. See the exchange between Judith Butler and Seyla Ben-Habib in "Feminism and Post-Modernism." Also, Judith Butler, "Contingent Foundations." Cf. e.g. Teresa De Lauretis, who argues for identity as a "strategy"; "Introduction," *Feminist Studies /Critical Studies*, 9; or, conversely, Susan Bordo, "Feminism, Post-Modernism and Gender Skepticism," who reminds, against

notions of free self-construction out of heterogeneity, that the body is not simply free to change shape and is "a metaphor of our locatedness in space and time," 144.
12. Nancy Fraser, "The Uses and Abuses of French Discourse Theories," notes this tendency in psychoanalytic discussion to intrasubjective over intersubjective engagements, 189. Cf. Elizabeth Grosz *space, time and perversion*. Mary Ryan, "Gender and Public Access," 260: "To this day much of feminist theory is still occupied in the private side of this political project, debating gender identity as it takes form in the private spaces of the psyche, infant development and the family."
13. Shira Wolosky, "Harvard Formalism," *Cambridge History*, 310–323.
14. Misha Kavka, "Introduction" to the retrospective *Feminist Consequences*. Cf. e.g. Elizabeth Grosz, etc.
15. Books on postfeminism include Angela McRobbie, *Third Wave Agenda*; Ann Brooks, *Postfeminisms*; Natasha Walter, *On the Move*; and Rebecca Walker, "Introduction: To Be Real." Also see *Hypatia* 12(3) issue on "Third Wave Feminisms." Second Wave feminism is reassessed in Linda Nicholson, ed., *The Second Wave*. The Third Wave critique of the Second Wave is discussed in Cathryn Bailey, "Making Waves and Drawing Lines: The Politics of Defining the Vicissitudes of Feminism." For an analysis of the "genealogy" of the Third Wave, see Alison Stone, "On the Genealogy of Women." Third Wave in fact remains a term with a wide range of meanings, and critiques Second Wave both from a left Marxian direction as not radical enough, and from a conservative 'postfeminism' that claims the feminist project has been fulfilled and should be dissolved. In general, there is a greater sense of the diversity of women, often in postmodern senses of fragmentation of the self.
16. Alison Jagger, 5. On conflicts between Marxism and feminism, see Heidi Harmann, "The Unhappy Marriage of Marxism and Feminism."
17. Sabah Mahmood, *Politics of Piety*, 6.
18. Mary Douglas, *Purity and Danger*, 60–62.
19. E.g. in *Feminist Practice*, Chris Weedon underscores Foucauldian "reverse" and "resistant discourses" within a multiplicity of discourses that creates "conditions of resistance," 109–110. Cf. Terry Threadgold, *Feminist Poetics*, 11.

NOTES TO CHAPTER 1

1. Elaine Showalter offers a classic overview of the questions of feminist literary criticism in *New Feminist Criticism*. Cf. Sydney Janet Kaplan, "Varieties of Feminist Criticism."
2. On the recasting of imagery in women's poetry, specifically in the American context, see, for example, Alicia Ostriker, *Stealing the Language*. For a discussion of how classical poetic genres are gendered, see especially Ann Rosalind Jones, *Currency of Eros*; John Freccero, "Petrarchan Poetics"; and Barbara Lewalski, *Writing Women*.
3. For rewritings of the Bible by nineteenth-century American women, see Shira Wolosky, "Women's Bibles," *Cambridge History*, 216–233.
4. Adrienne Rich specifically defines her project as "Re-vision—the act of looking back, of seeing with fresh eyes, of entering an old text from a new direction," *On Lies*, 127.
5. Elaine Showalter's *Literature of Their Own*, 11–12; Margaret Ezell, *Writing Women's Literary History*, chapter 1.

6. Gerda Lerner, *Creation of Feminist Consciousness*, 50. Cf. David Cressy, *Literacy*; *Beyond Their Sex*; Patricia Crawford, "Women's Published Writings 1600–1700."
7. On women's writings in early religious contexts, see Caroline Bynum, "Patterns of Female Piety"; see also Caroline Bynum, *Jesus as Mother*.
8. Harold Bloom presents these theories through many books; see especially *Anxiety of Influence*, 60–66.
9. One pivotal essay providing core patterns in Bloomian theory is "The Internalization of Quest Romance."
10. Sandra Gilbert and Susan Gubar, *Madwoman*; Margaret Homans, *Women Writers*; Joanne Feit Diehl, *Dickinson and the Romantic Imagination*; and Suzanne Juhasz *Naked and Fiery Forms*.
11. For collaborative feminized models, see Elizabeth Abel, "(E)merging Identities"; and Ellen Moers, *Literary Women*. See also Bonnie Costello, "Marianne Moore and Elizabeth Bishop."
12. Gilbert and Gubar, *Madwoman*, 59–60; cf. Juhasz, *Naked and Fiery Forms*.
13. Suzanne Hull has collected such instructions manuals in *Chaste, Silent and Obedien*. Cf. Angeline Goreau, *Whole Duty*.
14. Gilbert and Gubar, 73.
15. Gilbert and Gubar, 17.
16. Homans, 17, 33.
17. Barbara Welter, "The Cult of True Womanhood," 152.
18. Mary Kelley, *Private Woman*, 111.
19. Gilbert and Gubar, *Madwoman*, 16, 23
20. Mary Poovey, *Proper Lady*, 36.
21. Elaine Hobby, *Virtue of Necessity*, 9.
22. Joanne Dobson, *Dickinson and Strategies of Reticence*. Elaine Hobby sees modesty as a strategic decision to "prove their obedience and hence their modesty by doing as they are told," 9. Tina Krontiris similarly adopts this strategic argument in *Oppositional Voice*.
23. Anne Rosalind Jones discusses the complex structures of humility in "Nets and Bridles," claiming that women writers succeeded in diverting "early modern controls upon women into channels for their survival through literary self-representation. Nets and bridles that restrained women's participation in literary culture also provided them with entries into it," 67. See also Marion Wynne-Davies, "Literary Dialogues."
24. Margaret Ezell, 25–26.
25. The extent to which conservative and radical societal impulses could intercross is discussed by Catherine Gallagher, "Embracing the Absolute" in relation to "Tory feminism." See also William Kolbrener, "Mary Astell's Feminist Historiography"; Hilda Smith, *Reason's Disciples*; and Carole Pateman, "Women's writing."
26. Joan Landes argued that this was not the case in France in *Women and the Public Sphere*.
27. Cf. Mary Kelley's discussion on novelists, *Private Woman*, chapter 8, where, however, she sees the entry into publicity as an ironic exposure of the private.
28. Joanne Feit Diehl explicates the gender of the Muse in Bloomian terms, *Dickinson*. Suzanne Juhasz discusses the ambivalence of Dickinson and the woman writer in general, *Naked*.
29. For fuller discussion of Dickinson, see Shira Wolosky, *Cambridge History* 427–480.
30. Arguments for Bradstreet as incipiently either secular or feminist are common. See, for example, Wendy Martin, *American Triptych*. This reading is contested by Jeannine Hensley in her introduction to *Works of Anne Bradstreet*.

31. Cristanne Miller, *Marianne Moore*, 21; Randall Jarrell, "Her Shield," 122.
32. Cristanne Miller, *Moore*, 23; and Cheryl Walker, *Masks Outrageous*, 7.
33. Cristanne Miller, *Moore*, 24; and Betsy Erkkila, *Wicked Sisters*, 103, 126.
34. Elizabeth Bishop, *Poems*, 94.
35. Elizabeth Bishop, *Prose*, 156.
36. Marianne Moore, *Prose*, 406
37. Moore's modesty is often linked to her ethics. See Bonnie Costello, "Feminine Language"; see also Costello, *Marianne Moore*; and Cynthia Hogue, "Another Postmodernism." Jeredith Merrin discusses humility in traditional religious terms in *Enabling Humility*.
38. Patricia Crawford, *Women and Religion in England*, 41. Bonnie Costello calls "To a Snail" Moore's "most self-reflective poem," 51.
39. Some of the discussions on modesty include Owen Flanagan, "Virtue and Ignorance," Ben-Ze'ev, "The Virtue of Modesty"; Statman, "Modesty, Pride, and Realistic Self-Assessment," A. T. Nuyen, "Just Modesty," 102–103; Julia Driver, "Virtues of Ignorance"; and Norvin Richards, "Is Humility a Virtue"; G. F. Schueler systematically reviews and critiques prior discussions in "Why Modesty Is a Virtue" but ultimately argues that modesty is the virtue of "not caring" for the opinions of others, a strange sort of argument since this seems more like defiance, while modesty in contrast is deeply concerned with the views of others. This, however, is modified in G. F. Schueler, "Why Is Modesty a Virtue," where the author does turn from the question of self-regard to modesty as instead oriented toward others: "not generated from herself but from those around her," so that, "the direction of her life comes not from within herself but from others." Cf. Valerie Tiberius and John Walker, "Arrogance," 383.

NOTES TO CHAPTER 2

1. Sherry B. Ortner, "Is Female to Male as Nature Is to Culture?"
2. Nancy Chodorow, "Family Structure." Chodorow is more fully discussed in Chapter 3; Michelle Zimbalest Rosaldo, "Women, Culture and Society."
3. Sandra Morgen, "Introduction."
4. Henrietta Moore, *Feminism and Anthropology*, 13, 25.
5. Margaret Mead, *Male and Female*.
6. Gayle Rubin, "The Traffic in Women,"160. Judith Butler, *Gender Trouble*.
7. Michelle Zimbalist Rosaldo, "The Use and Abuse of Anthropology," 393.
8. Shirley Ardener, "Introduction," xviii.
9. Cheris Kramare, Barrie Thorne, and Nancy Henley, "Perspectives," 638. Cf. *Women and Language in Literature and Society*, eds. Sally McConnell-Ginet, Ruth Borker, and Nelly Furman.
10. Robin Lakoff offers these suggestions in *Language and Woman's Place*. An overview of attempts to specify sex difference in language is given by Cheris Kramarae, Barrie Thorne, and Nancy Henley in "Perspectives," with due warnings that empirical findings are inconclusive and must be assessed in terms of myriad nonverbal and social contexts. Cheris Kramarae in "Women and Men Speaking" directly discuss the Ardener model. A collection of classic discussions on the difficulties of characterizing either men's or women's language appears in Roman, Camille, Suzanne Juhasz, and Cristanne Miller, eds. *The Women and Language Debate*; Cate Poynton, *Language and Gender*; Marsha Houston and Cheris Kramarae,*Women Speaking from Silence*; and Francine Frank and Frank Anshen, *Language and the Sexes*.

11. Lakoff, *Language and Woman's Place*; and Ruth Borker, "Antrhropological Perspectives on Gender and Language," 412.
12. Jane Mansbridge "Feminism and Democratic Community," sums up a series of different studies, 363.
13. Dean MacCannell and Juliet Flower MacCannell note, for example, that there are Australian aboriginal groups in which males speak a language forbidden to females, "The Body System," 208.
14. Natalie Zeman Davis, *Women on the Margins*, 24.
15. Edwin Ardener, "Belief and the Problem of Women."
16. Shirley Ardener, "Introduction," xvi.
17. Hélène Cixous, "The Laugh of the Medusa," 280, 283, 285; and Luce Irigaray, *This Sex Which Is Not One*.
18. This is the case in Julia Kristeva's *Revolution in Poetic Language*, which in many ways dehistoricizes Bakhtin. See Chapter 8 for discussion.
19. There have been sustained critiques of French feminist theory as unhistorical, unempirical, and privatizing. See Nancy Fraser, "Uses and Abuses,"178, and other essays in *Revaluing French Feminism*.
20. For Marxist discussions of dominant values, see Raymond Williams, *Marxism and Literature*, 121–127. Ann Rosalind Jones, "Nets," discusses such "Marxist cultural studies" in terms of poetry as a contest between "dominant cultural forms and systems of representation" and "acceptance and resistance" by women, 2–3. For the reductive potential of Marxist categories, see Saba Mahmood, "Feminist Theory," 206.
21. Elaine Showalter, "Feminist Criticism in the Wilderness," 261–262. She compares Ardener's to Gilbert and Gubar's image of the "palimpsest," 73.
22. See Chapter 8 on poetics for fuller discussion.
23. See Mikhail Bakhtin, "Discourse in the Novel," 264–265, 273, 285–288.
24. The topic of Bakhtin and gender is taken up in Chapter 8 below.
25. Alicia Ostriker, *Stealing the Language*.
26. Shira Wolosky, *Emily Dickinson*.
27. Dickinson's "Wife" poems include: J 199/F 225, J 271/F 307, J 273/F 330, J 461/F 185, J 493/F 467, J 528/F 411, J 613/F 445, J 616/F 454, J 732/F 857, J 959/F1072, J 1072/F 194, and J 1737/F 267.
28. Homi Babha, *The Location of Culture*, p. 87.
29. Luce Irigaray, *This Sex Which Is Not One*," p. 76.
30. On the relation between the double standard and women as property, see Keith Thomas, "Double Standard."
31. Mikhael Bakhtin, *Problems of Dostoevsky's Poetics*, 184.
32. Hazel Carby, *Reconstructing Womanhood*, points in this direction with reference to Bakhtin: "Language is accented differently by competing groups, and therefore the terrain of language is a terrain of power relations," 17.
33. W. E. B. DuBois, *Souls of Black Folks*, 34.
34. Daved Grimsted, "Anglo American Racism," 356.
35. For Harper's biography, see Frances Smith Foster, "Introduction."
36. For a discussion of African-American dialects and its importance to Paul Laurence Dunbar, see Shira Wolosky, *Cambridge History* Vol. IV, 336–350.
37. Cf. discussion of Phyllis Brian Harper, 95.
38. Cf. Stanlie M James, "Mothering."

NOTES TO CHAPTER 3

1. Jean Bethke Elshtain argues, for example, that certain forms of feminism seem to presume that "in order to have a revolutionary or feminist

consciousness one must disconnect oneself from particular ties," "Feminism, Family and Community," 264. Criticisms of liberal Second Wave feminism appear in the collection *Third Wave*; also Rebecca Walker, *To Be Real*. Some Third Wave discussions fall into what has been called 'backlash' as a retreat from feminism's critical project into a renewed privatism that, however, is also a product of contemporary commercial culture. This critique can then turn around into Marxian materialist analysis of women's commodification. See Susan Faludi *Backlash*; Rebecca Munford, "'Wake Up and Smell the Lipgloss.' A major challenge remains how to balance equality and difference, e.g. Ann Snitow, "A Gender Diary."
2. Linda Kerber, "Some Cautionary Words," 306. Other critiques of Gilligan's methodologies and assumptions include Judy Auerbach, Linda Blum, Vicki Smith, and Christine Williams, "On Gilligan's 'In a Different Voice.'" Questions have been raised as to whether Gilligan's model is general or gendered, biological or social, how research-based it is, as in Nancy Hirschmann, "Rethinking Obligation for Feminism," 164; and Jane Mansbridge, *Democratic Community*, 351.
3. Catherin MacKinnon, *Feminism Unmodified*, 38. Cf. *Toward a Feminist Theory of the State*, "By establishing that women reason differently from men on moral questions, she revalues that which has accurately distinguished women from men by making it seem as though women's moral reasoning is somehow women's, rather than what male supremacy has attributed to women for its own use," 51.
4. See e.g. Susan Moller Okin, *Justice*, 15. Okin provides a bibliography of discussion on Gilligan's work, notes 25 and 26, 188–189. Cf. Okin, "Thinking Like a Man." Also, Cynthia Fuchs, *Deceptive Distinctions*.
5. As Nancy Hirschmann elucidates, in Gilligan, "care is characterized by theme, not necessarily by gender," "Rethinking Obligation for Feminism," 164. Cf. Judy Auerbach, Linda Blum, Vicki Smith, and Christine Williams, "On Gilligan's 'In a Different Voice,'" who acknowledge that Gilligan intends a "dialectic" between different moral approaches, although they question aspects of her methodology as well as of her developmental models, 155.
6. In this discussion, Gilligan's theoretical vision rather than her clinical work will be the focus. Carol Gilligan, *In a Different Voice*, hereafter DV.
7. Evelyn Fox Keller, "Feminism and Science." Recent research has gone so far as to suggest that experiments done on the cellular level should be labeled according to the gender of the cells, which each carry genetic markers of sex.
8. "This discovery occurs," writes Gilligan, "when theories formerly considered to be sexually neutral in their scientific objectivity are found instead to reflect a consistent observational and evaluative bias . . . we begin to notice how accustomed we have become to seeing life through the eyes of men," DV 6.
9. For an early critique of Freud, yet exploring what he still offers feminism, see Juliett Mitchell, *Woman's Estate*. Mari Jo Buhle thoroughly reviews and discusses the complex relations between feminism and psychoanalysis in *Feminism and Its Discontent*. French feminists such as Luce Irigaray of course take feminism and psychoanalysis as a major topic. For critiques of Freud in terms of Lesbian sexuality, see Teresa De Lauretis, *Practice of Love*; also Elizabeth Grosz, *Space, Time and Perversion*.
10. Sigmund Freud, "Some Psychical Consequences of the Anatomical Distinction Between the Sexes," 257–258; and S. Freud, "A Case of Homosexuality in a Woman" (1920).
11. Erik H. Erikson, *Childhood and Society*, 247–274.

12. Jean Baker Miller, *Toward a New Psychology of Women*, especially chapter 8, "Ties to Others," 83–97.
13. Baker, 83, 86.
14. Jean Baker Miller, "The Development of Women's Sense of Self," 11–26.
15. Dorothy Dinnerstein, *Mermaid and the Minotaur*.
16. Nancy Chodorow, *Reproduction of Motherhood*, 166–169; see also her earlier piece, "Family Structure and Feminine Personality."
17. Chodorow, "Toward a Relational Individualism," 199, 204.
18. Gilligan, "Reply to Critics," 207–208.
19. Gilligan, "Remapping the Moral Domain" 14.
20. Gilligan, "Remapping the Moral Domain," 4–5.
21. Gilligan, *Mapping the Moral Domain*, 15–16.
22. Gilligan, "Preface," *Making Connections*, 9.
23. Gilligan, "Women's Psychological Development," 7, 16, 17.
24. Gilligan, *Mapping the Moral Domain*, 17.
25. DV xiv; *Mapping the Moral Domain*, 16.
26. Virginia Held, "Non-Contractual Society," 217; and Held, "Mothering vs. Contract," "Feminism and Moral Theory," Held, *On Feminist Ethics and Politics*, ed. Claudia Card (University Press of Kansas, 1999), 288–309. Cf. Sara Ruddick, *Maternal Thinking*; Nel Noddings, *Care*; Annette Baier, "The Need for More than Justice," as well as many other writings on feminist ethics.
27. Hannah Arendt, *On Revolution*, 81.
28. Nancy Fraser and Linda Nicholson regarding accounts of "mothering" as a new "quasi-metanarrative," which treats theory as a "putatively unitary, culturally universal type of activity," in their case, "generally an activity conceived as domestic and located in the family," "Social Criticism without Philosophy." Cf. also Fox-Genovese, "Beyond Sisterhood"; Lorraine Code, "Second Persons," criticizes the idealization of maternal models, 367–370. Her preference is for models based on friendship, 370.
29. Elizabeth Fox-Genovese, *Feminism Without Illusions*, 11; see chapter 1, "Beyond Sisterhood." Cf. Carol Gould, "Feminism and Democratic Community Revisited."
30. Okin, *Justice*.
31. Mary G. Dietz, "Citizenship with a Feminist Face," 20, 27, 28. As Mary Dietz points out, the image of motherhood has been highly volatile in feminist discourse, from radical feminist denunciations as the force of patriarchal oppression, as in Shulamith Firestone's *Dialectic of Sex*, to motherhood's adoption as model in Sarah Ruddick.
32. Barbara Johnson, "Apostrophe, Animation, and Abortion," 191.
33. Like the "involuntary plan" in the poem "Kitchenette," such "layaway" plans were often scams perpetrated by banks, realtors, gangs, police, and politicians; James Edward Smethurst, *The New Red Negro*, 165.
34. Hirschmann, 165.

NOTES TO CHAPTER 4

1. Alexis de Tocqueville, *Democracy in America*, Book 3: IX. On the geography of the separate spheres, see Linda Kerber, "Separate Spheres, Female Worlds," 9–10.
2. Michelle Zimbalist Rosaldo argues that whatever activities women do, they are less prestigious than when men do them, "Woman, Culture and Society," 19. For Rosaldo's later rethinking of the public/private categories, see "The Use and Abuse of Anthropology."

3. Linda Imray and Audrey Middleton interestingly argue that gender determines, rather than merely reflects, the public/private demarcation but focus on the (de)valuation of domestic work. "Public and Private: Marking the Boundaries," in *Public and the Private*, eds. Eva Gamarnikow, David Morgan, Jane Purvis, Daphne Taylorson. London, Heinemann, 1983, 12–27; 14, 16.
4. Jane Tompkins, *Sensational Designs*. Richard Brodhead similarly expands the discourse of sentimentality in "Sparing the Rod." Ann Douglas had discussed sentimentalism as "the political sense obfuscated or gone rancid [which] never exists except in tandem with failed political consciousness," *Feminization of American Culture*, 254. Other works that critique Douglas's account include Nina Baym, *Women's Fiction*; and Philip Fisher, *Hard Facts*. Laura Wexler reviews the Anne Douglas/Jane Tompkins debate in "Tender Violence."
5. Nina Baym, *American Women Writers*, explores how "even when the focus is subjective . . . history is still there with all its public implications," 70.
6. Amy Kaplan, *Anarchy of Empire*, 23–50. The question of mutual implication between domesticity and imperialism was first posed by Gayatri Chakravorty Spivak, "Three Women's Texts and a Critique of Imperialism." Other works that address ideologies of domestic fiction include: Ann Romines *Home Plot*; Nancy Armstrong, *Desire and Domestic Fiction*; Lora Romero, *Home Fronts*; and Caren Kaplan, *Questions of Travel*. These discussions, however, focus on sentimental and domestic writing, not on women's public writings, and on fiction, not poetry. Joanne Dobson's "Reclaiming Sentimental Literature" offers a thorough overview of discussions of sentimental literature, including discussions of poetry. She interprets sentimentality as celebrating "human connection," 266, as against male texts, which fear "social bonds" as a "threat to individual existence," 267, thus suggesting civic implications.
7. Mary Ryan, for example, presents women's literature as essentially complicitous with restrictive domesticity, as in *Womanhood in America*, where Ryan speaks of "gilded literary package[s] of domestic piety and pathos," 76; cf. Mary Ryan, "Gender and Public Access," 272. "To this day much of feminist theory is still occupied in the private side of this political project, debating gender identity as it takes form in the private spaces of the psyche, infant development and the family," 260. Ryan tends to describe domesticity as a "retreat into the home," with suffrage alone a genuinely progressive movement, 272, 282. See also Mary Ryan, *Empire of the Mother*.
8. As Barbara Sicherman writes in her review essay on feminist revisions in "American History," "recent studies of women's work shows that the contrast between pre-industrial and industrial patterns has been exaggerated," 463.
9. For overviews of women's history in America, see Glenda Riley, *Inventing the American Woman*; Sara M. Evans, *Born For Liberty*; and Mary Ryan, *Womanhood in America*.
10. Susan Amussen, *An Ordered Society*, reviews the earlier history of women's and men's work distributions and the changes these went through in the seventeenth century.
11. Linda Kerber, "Separate Spheres," 9–10.
12. On legal restrictions, see Linda Kerber, "Disabilities," and other essays in *Women of the Republic*.
13. Linda Kerber, "The Paradox of Women's Citizenship"; and Linda Kerber, "A Constitutional Right," *Towards and Intellectual History of Women*.
14. Blackstone defines Femme Covert as: "the very being of legal existence of the wife is suspended during marriage, or at least is incorporated and

consolidated into that of the husband," 442. See Marylyn Salmon, "Equality or Submersion?"; and Mary Poovey, *Proper Lady*, 6–7.
15. Mary Ryan offers an overview of women's work in *Womanhood in America*. Glenna Matthews describes the labor of housework in *"Just a Housewife."* On the multiplicity of women's communities, see Nancy Hewitt, "Beyond the Search for Sisterhood"; and Nancy Cott, *The Bonds of Womanhood*, 64–70.
16. Carl Degler, *At Odds*, 381. He also provides a survey on education and teaching, 380. Already by 1834, women constituted 56% of all teachers; by 1860, 78%.
17. For the importing of white middle-class values into African-American representation, see Claudia Tate, *Domestic Allegories*.
18. That is, other than churches and cathedrals, as Rachel Bowlby points out in "Modes of Modern Shopping," 189. John F. Kasson, *Rudeness and Civility*, discusses the rise of shopping in women's culture, 131. Also Falk, Pasi, and Colin Campbell, Eds. *The Shopping Experience*. Department stores were the first public places that women could visit unaccompanied, and they were designed to be between public and private spheres, with domestic settings and saleswomen like domestic servants.
19. Mary Beth Norton, *Founding Mothers & Fathers*; Riley, *Inventing the American Woman*, 10–11; and Nancy Cott, *Public Vows*.
20. Linda Kerber, *Women of the Republic*; and Mary Beth Norton, *Liberty's Daughters*.
21. Rosemarie Zagarri, "The Rights of Man and Woman."
22. March 31, 1776. In a later, equally ineffective letter of May 7, 1776, Abigail Adams wrote: "I cannot say that I think you very generous to the Ladies, for whilst you are proclaiming peace and good will to Men, Emancipating all Nations, you insist upon retaining an absolute power over Wives." John Adams presciently responded that the Revolution had "loosened the bands of Government everywhere," April 14, 1776.
23. Bernard Bailyn, *Education in the Forming of American Society*; Edmund Morgan, *Puritan Family*; and H. G. Good, *History of American Education*, 41.
24. Roger Thompson, *Women in Stuart England*, compares Puritan women in England and America in terms of legal norms, education, demography, and so on. However, in *Literacy in Colonial New England*, Kenneth Lockridge finds that women's literacy, after a significant increase in the seventeenth century (45% compared to 33.5%), remained stable whereas men's continued to increase through the eighteenth century, creating a gap in gendered literacy.
25. Pangle and Pangle, *Learning of Liberty*. Nina Baym, *American Women Writers*, underscores the importance of history for women's Republican education, of history writing for women's ability to participate in the public sphere, and of the home as educating citizens, 11–12, 67.
26. Kerber, *Women of the Republic*.
27. Benjamin Rush, "Thoughts upon Female Education," 28.
28. For discussion of this new public meaning of the domestic sphere, see Norton, *Liberty's Daughters*; and Kerber, *Women of the Republic*. For discussion of the meanings of citizenship in the context of women's history, see Linda Kerber, "Paradox of Women's Citizenship in the Early Republic"; and "A Constitutional Right to Be Treated Like American Ladies." Cf. Noah Webster, "On the Education of Youth," arguing that women educating the youths of America must themselves be educated to "enable them to implant in the tender mind such sentiments of virtue, propriety, and dignity as are suited to the freedom of our governments," 68.

29. In this ongoing argument over whether activities undertaken within traditional women's definitions were more constraining or progressive, Daniel Scott Smith's "Family Limitation" defends domesticity as a resource for women. Carol Smith Rosenberg's "Female World of Love and Ritual" traces the "two cultures of gender, arguing that women found strength in their separate gendered world." Barbara Sicherman argues that, despite the separate spheres, "women gained considerable influence and even power in nineteenth century," with the separation of spheres providing "at least as many opportunities as liabilities," giving "access even to the 'public' sphere," 464. Sicherman also reviews counter-readings and ambivalence regarding the spheres and women's advancement. Nancy Cott explores domesticity and separatism as an ambivalent structure, *Bonds of Womanhood*. See also Estelle Freedman, "Separatism as Strategy"; Mary Ryan, *Empire*; and Glenna Matthews, *Rise of Public Woman*.
30. For discussions of women's education, see Kathryn Kish Sklar, "Founding of Mount Holyoke College"; Linda Kerber, *Women of the Republic*, 189–231; Norton, *Liberty's Daughters*, 256–299; Carl Degler, *At Odds*, 308–310; Carol Ruth Berkin and Mary Beth Norton, eds., *Women of America: A History* 15, 69–74; and "Family Patterns and Social Values in America," William E. Bridges, *Education*, 3–12.
31. Noah Webster, "On the Education of Youth," 45, 59; and Carl Degler, *At Odds*, 308–310. For arguments over just how genuinely civic education was and women's places in it, see Cathy Davidson, *Revolution of the Word*, 61–64.
32. Janet Carey Eldred and Peter Mortensen, "Persuasion Dwelt on Her Tongue."
33. Thomas F. Green, *Voices*.
34. Carl Degler, *At Odds*; Mary Ryan, *Cradle of the Middle Class* and *Womenhood in America*; Carroll Smith-Rosenberg, *Disorderly Conduct*; and Nancy Hewitt, *Women's Activism and Social Change*. See also Judith Hole and Ellen Levine, "The First Feminists."
35. See Paula Baker, "The Domestication of Politics," 621; Carl Degler, *At Odds*; and Mary Ryan, *Womanhood in America*.
36. Lori Ginzberg, *Women and the Work of Benevolence*. It is interesting to note that these activities of letter writing, petitions, lobbying, and so on are the heart of civic culture in G. A. Almond and S. Verba, *Civic Culture*.
37. Paula Baker, "Domestication," 640; Estelle Freedman, "Separatism as Strategy"; Glenna Matthews, *Rise of Public Woman*, offers an overview of women's clubs, 159; Mary Ryan, "The Power of Women's Networks."
38. Mary Ryan, *Women in Public*, although Ryan to a large extent is also tracing the restrictions on women's access to public spaces. See also Christine Stansell, *City of Women* and "Women, Children and the Uses of the Street."
39. Sara Evans, "Women's History and Political Theory," 120. Paula Baker, for example, even while uncovering women's activism in relief societies and hospitals, schools and anti-slavery protest, moral reform and suffrage, urban planning and employment, still refers to them through the language of domesticity, as "virtues exercised in the private sphere" or as "working from the private sphere," *Moral Frameworks*, xiv, xiii; "Domestication of Politics," 621.
40. Gayatry Spivak, "Three Women," 244. Nancy Armstrong's *Desire and Domestic Fiction* also argues for a complicit connection between domestic fiction as creating "a private domain of culture that was independent of the political world and overseen by a woman" and a process of individuation that proved, however, to be "techniques of social control," 98.

41. Ryan, "Gender and Public Access," 280, 268–269. Nina Baym, *American Women Writers*, sees political and civic writing as consistent with "female decorum" and not as challenging "the boundaries of home space," 67; but rather as exposures to the public eye of personal "subjective" writing, 68.
42. Hazel Carby, *Reconstructing Womanhood*; Claudia Tate, *Domestic Allegories*, 97—98. Here again the focus is on novelists, not poets.
43. On the battle for suffrage, see Ellen Carol DuBois, *Feminism and Suffrage*; Aileen S. Kraditor, *Ideas of the Woman Suffrage Movement*; Carl Degler, *At Odds*; Jean Bethke Elshtain, "Moral Woman and Immoral Man"; and Mary Beth Norton, "The Paradox of the Woman's Sphere."
44. Rufus Griswold, *Female Poets*, 7.
45. See Mary Kelley, *Private Woman*, ix. Many works now available investigate the circulation of women's writing as "public" for prose mainly but also for poetry.
46. On sentimental literature, see discussion of Jane Tompkins above.
47. Caroline Field Levander, *Voices of the Nation*. Janet Carey Eldred and Peter Mortensen, "Persuasion Dwelt on Her Tongue."
48. Paula Bennet's *Poets in the Public Sphere* addresses nineteenth-century women's poetry in public contexts. Her emphasis is on those nineteenth-century women poets who were committed to leftist politics; see also Mary Loeffelholtz and Martin Griffin. See also Wolosky, *Emily Dickinson* and *Poetry and Public Discourse*. For the twentieth century, see Suzanne Scweik, *A Gulf So Deeply Cut*.
49. See discussion in Chapter 1. Works examining the constraints and challenges to women poets include: Alicia Ostriker, *Stealing the Language*, which explores the "painful tension between aspiration and self-effacement" in women's poetry, 10; Margaret Homans' *Woman Writers* declares that, "without subjectivity, women are incapable of self-representation, the fundamental of masculine creativity," 17, but women have "difficulty in creating a central sense of self in poetry," 36. Suzanne Juhasz explores this "double bind" of women's writing in *Naked and Fiery Forms*, 1–2, where "women lack that sense of self" of male poets. Cheryl Walker's *Nightingale's Burden* defines the tradition of women's poetry as "ambivalent, personal, passionate lyrics claiming some special wisdom derived from female experience," and "lacking authority in this culture, American women poets have still spoken, but they have spoken obliquely, sometimes in cramped forms, and often without the confidence to range widely," xi, xiii. Joanne Feit Diehl, *Women Poet*s, "Emerson's faith in the self"'s ability . . . presents difficulties not easily overcome by poets of lesser confidence or by those who lack support of a tradition. . . . Women poets experience the burden of these difficulties in ways that bar their free access to the Sublime," 1.
50. For discussion of Emerson's model of the individual in its social and ethical dimensions, see Sacvan Bercovitch, *The Rites of Assent*; and Stanley Cavell, *Conditions Handsome and Unhandsome*, 9–11, 28–32.
51. I have more fully explored Dickinson's contexts and connections to the Civil War in *Emily Dickinson*. For an overview of treatments of Dickinson and the Civil War, see Faith Battet, "Public Selves and Private Spheres: Studies of Emily Dickinson and the Civil War, 1984-2007."
52. Cristanne Miller, "Pondering 'Liberty.'"
53. Cf. James McPherson, *Battle Cry of Freedom*.
54. Nina Baym, "Reinventing Lydia Sigourney." Baym writes mainly on fiction but devotes a chapter in *American Women Writers, 1790–1860* to women's poetic publications, 67–91, focusing on texts with historical implications. For arguments on the way intensified domesticity also included family

limitation and an enhanced authority for the woman in the household, see Daniel Scott Smith's "Family Limitation." See also Nancy Armstrong's argument in *Desire and Domestic Fiction* on women's increasing authority in the household as a significant political event, 3.
55. Cf. Shira Wolosky, *Cambridge History IV*, 163–176.
56. Amy Kaplan, "Manifest Domesticity."
57. Joan Kelly–Gadol's "Did Women Have a Renaissance" raises questions of periodization when seen from women's history as opposed to men's.
58. Joan Scott discusses the variety of women's histories in "Rewriting History."
59. Isabelle Lehuru, "Sentimental Figures," 75.
60. Lora Romero, *Home Fronts*, 77.
61. Dickson Bruce, Jr., *Black American Writing*, 19.
62. Hazel Carby, *Reconstructing Womanhood*, 39.
63. Claudia Tate, *Domestic Allegories*, 120–121, 13.
64. Karen Sanchez Eppler offers an interesting discussion of the relationship between abolitionist and feminist discourses in "Bodily Bonds," 100–105.
65. Audre Lorde, *Sister Outsider*; Patricia Hill Collins, *Black Feminist Thought*; Stanlie James, "Mothering," 44–45, 47; and Claudia Tate, *Domestic Allegories*, 4.
66. Cf. M. Dickie and T. Travisano, eds., *Gendered Modernisms*; and Cristanne Miller, *Cultures of Modernism*. Suzanne Clark in *Sentimental Modernism* discusses modernism as an "aesthetic anti-sentimentality." But her counter-argument to "restore the sentimental within modernism" involves its own retreat into the interiority of "text," 5–7.
67. This argument will be developed in Chapter 8 on feminist poetics.
68. Helen Vendler, "Domestication, Domesticity and the Otherwordly."
69. Plath's Holocaust imagery has been repeatedly an object of controversy. Irving Howe wrote that "there is something monstrous, utterly disproportionate, when tangled emotions about one's father are deliberately compared with the historical fate of the European Jews," "Plath," 158. M. L. Rosenthal comments, "Sometimes Sylvia Plath could not distinguish between herself and the facts of, say, Auschwitz or Hiroshima," 74. Leon Wieselthier similarly wrote, "Whatever her father did to her, it could not have been what the Germans did to the Jews," "Ghosts," 20. George Steiner calls Plath's "Daddy" "one of the very few poems . . . to come near the last horror" but then also asks whether it isn't "larceny" to invoke "the echoes and trappings of Auschwitz . . . [for] his own private design," "Dying Is an Art," 304. Marjorie Perloff, "Sylvia Plath's 'Sivvy'" poems likewise question Plath's "identification with the Jews at Auschwitz," 173. Cf. James Young, *Writing and Rewriting the Holocaust*, 118, 133. Janet Malcolm discusses Plath's use of the Holocaust in *The Silent Woman*, 63–64. However, in *Poetry After Auschwitz*, Susan Gubar challenges, "What if Plath is really writing about what she claims to be writing about, namely the Holocaust?", 181, 178, 195. For fuller discussion of Plath's historicity, see Lisa Katz, "World War II and the Gender of History."
70. Cf. Hannah Arendt, *On Totalitarianism*, 152.
71. The historical importance of this Plath poem is discussed by Lisa Katz; unpublished dissertation and "World War II." Recently, more attention has been given to Plath's historical dimension. See Claire Brenna, *The Poetry of Sylvia Plath*.
72. Margaret Randolph Higonnet, *Introduction: Behind the Lines* discusses women on the "home front," 15.

73. Jeffrey Berman's *Surviving Literary Suicide* treats Sexton this way, with her poetry both generated by and representing suicidal urges seeking "release from private torment," 182. Cf. Gale Swiontkowski, *Imagining Incest*. This confessional and psycho-analytic reading connects to wider cultural issues in terms of archetypes and universal symbols, rather than historical events and structures, 41. Cassue Oreni Steeke, *We Heal from Memory*, similarly treats Sexton and Audre Lorde in psycho-analytical terms of trauma due to sexual abuse. Deborah Nelson, "Penetrating Privacy," 61, argues that the Sexton poem "Her Kind," for instance, is tied to how "sufferers of abuse see themselves as whores and witches."
74. This is part of the answer to Joan Kelly Gadol's question, "Did women have a Renaissance?" and the differences between women's and men's historical periodization. The witch-craze in fact took place not during the medieval period but after it, in early modern Europe, thus distinguishing women's historical experience radically from men's. For a consideration that emphasizes the gendered elements in the witch hunts (more than 90% of witches were women), see Carol Karlsen, *The Devil in the Shape of a Woman*.

NOTES TO CHAPTER 5

1. Ann Rosalind Jones makes the interesting point that early books for courtiers used different terminology for ladies at court than for men since "cortigiana" as "courtesan" had already been assigned to prostitutes, "Nets," 44.
2. C. P. Macpherson, *Possessive Individualism*. For a careful analysis of these terms in liberal discourse, see Susan Moller Okin, "Gender, the Public and the Private," 67.
3. Linda Kerber, "Can a Woman Be an Individual?"
4. In political theory, two central figures offering this critique of liberalism are Okin, *Justice*; and Pateman, *Disorder of Women*.
5. Hannah Arendt in *Human Condition* investigates this opposition and limitation of the private to public space, e.g. 28; cf. Jean Bethke Elshtain, *Public Man*, for a full discussion of domestic privacy in the classical model.
6. For an astute discussion of the differences between these notions of public space, see especially Seyla Benhabib, "Models of Public Space." Benhabib (as do others) criticizes classical republicanism in Hannah Arendt's model as excluding women and slaves. Habermas's modern democratic discourse theory of participation is also criticized for its exclusions, in a call for a more pluralistic public discussion.
7. Hannah Arendt, *Between Past and Future*, 245; and Arendt, *Human Condition*, 24, 28, 55.
8. J. A. G. Pocock, *Machiavellian Moment*, 68. As Pocock goes on to examine, this commitment to a common good existed alongside one that saw "the same individual engaged in the particular activity of pursuing and enjoying the goods he preferred."
9. Jürgen Habermas, "Public Sphere."
10. Joan Landes, "Introduction," *Feminism, the Public and the Private*, 2: As to the private, "republicans regard the private, which they associate with the body and its needs, as pertaining to those things that ought to be hidden from view."
11. This sense of public includes, but goes beyond, Mary Beth Norton's notion of the "informal public" as involvement in community affairs in which, as she shows, women were fully active. *Founding Mothers and Fathers*, 20.
12. Theodore Lowi, "Public Philosophy," 81.

13. Paula Baker, "Domestication," 625–626.
14. Arendt, *Human Condition*, 29, 33, 58; and Elshtain, *Public Man*.
15. Gordon Wood, *Creation of the American Republic*, 68.
16. Pateman, *Disorder*, 34; and Okin, "Gender," 68.
17. The unstable placement of economics is attested in Gillian Brown's argument in *Domestic Individualism*, where she aligns domesticity with the individualism of property rights and self-determination, which she sees as "coming to be associated with the feminine sphere of domesticity," 2. Here individualism tends to mean "privacy" in terms of "personal life," 3; while Brown groups "self-denial" with "collectivity" as sentimental rather than seeing collectivity as public, 6.
18. Frances Olsen, "The Family and the Market," 1501.
19. See Kate Millett, *Sexual Politics*, 25–26.
20. Marxism represents a whole further discourse that I cannot enter into here. For fuller discussion, see Linda J. Nichols, *Gender and History*; and Iris Marion Young, "Impartiality and the Civic Public," 431.
21. For a fuller discussion of Foucault, see Chapter 7.
22. Carole Pateman, "The Patriarchal Welfare State," 243.
23. J. A. G. Pocock, *Machiavellian Moment*, 74.
24. Joyce Appleby, *Liberalism and Republicanism in the Historical Imagination* and *Capitalism and a New Social Order*.
25. For discussion of religious association in relation to civic community, see Chapter 6.
26. Most discussions of communitarianism and liberalism pose a collective as against a contractual association of private individuals. But the ideal American community, as so forcefully projected in, for example, Emerson and Whitman, is neither authoritarian collective nor privately interested individuals but a community of responsible and expressive selves. Cf. Bella, *Habits of the Heart*.
27. Joyce Appleby, *Liberalism*, 29.
28. Sidney Verba, *Voice and Equality*, 253. Note that Geoffrey Eley, "Nations, Publics and Political Cultures," claims that women were excluded from associations. But this was not the case in America, 312.
29. Elizabeth Fox-Genovese, *Feminism without Illusion*, 36, 17.
30. Jane Mansbridge, "Feminism and Democratic Community," 347. Cf. Sybil Schwarzenbah, "On Civic Friendship": "much of the important activity which de facto binds people together in a just society has continued to be performed throughout the centuries, but performed outside the official version of the modern state, primarily although not exclusively by women," 99.
31. Jean Bethke Elshtain, "Moral Woman and Immoral Man."
32. Ruth Bloch, "Virtue in Revolutionary America," 38, 56–57. Joan Landes in *Women and the Public Sphere* sees virtue as antithetical to women in the discourses of Revolutionary France, as does Hannah Pitkin in the Machiavellian Tradition *Fortune Is a Woman*. However it was traditionally defined, in practice, women came to inherit its stances in America. For further discussion of women in the republican tradition, see Judith A. Vega, "Feminist Republicanism and the Political Perception of Gender," where she describes this opposition between classic republicanism and feminism, 157–158.
33. Bloch, 56–57. Cf. Caroll Smith-Rosenberg, "Domesticating "Virtue," examines complex meanings of virtue in terms of gender and republicanism. Smith-Rosenberg interestingly refers to Bakhtinian "heterogeneous voices" through which "different social and subgroups challenge even the meanings of words," 162.
34. Mary Ryan, "Gender and Public Access," 213.

35. Anne Douglas, *Feminization*, 12.
36. This is a central point of Carol Gilligan's *Different Voice*. See also Seyla Benhabib, *Situating the Self*; and Marilyn Friedman, "Autonomy and Social Relationships." Communitarian philosophers also offer this critique of liberalism, although largely without reference to its feminist sources and implications.
37. This is Arendt's critique in *Human Condition* and is also a communitarian critique; see *Liberals and Communitarians*, eds. Stephen Mulhall and Adam Swift. A major feminist voice in this is Jean Bethke Elshtain, e.g "Individual Rights and Social Obligation."
38. See in particular Michael Sandel, *Democracy and Its Discontents*. Charles Taylor, *The Resources of the Self*, is perhaps the most extensive discussion of contexts of self- formation.
39. Mary G. Dietz makes this critique of Elshtain in "Citizenship with a Feminist Face"; Cf. the exchange between Jean Bethke Elshtain and Barbara Ehrenreich in "Feminism, Family, and Community" and Reply to Reply. See also Judith Stacey, "The New Conservative Feminism."
40. See Susan Bordo's defense of Gilligan, "Afterward: The Feminist as Other," 304–305.
41. Elshtain is somewhat contradictory on this score, seeming to place all social ethics in the private sphere and the private family, 333ff.
42. Charlotte Perkins Gilman, *Home*, 39.
43. See, for example, Hegel's Philosophy of Right, 166: "Thus one sex is mind . . . in the knowledge and volition of free universality, i.e. the self-consciousness of conceptual thought and the volition of the objective final end. The other sex is mind . . . but [with] knowledge and volition in the form of concrete individuality and feeling. In relation to externality, the former is powerful and active, the latter passive and subjective. It follows that man has his actual substantive life in the state, in learning, and so forth, as well as in labour and struggle with the external world and with himself. . . . In the family he has a tranquil intuition of this unity, and there he lives a subjective ethical life on the plane of feeling. Woman, on the other hand, has her substantive destiny in the family, and to be imbued with family piety is her ethical frame of mind." Cf. Joan B. Landes, "Hegel's Conception of the Family."
44. John Tomasi, in "Individual Rights and Community Virtues," argues that the opposition between liberal and communitarian norms as framed by Rawls and Sandel can be overcome through a notion of virtue as the withholding of rights. Rights in this way would be exercised and limited at the same time, 530–532.
45. Kathleen Jones's "Citizenship in a Woman Friendly Polity" reimagines public life as this would recognize and incorporate the values of feminism.
46. Headnote, Cheryl Walker, 342; Headnote, 223; and Janet Grey, ed., *She Wields a Pen*.
47. Nancy Cott, *Public Vows*, 1.
48. Stephanie Coontz, *Marriage*.
49. Keith Thomas, "Double Standard."
50. Mary Ryan, *Women in Public*, 100–102. Cf. Carl Degler's account in *At Odds*. Carol Smith-Rosenberg did original work on 1834 Female Society in New York. See also Paula Baker. The Purity movements were, however, successful in blocking the licensing and regulation of prostitution.
51. Charlotte Perkins Gilman, *Women and Economics*, 63–64. For discussion of Gilman's poems on the double standard, see Chapter 2.
52. Shira Wolosky, "Emerson's Figural Religion: From Poetics to Politics" *Religion and Literature* ed. Paul Kane, 41.1 Spring 2009, 25–48

53. All quotations taken from Stephen E. Whicher, *Selections from Ralph Waldo Emerson*.
54. Cf. David Leverenz, *Manhood and the American Renaissance*.
55. Lowell letter to Lazarus. Cf. Wolosky, *Poetry and Public Discourse*, 139–152.
56. Nancy Cott, *Grounding of Modern Feminism*.
57. Adrienne Rich, "Compulsory Heterosexuality and Lesbian Experience."
58. Kate Daniels, "Muriel Rukeyser and Her Literary Critics."
59. bell hooks, *Feminist Theory*, 19, 24, 36, 38. Cf. Patricia Collins' *Black Feminist Theory*'s discussion of motherhood as a form of social organization, 118–119.
60. Audre Lorde, *Sister/Outsider*, 112.
61. Kim Whitehead discusses Grahn in *Feminist Poetry Movement*, calling hers a "coalitional voice" committed to "blending subjective and collective voice without eliding difference," xxi. Poetry is embraced as "cultural work" that seeks "a collective voice by defining common concerns and publicly performing poetry," 30. Whitehead defines the Feminist Poetry Movement as a realignment of public and private, although in doing so she tends to rely on rather than critically analyze these terms. She thus says of the "coalitional voice" that it is in "speaking out of the integrity of her own personal experience that the feminist poet establishes her relationship to the community," 32.
62. Judy Grahn, "From a Public Dialogue," 94, discussed in Whitehead, 63–66.
63. Christopher Lasch, *Haven in a Heartless World*.

NOTES TO CHAPTER 6

1. Saba Mahmood notes this neglect of religious discussion in feminist theory in "Feminist Theory, Embodiment, and the Docile Agent," 202. Historians similarly tend to segregate religious from other feminist topics. Laurel Thatcher Ulrich notes how historians of the American Revolution "have shown little interest in religion. This is a striking omission given the importance of religion not only in the larger history of American women but in the recent history of the American Revolution." "Daughters of Liberty," 211. In literary contexts, Paula Bennet's *Poetry in the Public Sphere* does not mention religion.
2. Rosemarie Zagarri, for example, sees religion in opposition to the development of women's rights in "The Rights of Man and Woman," 218.
3. Roger Thompson, *Women in Stuart England and America*, provides statistics on church membership. Jon Butler and Grant Wacker, *Religion in American Life*, note that by 1680, 55% to 70% of church membership were made up by women, 71.
4. See e.g. Nancy Hardesty's *Your Daughters*; and Joyce L. Irwin, *Womanhood in Radical Protestantism*.
5. Anne Douglas, *Feminization*; cf. Richard Shiels, "The Feminization of America Congregationalism."
6. Such bifurcation of religious from economic life is traced in Richard Bushman's *From Puritans to Yankees*, where, however, gender is not discussed. Cf. Mary Maples Dunn, who observes that church life came to be assigned as 'domestic' and not 'public' when women become preponderant in church membership, "Saints and Sisters," 37.
7. Barbara Welter, "Clio's Consciousness Raised," sees religion as a repository for feminine values in a period when nation building no longer required them, 151.

8. Peter Berger and Richard Neuhaus, in their discussion of voluntary associations, point out that while "religious institutions form by far the largest network of voluntary associations in American society, yet, for reasons both ideological and historical, their role is frequently belittled or totally overlooked in discussions of social policy." The working assumption tends to be that religion "deals purely with the private sphere of life and is therefore irrelevant to public policy," *To Empower People*, 185–186. Feminist historians also tend to call the religious sphere 'private,' e.g. Margaret Bendroth, *Fundamentalism and Gender*, 3; and Westerkamp, *Women and Religion in Early America*, 79
9. For the communal dimension of Puritan selfhood, see e.g. Sacvan Bercovitch's *Puritan Origins*.
10. For rewritings of the Bible by nineteenth-century American women, see Shira Wolosky, "Women's Bibles," *Poetry and Public Discourse*, 97–112.
11. Wolosky, "Harvard Formalism," *Poetry and Public Discourse*, 163–175.
12. Gilbert and Gubar, *Madwoman*. See Chapter 1 for discussion.
13. Natalie Zemon Davis, *Society and Culture*, 93. Arguments over the gains and losses for women in the move into Protestantism are argued in, for example, Patricia Crawford, *Women and Religion in England*, who emphasizes the benefits of the monastic option for women in Catholicism, 73. Lyle Koehler, *A Search for Power*, contests claims that Puritans provided a context of greater equality for women. Cf. Kathleen M. Davies, "The Sacred Condition of Equality." Amanda Porterfield, *Female Piety*, argues that religion and domestic life enhanced women's status by locating grace within the family, where they, however, remained subordinate. Certain forms of women's communities reminiscent of convents also persisted in Protestantism.
14. See Lawrence Stone, *The Family, Sex and Marriage*; Cf. Stone, *Family in Early Modern England*.
15. Cf. *Literacy in Traditional Societies*, ed. Jack Goody; Michael Subbs, *Language and Literacy*; and Elizabeth Einstein, *The Printing Press as an Agent of Change*.
16. Emile Doumerge, ""Calvin a source of Democracy," 1–7; and Jane Dempsey Douglass, *Women, Freedom and Calvin*.
17. Natalie Zemon Davis, *Society and Culture*, 79.
18. Roger Thompson, 188, 195, 207, 209. On the relation of education to Puritanism, see Lawrence Stone, "Literacy and Education in England"; and David Zaret, on the importance of Reformation commitments to literacy, *Heavenly Contract*, 26–40. Patricia Crawford notes that during the Civil War in England, publication radically increased, with nearly half the total publications by women, of which all were works of religion, *Women and Religion in England*; also Keith Thomas, "Women and the Civil War Sects."
19. Marilyn Westerkamp, *Women and Religion in Early America*, 17; and Thompson, 85.
20. Laurel Thatcher Ulrich, *Good Wives*, 10, 216. Mary Ryan's "A Women's Awakening" describes women joining churches alone in a context of "evangelical disregard for the distinctions of sex, as well as age." Female preaching is also defended, although speaking out is still restrained, and there is no direct defiance of male authority, 91, 95–96.
21. Joyce L. Irwin, *Womanhood in America*, 161; Phyllis Mack, *Visionary Women*; and Roger Thompson, 97, 224. Jon Butler and Grant Wacker record a 1683 report on the abundance of Quaker and women preachers, 71. Much public speaking, however, stopped after the American Revolution, 125.
22. Perry Miller, "Puritan State." David Zaret sees lay activism as the key force in Puritan religious initiatives and their civic extensions, although he does

not specifically address the roles of women. Christopher Hill, *Puritanism and Revolution*, describes the effects of new church architecture, which were not large enough for processions but rather were designed as small meeting houses like lecture rooms, with pews for families, and emphasizing the Sabbath rather than parish festivals, 494–496.
23. For discussion of Quaker women's preaching and writing, see Mary Maples Dunn, "Women of Light," 117–119, 122; Pamela Walker, "A Chaste and Fervid Eloquence," describes the public activism of women in the Salvation Army.
24. Susan Juster, *Disorderly Women*, 124. Juster recounts records that show women voting at Newport and Providence, 4, 19–21, 30, 46, 41, 86. Both Quakers and Baptists, however, retreated from egalitarianism as they became more institutional.
25. A. S. P. Woodhouse underscores Puritanism as a continuity from the Presbyterian right to Independents at center through separating Congregationalists and verging into the outer boundary with Quakers, 38, 43. Cf. Thomas Sanders, *Protestant Concepts*, on the continuity among "variant expressions of a dominant and all pervasive Puritanism," 115. Also David Zaret, who claims, "There is a thin line dividing outright separation from Puritan nonconformity," 95.
26. David Donald Hall, *Colonial British America*, argues for a less rigid and more flexible understanding of Puritan orthodoxy, 325–326. Stephen Foster examines the construction of social cohesion across differences in "The Puritan's Greatest Achievement." William Mcloughlin, *Revivals, Awakenings, and Reform*, similarly groups as Puritan a range of sects, all of whom shared notions of private conscience, the spiritually inspired individual right to interpret God's will for himself, 30–32, although also with a variety of constraints. David Lovejoy, *Religious Enthusiasm*, explores how differences between "Puritans" and "Enthusiasts" are unstable and constantly changing, with movement between groups, 13, both participating in revivals and its emotional appeal and sharing orthodox doctrines. As Lovejoy cites, Emerson remarked in 1841, "the history of religion betrays a tendency to enthusiasm," 15.
27. Sidney Ahlstrom, *Religious History*, describes Protestantism as just this reform principle, 637. Richard Bushman, *From Puritan to Yankee*, connects liberty to Puritan individualism and egalitarianism, 53. In America, however, Puritans had to adjust to establishing government and not just resisting it, ultimately re-creating institutions it had sought to overcome, 147. Philip Gura argues for a different balance between religious spirituality and institutions, *A Glimpse of Zion's Glory*, 4.
28. Ruether, "Introduction," *Women and Religion in America*, Vol. 1, 17.
29. Ulrich in "Daughters of Liberty," 211–243, 211, 228, 213. Cotton Mather, *Ornaments for the Daughter's of Zion* (Boston: S. Green and B. Green, 1692). Cf. Janet Wilson James, *Women in American Religion*, 87.
30. Christopher Hill, *Puritanism and Revolution*, 494–496.
31. For Hutchincon and conventicles, Stephen Foster, 55. At Plymouth, women claimed prophetic gifts at home in the company of other women, as Hutchinson did.
32. Harry Stout, *The New England Soul*, 13–14. Stout, citing church covenantal language—"We covenant with the Lord and one with an other"—describes the Church as a corporate extension of each member, 18.
33. Harry Stout, Nathan Hatch, and others emphasize the Puritan transformations into popular rhetoric, already evident in the First Great Awakening but then accelerating, Stout, 81, and its trends toward individual textual

interpretation, Hatch, *Democratization*, 73. Cf. D. D. Hall, "World of Print," on the impact of cheap publishing on bringing the Puritan ministry to a general audience, 173–175.
34. Alan Heimert, *Religion and the American Mind*, among others charts the complex relationships between the Great Awakening and the Revolution; and Nathan Hatch, *Sacred Cause*.
35. Ralph Barton Perry, "The Ultimate Individual," remarks that the Awakenings "sowed the seeds of that very tolerance which in his theocracy he sought to suppress," 58.
36. Harry Stout, *New England Soul*; cf. Harry Stout, "Religion, Communications and Ideological Origins of the American Revolution," 527.
37. David Zaret, "Religion, Science and Printing in the Public Sphere in Seventeenth Century England," 218–221. Habermas emphasizes the privatizing effects of the Reformation, but its lay activism expressed itself and was in turn shaped by critical discussions in taverns as well as conventicles, markets, and homes. Writes Zaret, "Popular initiatives in religion had profound implications for political discourse. Even when Protestant doctrines opposed liberal politics, popular developments created a public sphere in religion," 221. Cf. Geoff Eley, "Nations, Publics and Political Cultures," who notes the start of the public sphere in religious sects, 304.
38. In light of the "tendency to overlook women's roles" in the usual linkage of politics to male activity, while "the religious sphere is traditionally separated from the political arena for women," Elaine Forman Crane argues that what is required is "to review traditional definitions of what is political," to include "political decisions based on religious orientation," "Religion and Rebellion," 53–54.
39. Joyce L. Irwin, *Womanhood in Radical Protestantism*, 161; and Roger Thompson, *Women in Stuart England*, 97, 224. Jon Butler and Grant Wacker record a 1683 report on the abundance of Quaker and women preachers, *Short History*, 71. Much public speaking, however, stopped after the American Revolution, 125.
40. Perry Miller, "Puritan State."
41. Rosemary Skinner Keller, "Civil Religion," sees a religious patriotism combining Puritanism and Enlightenment at work in the Revolution, with activist women drawing on Puritan discussions of the right to rebel and of sacred compact.
42. As with other arguments concerning women's values, so also with religious history, it is difficult to measure constraint against inspiration. Nancy Cott argues that religious identity allowed women to assert themselves in both public and in private, giving them an authority beyond the world of men. Yet she adds that if evangelicism gave women some personal authority, it finally reinforced the conservatism of traditional female values. To attain further rights, it was necessary to disengage from Protestantism, *Bonds*, 139, 204. Rosemarie Zagarri sees spiritual equality as involving "no expectation of equal rights on earth" and instead substituted for and diverted the civic claims that natural rights talk suggested, 217–218. Despite this, the granting of "dignity and moral standing in the eyes of nature's God ultimately let 'the genie out of the bottle,'" 224. Ruether describes a general ambivalence between "conservative and radical," between "helpmeet and co-authority," "Introduction," *Women and Religion in America*, Vol. 2, xii. Yet she points out, "Introduction," *Women and Religion in America*, Vol. 1, that "religion [was] an infinitely variable instrument for enlarging women's sphere," so that when seen from the perspective of the nineteenth century itself, "the liberating rather than the repressive power of religion predominates," x. Cf.

Zikmund, "Struggle for the Right to Preach," on the tension between liberal and conservative church ideologies, 193.
43. Hardesty contests Aileen Kraditor's argument that women's suffrage originated (only) in natural rights, *Ideas of the Woman Suffrage Movement*, 5–6, 21, 111, 116, 127, citing, for example, Angelina's Grimke letters to Beecher, 108. Cf. Zikmund, *Stuggle*, 205.
44. Dorothy Bass, "Prodigious," 280.
45. Alice Rossi, *Feminist Papers*, 241, 247.
46. Carolyn Haynes, "Women and Protestantism," 300–318, 302, 303, 315–316. Cf. Hardesty, who sees religious claims as palliative but then also as escaping conservative control, 288.
47. As Westerkamp puts it, "the voice belonged not to the Holy Spirit but to herself," 180. Westerkamp comments that "whether they believed themselves the captives of the spirit or deliberately manipulated language to justify fulfilling their desire, their very activism belied this construction of passivity," 180. Nancy Cott explores ambiguities of religious affirmation as "allowing women to assert themselves, both in private and in public ways; proposing a way of submission of the self that was simultaneously a pronounced form of self-assertion," *Bonds*, 155. Bernard Capp, "Separate Domains? Women and Authority in Early Modern England": Although women had "no formal place in the hierarchy of public authority, they would challenge it in defense of family and religion," 128, 138.
48. Maria Stewart, 1832 lecture on religion, cited by Carla Peterson, *Doers of the Word*. Peterson emphasizes the role of the black church and women in it toward "self-empowerment and community building," 14, and "authorization to act in the world," 56, 68.
49. William Andrews, *Sisters of Spirit*, 35, 67–68, 136, 164, 201
50. See footnote 10.
51. For discussion of John Locke's religious resources, see Jeremy Waldron, *God Locke and Equality*, and "Image of God"; and Gary Dorrien, "Making," 11–21.
52. Woodhouse, 367. Cf. Keith Thomas, "Civil War Sects," 337. Thomas notes that "From the beginning the separatists laid great emphasis upon the spiritual equality of the two sexes ... once admitted to the sect women had an equal share in church government," 320; Cf. Christopher Hill, *World Turned Upside Down*, 73. David Zaret, *Heavenly Contract*, chapter 4, sees as central to English Puritanism the tension between lay activism, founded in Bible reading and discussion, and clerical attempts to retain authority over lay initiatives.
53. Nancy Hardesty, *Your Daughters*, 66. Luther's *sola scriptura* did not promote independent subjective interpretations outside the guidance of the church.
54. Zikmund tends to polarize and oppose radical as against conservative impulses, splitting apart notions of free church polity and holy spirit as against the authority of scripture and the order of the church, *Women and Religion in America*, Vol. 1, 193.
55. Both prophetic gifts and biblical interpretation took place embedded in social settings. David Lovejoy, *Religious Enthusiasm*, describes religious truths as discovered democratically through prophesying, with church services open to membership for biblical discussion, 193. "Almost every woman prophet preached as a member of an independent church or sect and relied on the physical, oral and financial support of her spiritual family. Religious ecstasies were profoundly social events often in rooms crowded with congregational members who supported them," Mack, 122. Rosemary Ruether, however,

opposes prophetic against institutional Christianity in, for example, "The Liberation of Christology," 143–145.
56. Hardesty, *Daughters*, 12; Cady Stanton later repudiated evangelicism. Haynes describes a women's oriented hermeneutic against conservative readings of the Bible, 305. Of course biblical hermeneutics was no less enlisted in slavery controversy, as in, for example, Theodore Weld's *Bible Against Slavery*, which was written to counter southern biblical accounts. William Garrison was an earnest Calvinist who joined Lyman Beecher's Boston congregation. See Milton Rugoff, *The Beechers*, 109.
57. Hardesty, *Women Called to Witness*, 3. For discussion of Willard, see Suzanne M. Marilley, "Frances Willard and the Feminism of Fear," 135. Marilley attempts to counter arguments that Willard's traditionalist approach either betrayed or compromised possibilities of real advance. Yet her positing a "feminism of fear" as the alternative to a "feminism of rights" weakens her argument. She also leans toward presenting Willard's biblical and religious appeals as strategies "to convince women in her audience that their God-given motherly duties required political action," 131. Yet Marilley does show how Willard extended women's senses of their roles into a model of political action.
58. For discussion, see Carolyn De Swarte Gifford, "American Women and the Bible," 17–21.
59. Sarah Grimké, *Letters on Equality*, Letter I.
60. Angelina Grimké, *Letters*, Letter XII.
61. Rosemary Ruether, "Introduction," *Women and Religion in America*, Vol. 1, 17.
62. Cf. Zikmund, "Feminist Thrust," who distinguishes between "soft feminism" and feminism proper among sects in the matter of upholding social order, 207.
63. Shira Wolosky, "Hymnal Tropes," 232.
64. Jualyne Dodson and Cheryl Townsend Gilkes, "Something Within: Social Change and Collective Endurance in the Sacred World of Black Christian Women," 80–130, 81–83. They note that 75% of church membership generally and 90% in the more prophetic, Pentecostal Sanctified Church movements is made up of women, *Women and Religion in America*, Vol. 3, 87. Peter L. Berger and Richard John Neuhaus, *To Empower People*, affirm that the "black community cannot be understood apart from black church," 187. They, however, do not discuss women.
65. Cheryl Townsend Gilkes, "Women's Traditions in the Sanctified Church," 214–15. Cf. *Black Women in White America: A Documentary History*, ed. Gerda Lerner.
66. Evelyn Brooks Higgenbotham, *Righteous Discontent*, argues that there remained sexism in black churches. She quotes DuBois, who said in 1918 that "Black women are the main pillars of those social settlements which we call churches," 120–121. *Sisters of Spirit* describes both black women's roles and their limits: women were permitted to be exhorters but not ministers in the African Methodist Church, 14. They could address individual congregations but needed permission to do so; they could lead Sunday school classes and prayer meetings, but they spoke in formal church services only with permission, 20. Daniel Mathews, *Religion in the Old South*, recounts how, despite the severe compromise of egalitarian religious principles in the southern context of slavery, blacks did develop leadership; they were allowed to preach from the eighteenth-century revivals onward but only under church supervision. Jon Butler, *Awash in a Sea of Faith*, describes southern religion as severely compromised,

with Christianity and colonial slavery molding each other after 1680. "The Church articulated a planter ethic of absolute slave obedience running counter to English political and social theory and became a principle foundation of American slavery's distinctive paternalism, violence and sentimentalism," 129.
67. Melba Joyce Boyd, *Discarded Legacy*, 36; and Carla L. Peterson, *Doers of the Word*, 124. These writers contest readings of Harper as a merely sentimental poet. Hazel Carby, *Reconstructing Womanhood*, describes black women's activisms in the formation of mutual aid societies, benevolent associations, and the many organizations of the various black churches, although not in suffrage, 4. She discusses Frances Harper as contesting the white women's suffrage failure to endorse suffrage for black men's: "Between the white people and the colored there was a community of interests, but not for increasing the privileges of one class and curtailing the rights of the other," 67. In her speech at the Chicago Fair World's Congress of Representative Women, Harper encouraged women to enter the "political estate" in order to transform society toward "the grand and holy purpose of uplifting the human race against the aims of a society dominated by the greed of gold and the lust for power," 70.
68. For fuller discussion of the spirituals' treatments of biblical pattern, see Wolosky, "Slave Spirituals and Black Typology," *Cambridge History* IV, 200–216. Harper's work, like the spirituals, can be seen as a hybrid form, crossing African-American with white American Christianity.
69. Paula Bennet discusses Sarah Forten's "My Country," who questions the "proud name" of the "Home of the Free," 80, and "The Grave of the Slave," who only finds "freedom and rest" in "death," 77. See also Harper's "Eliza Harris" based on *Uncle Tom's Cabin*, where Eliza, fleeing from slavery, demands: "How shall I speak of my proud country's shame / How say that her banner in mockery waves—Her star—spangled banner—o'er millions of slaves?"
70. Ruether, "Introduction," *Women and Religion in America*, Vol. 3, xiii.
71. George Kent, *A Life of Gwendolyn Brooks*, mentions various church involvements of Brooks and her family, including her mother Keziah's regular church attendance throughout her life, 258. Brooks's essay, "What Prayer Did for Me," describes her recognition of a "strength superior to any that I have known." However, she continues: "I rarely ask for anything, a little lingering independence of spirit," 129, 147.
72. *Report from Part I*, 183. See D. H. Melham, "Gwendolyn Brooks: The Heroic Voice of Prophecy," *Studies in Black Literature Autumn*, 1–3, which describes "In the Mecca" as an "oracular voice, prescriptive and poetic."
73. Cf. discussion by Gary Smith, "Gwendolyn Brooks's 'Children of the Poor.'"
74. Charlotte Gilman, *His Religion and Hers*, 46–48.
75. Katherine Ludwig Jansen, "Maria Magdalena: Apostolorum Apostola," in *Women's Preachers and Prophets*, 57–96, 59–60. Cf. Elisabeth Schussler Fiorenza, *In Memory of Her*, and its project to recover women discipleship suppressed in the androcentric accounts that came to make up the Christian scriptures, xiii–xxiv.
76. Plath, *Poems*, 148, 257, 258.
77. See Shira Wolosky, "What Do Jews Stand For? Muriel Rukeyser's Ethics of Identity."
78. Cristanne Miller, "Marianne Moore and a Poetry of Hebrew (Protestant) Prophecy"; and Cristanne Miller, *Cultures of Modernism*, 240, 152.
79. Marianne Moore, "Feed Me, Also, River God," *Egoist*, 118.

NOTES TO CHAPTER 7

1. It is fascinating that Foucault includes a discussion on Augustinian will and autonomy in "Sexuality and Solitude," *Ethics*, 181. Herafter cited as *E*.
2. Michel Foucault, *Discipline and Punish*, 136–139. Hereafter cited as *DP*.
3. Michel Foucault, *Power/Knowledge*, 192. Hereafter cited as *P/K*. This, of course, has been much discussed by feminist theorists, such as Linda Alcoff, "Feminism and Foucault."
4. Cf. Jürgen Habermas, "Foucault raises power to a basic transcendental-historicism concept of historiography as a critique of reason," *Philosophical Discourses of Modernity*, 254
5. Michel Foucault, "The Subject and Power," 212. Hereafter cited as *SP*.
6. Michael Walzer, Charles Taylor, and Jürgen Habermas in David Couzens Hoy, ed. *Foucault: A Critical Reader*. Foucault in fact does not give much of an account of electoral politics, e.g. *E* 59, *S/P* 55. As he writes, "The phenomenon of the social body is the effect not of a consensus but of the materiality of power operating on the very bodies of individuals," *P/K* 55.
7. Isaac Balbus, "Disciplining Women: Michel Foucault and the Power of Feminist Discourse," 110–128; Nancy Harstock, "Foucault on Power: A Theory for Women," 157–173; Jana Sawicki, *Disciplining Foucault*; Seyla Benhabib, "Feminism and Post-Modernism: An Uneasy Alliance," 17–34; and Susan Bordo, "Feminism, Post-Modernism and Gender Skepticism."
8. See, for example, Foucault, *History of Sexuality I*, 131, where there is the notorious apologia for a mad sexual abuser. Cf. discussion of rape, 163–164.
9. Sandra Lee Bartky, "Foucault, Femininity, and Patriarchal Power," 64.
10. Sylvia Plath, *Collected Poems*, 155.
11. Susan Bordo, *Unbearable Weight*. Simone de Beauvoire already observed: "The purpose of the fashions to which woman is enslaved is not to reveal her as an independent individual but rather to offer her as prey to male desires, within an ideology of consumption," 138–139. See Sue Thornham, *Feminist Theory and Cultural Studies*, for discussion of the production of women through commercialization of the body from Charlotte Gilman onward: "He is the market, the demand. She is the supply," 127. Thornham also provides an overview of how Foucault's body is male, 167. Cf. Luce Irigaray's discussion of women as "fabrications disinvested of the body and reclothed in a form that makes [them] suitable for exchange among men," "Women on the Market," 173, 180.
12. Hilary Radner, "Roaming the City," 88, 92.
13. Bartky, "Foucault, Femininity," 66, 73.
14. Susan Bordo, *Unbearable Weight*.
15. See Alfred Alvarez, *Savage God*, for a powerful account of Plath's body practices.
16. Kate Daniels, "Muriel Rukeyser and Her Literary Critics."
17. Stephanie Hartman notes the "X-Ray likeness between worker's body and the land created by silicosis," with the human body "eclipsed by its own technological representation," "Muriel Rukeyser's "The Book of the Dead," 213.
18. David Kadlec, "X-Ray Testimonials in Muriel Rukeyser," 31.
19. Sacvan Bercovitch explicates these varieties of meanings of individualism and its specifically Emersonian-American senses in "Emerson, Individualism, and Liberal Dissent," 307–352.
20. Michel Foucault, *History of Sexuality I*, 95–96. Hereafter cited as *HS I*.

21. Michel Foucault, *History of Sexuality II*, 43. Hereafter cited as *HS II*.
22. Michel Foucault, *The Foucault Reader*, 380. Hereafter cited as *FR*.
23. Cf. Nancy Fraser, in *Unruly Practices*, observes, "I find no clues as to what his alternative norms might be," 29; and Jean Grimshaw "Practices of Freedom," on the failure of the late Foucault's ethics of self, 65–70.
24. Michel Foucault, *Aesthetics*, 339. Hereafter cited as *A*.
25. See especially Judith Butler, "Contingent Foundations."
26. See Chapter 3.
27. Patricia Hill Collins, *Black Feminist Thought*, describes the particularly communal norms of African-American motherhood, as well as its complex political meanings. Rather than a privatized domesticity, motherhood is a site where black women "express and learn the power of self-definition, importance of valuing and respecting themselves." Tensions of course remain, in which motherhood is seen as a "burdensome" labor, but it also serves as a base for self-actualization, status in black community, and catalyst of activism. "These alleged contradictions can exist side by side in African American communities and families and even within individual women." Collins underscores the participation of "othermothers" who share mothering responsibilities as traditionally central to the institution of black motherhood alongside "bloodmothers," 118–119.

NOTES TO CHAPTER 8

1. Marjorie Perloff theorizes the poetic text in ways that "open the field so as to make contact with the world as well as the word," *Dance of the Intellect*, 181. But she is also ambivalent about whether reference "to an external reality even as its compositional thrust [also] undercut[s] the very referentiality it seems to assert," *Futurist Moment*, 49.
2. Roman Jakobson, "Linguistics and Poetics."
3. For review and discussion of definitions of "woman," see Toril Moi, *What Is a Woman?*
4. The absence of gender in Bakhtin is raised by Wayne C. Booth, "Freedom of Interpretation," and subsequently by many others.
5. Stephen Greenblatt, *Shakespearean Negotiations*, 5–6.
6. Judith Lowder Newton, "History as Usual?"
7. Raymond Williams, *Keywords*, 32; and Raymond Williams, *Marxism and Literature*, 154.
8. Terry Eagleton, *Ideology of the Aesthetic*, 86 196, 2, 3, 9, 4, 206–207, 9.
9. Eagleton, 3. Cf. Isobel Armstrong's critique of Eagleton as himself perpetrating the idealist aesthetic he is attacking, *Radical Aesthetic*, 32–33.
10. Eagleton, 252. Ian Hunter, "Aesthetics and Cultural Studies," traces a genealogy of aesthetics as withdrawal "from the world as a sphere of mundane knowledge and action," 354, 362. This "ethic of withdrawal," however, persists into his own account of aesthetics as "a means by which individuals set themselves apart from 'ordinary' existence and conduct themselves as subjects of a heightened form of being," 361.
11. Winfried Fluck, "Aesthetics and Cultural Studies," 92. Cf. Ian Hunter, "Aesthetics and Cultural Studies": "The task confronting the political analysis of aesthetics, therefore, is not to unmask it as the disguised expression of political domination," 358.
12. Christopher Castiglia and Russ Castronovo, "A Hive of Subtlety," 428.
13. Laurie A. Finke, *Feminist Theory, Women's Writing*, 11. Cf. Terry Threadgold's discussion of Foucault, *Feminist Poetics*.

14. Rita Felski, *Doing Time*, 8. Cf. *Literature and Feminism*, where Felski argues against either/or claims regarding formal vs historicist criticism, 13–14.
15. Max Weber, "Social Psychology of the World Religions," 269–270.
16. Dale Bauer, *Feminist Dialogics*, xiii–xiv, xi; and Teresa De Lauretis, *Alice Doesn't*, 7. Cf. Peter Stallybrass and Allon White, *The Politics and Poetics of Transgression*, 13.
17. Julia Kristeva has particularly absorbed Bakhtinian discourses into psychoanalytic problematics. For the problem of ahistoricity in French Feminism, see, for example, Ann Rosalind Jones, "Inscribing Femininity:; Domna Stanton, "Difference on Trial: A Critique of the Maternal Metaphor in Cixous, Irigaray, and Kristeva," *Poetics of Gender*; Toril Moi discusses Kristeva at length in *Sexual/Textual Politics*, 156–170.
18. Rita Felski, *Beyond Feminist Aesthetics*, 2; cf. 7–8, 30. Felski likewise questions Kristeva's notion of "women's time" as ahistorical, *Beyond Feminist Aeshtetics*, 150.
19. De Lauretis Alice, 7.
20. Bauer, *Feminist Dialogics*, 7.
21. Suzanne Kehde, "Voices from the Margin," 27. Kehde interestingly cites Caryl Emerson's discussion of Vyogotsky, a contemporary to Bakhtin, who, against Piaget, proposed theories of language acquisition as a "development in thinking [which] is not from the individual to the socialized but from the social to the individual." Caryl Emerson, "The Outer Word and Inner Speech," 27–30. This recalls similar redefinitions of the self in terms of social belonging in e.g. Goffman and Meade. Cf. Patrick D. Murphy's contrast of Bakhtin to Freud in "Prolegomenon for an Ecofeminist Dialogics," where Bakhtin's is a "dialogical conception of the self" that recognizes the "social/self" as a "construct developing within social, economic political historical and environmental parameters," 45.
22. Jan Montefiore, for example, speaking of the "need for a coherent feminist theory of poetic language," *Feminism and Poetry*, 8, proposes a "multiply authored poetry as a highly collective repository of female experience" with "women speaking to each other," 11.
23. Diane Price Herndl, "Dilemmas,"16. Cf. Bauer, *Feminist Dialogics*, who posits the problem of internalization as a threat to independent selfhood but then responds that "Each internalization of repression contains the possibility of rebellion," xii, such that personal activism only occurs as a rejection of social norms.
24. Diane Price Herndl, "Dilemmas,"11. Here she is explicating Irigaray.
25. Cf. Jane Gallop, "Snatches of Conversation," feminine language does not conform "to solid male rules of logic, clarity, consistency," 274. Cf. Josephine Donovan, "Style and Power," 85–94, 88, generalizes women's language as paratactic.
26. *Revolution in Poetic Language*, 36. The "space of a given text" is where "several utterances, taken from other texts, intersect and neutralize each other," organized through a typology that "defines the specificity of different textual arrangements by placing them within the general text (culture) of which they are part." As Susan Stewart points out, "the major heirlooms of Saussurian linguistics—langue and parole, the arbitrary nature of the sign, and more indirectly, the distinction between poetic and ordinary language—reappear in transformational grammar, in the old (and the new) stylistics, and even, surprisingly, in quasi-Marxist theories of language such as Julia Kristeva's." "Shouts on the Street: Bakhtin's Anti-Linguistics," 43.
27. Cf. Simon Dentith distinguishes Kristeva's "intertextuality" from Bakhtin's "heterogeneity of the historical process," *Bakhtinian Thought*, 94–98.

28. Kristeva, *Desire*, 32; *Reader*, 52; and *Desire*, 137. For a critique of Kristevan psychoanalytics as ahistorical and politically problematic, see Diana Leland, "The Subversion of Women's Agency in Psychoanalytic Feminism: Chodorow, Flax, Kristeva"; and Judith Butler, "The Body Politics of Julia Kristeva," 162–176. Cf. in the same volume Diana T. Meyers, "The Subversion of Women's Agency," 136–161.
29. Nancy Fraser, "Uses and Abuses," 177–179, 186–187.
30. Kristeva cites Jakobson: *Desire*, 26–34.
31. Psychoanalytic categories may intersect with literary tradition through Bloomian scenes of Oedipal agon as revised through feminized categories, as we saw in Chapter 1. But Bloom still largely veers away from concrete social territories, addressing literary history as a near autonomous domain.
32. There are many discussions of French Feminism. See, for example, Ann Rosalind Jones, "Inscribing Femininity," who argues that écriture feminine "privileges changes in subjectivity over change in economic and political systems" and asks, "can parler femme escape the boundaries of discourse?" 107. Also Judith Kegan Gardiner, "Mind Mother," who argues that women's "mind" in French Feminism is "neither historical nor socially constructed," 113, 120. Domna Stanton, "Difference on Trial," says of Cixous, Irigaray, and Kristeva that "their analyses are basically unconcerned with 'the real' or the historical despite occasional references to the radical transformations in socio-political structures [which] would create a radically different inscription of difference" (citing Cixous), 160. Toril Moi discusses Kristeva at length in *Sexual/Textual Politics*, 156–170, arguing in the end that Kristeva's remains a theory that does not account for the "relations between the subject and society," 171. It is worth noting that Daniel Stern's *The Interpersonal World of the Infant* has called into question the whole notion of an undifferentiated pre-Oedipal experience on which Lacanian French Feminism is based. This empirical critique, however, works beside the more theoretical objection of the problematic reduction of the female to nonrational language. This is discussed in Suzanne Juhasz, "Adventures in the World of the Symbolic: Dickinson and Metaphor," who poses Stern's work on linguistic intersubjectivity against French Feminism's posting of women as outside language in a pre-Oedipal body, 141.
33. Felski, *Beyond Feminist Aesthetics*, 2; cf. 7–8, 30. Felski likewise questions Kristeva's notion of "women's time" as ahistorical, *Beyond Feminist Aesthetics*, 150. In a discussion of American women's poetry, Leigh Gilmore, "The Gaze of the Other Woman," sees psychoanalytic criticism as assuming an ahistorical "self:" In these interpretations, literary texts may be transformed into elegant instances of psychosocial dynamics," 82. Psychoanalysis describes "transhistorical features of identity," and thus "subordinates the process [of interpretation] to a conclusion that must seem self-evident, existing prior to and independent of the reading that produced it," 87.
34. Mikhail Bakhtin, *Problems of Dostoevsky's Poetics*, 184. Hereafter cited as Dost.
35. Josephine Donovan, "Style and Power," 85; Cf. Diane Price Herndl, "Dilemmas," 7–24. "Bakhtin describes dialogue as important to the extent that it is political and raises questions of power by asking whose voice is dominant," 7. Cf. Zofia Burr, *Of Women, Poetry and Power*, 9–10. Burr also tends to use the terms "aesthetic" to mean constructing a "hermetic inviolability around the poem as aesthetic artifact" as against "motivated utterance addressed to its auditors," 157. Nigel Smith in *Literature and Revolution* attempts to bridge historical and formal discussion through reference to Bakhtinian genre theory. Yet he still poses texts as, on the one hand, "part of lived,

social reality," but, "on the other," as "constellations of linguistic signs, tied together by grammar rules and other systems of signification," 3–4.
36. Tzvetan Todorov, *Mikhail Bakhtin*, 54–55.
37. For Bakhtin, to become dialogical, utterances must "become the positions of various subjects expressed in discourse," *Dostoevsky*, 183. Cf. *Dialogical Imagination*, 323.
38. M. M., Bakhtin *Speech Genres*, 62. Hereafter cited as *SG*.
39. Paul de Man, "Dialogue and Dialogism," 104–105.
40. To take one influential case, Paul Ricoeur distinguishes his own position from what he calls a Derridean "hypostasis of language," which sets up "language as an absolute," *Philosophy of Paul Ricoeur*, 101.
41. Allon White, *Carnival, Hysteria and Writing*, 150.
42. Jacques Derrida, *Acts of Literature*, 63–64.
43. Jacques Derrida, *Speech and Phenomena*, 30.
44. Jacques Derrida, "Signature, Event, Context," 318, 317.
45. Diane Elam, *Feminism and Deconstruction*, 31.
46. Jacques Derrida, *Limited Inc.*, 190, 198; 203. cf. "Signature, Event, Context," 317. Hereafter cited as *LTD* followed by page number.
47. Marjorie Perloff, "Language Poetry and the Lyric Subject," 412–419, 432.
48. Diane Price Herndl, " Dilemmas," 10.
49. Jacques Derrida and Christie McDonald, "Interview: Choreographies," 76, 72–73. See also *Spurs*.
50. Derrida, *LTD*, 148.
51. Lynn Keller, *Forms of Expansion*, and Yopie Prins and Maeera Shreiber, eds., *Dwelling in Possibility: Women Poets and Critics on Poetry*, address the move of contemporary poetry into public performance in ways that are reviewed by Kathleen Crown, "Poetry, Feminism and the Public Sphere." Cf, Linda Kinnahan, *Poetics of the Feminine*; and Cristanne Miller, *Marianne Moore*, 173–179.
52. Cristanne Miller, "Corpses of Poetry," discusses Moore in terms of Bakhtin in bringing "into poetry the density of social analysis," 77. Cf. Lynn Keller, "For inferior who is free," *Influence and Intertextuality*, 220.
53. Marianne Moore, *Complete Poems*, 173, Notes: 289.
54. Most discussions of Moore investigate this question of feminized modesty, as part of Moore's complex gender evasions as well as invocations and performances. Cristanne Miller extensively reviews the question of Moore's modesty, arguing that it ultimately grounds "her construction of an alternative authority," 32, 33, 173.
55. Betsy Erkkila sees Moore's "seemingly ladylike timidity and modesty" as "mask[ing] an ambition to invent herself as an American original"; but also describes Moore's as an assertive critique of social norms from a position at once ethical and historically feminized, *Wicked Sisters*, 102–104.
56. James Bryant Conant, *Citadel of Learning*, 5, 8, 67.

References

PRIMARY SOURCES

Note: almost all poems cited in this study can be read online. Citations for poetry will be from the texts listed below, cited by abbreviation and page number.

Bishop, Elizabeth. *The Complete Poems*. New York: Farrar Straus Giroux, 1983. Cited as *CP*.
———. *The Collected Prose*. London: The Hogarth Press, 1984. Cited as *CPr*.
Bradstreet, Anne. *Works of Anne Bradstreet*, Ed. Jeannine Hensley. Cambridge, MA: Harvard University Press, 1967. Cited as *Works*.
Brooks, Gwendolyn. *Blacks*. Chicago, IL: Third World Press. 1981. Cited as *B*.
———. "Interview" with Martha H. Brown. *The Great Lakes Review* 6 (Summer 1979).
———. *Report from Part I, Part II*.
———. "What Prayer Did for Me." *Chicago American* (February 26, 1958).
Cary, Alice, and Cary, Phoebe. *The Poems of Alice and Phoebe Cary*. New York: Hurst and Co. Pub., 1850; also from the Making of America internet archive at the University of Michigan. Cited as *P*.
Dickinson, Emily. *Poems of Emily Dickinson*. Ed. Thomas Johnson. Cambridge, MA: Harvard University Press, 1951. Cited as *J*.
———. *The Poems of Emily Dickinson*. Ed. R. W. Franklin. Cambridge, MA: Harvard University Press, 1998. Cited as *F*.
Gilman, Charlotte. *In This Our World*. New York: Arno Press, 1974 (reprint of 1899). Cited as *World*.
———. *The Later Poetry of Charlotte Gilman*. Ed. Denise D. Knight. Newark: University of Delaware Press, 1996. Cited as *LP*.
———. *His Religion and Hers*. Westport, CT: Hyperion Press Inc., 1976.
———. *The Home, Its Work and Influence*. New York: Charlton Co., 1910.
———. *Women and Economics*. New York: Prometheus Books, 1994.
Grahn, Judy. "From a Public Dialogue between Grahn and Felstiner." *Women Writers of the West Coast*. Ed. Mailyn Yalom. Santa Barbara, CA: Capra Press, 1983.
Harper, Frances. *Complete Poems*. Ed. Maryemma Graham. New York: Oxford University Press, 1988. Cited as *CP*.
H. D. *Collected Poems 1912–1944*. Ed. Louis Martz. New York: New Directions, 1983. Cited as *CP*.
Howe, Julia Ward. *From Sunset Ridge*. Boston: Tilton and Co., 1898. Cited as *SR*.

Jackson, Helen Hunt. *Complete Poems*. Boston: Roberts Brothers, 1873 (reprint, New York: Arno Press, 1972). Cited as *CP*.
Larcom, Lucy. *The Poetical Works*. Boston: Houghton Mifflin, 1868. Cited as *PW*.
Lorde, Audre. *Collected Poems*. New York: Norton, 1997.
———. *Sister Outsider*. New York: The Crossing Press 1984.
Moore, Marianne. *The Complete Poems*. New York: Macmillan, 1956. Cited as *CP*.
———. *Complete Prose*. New York: Viking, 1986. Cited as *CPr*.
Plath, Sylvia. *Collected Poems*. New York: Harper and Row, 1981. Cited as *CP*.
Rich, Adrienne. *The Fact of a Doorframe*. New York: Norton, 1984. Cited as *Facts*.
———. *Poems Selected and New 1950–1974*. New York: Norton, 1975. Cited as *PS*.
———. *Poems*. New York: Norton, 1975. Cited as *P*.
———. "Compulsory Heterosexuality and Lesbian Experience." *Blood, Bread and Poetry*. New York: Norton, 1986.
———. *On Lies, Secrets, and Silence: Selected Prose 1966–1978*. New York: Norton, 1986.
Rukeyser, Muriel. *The Collected Poems of Muriel Rukeyser*. New York: McGraw-Hill Book Company, 1978. Cited as *CP*.
Sexton, Anne. *The Complete Poems*. Boston: Houghton Mifflin, 1981. Cited as *CP*.
Sigourney, Lydia. *Select Poems*. Boston: Edward C. Riddle, 1843. Cited as *SP*.
Wheatley, Phyllis. http://www.poetryfoundation.org/bio/phillis-wheatley Sept. 2012
Wilcox, Ella Wheeler. Project Gutenberg: http://www.gutenberg.org/ebooks Sept. 2012
———. *Poems of Problems*. Chicago: W. B. Conkey Co., 1914. Cited as *PProb*.
———. *Poems of Progress*. Chicago: W. B. Conkey Co., 1909. Cited as *PProg*.

Note: Nineteenth-century poems discussed here are reprinted in Shira Wolosky. *Major Voices: Nineteenth-Century American Women's Poetry*. London: Toby Press, 2003.

SECONDARY SOURCES

Abel, Elizabeth. "(E)merging Identities: The Dynamics of Female Friendship in Contemporary Fiction by Women." *Signs* (Spring 1981): 413–435.
Ahlstrom, Sidney. *A Religious History of the American People*. New Haven, CT: Yale University Press, 1972.
Alcoff, Linda. "Feminism and Foucault: The Limits to a Collaboration." *Crises in Continental Philosophy*. Eds. Arlene Dallery and Charles Scott. New York: State University of New York Press, 1990.
Almond, G. A., and Verba, Sidney. *The Civic Culture: Political Attitudes and Democracy in Five Nations*. Princeton NJ: Princeton University Press, 1963.
Alvarez, A. *The Savage God*. Hammondsworth, Middlesex: Penguin, 1975.
Amussen, Susan. *An Ordered Society: Gender and Class in Early Modern England*. Oxford: Basil Blackwell, 1988.
Andrews, William. *Sisters of the Spirit*. Bloomington: Indiana University Press, 1986.

Appleby, Joyce. *Capitalism and a New Social Order.* New York: New York University Press, 1984.
———. *Liberalism and Republicanism in the Historical Imagination.* Cambridge, MA: Harvard University Press, 1992.
Ardener, Edwin. "Belief and the Problem of Women." *Perceiving Women.* Ed. Shirley Ardener. London: Dent & Sons, 1975, 1–8.
Ardener, Shirley. "Introduction." *Perceiving Women.* Ed. Shirley Ardener. London: Dent & Sons, 1975, vii–xxiii.
Arendt, Hannah. *Between Past and Future.* New York: Viking, 1954.
———. *The Human Condition.* Chicago: University of Chicago Press, 1958.
———. *On Revolution.* Harmondsworth: Penguin Books, 1977.
———. *Totalitarianism, The Origins of Totalitarianism III.* New York: Harcourt, Brace & World, 1968.
Armstrong, Isobel. *The Radical Aesthetic.* Oxford: Basil Blackwell, 2000.
Armstrong, Nancy. *Desire and Domestic Fiction.* New York: Oxford University Press, 1987.
Auerbach, Judy, Blum, Linda, Smith, Vicki, and Williams, Christine. "On Gilligan's 'In a Different Voice.'" *Feminist Studies* 11.1 (Spring 1985): 149–161.
Babha, Homi. *The Location of Culture,* New York: Routledge, 1994.
Baier, Annette. "The Need for More than Justice." *Science, Morality and Feminist Theory.* Eds. Marsha Hanen and Kai Nielsen. Calgary, Alberta, Canada: University of Calgary Press, 1987, 41–58.
Bailey, Cathryn. "Making Waves and Drawing Lines: The Politics of Defining the Vicissitudes of Feminism." Hypatia 12.3 (1997): 17–28.
Bailyn, Bernard. *Education in the Forming of American Society.* Chapel Hill, NC: University of North Carolina Press, 1960.
Baker, Paula. "The Domestication of Politics." *American Historical Review* 89:3 (June 1984): 620–647.
———. *The Moral Frameworks of Public Life.* New York: Oxford University Press, 1991.
Bakhtin, M. M. *The Dialogic Imagination.* Ed. Michael Holquist, Trans. Caryl Emerson and Michael Holquist. Austin: University of Texas Press, 1982.
———. *Problems of Dostoevsky's Poetics.* Minneapolis: University of Minnesota Press, 1984.
———. *Speech Genres & Other Late Essays.* Eds. Caryl Emerson and Michael Holquist. Trans. Vern W. McGee. Austin: University of Texas Press, 1986.
Balbus, Isaac. "Disciplining Women: Michel Foucault and the Power of Feminist Discourse." *Feminism as Critique.* Eds. Seyla Benhabib and Drucilla Cornell. Oxford: Polity Press. 1987, 110–128.
Barret, Faith. "Public Selves and Private Spheres: Studies of Emily Dickinson and the Civil War, 1984–2007." *Emily Dickinson Journal* 16:1 (2007): 92–104.
Bartky, Sandra Lee. "Foucault, Femininity, and Patriarchal Power." *Feminism and Foucault.* Eds. Irene Diamond and Lee Quinby. Boston: Northeastern Press, 1988, 61–86.
Barzilai, Shuli. "Reading Snow White: The Mother's Story." *Signs* 15.3 (1990): 515–534.
Bass, Dorothy. "Their Prodigious Influence." *Women of Spirit.* Eds. Rosemary Ruether and Eleanor McLaughlin. New York: Simon and Schuster, 1979, 280–300.
Bauer, Dale. *Feminist Dialogics: A Theory of Failed Community.* Albany: State University of New York Press, 1988.
Baym, Nina. "Reinventing Lydia Sigourney." *Feminism and American Literary History.* New Brunswick, NJ: Rutgers University Press, 1992, 151–166.

———. *American Women Writers and the Work of History, 1790–1860.* New Brunswick, NJ: Rutgers University Press, 1995.

———. *Women's Fiction.* Ithaca, NY: Cornell University Press, 1978.

Bellah, Robert. *Habits of the Heart.* Berkeley: University of California Press, 1985.

Bendroth, Margaret. *Fundamentalism and Gender.* New Haven, CT: Yale University Press, 1993.

Benhabib, Seyla. "Feminism and Post-Modernism: An Uneasy Alliance." *Feminist Contentions: A Philosophical Exchange.* Ed. Linda Nicholson. New York: Routledge, 1995, 17–34.

———. "Models of Public Space: Hannah Arendt, the Liberal Tradition, and Jürgen Habermas." *Feminism, the Public and the Private.* Ed. Joan B. Landes. New York: Oxford University Press, 1998, 65–99.

———. *Situating the Self: Gender, Community and Postmodernism.* New York: Routledge, 1992.

Bennett, Paula. *Poets in the Public Sphere: The Emancipatory Project of American Women's Poetry, 1800–1900.* Princeton: Princeton University Press, 1998.

Ben-Ze'ev, Aaron. "The Virtue of Modesty." *American Philosophical Quarterly* 30 (1993): 235–246.

Bercovitch, Sacvan. *Puritan Origins of the American Self.* New Haven, CT: Yale University Press, 1975.

———. "Emerson, Individualism, and Liberal Dissent." *The Rites of Assent.* New York: Routledge, 1993, 307–352.

Berger, Peter, and Neuhaus, Richard. *To Empower People.* Ed. Michael Novak. Washington, DC: AEI Press, 1996.

Berman, Jeffrey. *Surviving Literary Suicide.* Amherst: University of Massachusetts Press, 1999.

Berry, Helen, and Foyster, Elizabeth, eds. *The Family in Early Modern England.* New York: Cambridge University Press, 2007.

Blackstone, William. *Commentaries on the Laws of England.* Boston: Beacon Press, 1966.

Bloch, Ruth. "Virtue in Revolutionary America." *Signs* 13.1 (1987): 37–58.

Bloom, Harold. *The Anxiety of Influence.* New York: Oxford University Press, 1979.

———. "The Internalization of Quest Romance." London: Henry Schwab, 1988, 17–41.

Booth, Wayne C. "Freedom of Interpretation: Bakhtin and the Challenge of Feminist Criticism." *Bakhtin: Essays and Dialogues on His Work.* Ed. Gary Saul Morson. Chicago: University of Chicago Press, 1986.

Bordo, Susan. "Afterward: The Feminist as Other." *Philosophy in a Feminist Voice.* Ed. Janet A. Kourany. Princeton: Princeton University Press, 1988, 296–312.

———. "Feminism, Post-Modernism and Gender Skepticism." *Feminism/Postmodernism.* Ed. Linda J. Nicholson. New York: Routledge, 1990, 133–156.

———. *Unbearable Weight.* Berkeley: University of California Press, 1993.

Borker, Ruth. "Anthropological Perspectives on Gender and Language." *Gender and Anthropology.* Ed. Sandra Morgen. Washington, DC: American Anthropological Association, 1989,. 411–437.

Bowlby, Rachel. "Modes of Modern Shopping." *The Ideology of Conduct.* Eds. Nancy Armstrong and Leonard Tennenhouse. New York: Methuen, 1987, 185–205.

Boyd, Melba. Joyce *Discarded Legacy.* Detroit: Wayne State University Press, 1994.

Braude, Anne. *Women and Religious History.* New York: Oxford University Press, 2000.

Brennan, Claire, ed. *The Poetry of Sylvia Plath*. Cambridge, England: Icon Books, 2000.
Bridges, William E. "Family Patterns and Social Values in America." *Education in American History*. Ed. Michael Katz. New York: Praeger Publishers, 1973, 3–12.
Brodhead, Richard. *Cultures of Letters: Scenes of Reading and Writing in Nineteenth-Century America*. Chicago: University of Chicago Press, 1993.
Brooks, Ann. *Postfeminisms: Feminism, Cultural Theory, and Cultural Forms*. New York: Routledge, 1997.
Brown, Gillian. *Domestic Individualism*. Berkeley: University of California Press, 1990.
Bruce, Jr., Dickson. *Black American Writing from the Nadir: The Evolution of a Literary Tradition 1877–1915*. Baton Rouge: Louisiana State University Press, 1989.
Buhle, Mari Jo. *Feminism and Its Discontents: A Century of Struggle with Psychoanalysis*. Cambridge, MA: Harvard University Press, 1998.
Burr, Zofia. *Of Women, Poetry and Power*. Urbana: University of Illinois Press, 2002.
Bushman, Richard. *From Puritan to Yankee*. New York: Norton, 1967.
Butler, Jon. *Awash in a Sea of Faith*. Cambridge, MA: Harvard University Press, 1992.
———, and Grant Wacker. *Religion in American Life: A Short History*. New York: Oxford University Press, 2000.
Butler, Judith. "The Body Politics of Julia Kristeva." *Revaluing French Feminism: Critical Essays on Difference, Agency, & Culture*. Eds. Nancy Fraser and Sandra Lee Bartky. Bloomington: Indiana University Press, 1992, 162–176.
———. "Contingent Foundations: Feminism and the Question of Post-Modernism." *Feminist Contentions: A Philosophical Exchange*. Ed. Linda Nicholson. New York: Routledge, 1995, 35–57.
———. "Feminism and Post-Modernism: An Uneasy Alliance." *Feminist Contentions: A Philosophical Exchange*. Ed. Linda Nicholson. New York: Routledge, 1995, 17–34.
———. *Gender Trouble*. New York: Routledge, 1990.
Bynum, Caroline. *Jesus as Mother*. Berkeley: University of California Press, 1982.
———. "Patterns of Female Piety in the Later Middle Ages." *Crown and Veil*. Eds. Jeffrey Hamburger and Susan Marti. New York: Columbia University Press, 2008.
Capp, Bernard. "Separate Domains? Women and Authority in Early Modern England." *The Experience of Authority in Early Modern England*. Eds. Paul Griffiths, Adam Fox, and Steve Hindle. New York: St. Martin's Press, 1996.
Carby, Hazel. *Reconstructing Womanhood: The Emergence of the Afro-American Woman Novelist*. New York: Oxford University Press, 1982.
Castiglia, Christopher, and Castronovo, Russ. "A 'Hive of Subtlety': Aesthetics and the End(s) of Cultural Studies." *American Literature* 76:3 (September 2004): 423–435.
Cavell, Stanley. *Conditions Handsome and Unhandsome*. Chicago: The University of Chicago Press, 1990.
Chodorow, Nancy. "Family Structure and Feminine Personality." *Woman, Culture and Society*. Eds. Michelle Zimbalest, Rosaldo Rosaldo, and Louise Lamphere. Stanford, CA: Stanford University Press, 1974, 43–66.
———. *The Reproduction of Motherhood*. Berkeley: University of California Press, 1978.

———. "Toward a Relational Individualism." *Reconstructing Individualism: Autonomy, Individuality, and the Self.* Eds. Thomas Heler, Morton Sosnor, and David Bellbery. Stanford, CA: Stanford University Press, 1986, 197–208.
Cixous, Hélène. "The Laugh of the Medusa." *The Signs Reader.* Chicago: University of Chicago Press, 1983, 279–297.
Clark, Suzanne. *Sentimental Modernism: Women Writers and the Revolution of the Word.* Bloomington: Indiana University Press, 1996.
Code, Lorraine. "Second Persons." *Science, Morality and Feminist Theory.* Eds. Marsha Hanen and Kai Nielsen. Canada: University of Calgary Press, 1987, 357–385.
Collins, Patricia Hill. *Black Feminist Thought: Knowledge, Consciousness, and the Politics of Empowerment.* New York: Routledge, 1991.
Conant, James Bryant. *The Citadel of Learning.* New Haven, CT: Yale University Press, 1956.
Coontz, Stephanie. *Marriage: A History.* New York: Penguin Books, 2005.
Costello, Bonnie. "The 'Feminine' Language of Marianne Moore." *Women and Language in Literature and Society.* Eds. Sally McConnel-Ginet, Ruth Borker, and Nelly Furman. New York: Praeger Special Studies, 1980, 222–239.
———. *Marianne Moore: Imaginary Possessions.* Cambridge, MA: Harvard University Press, 1981.
———. "Marianne Moore and Elizabeth Bishop: Friendship and Influence." *American Women Poets.* Ed. Harold Bloom. New York: Chelsea House, 1986.
Cott, Nancy. *The Bonds of Womanhood.* New Haven, CT: Yale University Press, 1977.
———. *The Grounding of Modern Feminism.* New Haven, CT: Yale University Press, 1987.
———. *Public Vows.* Cambridge, MA: Harvard University Press, 2000.
Crane, Elaine Forman. "Religion and Rebellion: Women of Faith in the American Way of Independence." *Religion in a Revolutionary Age.* Eds. Ronald Hoffman and Peter Albert. Charlottesville: U.S. Capitol Historical Society, University Press of Virginia, 1994, 52–86.
Crawford, Patricia. *Women and Religion in England 1500–1720.* London: Routledge, 1996.
———. "Women's Published Writings 1600–1700." *Women in English Society 1500–1800.* Ed. Mary Prior. London: Methuen, 1985, 211–282.
Cressy, David. *Literacy and the Social Order: Reading and Writing in Tudor and Stuart England.* Cambridge: Cambridge University Press, 1980.
Crown, Kathleen. "Poetry, Feminism and the Public Sphere." *Contemporary Literature* 39:4 (Winter 1998): 644–668.
Daniels, Kate. "Muriel Rukeyser and Her Literary Critics." *Gendered Modernism.* Eds. M. Dickie and T. Travisano. Philadelphia: University of Pennsylvania Press, 1966, 247–263
Davidson, Cathy. *Revolution and the Word: The Rise of the Novel in America.* New York: Oxford University Press, 1986.
Davies, Kathleen M. "The Sacred Condition of Equality—How Original Were Puritan Doctrines of Marriage?" *Social History* 2.5 (1977): 563–580.
Davis, Natalie Zemon. *Society and Culture in Early Modern France.* Stanford, CA: Stanford University Press, 1975.
———. *Women on the Margins, Three Seventeenth Century Lives.* Cambridge, MA: Harvard University Press, 1995.
De Beauvoir, Simone. *The Second Sex.* New York: Alfred Knopf, 1971.
De Lauretis, Teresa. *Alice Doesn't.* Bloomington: Indiana University Press, 1984.
———. "Introduction." *Feminist Studies/Critical Studies.* Ed. Teresa De Lauretis. Bloomington: Indiana University Press, 1986.

———. *The Practice of Love: Lesbian Sexuality and Perverse Desire.* Bloomington: Indiana University Press, 1994.
De Man, Paul. "Dialogue and Dialogism." *Poetics Today* 4:1 (1983): 99–107.
De Tocqueville, Alexis. *Democracy in America.* New York: Vintage Books, 1957.
Degler, Carl. *At Odds.* New York: Oxford University Press, 1980.
Dentith, Simon. *Bakhtinian Thought.* London: Routledge 1991.
Derrida, Jacques. *Acts of Literature.* New York: Routledge, 1992.
———, and Christie McDonald. "Interview: Choreographies." *Diacritics* 12.2 (Summer 1982): 66–76.
———. *Limited Inc.* Evanston, IL: Northwestern University Press, 1988.
———. "Signature, Event, Context." *Margins of Philosophy.* Trans. Alan Bass. Brighton, Sussex: Harvester Press, 1982.
———. *Speech and Phenomena and Other Essays on Husserl's Theory of Signs.* Evanston: Northwestern University Press, 1973.
———. *Spurs.* Chicago: University of Chicago Press, 1978.
Diehl, Joanne Feit. *Dickinson and the Romantic Imagination.* Princeton, NJ: Princeton University Press, 1981.
———. *Women Poets and the American Sublime.* Bloomington: Indiana University Press, 1990.
Dinnerstein, Dorothy. *The Mermaid and the Minotaur.* New York: Harper and Row, 1976.
Dietz, Mary G. "Citizenship with a Feminist Face: The Problem with Maternal Thinking." *Political Theory* 13.1 (February 1985): 19–37.
Dobson, Joanne. *Dickinson and Strategies of Reticence.* Bloomington: Indiana University Press, 1989.
———. "Reclaiming Sentimental Literature." *American Literature* 69:2 (June 1997): 263–288.
Dodson, Jualyne, and Gilkes, Cheryl Townsend. "Something Within: Social Change and Collective Endurance in the Sacred World of Black Christian Women." *Women and Religion in America.* Vol. 3. Eds. Rosemary Ruether and Rosemary Skinner Keller. New York: Harper and Row, 1986, 80–130.
Donovan, Josephine. *Feminist Theory.* New York: Unger, 1985.
———. "Style and Power." *Feminism, Bakhtin and the Dialogic.* Eds. Dale Bauer and S. Jaret McKinstry. Albany: State University of New York Press, 1991.
Dorrien, Gary. *The Making of American Liberal Theology: Imagining Progressive Religion.* Louisville: Westminster John Knox Press, 2001.
Douglas, Ann. *The Feminization of American Culture.* New York: Anchor Books, 1977.
Douglas, Mary. *Purity and Danger.* London: Ark Paperbacks, 1984.
Douglass, Jane Dempsey. *Women, Freedom and Calvin.* Philadelphia: Westminster Press, 1985.
Doumerge, Emile. "Calvin a Source of Democracy." *Calvin and Calvinism: Sources of Democracy.* Eds. Robert Kingdon and Robert Linder. Lexington, MA: D.C. Heath and Co., 1970, 1–7.
Driver, Julia. "The Virtues of Ignorance." *Journal of Philosophy* 86 (1989): 373–384.
DuBois, Ellen Carol. *Feminism and Suffrage: The Emergence of an Independent Women's Movement in America.* Ithaca, NY: Cornell University Press, 1978.
DuBois, W. E. B. *The Souls of Black Folks.* New York: Bantam Books, 1989.
Dunn, Mary Maples. "Saints and Sisters." *Women in American Religion.* Ed. Janet Wilson James. Philadelphia: University of Pennsylvania Press, 1980.

———. "Women of Light." *Women of Spirit.* Eds. Rosemary Ruether and Elanor McLaughlin. New York: Simon and Schuster, 1979, 114–133.

Eagleton, Terry. *The Ideology of the Aesthetic.* Oxford: Basil Blackwell, 1990.

Einstein, Elizabeth. *The Printing Press as an Agent of Change.* New York: Cambridge University Press, 1979.

Elam, Diane. *Feminism and Deconstruction.* New York: Routledge, 1994.

Eldred, Janet Carey, and Peter Mortensen. "Persuasion Dwelt on Her Tongue: Female Civic Rhetoric in Early America." *College English:* 60:2 (February 1998): 173–188.

Eley, Geoff. "Nations, Publics and Political Cultures." *Habermas and the Public Sphere.* Ed. Craig Calhoun. Cambridge, MA: MIT Press, 1992, 289–339.

Elshtain, Jean Bethke. "Feminism, Family and Community." *Feminism and Community* . Philadelphia: Temple University Press, 1995.

———. "Individual Rights and Social Obligation." *Common Knowledge* 7.3 (Winter 1998): 118–128.

———. "Moral Woman and Immoral Man: A Consideration of the Public-Private Split and Its Political Ramifications." *Politics and Society* 4 (1974), 453–473

———. *Public Man, Private Woman.* Princeton, NJ: Princeton University Press, 1981.

———,. and Ehrenreich, Barbara. "Feminism, Family, and Community." *Dissent* 29 (Fall 1982): 442–449.

———. "Reply," *Dissent* 30 (Winter 1983): 103–109.

———. "Reply to Reply." *Dissent* 30 (Spring 1983): 247–255.

Emerson, Caryl. "The Outer Word and Inner Speech." *Bakhtin: Essays and Dialogues on His Work.* Ed. Gary Saul Morson. Chicago: University of Chicago Press, 1986, 21–40.

Emerson, Ralph Waldo. "Circles." *Selected Prose and Poetry.* Ed. Reginald Cook. New York: Holt Rinehart, 1969, 110–120.

Eppler, Karen Sanchez. "Bodily Bonds: The Intersecting Rhetorics of Feminism and Abolition." *The Culture of Sentiment: Race Gender and Sentimentality in Nineteenth-Century American Culture.* Ed. Samuels, Shirley. New York: Oxford University Press, 1992, 92–114.

Erkkila, Betsy. *The Wicked Sisters.* New York: Oxford University Press, 1992.

Erikson, Erik H. *Childhood and Society.* New York: Norton, 1963.

Evans, Sara. *Born For Liberty.* New York: Free Press, 1989.

———. "Women's History and Political Theory." *Visible Women.* Eds. Nancy A. Hewitt and Suzanne Lebsock. Urbana: University of Illinois Press, 1993, 117–139.

Ezell, Margaret. *Writing Women's Literary History.* Baltimore: Johns Hopkins University Press, 1993.

Falk, Pasi, and Colin Campbell, eds. *The Shopping Experience.* London: Sage, 1997.

Faludi, Susan. *Backlash: The Undeclared War Against American Women.* New York: Anchor, 1991.

Felski, Rita. *Doing Time: Feminist Theory and Postmodern Culture.* New York: New York University Press, 2000.

———. *Literature and Feminism.* Chicago: University of Chicago Press, 2003.

Finke, Laurie. A. *Feminist Theory, Women's Writing.* Ithaca, NY: Cornell University Press, 1992.

Fisher, Philip. *Hard Facts.* New York: Oxford University Press, 1987.

Flanagan, Owen. "Virtue and Ignorance." *Journal of Philosophy* 87 (1990): 420–428.

Flax, Jane. "Postmodernism and Gender Relations in Feminist Theory." *Feminism/Postmodernism.* Ed. Linda Nicholson. New York: Routledge, 1990.

Fluck, Winfried. "Aesthetics and Cultural Studies." *Aesthetics in a Multicultural Age*. Ed. Emory Elliott. New York: Oxford University Press, 2002.
Foster, Frances Smith, ed. *A Brighter Coming Day: A Frances Harper Reader*. New York: Feminist Press at the City University of New York, 1990.
Foster, Stephen. "The Puritan's Greatest Achievement: A Study of Social Cohesion in 17th Century Massachusetts." *The Journal of American History* 60.1 (June 1973): 5–22.
Foucault, Michel. *Aesthetics, Method and Epistemology, Essential Works of Foucault 1954–1984*, Vol. II. Ed. James Faubion. London: Allen Lane, The Penguin Press, 1998.
———. *Discipline and Punish*. New York: Vintage Books, 1979.
———. *Ethics. Essential Works of Foucault 1954–1984*, Vol. 1. Ed. Paul Rabinow. London: Penguin, 1977.
———. *History of Sexuality I: The Will to Know*. New York: Pantheon, 1978.
———. *History of Sexuality II: The Care of the Self*. New York: Vintage, 1988.
———. *Power/Knowledge*. Ed. Colin Gordon. New York: Prentice Hall, 1980.
———. *The Foucault Reader*. Ed. Paul Rabinow. New York: Pantheon Books, 1984.
———. "The Subject and Power." *Michel Foucault: Beyond Structuralism and Hermeneutics*. Eds. Hubert Dreyfus and Paul Rabinow. Chicago: University of Chicago Press, 1982.
Fox-Genovese, Elizabeth. *Feminism Without Illusions*. Chapel Hill: University of Chapel Hill Press, 1991.
Fraser, Nancy, and Nicholson, Linda. "Social Criticism without Philosophy: An Encounter between Feminism and Postmodernism." *Feminism/Postmodernism*. New York: Routledge, 1990, 19–38.
Fraser, Nancy. *Unruly Practices*. Cambridge, MA: Polity Press, 1989.
Linda. "The Uses and Abuses of French Discourse Theories for Feminist Politics." *Revaluing French Feminism: Critical Essays on Difference, Agency and Culture*. Eds. Nancy Fraser and Sandra Lee Bartky. Bloomington: Indiana University Press, 1992, 177–194.
Freccero, John. "The Fig Tree and the Laurel: Petrarchan Poetics." *Diacritics* 5 (1975): 34–40.
Freedman, Estelle. "Separatism as Strategy." *Feminist Studies* 5.3 (Fall 1979): 512–529.
Friedman, Marilyn. "Autonomy and Social Relationships." *Feminists Rethink the Self*. Ed. Diana Tietjens Meyers. New York: Westview Press, 1997, 40–61.
Freud, Sigmund. "Some Psychical Consequences of the Anatomical Distinction Between the Sexes" (1925). *The Standard Edition of the Complete Psychological Words of Sigmund Freud* 19. Ed. James Strachey. London: Hogarth Press, 1961, 257–258.
———. "A Case of Homosexuality in a Woman" (1920). *Standard Edition* 18. Ed. James Strachey. London: Hogarth Press, 1955, 145–172.
Fuchs, Cynthia. *Deceptive Distinctions*. New Haven, CT: Yale University Press, 1988.
Gallagher, Catherine. "Embracing the Absolute." *Genders* 1 (1988): 24–39.
Gallop, Jane. "Snatches of Conversation." *Women and Language in Literature and Society*. Eds. Sally McConnel-Ginet, Ruth Borker, and Nelly Furman. New York: Praeger, 1980, 274–283.
Gardiner, Judith Kegan. "Mind Mother: Psychoanalysis and Feminism." *Making a Difference: Feminist Literary Criticism*. Eds. Gayle Greene and Coppelia Kahn. New York: Routledge, 2005, 114–145.
Gayle, Greene, and Kahn, Coppelia, eds. *Making a Difference: Feminist Literary Criticism*. New York: Routledge, 2005.

Geertz, Clifford. *The Interpretation of Cultures*. New York: Basic Books, 1973.
Gifford, Carolyn De Swarte. "American Women and the Bible." *Feminist Perspectives on Biblical Scholarship*. Ed. Adela Yarbro Collins. Cico, CA: Scholars Press, 1985, 11–34.
Gilbert, Sandra, and Gubar, Susan. *The Madwoman in the Attic*. New Haven, CT: Yale University Press, 1979.
Gilkes, Cheryl Townsend. "Together in Harness: Women's Traditions in the Sanctified Church." *Women and Women's Issues: Modern Protestantism and its World*. New York: K. G. Sauss 1993, 214–235.
Gilligan, Carol. *In a Different Voice*. Cambridge, MA: Harvard University Press, 1982, 1993.
———. "Reply to Critics." *An Ethic of Care*. Ed. Mary Jeanne Larrabee. New York: Routledge, 1992, 207–214.
———. "Remapping the Moral Domain: New Images of Self in Relationship." *Mapping the Moral Domain*. Eds. Carol Gilligan, Janie Victoria Ward, and Jill McLean Taylor. Cambridge, MA: Harvard University Press, 1988, 3–19.
———. "Preface." *Making Connections*. Eds. Carol Gilligan, Nora Lyons, and Trudy Hanmer. Cambridge, MA: Harvard University Press, 1990, 6–29.
———. "Women's Psychological Development: Implications for Psychotherapy." *Women, Girls and Psychotherapy*. Ed. Carol Gilligan, Annie G. Rogers, and Deborah L. Tolman. New York: Haworth Press, 1991, 5–32.
Gilmore, Leigh. "The Gaze of the Other Woman: Beholding and Begetting in Dickinson, Moore, and Rich." *Engendering the Word: Feminist Essays in Psychosexual Poetics*. Eds. Temma F. Berg et al. Urbana: University of Illinois Press, 1989, 81–102.
Ginzberg, Lori. *Women and the Work of Benevolence*. New Haven, CT: Yale University Press, 1990.
Good, H. G. *A History of American Education*. New York: Macmillan, 1956.
Goody, Jack, ed. *Literacy in Traditional Societies*. New York: Cambridge University Press, 1968.
Goreau, Angeline. *The Whole Duty of a Woman: Female Writers in Seventeenth Century England*. New York: Dial Press, 1985.
Gould, Carol. "Feminism and Democratic Community Revisited." *Democratic Community*. Eds. John Chapman and Ian Shapiro. *Nomos* 35: 396–413.
Grant, Judith. *Fundamental Feminism*. New York: Routledge, 1993.
Gray, Janet, ed. *She Wields a Pen*. London: J.M. Dent, 1997.
Green, Thomas F. *Voices: The Educational Formation of Conscience*. Notre Dame, IN: The University of Notre Dame Press, 1999.
Greenblatt, Stephen. *Shakespearean Negotiations*. Berkeley: University of California Press, 1988.
Grimké, Angelina. *Letters to Catherine Beecher*. Boston: Isaac Knapp, 1838.
Grimké, Sarah. *Letters on the Equality of the Sexes and the Condition of Women*, 1837. Bibliobazaar, 2008.
Grimshaw, Jean. "Practices of Freedom." *Up Against Foucault*. Ed. Caroline Ramazanoglu. New York: Routledge, 1993, 51–72.
Griswold, Rufus. *Female Poets of America*. 2nd edition. Philadelphia: H. C. Baird, 1853.
Grosz, Elizabeth. *Space, time and perversion*. New York: Routledge, 1995.
Gubar, Susan. *Poetry After Auschwitz*. Bloomington: Indiana University Press, 2003.
Gura, Philip. *A Glimpse of Zion's Glory*. Middletown, CT: Wesleyan University Press, 1984.

Habermas, Jürgen. "The Public Sphere: An Encyclopedia Article," 1964. *New German Critique* 5.2 (1974): 49–55.
———. *Philosophical Discourses of Modernity*. Cambridge, MA: MIT Press, 1987.
Hall, David Donald. "Religion and Society: Problems and Considerations." *Colonial British America*. Eds. Jack P. Greene and R. Poole. Baltimore: Johns Hopkins University Press, 1984, 317–344.
———. "World of Print and Collective Mentality in 17th century New England." *New Directions in American Intellectual History*. Eds. John Higham and Paul Conkin. Baltimore: Johns Hopkins University Press, 1979, 166–180.
Hardesty, Nancy. *Women Called to Witness: Evangelical Feminism in the Nineteenth Century*. Knoxville: University of Tennessee Press, 1999.
———. *Your Daughters Shall Prophecy*. Brooklyn: Carlson Publishers, 1990.
Harmann, Heidi. "The Unhappy Marriage of Marxism and Feminism: Toward a More Progressive Union." *The Second Wave: A Reader in Feminist Theory*. Ed. Linda Nicholson. New York: Routledge, 1997, 97–122.
Harper, Phyllis Brian. *Framing the Margins: The Social Logic of Postmodern Culture*. New York: Oxford University Press, 1994.
Hartman, Stephanie. "All Systems Go: Muriel Rukeyser's 'The Book of the Dead,' and the Reinvention of Modernist Poetics." *How Shall We Tell Each Other of the Poet: The Life and Writing of Muriel Rukeyser*. Eds. Anne Herzog and Janet Kaufman. New York: St. Martin's Press, 1999, 209–223.
Hartsock, Nancy. "Foucault on Power: A Theory for Women." *Feminism/PostModernism*. Ed. Linda Nicholson. New York: Routledge, 1990, 157–173.
Hatch, Nathan. *The Democratization of American Christianity*. New Haven, CT: Yale University Press, 1989.
———. *The Sacred Cause of Liberty*. New Haven, CT: Yale University Press, 1979.
Haynes, Carolyn. "Women and Protestantism in Nineteenth-Century America." *Perspectives in American Religion and Culture*. Ed. Peter Williams. Oxford: Blackwell, 1999, 300–318.
Hegel, G. W. F. *Philosophy of Right*. London: Oxford University Press, 1952.
Heimert, Alan. *Religion and the American Mind*. Cambridge, MA: Harvard University Press, 1963.
Held, Virginia. "Non-Contractual Society: A Feminist View." *Feminism and Community*. Eds. Penny Weiss and Marilyn Freedman. Philadelphia: Temple University Press, 1995.
———. "Mothering vs. Contract." *Beyond Self Interest*. Ed. Jane Mansbridge. Chicago: University of Chicago Press, 1990, 287–347.
———. "Feminism and Moral Theory." *Women and Moral Theory*. Eds. Eva Feder Kittay and Diana Meyers. Totowa, NJ: Rowman and Littlefield, 1987, 166–171.
———. *On Feminist Ethics and Politics*. Ed. Claudia Card. Lawrence, KS: University Press of Kansas, 1999.
Hensley, Jeannine. *The Works of Anne Bradstreet*. Cambridge, MA: Harvard University Press, 1967.
Herndl, Diane Price. "The Dilemmas of a Feminine Dialogic." *Feminism, Bakhtin and the Dialogic*. Eds. Dale Bauer and S. Jaret McKinstry. Albany: State University of New York Press, 1991, 7–24.
Hewitt, Nancy. "Beyond the Search for Sisterhood." *Unequal Sisters*. Eds. Ellen Carol Dubois and Vicki L. Ruiz. New York: Routledge, 1990, 1–18.
———. *Women's Activism and Social Change*. Ithaca, NY: Cornell University Press, 1984.
Heyes, Cressida J. "Anti-Essentialism in Practice: Carol Gilligan and Feminist Philosophy." *Hypatia* 12.3 (1997): 142–163.

Heywood, Leslie, and Jennifer Drake, eds. *Third Wave Agenda: Being Feminist, Doing Feminism* Minneapolis: University of Minnesota Press, 1997.
Higgenbotham, Evelyn Brooks. *Righteous Discontent.* Cambridge, MA: Harvard University Press, 1993.
Higonnet, Margaret Randolph. "Introduction." *Behind the Lines: Gender and the Two World Wars.* New Haven, CT: Yale University Press, 1987.
Hill, Christopher. *Puritanism and Revolution.* New York: Schocken Books, 1958.
Hirschmann, Nancy. "Rethinking Obligation for Feminism." *Revisioning the Political.* Eds. Hirschmann and Christine Di Stefano. Boulder, CO: Westview Press, 1996, 157–180.
———. "Revisioning Freedom" *Revisioning the Political.* Eds. Nancy Hirschmann and Christina Di Stefano. New York: Westview Press, 1996, 51–74.
Hobby, Elaine. *Virtue of Necessity: English Women's Writing 1649–88.* London: Virago Press, 1988.
Hogue, Cynthia. "Another Postmodernism: Towards an Ethical Poetics." *How2 Online Journal* 1.7 (Spring 2002).
Hole, Judith, and Ellen Levine. "The First Feminists." *Radical Feminism.* Eds. Anne Koedt, Ellen Levine, and Anita Rapone. New York: Quadrangle, 1973, 3–16.
Homans, Margaret. *Women Writers and Poetic Identity.* Princeton: Princeton University Press, 1980.
hooks, bell. *Feminist Theory: From Margin to Center.* Cambridge, MA: South End Press, 1984.
Howe, Irving. "The Plath Celebration: A Partial Dissent." *The Critical Point.* New York: Horizon Press, 1973, 158–169.
Hoy, David Couzens, ed. *Foucault: A Critical Reader.* Oxford: Basil Blackwell, 1986.
Hull, Suzanne. *Chaste, Silent and Obedient: English Books for Women 1475–1640.* San Marino, CA: Huntington Library, 1982.
Hunter, Ian. "Aesthetics and Cultural Studies." *Cultural Studies.* Eds. Lawrence Grossberg, Cary Nelson, and Paula Treichler. New York: Routledge, 1992.
Iannello, Kathleen. "Women's Leadership and Third Wave Feminism." *Hypatia* 12.3 1997: 70–77.
Imray, Linda, and Middleton, Audrey. "Public and Private: Marking the Boundaries." *The Public and the Private.* Eds. Eva Gamarnikow, David Morgan, Jane Purvis, and Daphne Taylorson. London: Heinemann, 1983, 12–27.
Irigaray, Luce. *This Sex Which Is Not One.* New York: Cornell University Press, 1985.
Irwin, Joyce L. *Womanhood in Radical Protestantism 1525–1675.* Lewiston, NY: E. Mellen Press, 1979.
Jaggar, Alison. *Feminist Politics and Human Nature.* Totowa, NJ: Rowman and Allanheld, 1983.
Jarrell, Randall. "Her Shield." *Marianne Moore: A Collection of Critical Essays.* Ed. Charles Tomlinson. New York: Prentice Hall, 1969, 114–124.
Jakobson, Roman. "Linguistics and Poetics." *Style in Language.* Ed. Thomas Sebeok. Cambridge, MA: MIT Press, 1960, 350–377.
James, M. "Mothering: A Possible Black Feminist link to Social Transformation." *Theorizing Black Feminists: The Visionary Pragmatism of Black Women.* Eds. Stanlie M. James and Abena P. A. Busia. New York: Routledge, 1993, 44–54.
Jansen, Katherine Ludwig. "Maria Magdalena: Apostolorum Apostola." *Women Preachers and Prophets Through Two Millennia of Christianity.* Eds. Beverly M. Kienzle and Pamela J. Walker. Berkeley: University of California Press, 1998, 57–96.

Johnson, Barbara. "Apostrophe, Animation, and Abortion." *A World of Difference*. Baltimore: Johns Hopkins University Press, 1987, 184–199.
Jones, Ann Rosalind. *The Currency of Eros*. Bloomington: Indiana University Press, 1990.
———. "Nets and Bridles: Early Modern Conduct Books." *The Ideology of Conduct: Essays on Literature and the History of Sexuality*. Eds. Nancy Armstrong and Leonard Tennenhouse. New York: Methuen, 1987, 39–72
———. "Inscribing Femininity: French Theories of the Feminine." *Making a Difference: Feminist Literary Crticism*. Ed. Gayle Greene and Coppelia Kahn. London: Methuen and Co. Ltd., 1985, 80–112.
Jones, Kathleen. "Citizenship in a Woman Friendly Polity." *Signs* 15:4 (Summer 1990): 781–814.
Juhasz, Suzanne. "Adventures in the World of the Symbolic: Dickinson and Metaphor." *Feminist Measures: Soundings in Poetry and Theory*. Eds. Lynn Keller and Cristanne Miller. Ann Arbor: University of Michigan Press, 1994, 139–162.
———. *Naked and Fiery Forms*. New York: Harper and Row, 1976.
Juster, Susan. *Disorderly Women*. Ithaca, NY: Cornell University Press, 1994.
Kadlec, David. "X-Ray Testimonials in Muriel Rukeyser." *Modernism/Modernity* 5.1 (1988): 23–37.
Kaplan, Amy. *The Anarchy of Empire in the Making of U.S. Culture*. Cambridge, MA: Harvard University Press, 2002.
Kaplan, Caren. *Questions of Travel: Postmodern Discourses of Displacement*. Durham, NC: Duke University Press, 1998.
Kaplan, Sydney Janet. "Varieties of Feminist Criticism." *Making a Difference: Feminist Literary Criticism*. Eds. Gayle Greene and Coppelia Kahn. London: Methuen, 1985, 37–58.
Karlsen, Carol. *The Devil in the Shape of a Woman*. New York: Norton, 1987.
Kasson, John F. *Rudeness and Civility*. New York: Hill and Wang, 1990.
Katz, Lisa. "World War II and the Gender of History: The Poetry of Sylvia Plath." *Tales of the Great American Victory: World War II in Politics and Poetics*. European Contributions to American Studies no. 62, 2006.
Kavka, Misha. "Introduction." *Feminist Consequences: Theory for the New Century*. Eds. Elisabeth Bronfen and Misha Kavka. New York: Columbia University Press, 2001, ix–xxvi.
Kehde, Suzanne. "Voices from the Margin." *Feminism, Bakhtin and the Dialogic*. Eds. Dale Bauer and S. Jaret McKinstry. Albany: State University of New York Press, 1991, 25–38.
Keller, Evelyn Fox. "Feminism and Science." *The Signs Reader*. Eds. Elizabeth Abel and Emily Abel. Chicago: University of Chicago Press, 1983, 109–122.
Keller, Lynn. "For Inferior Who Is Free." *Influence and Intertextuality in Literary History*. Eds. Jay Clayton and Eric Rothstein. Madison: University of Wisconsin Press, 1991, 219–244.
———. *Forms of Expansion: Recent Long Poems by Women*. Chicago: University of Chicago Press, 1997.
Keller, Rosemary Skinner. "Women, Civil Religion, and the American Revolution." *Women and Religion in America, Colonial and Revolutionary Periods*, Vol. 2. Eds. Rosemary Ruether and Rosemary Skinner Keller. New York: HarperCollins, 1983, 358–382.
Kelley, Mary. *Private Woman, Public Stage*. New York: Oxford University Press, 1984.
Kelly, Joan. "The Doubled Vision of Feminist Theory." *Feminist Studies* 5.1 (Spring 1979): 216–227.

Kelly-Gadol, Joan. "Did Women Have a Renaissance." *Becoming Visible: Women in European History*. Eds. Renate Bridenthal and Claudia Koonz. New York: Houghton Mifflin Co., 1977, 137–164.

———. "The Social Relations of the Sexes: Methodological Implications of Women's History." *Signs* 1 (1976): 809–823.

Kent, George. *A Life of Gwendolyn Brooks*. Lexington: University Press of Kentucky, 1990.

Kerber, Linda. "A Constitutional Right to Be Treated Like Ladies." *U.S. History as Women's History*. Chapel Hill, NC: University of North Carolina Press, 1995, 17–35.

———. "Can a Woman Be an Individual." *Towards an Intellectual History of Women*. Chapel Hill: University of North Carolina Press, 1997, 201–223.

———. "Separate Spheres, Female Worlds, Woman's Place: The Rhetoric of Women's History." *Journal of American History* 75.1 (June 1988): 9–39.

———. "The Paradox of Women's Citizenship in the Early Republic." *Towards and Intellectual History of Women*. Chapel Hill: University of North Carolina Press, 1997, 261–301.

———. "Some Cautionary Words for Historians." *Signs* 11.2 (Winter 1986): 304–310.

———. *Women of the Republic*. Chapel Hill: University of North Carolina Press, 1980.

Kinnahan, Linda. *Poetics of the Feminine*. New York: Cambridge University Press, 2008.

Koehler, Lyle. *A Search for Power: The Weaker Sex in Seventeenth-Century New England*. Urbana: University of Illinois Press, 1980.

Kristeva, Julia. *Desire in Language*. New York: Columbia University Press, 1980.

———. *Kristeva Reader*. Ed. Toril Moi. New York: Columbia University Press, 1986.

———. *Revolution in Poetic Language*. New York: Columbia University Press, 1984.

Kolbrener, William. "Mary Astell's Feminist Historiography." *18th Century* 44.1 2004: 1–24.

Kraditor, Aileen S. *The Ideas of the Woman Suffrage Movement 1890–1920*. New York: Doubleday Anchor Book, 1971.

Kramarae, Cheris. *Women and Men Speaking: Frameworks for Analysis*. Rowley, MA: Newbury House Publishers, 1981.

———, Barrie Thorne, and Nancy Henley. "Perspectives on Language and Communication." *Signs* 3:3 (Spring 1978): 638–652.

Krontiris, Tina. *Oppositional Voices: Women as Writers and Translators of Literature in the English Renaissance*. London: Routledge, 1992.

Lakoff, Robin. *Language and Woman's Place*. Stanford, CA: Stanford University Press, 1973.

Landes, Joan B. "Hegel's Conception of the Family." *The Family in Political Thought*. Ed. J. B. Elshtain. Amherst: University of Massachusetts Press, 1982, 125–144.

———. "Introduction." *Feminism, the Public and the Private*. Ed. Joan B. Landes. New York: Oxford University Press, 1998, 1–20.

———. *Women and the Public Sphere in the Age of the French Revolution*. Ithaca, NY: Cornell University Press, 1988.

Lasch, Christopher. *Haven in a Heartless World*. New York: Basic Books, 1977.

Lehuru, Isabelle. "Sentimental Figures: Reading Godey's Lady's Book in Antebellum America." *The Culture of Sentiment*. New York: Oxford University Press, 1992, 73–91.

Leland, Diana. "The Subversion of Women's Agency in Psychoanalytic Feminism: Chodorow, Flax, Kristeva." *Revaluing French Feminism: Critical Essays on Difference, Agency, & Culture*. Eds. Nancy Fraser and Sandra Lee Bartky. Bloomington: Indiana University Press, 1992, 136–161.
Lerner, Gerda. *The Creation of Feminist Consciousness*. New York: Oxford University Press, 1993.
———, ed. *Black Women in White America: A Documentary History*, NY: Vintage Books, 1973.
Levander, Caroline Field. *Voices of the Nation: Women and Public Speech in the Nineteenth Century*. New York: Cambridge University Press, 1998.
Leverenz, David. *Manhood and the American Renaissance*. Ithaca, NY: Cornell University Press, 1989.
Lewalski, Barbara. *Writing Women in Jacobean England*. Cambridge, MA: Harvard University Press, 1993.
Lockridge, Kenneth. *Literacy in Colonial New England*. New York: Norton, 1974.
Lovejoy, David. *Religious Enthusiasm in the New World*. Cambridge, MA: Harvard University Press, 1985.
Lowi, Theodore. "The Public Philosophy: Interest-Group Liberalism." *The Bias of Pluralism*. Ed. William Connolly. Redwood City, CA: Atherton Press, 1969, 81–122.
MacCannell, Dean, and Juliet Flower MacCannell. "The Body System." *The Ideology of Conduct*. Eds. Nancy Armstrong and Leonard Tennenhouse. New York: Methuen, 1987, 206–238.
Mack, Phyllis. *Visionary Women: Ecstatic Prophecy in Seventeenth-Century England*. Berkeley: University of California Press, 1992.
MacKinnon, Catherine. *Feminism Unmodified*. Cambridge, MA: Harvard University Press, 1987.
———. *Toward a Feminist Theory of the State*. Cambridge, MA: Harvard University Press, 1989.
Macpherson, C. P. *The Political Theory of Possessive Individualism*. London: Oxford University Press, 1962.
Mahmood, Saba. "Feminist Theory, Embodiment, and the Docile Agent." *Cultural Anthropology* 16.2 (May 2001): 202–237.
———. *The Politics of Piety*. Princeton, NJ: Princeton University Press, 2005.
Malcolm, Janet. *The Silent Women*. New York: Alfted A. Knopf, 1994.
Mansbridge, Jane. "Feminism and Democratic Community." *Democratic Community Nomos 35*. Eds. John Chapman and Ian Shapiro. New York University Press, 1993, 339–395.
Marilley, Suzanne M. "Frances Willard and the Feminism of Fear." *Feminist Studies* 19.1 (Spring 1993): 123–146.
Martin, Wendy. *An American Triptych: Anne Bradstreet, Emily Dickinson, Adrienne Rich*. Chapel Hill: University of North Carolina Press, 1984.
Mathews, Daniel. *Religion in the Old South*. Chicago: University of Chicago Press, 1977.
Matthews, Glenna. *"Just a Housewife": The Rise and Fall of Domesticity in America*. New York: Oxford University Press, 1989.
———. *The Rise of Public Woman*. New York: Oxford University Press, 1994.
McConnell-Ginet, Ruth Borker, and Nelly Furman, eds. *Women and Language in Literature and Society*. New York: Praeger, 1980.
McLoughlin, William. *Revivals, Awakenings, and Reform*. Chicago: University of Chicago Press, 1978.
McPherson, James. *Battle Cry of Freedom*. New York: Oxford University Press, 1988.

McRobbie, Angela. *The Aftermath of Feminism*. London: Sage, 2009.
Mead, Margaret. *Male and Female*. New York: New American Library, 1955.
Melham, D. H. "Gwendolyn Brooks: The Heroic Voice of Prophecy." *Studies in Black Literature Autumn* 8 (1977): 1–3.
Merrin, Jeredith. *An Enabling Humiliy*. New Brunswick, NJ: Rutgers University Press, 1990.
Meyers, Diana T. "The Subversion of Women's Agency in Psychoanalytic Feminism." *Revaluing French Feminism: Critical Essays on Difference, Agency, & Culture*. Eds. Nancy Fraser and Sandra Lee Bartky. Bloomington: Indiana University Press, 1992, 136–161.
Miller, Cristanne. *Cultures of Modernism : Marianne Moore, Mina Loy, & Else Lasker-Schüler: Gender and Literary Community in New York and Berlin*. Ann Arbor: University of Michigan Press, 2005.
———. "Corpses of Poetry." *Feminist Measures: Soundings in Poetry and Theory*. Eds. Lynn Keller and Cristanne Miller. Ann Arbor: University of Michigan Press, 1994, 69–95.
———. "Marianne Moore and a Poetry of Hebrew (Protestant) Prophecy." *20th-Century American Women's Poetries of Engagement*. Special Issue Eds. Cristina Giorcelli, Cristanne Miller, and Shira Wolosky. *Sources*. 12 (Spring 2002): 29–47.
———. "Pondering 'Liberty': Emily Dickinson and the Civil War." *American Vistas and Beyond: A Festschrift for Roland Hagenbüchle*. Eds. Marietta Messmer and Josef Raab. Trier: Wissenschaftlicher Verlag Trier, 2002, 45–64.
———. *Marianne Moore: Questions of Authority*. Cambridge, MA: Harvard University Press, 1995.
Miller, Howard. *The Revolutionary College*. New York: New York University Press, 1976.
Miller, Jean Baker. *Toward a New Psychology of Women*. Boston: Beacon Press, 1976/1986.
———. "The Development of Women's Sense of Self." *Women's Growth in Connection*. Eds. Judith V. Jordan, Alexandra Kaplan, Jean Beker Miller, Irene Stiver, and Janet Surrey. New York: The Guilford Press, 1991, 11–26.
Miller, Perry. "Puritan State and Puritan Society." *Errand into the Wilderness*. Cambridge, MA: Harvard University Press, 1956, 141–152.
Millett, Kate. *Sexual Politics*. London: Hart-Davis, 1971.
Mitchell, Juliett. *Woman's Estate*. New York: Vintage Books, 1971.
Moers, Ellen. *Literary Women*. New York: Doubleday, 1976.
Moi, Toril. *Sexual/Textual Politics*. New York: Routledge, 1985.
———. *What Is a Woman*. New York: Oxford University Press, 1999.
Montefiore, Jan. *Feminism and Poetry* London: Pandora, 1987.
Moore, Henrietta. *Feminism and Anthropology*. London: Polity Press, 1988.
Morgan, Edmund. *The Puritan Family*. New York: Harper and Row, 1966.
Morgen, Sandra. "Introduction." *Gender and Anthropology*. Ed. Sandra Morgen. Washington, DC: American Anthropological Association, 1989, 1–20.
Munford, Rebecca. "'Wake Up and Smell the Lipgloss': Gender, Generation and the (A)politics of Girl Power." *Third Wave Feminism: A Critical Exploration*. Eds. Stacy Gillis, Gillian Howie, and Rebecca Munford. Palgrave Macmillan, 2004, 142–153.
Murphy, Patrick D. "Prolegomenon for an Ecofeminist Dialogics." *Feminism, Bakhtin and the Dialogic*. Eds. Dale Bauer and S. Jaret McKinstry. Albany: State University of New York Press, 1991, 39–56.
Nelson, Deborah. "Penetrating Privacy: Confessional Poetry and the Surveillance Society." *Homemaking: Women Writers and the Politics and Poetics of Home*. Eds. Catherine Wiley and Fiona Barnes. New York: Garland Publishing, 1996, 87–114.

Newton, Judith Lowder. "History as Usual? Feminism and the 'New Historicism.'" *The New Historicism*. Ed. H. Aram Veeser. New York: Routledge, 1989, 152–167.
Nichols, Linda J. *Gender and History*. New York: Columbia University Press, 1986.
Noddings, Nel. *Care*. Berkeley: University of California Press, 1984.
Norton, Mary Beth. *Founding Mothers and Fathers*. New York: Alfred A. Knopf, 1996.
———. *Liberty's Daughters*. Boston: Little, Brown Press, 1980.
———. "The Paradox of the Woman's Sphere." *Women of America: A History*. Eds. Carol Ruth Berkin and Mary Beth Norton. Boston: Houghton Mifflin Co., 1979, 139–149.
Nuyen, A.T. "Just Modesty." *American Philosophical Quarterly* 35 (1998): 101–109.
Okin, Susan Moller. *Justice, Gender and the Family*. New York: Basic Books, 1989.
———. "Thinking Like a Man."*Theoretical Perspectives on Sexual Difference*. Ed. Deborah Rowe. New Haven, CT: Yale University Press, 1990.
———. "Gender, the Public and the Private." *Political Theory Today*. Ed. David Held. Cambridge: Polity Press, 1991, 67–90.
Olsen, Frances. "The Family and the Market: A Study of Ideology and Legal Reform." *Harvard Law Review* 96.7 (May 1883): 1495–1578.
Ortner, Sherry B. "Is Female to Male as Nature Is to Culture?" *Woman, Culture and Society*. Eds. Michelle Zimbalist Rosaldo and Louise Lamphere. Stanford, CA: Stanford University Press, 1974.
Ostriker, Alicia. *Stealing the Language: The Emergence of Women's Poetry in America*. Boston: Beacon Press, 1986.
Pangle, Lorraine Smith, and Thomas L. Pangle. *The Learning of Liberty*. Lawrence, KS: University of Kansas Press, 1993.
Pateman, Carole. "Feminist Critiques of the Public/Private Dichotomy." *Private and Public in Social Life*. Eds. Stanley Benn and Gerald Gaus. London: Croom Helm, 1983 (reprinted in *The Disorder of Women*).
———. *The Disorder of Women: Democracy, Feminism, and Political Theory*. Stanford, CA: Stanford University Press, 1989.
———. "The Patriarchal Welfare State." *Feminism, the Public and the Private*. Ed. Joan Landes. New York: Oxford University Press, 1998, 241–276.
———. "Women's Writing, Women's Standing: Theory and Politics in the Early Modern Period." *Women Writers in the Early Modern British Political Tradition*. Ed. Hilda Smith. New York: Cambridge University Press, 2001, 363–382.
Perloff, Marjorie. *The Dance of the Intellect*. New York: Cambridge University Press, 1985.
———. *The Futurist Moment*. Chicago: University of Chicago Press, 1986.
———. "Language Poetry and the Lyric Subject: Ron Silliman's Albany, Susan Howe's Buffalo." *Critical Inquiry* 25 (Spring 1999): 405–434.
———. "Sylvia Plath's 'Sivvy' Poems: A Portrait of the Poet as Daughter." *Sylvia Plath: New Views on the Poetry*. Ed. Gale Lane. Baltimore: John Hopkins University Press, 1979, 155–178.
Perry, Ralph Barton. "The Ultimate Individual." *Puritanism and the American Experience*. Ed. Michael McGiffert. New York: Addison-Wesley Publishing Company, 1969, 52–64.
Peterson, Carla. *Doers of the Word*. New York: Oxford University Press, 1995.
Pitkin, Hannah. *Fortune Is a Woman: Gender and Politics in the Thought of Niccolo Machiavelli*. Berkeley: University of California Press, 1984.

Pocock, J. A. G. *The Machiavellian Moment.* Princeton, NJ: Princeton University Press, 1975.
Porterfield, Amanda. *Female Piety in Puritan New England.* New York: Oxford University Press, 1992.
Poovey, Mary. *The Proper Lady and the Woman Writer: Ideology as Style in the Works of Mary Wollstonecraft, Mary Shelley, and Jane Austen,* Chicago: University of Chicago Press, 1984.
Prins, Yopie, and Maeera Shreiber, eds. *Dwelling in Possibility: Women Poets and Critics on Poetry.* Ithaca, NY: Cornell University Press, 1997.
Radner, Hilary. "Roaming the City: Proper Women in Improper Places." *Spaces of Culture.* Eds. Mike Featherstone and Scott Lash. London: Sage, 1999, 86–100.
Richards, Norvin. "Is Humility a Virtue." *American Philosophical Quarterly* 25 (1988).
Ricoeur, Paul. *The Philosophy of Paul Ricoeur.* Eds. Charles E. Reagan and David Stewart. Boston: Beacon Press, 1978.
Riley, Glenda. *Inventing the American Woman,* Wheeling, IL: Harlan Davidson, Inc., 1995.
Roman, Camille, Suzanne Juhasz, and Cristanne Miller, eds. *The Women and Language Debate: A Sourcebook.* New Brunswick, NJ: Rutgers University Press, 1994.
Romero, Lora. *Home Fronts: Domesticity and Its Critics in the Antebellum United States.* Durham, NC: Duke University Press, 1998.
Romines, Ann. *The Home Plot.* Amherst: University of Massachusetts Press, 1992.
Rosaldo, Michelle Zimbalist. "Woman, Culture and Society: A Theoretical Overview." *Women, Culture, Society.* Eds. Michelle Zimbalist Rosaldo and Louise Lamphere. Stanford, CA: Stanford University Press, 1975, 17–42.
——. "The Use and Abuse of Anthropology: Reflections on Feminism and Cross-cultural Understanding." *Signs* 5.3 (Spring 1980): 389–417.
Rosenthal, M. L. "Sylvia Plath and Confessional Poetry." *The Art of Sylvia Plath.* Ed. Charles Newman. Bloomington: Indiana University Press, 1971, 74–90.
Rossi, Alice. *The Feminist Papers: From Adams to Beauvoir.* New York: Columbia University Press, 1973.
Rubin, Gayle. "The Traffic in Women." *Toward an Anthropology of Women.* Ed. Rayna Reiter. New York: Monthly Review Press, 1975.
Ruddick, Sara. *Maternal Thinking.* London: The Woman's Press, 1989.
Ruether, Rosemary. "Introduction." *Women and Religion in America: The Nineteenth Century Vol. 1.* Ed. Rosemary Ruether and Rosemary Skinner Keller. New York: Harper & Row, 1981, viii–xiv.
——. "Introduction." *Women and Religion in America: The Colonial and Revolutionary Periods.* Eds. Rosemary Ruether and Rosemary Skinner Keller. New York: HarperCollins, 1983, xiii–xxi.
——. "Introduction." *Women and Religion in America*: 1900–1968, Vol. 3. Eds. Rosemary Ruether and Rosemary Keller. New York: Harper & Row, 1986, xiii–xxi.
——. "The Liberation of Christology from Patriarchy." *Feminist Theology: A Reader.* Ed. Ann Loades. London: SPCK, 1990, 138–147.
——, and Elanor McLaughlin, eds. *Women of Spirit.* New York: Simon and Schuster, 1979.
Rugoff, Milton. *The Beechers.* New York: Harper and Row, 1981.
Rush, Benjamin. "Thoughts upon Female Education." *Essays on Education in the Early Republic.* Ed. Frederick Rudolf. Cambridge, MA: Harvard University Press, 1965, 32–43.

Ryan, Mary. "A Women's Awakening." *Women in American Religion*. Ed. Janet Wilson James. Philadelphia: University of Pennsylvania Press, 1980, 89–110.
———. *Cradle of the Middle Class*. New York: Cambridge University Press, 1981.
———. *The Empire of the Mother*. New York: Howarth Press, 1982.
———. "The Power of Women's Networks: A Case Study of Moral Reform in Antebellum America." *Feminist Studies* 5.1, 1989: 66–85.
———. "Gender and Public Access: Women's Politics in Nineteenth Century America." *Habermas and the Public Sphere*. Ed. Crag Calhoun. Boston: MIT Press, 1992, 259–289.
———. *Womanhood in America*. New York: New Viewpoints, 1975.
———. *Women in Public*. Baltimore: Johns Hopkins University Press, 1990.
Salmon, Marylyn. "Equality or Submersion? Feme Covert Status in Early Pennsylvania." *Women of America: A History*. Eds. Mary Beth Norton and Carol Ruth Berkin. Boston: Houghton Mifflin Co., 1979, 93–113.
Sandel, Michael. *Democracy's Discontents*. Cambridge, MA: Harvard University Press, 1996.
Sanders, Thomas. *Protestant Concepts of Church and State*. New York: Holt, Rinehart, Winston, 1964.
Sawicki, Jana. *Disciplining Foucault: Feminism, Power and the Body*. New York: Routledge, 1991.
Schueler, G. F. "Why Modesty Is a Virtue." *Ethics* 107.3 (1997): 467–485.
Fiorenza, Elisabeth Schussler. *In Memory of Her*. New York: Crossroad, 1994.
Scott, Joan. "Gender: A Useful Category of Historical Analysis." *American Historical Review* 91 (1986): 1053–1075.
———. "Rewriting History." *Behind the Lines*. Ed. Margaret Randolph Higonnet. New Haven, CT: Yale University Press, 1987, 21–30.
Schwarzenbach, Sybil. "On Civic Friendship." *Ethics* 107 (October 1996): 97–128.
Scweik, Suzanne. *A Gulf So Deeply Cut: American Women Poets and the Second World War*. Madison, WI: University of Wisconsin Press, 1991.
Shiels, Richard. "The Feminization of America Congregationalism 1730–1835." *American Quarterly* 62 (1981): 46–62.
Showalter, Elaine. *A Literature of Their Own: British Women Novelists from Bronte to Lessing*. Princeton, NJ: Princeton University Press, 1977.
———. "Feminism and Literature." *Literary Theory Today*. Eds. Peter Collier and Helga Geyer-Ryan. Ithaca, NY: Cornell University Press, 1990, 179–202.
———. "Feminist Criticism in the Wilderness." *The New Feminist Criticism*. Ed. Elaine Showalter. New York: Pantheon Books, 1985, 243–270.
Sicherman, Barbara. "American History." *Signs* 1.2 (Winter 1975): 461–486.
———. "Feminist Revisions in 'American History.'" *Signs* 1.2 (Winter 1975): 461–485.
Sklar, Kathryn Kish. "The Founding of Mount Holyoke College." *Women of America: A History*. Eds. Carol Ruth Berkin and Mary Beth Norton. Boston: Houghtin Mifflin, 1979, 177–201.
Smethurst, James Edward. *The New Red Negro*. New York: Oxford University Press, 1999.
Smith, Daniel Scott. "Family Limitation, Sexual Control and Domestic Feminism in Victorian America." *A Heritage of Her Own*. New York: Simon and Schuster, 1979, 222–245.
Smith, Gary. "Gwendolyn Brooks's 'Children of the Poor,' Metaphysical Poetry and the Inconditions of Love." *A Life Distilled*. Eds. Maria Mootry and Gary Smith. Urbana: University of Illinois Press, 1987, 165–176.
Smith, Hilda. *Reason's Disciples*. Urbana: University of Illinois Press, 1982.

Smith, Nigel. *Literature and Revolution in England, 1640–1660*. New Haven, CT: Yale University Press, 1994.
Smith-Rosenberg, Carol. "Female World of Love and Ritual." *Signs* 1 (Autumn 1975): 1–29.
———. *Disorderly Conduct*. New York: Oxford University Press, 1985.
———. "Domesticating "Virtue," *Literature and the Body*. Ed. Elaine Scarry, Baltimore: Johns Hopkins Press, 1988, 160–184.
———. *Religion and the Rise of the American City*. Ithaca, NY: Cornell University Press, 1971.
Snitow, Ann. "A Gender Diary." *Conflicts in Feminism*. Eds. Mariane Hirsch and Evelyn Fox Keller. New Yrk: Routledge, 1990, 9–43.
Spivak, Gayatri Chakravorty. "Three Women's Texts and a Critique of Imperialism." *Critical Inquiry* 12.1 (Autumn 1985): 243–261.
Stacey, Judith. "The New Conservative Feminism." *Feminist Studies* 9.3 (Fall 1985): 559–583.
Stansell, Christine. *City of Women*. Urbana: University of Illinois Press, 1987.
———. "Women, Children and the Uses of the Street." *Unequal Sisters*. Eds. Ellen Carol Dubois and Vicki L. Ruiz. New York: Routledge, 1990, 92–108.
Stallybrass, Peter, and Allon White. *The Politics and Poetics of Transgression*. London: Methuen, 1986.
Stanton, Domna. "Difference on Trial: A Critique of the Maternal Metaphor in Cixous, Irigaray, and Kristeva." *The Poetics of Gender*. Ed. Nancy K. Miller. New York: Columbia University Press, 1986.
Statman, Daniel. "Modesty, Pride, and Realistic Self-Assessment." *Philosophical Quarterly* 42 (1992): 420–438.
Steeke, Cassue Oreni. *We Heal from Memory*. New York: Palgrave, 2000.
Steiner, George. "Dying Is an Art." *Language and Silence*. New York: Atheneum, 1976, 295–304.
Stern, Daniel. *The Interpersonal World of the Infant*. New York: Basic Books, 1973.
Stevenson, William R., Jr. *Sovereign Grace*. New York: Oxford University Press, 1999.
Stewart, Susan. "Shouts on the Street: Bakhtin's Anti-Linguistics." *Bakhtin: Essays and Dialogues on His Work*. Ed. Gary Saul Morson. Chicago: University of Chicago Press, 1986, 41–57.
Stone, Alison. "On the Genealogy of Women: A Defence of Anti-Essentialism." Third Wave Feminism: A Critical Exploration. Eds. Stacy Gillis, Gillian Howie, and Rebecca Munford. Palgrave Macmillan, 2004.
Stone, Lawrence. *The Family, Sex and Marriage in England 1500–1800*. New York: Harper and Row, 1979.
———. "Literacy and Education in England 1690–1900." *Past and Present* 42 (1969): 68–149.
Stout, Harry *The New England Soul*. New York: Oxford University Press, 1986.
———. "Religion, Communications and Ideological Origins of the American Revolution." *William and Mary Quarterly*, Third Series 34 (1977): 519–541.
Subbs, Michael. *Language and Literacy*. New York: Routledge, 1980.
Swiontkowski, Gale. *Imagining Incest: Sexton, Plath, Rich, and Olds*. London: Associated University Presses, 2003.
Tate, Claudia. *Domestic Allegories of Political Desire*. New York: Oxford University Press, 1992.
Taylor, Charles. *The Resources of the Self*. Cambridge, Massachusetts: Harvard University Press, 1989.
Thomas, Keith. "The Double Standard." *Journal of the History of Ideas* 20.2 (April 1959): 195–216.

———. "Women and the Civil War Sects." *Crisis in Europe 1560–1660*. Ed. Trevor Aston. London: Routledge, 1965, 317–340.
Thompson, Roger. *Women in Stuart England*. London: Routledge, 1974.
Thornham, Sue. *Feminist Theory and Cultural Studies*. London: Arnold, 2000.
Threadgold, Terry. *Feminist Poetics: Poeisis, Performance, Histories*. New York: Routledge, 1997.
Tiberius, Valerie, and Walker, John. "Arrogance." *American Philosophical Quarterly* (October 1998).
Todorov, Tzvetan. *Mikhail Bakhtin: The Dialogical Principle*. Minneapolis: University of Minnesota Press, 1984.
Tomasi, John. "Individual Rights and Community Virtues." *Ethics* 101.3 (April 1991): 521–536.
Tompkins, Jane. *Sensational Designs*. New York: Oxford University Press, 1985.
Tong, Rosemary. *Feminist Thought*. Boulder, CO: Westview Press, 1989.
Ulrich, Laurel Thatcher. "Daughters of Liberty: Religious Women in Revolutionary New England." *Women in the Age of the American Revolution*. Eds. Ronald Hoffman and Peter Albert. Charlottesville: University Press of Virginia, 1989, 211–243.
———. *Good Wives: Image and Reality in the Lives of Women in Northern New England 1650–1750*. New York: Oxford University Press, 1983.
Vega, Judith A. "Feminist Republicanism and the Political Perception of Gender." *Republicanism: A Shared European Heritage*. Eds. Martin Van Gelderen and Quentin Skinner. New York: Cambridge University Press, 2002, 157–174.
Verba, Sidney. *Voice and Equality: Civic Voluntarism in American Politics*. Cambridge: Harvard University Press, 1995.
Waldron, Jeremy. *God, Locke and Equality*. New York: Cambridge University Press, 2002.
———. "The Image of God: Rights, Reason, and Order." *NYU School of Law, Public Law Research Paper No. 10–85* (November 30, 2010). Online NEELCO Legal Scholar Depository, New York University Public Law and Legal Theory, Working Papers New York University Law School, http://lsr.nellco.org/cgi/viewcontent.cgi?article=1247&context=nyu_plltwp June, 2012
Walker, Cheryl. "Headnote." *She Wields a Pen*. Ed. Janet Grey. London: Dent, 1997, 342–344.
———. *Masks Outrageous and Austere*. Bloomington: Indiana University Press, 1991.
———. *The Nightingale's Burden*. Bloomington: Indiana University Press, 1982.
Walker, Pamela. "A Chaste and Fervid Eloquence: Catherine Booth and the Salvation Army." *Women Preachers and Prophets*. Eds. Beverly Kienzle and Pamela Walker. Berkeley: University of California Press, 1998, 288–302.
Walker, Rebecca. "Being Real: Introduction." *To Be Real: Telling the Truth and Changing the Face of Feminism*. Ed. Rebecca Walker. New York: Anchor Books, 1995, xxix–xxxix.
Walter, Natasha. *On the Move: Feminism for a New Generation*. London: Virago Press, 1999.
Weber, Max. "The Social Psychology of the World Religions." *From Max Weber*. New York: Oxford University Press, 1946, 267–301.
Webster, Noah. "On the Education of Youth." *Essays on Education in the Early Republic*. Ed. Frederick Rudolph. Cambridge. MA: Harvard University Press, 1965, 41–50.
Weedon, Chris. *Feminist Practice and Poststructuralist Theory*. Oxford: Basil Blackwell, 1987.

Welter, Barbara. "Clio's Consciousness Raised." *Shakespeare's Sisters.* Eds. Sandra Gilbert and Susan Gilbert. Bloomington: Indiana University Press, 1979, 137–157.
———. "The Cult of True Womanhood." *American Quarterly* 18.2 (Summer 1966): 151–174.
Westerkamp, Marilyn. *Women and Religion in Early America 1600–1850.* New York: Routledge, 1999.
Wexler, Laura. "Tender Violence: Literary Eavesdropping, Domestic Fiction, and Educational Reform." *The Culture of Sentiment.* Ed. Shirley Samuels. New York: Oxford University Press, 1992, 9–38.
White, Allon. *Carnival, Hysteria and Writing.* New York: Oxford University Press, 1993.
Whitehead, Kim. *The Feminist Poetry Movement.* Jackson: University of Mississippi, 1996.
Wieselthier, Leon. "In a Universe of Ghosts." *New York Review of Books* (November 25, 1976): 20.
Williams, Raymond. *Keywords: A Vocabulary of Culture and Society.* New York: Oxford University Press, 1985.
———. *Marxism and Literature.* New York: Oxford University Press, 1977.
Wolosky, Shira. *Cambridge History of American Literature,* Vol. IV. Ed. Sacvan Bercovitch. New York: Cambridge University Press, 2004.
———. *Emily Dickinson: A Voice of War.* New Haven, CT: Yale University Press, 1984.
———. *Poetry and Public Discourse.* New York: Palgrave Macmillan, 2010.
———. "Rhetoric or Not: Hymnal Tropes in Emily Dickinson and Isaac Watts." *New England Quarterly* LXI.2 (June 1988): 214–232.
———. "What do Jews Stand for? Muriel Rukeyser's Ethics of Identity." *Nashim* 19 (Spring 2010): 197–224.
Wood, Gordon. *The Creation of the American Republic.* Chapel Hill: University of North Carolina Press, 1969.
Woodhouse, A. S. P. *Puritanism and Liberty.* London: J. M. Dent, 1950.
Wynne-Davies, Marion. "Literary Dialogues in an English Renaissance Family." *This Double Voice: Gendered Writing in Early Modern England.* Eds. Danielle Clarke and Elizabeth Clarke. New York: St. Martin's Press, 2000, 164–184.
Young, Iris Marion. "Impartiality and the Civic Public." *Feminism, the Public and the Private.* Ed. Joan Landes. New York: Oxford University Press, 1998, 421–447.
Young, James. *Writing and Rewriting the Holocaust.* Bloomington: Indiana University Press, 1988.
Zagarri, Rosemarie. "The Rights of Man and Woman in Post-Revolutionary America." *William and Mary Quarterly* 3rd Series 55 (April 1998): 203–227.
Zaret, David. *The Heavenly Contract.* Chicago: University of Chicago Press, 1985.
———. "Religion, Science and Printing in the Public Sphere in Seventeenth Century England." *Habermas and the Public Sphere.* Ed. Craig Calhoun. Cambridge, MA: MIT Press, 1992, 212–235.
Zikmund, Barbara Brown. "The Struggle for the Right to Preach." *Women & Religion in America Vol. I.* Eds. Rosemary Ruether and Rosemary Skinner Keller. New York: Harper and Row, 1981, 193–241.
———. "The Feminist Thrust of Sectarian Christianity." *Women of Spirit.* Eds. Rosemary Ruether and Elanor McLaughlin. New York: Simon and Schuster, 1979, 206–224.

Index

A

Abolition 40, 60, 75, 76, 80, 85, 87, 116, 124, 128, 178–179, 192, 194

Adams, Abigail 73, 191

African-American 21, 27, 28, 39–46, 77, 84–87, 122, 127–132, 147, 156–160, 202, 203–204, 206

African-American Dialect 24, 41, 187

Appleby, Joyce 95, 98, 99

Ardener, Shirley and Edwin 24–28, 52, 55

Arendt, Hannah 65, 95, 96, 99

Awakenings (Revivals) 120, 122, 124, 126, 200, 201

B

Babha, Homi 29

Bakhtin, Mikhail 27–28, 36, 148, 164, 166–172, 174–175, 176, 196, 207, 208–209

Beecher, Catherine 74, 124

Bible 2, 3, 41, 73, 117, 118, 120, 123–126, 127–133, 135, 136, 152, 202

Bishop, Elizabeth: 20, 28, 62; 87, 88–89, 110; "Songs for a Colored Singer I and II," 62; "Squatter's Children," 88–89

Blackstone, William (Femme Couvert) 72, 190

Bloom, Harold Chapter 1 passim; 50, 208

Bordo, Susan 140, 146, 183

Bradstreet, Anne: xv, 15–19; "Prologue," 16–18; "Author to her Book," 18–19

Brooks, Gwendolyn: xviii, 21–23, 43, 44–46, 65–68, 131–132, 156–161, 177; "Children of the Poor," 43; "A Bronzeville Mother Loiters in Mississippi. Meanwhile, A Mississippi Mother Burns Bacon," 44–46; "Mrs. Small," 65–68; "Sonnet-Ballad," 160–161

Butler, Judith xiv, 24, 160, 208

C

Cary, Alice 42, 82–83

Cary, Phoebe: 42, 60, 108–109; "Homes for All," 108–109

Chodorow, Nancy 23, 52–53

Civic Feminism xii, xvi, xviii, xix–xx, 11, 12, 16, 37, 74, 85, 100–101, 103, 110, 196

Civic Virtue 11, 100, 180

Cixous, Hélène 26, 27, 208

Commercialism (Commodification) 3, 35, 103, 107, 112, 143, 145, 147, 153, 158, 171, 188, 205

Conservative Trends 11, 70, 74, 81, 84, 107, 116, 121, 123, 125, 127, 185, 201–202

Cott, Nancy 106, 110, 202

Culture Studies xv, xvi, xviii, Chapter 7 passim, 162, 165–166

D

Davis, Natalie Zemon 25, 118

De Beauvoir, Simone 205

De Lauretis, Teresa 167, 183

De Man, Paul 172

De Tocqueville, Alexis 69

Derrida, Jacques (deconstruction) 164, 171–176

Dickinson, Emily: 13–15, 29–32, 33, 57, 74, 79–81, 89, 110, 117,

234   Index

126–127, 136, 142; "Fitter to See Him," 14–15; "I'm Wife," 30–31; "A Solemn Thing it was," 31–32; "I Took my Power in my Hand," 126
Dinnerstein, Dorothy 52
Domesticity xii, xiii, 1, 8, 18, 20, 37, 38–39, 45–46, 67, Chapter 4 passim, 93–95, 97, 98, 102, 105, 110, 111, 112, 115, 117, 161, 189–191. *See* Domesticity, Sentimental Writing
Dominant/Muted Discourses xvii, 26, 33, 49, 52, 54–55, 61, 82, 91
Double Standard (prostitution) 34, 42, 72, 75, 92, 104, 106–107, 142, 197
Douglas, Anne 100
Douglas, Mary xx
Douglass, Frederick 41
DuBois, W. W. B. 40
Dunbar, Paul Laurence 41

E
Eagleton, Terry 165
Education (Literacy) xi, 3, 41, 73–75, 82, 117, 118–119, 191, 182, 199
Eliot, T. S. 79, 88, 136. *See* Modernism
Elshtain, Jean Bethke 97, 100, 187
Emerson, Ralph Waldo 69, 79, 108, 193
Erikson, Erik 50

F
Felski, Rita 166, 167, 169
Feminist Waves (First, Second, Third) xi–xii, xix, 5, 47, 76, 77, 106, 113, 131, 184, 188
Foucault, Michel xiv, xvii, 98, Chapter 7 passim, 166
Fraser, Nancy 168–169
French Feminism 26, 29, 167, 172, 184, 187, 188, 208
Freud, Sigmund 4, 5, 6, 50–51, 53, 167, 188, 207

G
Genre: 1, 2, 3, 4, 44, 45, 87, 117, 123, 125, 126, 157, 158, 160, 184, 209; ballad, 44, 45, 157; Bible, 117, 123; hymns, 87, 117, 125, 126; seduction, 4, 123; sonnet, 4, 21, 22, 132, 157, 160; speech genres, 171, 175

Gilbert, Sandra and Susan Gubar 5, 7–8, 9, 118
Gilligan, Carol xvii, Chapter 3 passim; 66, 102, 188
Gilman, Charlotte: 33–39, 42, 60, 83–84, 102, 104, 107, 109–111, 133–135, 142; "One Girl Too Many," 34–35; "To the Preacher," 35; "An Old Proverb," 35–36; "The Housewife," 37; "Homes: A Sestina," 38–39; "Exiles," 83–84; "Nationalism," 109–110; "The Real Religion," 133–135
Grahn, Judy: 114–115, 177; "The Work of a Common Woman," 114–115
Greenblatt, Stephen 165
Grimké, Sarah and Angelina 122, 123, 124
Griswold, Rufus 77

H
Habermas, Jürgen 95, 120, 140, 195, 201, 205
Harper, Frances: 28, 40–43, 83–87, 127–131, 133, 204; Aunt Chloe, 42–43; "A Double Standard," 43; "The Slave Auction," 85; "A Fairer Hope, A Brighter Morn," 85–87, 131; "A Bible Defense of Slavery," 128–129; "Bury Me in a Free Land," 130
H. D. (Hilda Doolittle) 2, 28, 61–62, 87–88, 110, 135–136
Hegel, G. W. F. xiii, 102, 197
Hirschmann, Nancy 68, 183
Holocaust 90, 91, 136, 194, 202. *See* War
hooks, bell 113
Howe, Julia Ward 42, 107, 125
Hutchinson, Anne 16, 120

I
Individualism xiii, xviii, 55, 68, 77, 94, 99, 103, 110, 114–115, 117, 128, 134, 148, 152–154, 196
Irigaray, Luce 26, 29, 205, 208

J
Jackson, Helen Hunt: 57–60, 107, 133; "Two Truths," 57–58; A Woman's Battle," 59
Jakobson, Roman 162, 168, 169, 170

K

Kerber, Linda 48, 71, 73, 94
Kohlberg, Lawrence 48, 50, 51
Kristeva, Julia 26, 27, 167–168, 207–208

L

Language (women's) 24, 26, 29, 167–169, 172, 207
Larcom, Lucy: 60–61, 62; "Getting Along," 60–61
Lazarus, Emma 109
Levertov, Denise 177
Liberalism xi, xii, xiii, xx, 47, 49, 93–95, 97, 98–99, 101–103, 109, 110–111, 113, 116, 124, 128, 148, 151, 153–154, 183, 188
Lincoln, Abraham 42, 85, 124, 176, 178, 179
Literacy. See Education
Locke, John xiii, 73, 97, 202
Lorde, Audre 133, 142, 177

M

MacKinnon, Catherine 48, 188
McPherson, C. P. 94, 99
Marriage 15, 24, 33, 35, 45, 60–61, 72, 90, 106, 107, 111, 146, 190. See Blackstone
Mather, Cotton 119–120
Miller, Jean Baker 51–52
Miller, Cristanne 136, 177
Marxism (Socialism) xi, xvii, xx, 27, 98, 104, 112, 147, 148, 165, 169, 170, 183, 184, 187, 188
Missed Dialogue 57–66, 82, 104, 150
Modernism 87–89, 118, 136, 149, 168, 177, 183, 194
Modesty, Chapter 1 passim, 57, 79, 84, 119, 122, 133, 136, 179, 180, 185, 186, 209
Moral Theory (Ethics) xvii, xx, 12, 20, 21, 34, 42, 43, Chapter 3 passim, 85, 100, 102, 103, 104, 109, 113, 122, 124–125, 126, 127, 136, 141, 150, 155–156, 158–160, 178–180, 188, 201. See Foucault.
Motherhood: 1, 4, 5, 16, 17, 18–19, 20, 21–22; 26, 27; 33; 37; 44–45; 50–52, 63, 64, 65–68, 73–74, 84–85, 89, 92, 100, 101, 108–109, 132, 133, 135, 136, 143–145, 152–153, 157, 160–161, 168, 185, 189; Maternal Care, 65, 101, 189; Republican Motherhood, 73–74
Moore, Marianne: 10, 19–21, 22, 87, 110, 136–138, 165, 176–180; "To a Snail," 19–21; "Feed Me, Also, River God," 137–138; "Blessed is the Man," 176–180
Muse, Chapter 1 passim

N

New Criticism 112, 114, 147

O

Okin, Susan 65, 97
Ortner, Sherry 23

P

Pateman, Carole xiii, 97, 98
Personal is Political 65, 98
Plath, Sylvia: 87, 89–90, 91, 110, 135, 136, 142–147, 156, 194; "Face Lift" 143–146
Pocock, J. G. A. 95, 98, 194
Poetics (aesthetics; formalism) xv–xvi, xviii, xix, 1, 22, 27, 88, 89, 110, 112, 114, 117–118, 135, 141–142, 147, 148, 156, 157, 159, Chapter 8 passim
Postfeminism xix, 47, 184. See Feminist Waves
Prophetic Call 117, 119, 122, 123, 125, 127–132, 136–137, 202, 209
Prostitution. See Double Standard
Psychoanalysis xi, xvi, 26–27, 50–51, 52, 64, 167–168, 172, 184, 188, 195, 208; (Oedipal Complex), 4–7, 13, 50, 208
Publishing (women's) 2, 3, 9, 15, 16, 18, 33, 70, 78, 79, 84, 199

R

Religion xiii, xvi, xviii, 3, 8, 9, 11, 14, 15, 16, 20, 28, 31, 34–36, 39, 41, 89, Chapter 6 passim, 155, 156, 163, 164, 166, 177, 178, 179, 181, 185, 198–203
Republicanism xii, xviii, xx, 11, 73–75, Chapter 5 passim, 100, 120, 123, 180, 191, 196
Revolution (American) 3, 11, 73, 81, 98, 100, 120, 180, 191, 196

Rich, Adrienne: 2, 20, 28, 63–64, 111, 177, 184; "Novella," 64
Rosaldo, Michelle Zimbalist 23, 70
Rosemary Ruether 100, 125, 131
Rukeyser, Muriel: xviii, 2, 28, 62–63, 104, 111–113, 114, 135–135, 147–154, 156, 177, 178–180; "Waiting for Icarus," 62–63; "Boy With His Hair Cut Short," 111–113; *Book of the Dead*, 149–153
Ryan, Mary 76, 77, 184

S

Selfhood: poetic selfhood (authorship, self-representation), xv, xvii, Chapter 1 passim, 54, 57, 78–79, 87, 88, 103, 117–118, 142, 179, 180, 185, 193; agent selfhood, 121, 127, 140, 142, 148, 149, 153–154, 161, 198; autonomy, xii, xiii, xvii, xx, 4, 7, 8, 9, 13, 47–56, 65–68, 84, 93–97, 99, 101–102, 117–118, 140, 145, 148, 153–154, 155, 158, 165–168; participatory selfhood, xv, xviii, xix, xx, xxi, 28, 55, 73, 74, 75, 115, 121, 97, 109, 110, 114, 115, 117, 119, 120, 121, 123, 125, 127, 157, 159, 165, 166, 176, 178, 179, 185, 191, 200, 206; multiple selfhood, xix, xx, 53, 55, 88, 159–161; relational selfhood, xx, 23, 53–56, 68, 104, 110, 156, 159, 160; religious selfhood, xviii, 117, 121–122, 127; self-in-community, 65, 68, 121, 156, 158–160
Sentimental Writing 70, 78, 80, 81, 82, 84, 85, 88, 91, 99, 100, 107, 108, 116, 190, 193, 194, 196, 204. *See* Domesticity, Separate Spheres
Separate Spheres xvii, Chapter 4 passim, 93–97, 100, 102, 122, 125, 189, 192. *See* Domesticity, Sentimental Writing

Sexton, Anne: 87, 91–92, 135, 136, 142, 195; "Her Kind," 91–92
Sigourney, Lydia 81–82, 125
Slavery 40, 41–42, 72, 79, 80, 85–87, 109, 124, 128, 129–131, 203, 204
Social Construction xiii, xiv, xvi, xvii, xx, 11, 22, 24, 29, 53, 78, 104, 117–118, 140, 141, 152, 155–156, 157, 160, 168, 183. *See* Selfhood
Stanton, Elizabeth Cady 121, 122, 124, 128, 203
Stowe, Harriet Beecher 85
Suffrage 40, 76–78, 110, 122, 190, 192, 204

T

Taylor, Charles 140, 197
Thoreau, Henry David 108
Topos/Topoi 2, 10, 11–12, 17, 18, 37, 57. *See* Modesty
Todorov, Tzvetan 170

W

Webster, Noah 73–74
Welter, Barbara 8, 117
Walzer, Michael 140
War 40, 42, 79–80, 85, 87, 90, 106, 112, 123, 124, 125, 128, 135, 136, 160–161, 193, 199, 202. *See* Holocaust
Weber, Max 166
Wheatley, Phyllis: 17, 40, 41; "On Being Brought from Africa," 40
Whitman, Walt 79, 117, 196
Wilcox, Ella Wheeler: 104–106, 133; "A Holiday," 104; "The Cost," 105, 133
Willard, Frances (Temperance) 75, 76, 77, 124, 203
Williams, Raymond 165
Witch Craze 91–92, 195
Wollstonecraft, Mary 11
Woolf, Virginia 3